W9-BPJ-424

THE
CHEMICALLY
DEPENDENT

*Phases of Treatment
and Recovery*

THE
CHEMICALLY
DEPENDENT

*Phases of Treatment
and Recovery*

Edited by

Barbara C. Wallace, Ph.D.

BRUNNER/MAZEL *Publishers* • NEW YORK

Library of Congress Cataloging-in-Publication Data
The Chemically dependent : phases of treatment and recovery / edited
by Barbara C. Wallace.
    p.   cm.
Includes bibliographical references and index.
ISBN 0-87630-675-X
1. Substance abuse—Treatment.   2. Narcotic addicts-
-Rehabilitation.   3. Psychiatry—Differential therapeutics.
I. Wallace, Barbara C.
RC564.C478   1992
616.86'06—dc20   92-1371
                                                              CIP

Published by
BRUNNER/MAZEL, INC.
19 Union Square West
New York, New York 10003

Manufactured in the United States of America

10   9   8   7   6   5   4   3   2   1

To dearest Grandmom, Ivy Booth Wallace, who perceived potential in playful antics on a red playground jungle gym and walked me to kindergarten on my first day of school—a path that never seems to end. I thank God my family walks alongside me, since the path is rough in spots.

For a generation in desperate need of quality chemical-dependency treatment and relapse prevention. A special dedication for professionals willing to sacrifice rigidity and dogma for the sake of elevating the field of chemical dependency to a level from which efficacious treatment can be delivered.

Contents

———————◆◆◆———————

Contributors

Kenneth Blum, Ph.D., Director, Laboratory of Pharmacogenetics, University of Texas Health Science Center, San Antonio, Texas

Eric Braverman, M.D., Medical Director, Princeton Associates for Total Health, Skillman, New Jersey

Karen Derby, Ph.D., CAC, Paul Group, New York, New York

Olivia Finley, M.D., 1344 Shepherd St. N.E., Washington, D.C.

Rosalyn Harris-Offutt, B.S., CRNA, NCC, CPC, Private Practice, Greensboro, North Carolina; Consultant, Office of Substance Abuse Prevention, Dept. of Health and Human Services of the United States of America; Consultant, Charter Hills Psychiatric Hospital, Greensboro, North Carolina; Member of Governor's Council on Alcohol and Other Drugs for the State of North Carolina

Raymond C. Hawkins II, Ph.D., Coordinator, Family Recovery Program, Austin Regional Clinic, Austin, Texas

Daniel A. Hoffman, M.D., Medical Director, The Neurotherapy Institute, Denver, Colorado

Sung-Yeon Kang, Ph.D., Narcotic and Drug Research Inc., New York, New York

Paula H. Kleinman, Ph.D., Assistant Professor, Cornell University Medical College, New York, New York

Douglas S. Lipton, Ph.D., Director, Narcotic and Drug Research Inc., New York, New York

Laurel Loeblich-Smith, Ph.D., 4207 Bradshire Court, Seabrook, Texas

Robert B. Millman, M.D., Professor of Psychiatry and Public Health, New York Hospital/Cornell University Medical College, New York, New York

James E. Payne, Executive Director, National Foundation of Addictive Diseases, Austin, Texas

Debra E. Rothschild, Ph.D., CAC, Paul Group; Private Practice, New York, New York

Andrew Tatarsky, Ph.D., Clinical Director, Washton Institute, New York, New York

Thomas C. Todd, Ph.D., Forest Hospital and Foundation, Des Plaines, Illinois

Therese M. Unumb, Ph.D., Arlington Psychological Services, Arlington Heights, Illinois

Barbara C. Wallace, Ph.D., Assistant Professor, Department of Health Education, Teachers College, Columbia University, New York, New York; Consultant, Damon House New York, Inc., Brooklyn, New York

Arnold Washton, Ph.D., Executive Director, Washton Institute, New York, New York

Arthur A. Weidman, Ph.D., ACSW, M.B.A., Executive Director, Jewish Family Service of Colorado, Denver, Colorado

George E. Woody, M.D., Drug Dependence Treatment Unit, Veterans Administration Medical Center, Philadelphia, Pennsylvania

Leon Wurmser, M.D., Clinical Professor of Psychiatry, University of West Virginia, Charleston, West Virginia; Clinical Assistant Professor of Psychology, Johns Hopkins University, Baltimore, Maryland

Daniel L. Yalisove, Ph.D., CAC, Program Director, START Program, Stuyvesant Polyclinic, New York, New York

Joan Ellen Zweben, Ph.D., Executive Director, East Bay Community Recovery Project and 14th Street Clinic and Medical Group, Oakland, California

Acknowledgments

Acknowledgments are due those loving family and friends who support me wholeheartedly in my endeavors. In addition, Jochanon Weisenfreund, M.D., Director of the Department of Psychiatry, must be recognized for his important role in establishing model inpatient detoxification units at Interfaith Medical Center, Brooklyn, New York. I remain grateful for the experience of working with the staff and patients at 10 West.

In a similar vein, I must thank Irwin Scheintaub, Executive Director of Damon House, Inc., Brooklyn, New York, who hired me as a consultant and has guided the development of a model residential therapeutic community. Staff members must also be recognized for their role in creating a treatment environment at Damon House conducive to serious group therapy work. Without the cooperation and openness of the female residents of Damon House, my knowledge of important group therapy dynamics would not have evolved; so my gratitude and thanks must also be extended to these very special women.

Perhaps most important, I must acknowledge the cooperation and perseverance of all of the contributors who had faith in my vision of this book and took seriously the challenge of sticking to often difficult deadlines. I must also thank them for their patience in remaining committed to the book, even when unforeseen delays were difficult to endure. Without their hard work, I would surely have fallen short of a goal that remains of primary importance to me—working with other professionals in elevating the field of chemical dependency to a level at which a well-articulated and refined theory dictates clinical interventions and research directions.

Introduction

The order of the alphabet for purposes of distributing degrees placed Andrew Tatarsky and myself side by side when we marched at our City University of New York graduation in May 1986. All along the procession, we debated our views on addiction as the only two members of our clinical-psychology doctoral program cohort with a firm interest in the area. In the fall of 1988, I called Andrew Tatarsky, aware that he knew both Karen Derby and Debra Rothschild better than I did, and suggested that the four of us might compose a competitive panel for inclusion at the 97th Annual Convention of the American Psychological Association (APA) to be held August 1989 in New Orleans, Louisiana. At a prior APA convention in New York City, I, along with Andy, had heard a compelling presentation by Derby and Rothschild, and it was my very positive impression of their progressive and clear views at that time that led to my desire to create the panel workshop. Also at that same New York City APA convention, Andy and I had criticized some of the other sessions we had attended that dealt with addiction and chatted about the directions in which the field of addiction needed to move.

The four of us met in November 1988 at the Washton Institute in New York where Andy works, and easily arrived at a consensus on the title of our panel and individual topics, which are reflected in the title of this book and those of our individual chapters. Having the time that academic life afforded me, I submitted a proposal for consideration, and upon its acceptance for presentation at the 97th annual APA convention, proceeded with a call for papers and plans for an edited book. This book represents the fruit of those efforts.

OVERVIEW OF THE BOOK

Part I of the book covers phases of treatment for specific phases of recovery by describing key concepts and focusing on three dominant treatment modalities—inpatient, outpatient, and long-term residential therapeutic communities. In the first chapter, Wallace (this editor) introduces the volume by explaining the guiding concept of phases of treatment and recovery, the utility of an integrated theory and biopsychosocial approach, and the critical role of relapse prevention in every phase of recovery. In Chapter 2, Wallace provides a discussion of inpatient treatment,

xv

drawing on her experiences in working with crack and cocaine patients, as well as with intravenous drug users. In Chapter 3, Tatarsky and Washton—drawing upon their clinical experience obtained within the context of refining treatment at the Washton Institute in Manhattan, New York—argue the utility of the intensive out-patient treatment model. Chapter 4 allows Wallace to expose readers to yet a third major treatment modality, the residential therapeutic community (TC), and to describe progressive developments in the delivery of services within a model residential program, Damon House New York Inc. Specifically, Wallace outlines the ways in which Damon House New York Inc. is different from other TCs and shares her professional consultation experiences developing a model of staff training and client treatment combining professionally led group and individual psychotherapy.

In this way, Part I of the book describes progressive contemporary treatment models for clients diagnosed as dependent upon chemicals. Further, this part illustrates several important principles underlying this book: (1) severely dependent clients negotiating a first phase of withdrawal or early abstinence may need to be matched to inpatient treatment; (2) the chemically dependent negotiating a second phase of recovery where the goal is to prolong the period of abstinence and avoid relapse should be matched to a six month to a year of outpatient treatment so they can successfully pursue lifetime recovery—a third phase of recovery spanning the first few years of abstinence; (3) the severely chemically dependent who have also experienced severe psychosocial deterioration (for example, homelessness, loss of employment, criminal activities, loss of child custody) may require residential therapeutic community treatment that extends into the first and second year of recovery, or a phase of pursuing lifetime recovery. The concept of phases of treatment for specific phases of recovery—which is central to this book—suggests that knowledge of the phase of recovery a chemically dependent client is negotiating dictates the appropriateness of a specific treatment modality (inpatient, outpatient, or long-term residential TC) designed to span that phase of recovery.

Part II covers, in substantial depth, psychoanalytic/psychodynamic approaches. In Chapter 5, Yalisove provides surveys of psychoanalytic approaches to treatment of the chemically dependent, and arrives at a summary description of the kind of modifications in technique appropriate within the various phases of recovery, ranging from early abstinence to stable sobriety. He essentially provides an invaluable synthesis of the historical and contemporary psychoanalytic/psychodynamic approaches to the chemically dependent. Chapter 6 permits Rothschild to articulate both practical clinical insights and theoretical understanding of the role and purpose of individual psychotherapy throughout the rather lengthy period of recovery that chemically dependent patients face. Her experience with a diverse group of intravenous heroin and cocaine patients, her grasp of psychoanalytic theory, and her sensitivity in deploying an appropriate clinical technique make this chapter's contribution particularly important. A seventh chapter permits Wurmser, one of the most eminent psychoanalytic practitioners in the field of chemical-dependency treatment, to articulate some of his most recent reflections on the dynamics of compulsive drug use. In Chapter 8, Derby demystifies the kind of countertransference reactions and transference states common in the treatment of the character-disordered patient. This chapter reflects the integration of clinical observation and an understanding of psychoanalytic theory in arriving at the kind of technique necessary to work effectively with the most difficult segment of the chemically dependent population.

Part III of the book examines cognitive-behavioral, self-help, and relapse-prevention approaches to the treatment of the chemically dependent. In Chapter 9, Hawkins presents a survey of research elucidating the role of stress and emphasizes the importance of stress-coping resources within a person's overall life context. In light of the growth in 12-step programs for a variety of addictions beyond alcoholism, Derby provides, in Chapter 10, an important perspective on the role and utility of these self-help programs, including an appreciation of how 12-step programs can be utilized by those also embracing an ego-psychological approach. This important chapter helps the field of chemical dependency to move toward greater acceptance of how both 12-step-program involvement and long-term individual psychotherapy, when used in combination, may best serve the goal of successful long-term recovery.

An 11th chapter permits Wallace to advance a multidimensional approach to relapse. Her view of relapse prevention includes biological approaches that reduce neurochemically based cravings, psychological treatment of underlying emotional problems, and social-environmental interventions that draw upon cognitive-behavioral theory. Wallace argues for the deployment of relapse-prevention interventions in all phases of treatment and recovery.

Part IV of the book provides an overview of contemporary trends in research, while also discussing implications for treatment. In an extremely important chapter (Chapter 12), Blum and his associates summarize the twin studies and historical research supporting a disease-model view of addiction and present a survey of their latest research findings—including the discovery of the alcogene. Their work builds a unifying biological foundation for understanding addiction to cocaine, alcohol, and heroin, and even the eating disorders. Also, in this section, Unumb discusses, in Chapter 13, recent research findings on the early object representations of female alcoholics. This chapter represents the kind of quality "model" research that draws on the latest object-relations theory, but also operationalizes these concepts and experimentally examines the level of internalized object relations the chemically dependent may possess. She integrates the use of both qualitative and quantitative research methods and urges the future inclusion of women in more alcohol research studies.

Kleinman and colleagues provide, in Chapter 14, a look at some of the first outcome-evaluation research with a population of cocaine- and crack-dependent patients. These findings are important and suggest the kind of modifications in current programs necessary to create "model" and effective treatment for this new and challenging treatment population. The findings suggest the need for intensive treatment models that go beyond once-a-week therapy—an inappropriate treatment model for the cocaine/crack addict. The last chapter (Chapter 15) in this section gives Weidman the opportunity to present his most recent research findings on the level of object relations possessed by adolescent chemically dependent patients and how the residential therapeutic community and its structure become internalized. This again demonstrates the exciting trend of operationalizing the latest object-relations theory and coming up with a methodology that permits elucidation of the level of internalized object relations that adolescent addicts possess. Weidman also reports on family therapy as an important adjunct to treatment with adolescents in the therapeutic community.

Part V attempts to draw the field of chemical dependency toward recognition of the importance of considering distinct population characteristics and how these characteristics may dictate modifications in treatment design. In Chapter 16, Harris-Offutt draws our attention to certain cultural factors that can affect the assessment and treatment of African-American addicts. Offering what she refers to as Africentric considerations, this author sensitizes clinicians to specific issues they need to consider in their work with African-American patients. Chapter 17 permits Zweben to point out the treatment needs of dually diagnosed patients. Zweben's work continues to break new grounds in the field of chemical dependency in repeatedly drawing our attention to modifications in treatment that are needed. Here, she provides a broad definition of who these dual-diagnosis clients actually are, suggests better integration/coordination of care between the historically opposed mental-health and chemical-dependency fields, and argues for improved training of treatment professionals. Wallace, in Chapter 18, describes the kind of treatment models needed for several special contemporary populations—criminals, pregnant women, uninsured patients, adolescents, AIDS victims, the Methadone-maintained, and the homeless.

And finally, Wallace concludes this volume by summarizing how the chapter authors have attempted to move the field of chemical dependency toward positive reform and evolution, and reiterates key goals and principles that should guide the future direction of treatment and research in the field. Wallace also draws on clinical experiences that suggest that yet another special population accounts for a significant segment of the chemically dependent—the victims of child abuse. She emphasizes the need to break the code of silence commonly characterizing society's approach to victims of incest and other forms of abuse, suggesting that prevention of and early intervention in childhood abuse may constitute a critical strategy for preventing adolescent and adult development of addictive disorders.

AUDIENCE FOR THE BOOK

The book is suitable as a text in a course on substance abuse or as a critical reference for anyone doing clinical work or research in the field of chemical dependency.

Social workers, psychiatrists, psychologists, and students in these disciplines all constitute the audience for the book—and not only students in graduate training programs, but also those pursuing certification for alcoholism and drug-addiction counseling.

Because of deficient graduate training curricula, most professionals are ill prepared to treat today's clients seeking assistance for chemical dependency, varied addictions, compulsive behaviors, and closely related problems stemming from childhood development in alcoholic and dysfunctional families. As a continuing education or subspecialization tool, the book can prepare professionals for the effective delivery of clinical services to these patients. It may also serve the goal of directing the development and modification of programs to meet the needs of special populations among the chemically dependent.

Barbara C. Wallace, Ph.D.

PART I

PHASES OF TREATMENT FOR SPECIFIC PHASES OF RECOVERY

1

Treatment and Recovery in an Evolving Field

Barbara C. Wallace, Ph.D.

Several factors justify the need for an edited volume on the chemically dependent that embraces the concept of phases of treatment and recovery. This chapter will discuss these factors. A summary of historical and social trends that stimulated the evolution of the field of chemical dependency is presented, followed by an explanation of the concept of phases of treatment and recovery, as well as of how an integrated biopsychosocial theory (Wallace, 1991a) and a multidimensional view of relapse prevention serve as other key areas from which a main thrust of the book derives.

HISTORICAL DEVELOPMENTS IN THE 1980s

The cocaine and crack epidemic of the 1980s challenged the traditional alcohol- and drug-addiction treatment programs in existence at that time. The 28- and 30-day inpatient rehabilitation program faced the difficulty of treating a new brand of client who was addicted to cocaine in addition to being an alcoholic. Other clients sought inpatient admission solely for cocaine abuse or dependence and were difficult to integrate into traditional program formats emphasizing involvement with Alcoholics Anonymous. Inpatient detoxification units with programs geared to the stabilization of the heroin addict or "speedballer" who used heroin and cocaine intravenously were particularly challenged by the flood of crack cocaine smokers in the middle to late 1980s. The residential therapeutic community (TC) tried hard to implement its self-help and confrontational approach in the face of a wave of much younger, but also quite debilitated, crack cocaine addicts. However, TCs found it

3

necessary to implement some changes to accommodate the needs and characteristics of crack addicts—even though they continued to embrace the philosophy that their treatment approach was fundamentally sound for any addict (except those who were on psychiatric medicine, had a severe mental disorder, or were suicidal, assaultive, or pyromaniacal).

CRITICAL ADVANCES IN OUTPATIENT TREATMENT

Outpatient treatment paid for by private insurance nearly developed into a mini-industry with the large number of referrals from employee-assistance programs that were trying to manage the cocaine and alcohol addictions of employees, from upper management to the assembly line. With the motivation to sustain this industry, private outpatient treatment programs pioneered truly state-of-the-art treatments worthy of continuing utilization by unions and employee-assistance programs (Rawson, 1990; Washton & Stone-Washton, 1990). Armed with modest treatment outcome data (Wallace, 1991a), these same addiction treatment centers—refined by treatment entrepreneurs who were brilliantly responsive to the cocaine epidemic—can now effectively compete with the old 28-day inpatient alcohol rehab as the state-of-the-art treatment model of the 1990s.

During the 1980s, employed cocaine addicts with excellent medical insurance policies guided the evolution of outpatient treatment toward high-quality service-delivery models. But cocaine use was considered so chic in the early 1980s, and drug dealers were so innovative, that low-income workers and inner-city African-Americans and Latinos could readily purchase $10 and $20 packages of powdered cocaine hydrochloride to sniff at Harlem parties and in after-hour social clubs—just as the elite did on Wall Street and at Hollywood social bashes. A resulting challenge involved treating those who were employed but did not have good medical insurance coverage, as well as those who eventually lost their jobs and so their insurance benefits.

THE IMPACT AND LEGACY OF CRACK

The advent of the packaging and marketing breakthrough of ready-to-smoke crack—converted by drug dealers from the powdered cocaine hydrochloride to the smokable alkaloid form called crack—permitted adolescents and women, juggling the most meager of budgets, to gain access to $5, $10, and $20 vials of crack (Wallace, 1991a). In response to this new wave of addicts, the residential TC and other treatment modalities struggled to meet the needs of surprisingly high numbers of adolescent and female addicts (Van Meter & Rioux, 1990; De Leon, 1989). Pregnant crack addicts' difficulty in gaining access to treatment and their vulnerability to criminal sanctions constitutes a sad dimension of the crack epidemic (Wallace, 1991b).

Our knowledge of the impact of dysfunctional family dynamics in childhood and fears of developmental delays in crack babies alerts us to the need for preventative treatment for crack-using family members to prevent a future generation of addicts. Along with the fear that children and adolescents in general would become users of chemicals, primary and secondary prevention efforts have reached new levels because of the cocaine and crack epidemic (Botvin, Baker, Filazzola, & Botvin, 1990; Bagnall, 1990; Klitzner, Bamberger, & Gruenwald, 1990; Bruvold, 1990; Klitzner, Gruenwald, & Bamberger, 1990; Caudill, Kantor, & Ungerleider, 1990; Massey & Neidigh, 1990).

In sum, the cocaine and crack epidemic of the 1980s provided the relatively nascent field of addiction treatment with an impetus to change and substantively evolve for the first time since the heroin epidemic of the 1960s.

THE CHEMICALLY DEPENDENT WITHIN A BROADER PERSPECTIVE

At the close of the 1980s, the possibility of an "ice" or methamphetamine epidemic, or a new surge in heroin use following on the heels of the crack epidemic, cautioned treatment practitioners and researchers against focusing too narrowly on specific drugs such as crack. The acquired immunodeficiency syndrome (AIDS) virus similarly prevented a singular focus on a single drug such as crack. Problems of intravenous drug users, needle-exchange program proposals, free needle distribution controversies, the development of safe-sex and needle-cleaning education, and those faced by methadone-maintenance programs (Des Jarlais & Friedman, 1990; Schilling et al., 1989; Kolar, Brown, Weddington, & Ball, 1990; Sorenson, Batki, Good, & Wilkinson, 1989) forced professionals to maintain a broad view of contemporary addiction problems. The reality that alcohol treatment had changed to include cocaine addiction and that cocaine treatment must address the use of sedative hypnotics and alcohol also suggests the need to avoid a narrow treatment focus. Thus, in the 1990s, it is appropriate to speak of chemical-dependency treatment as a generic or umbrella term that represents a marriage between the alcoholism treatment and drug treatment fields, while encouraging attention on a broad range of issues.

SOCIETAL SOPHISTICATION REGARDING ADDICTION

The term chemically dependent seeks to be all inclusive, but may still fall short of capturing refreshing trends in society's awareness of the various kinds of addictions and compulsions. The 1990s emerges as a decade in which commercial advertisements for weight-loss programs and liquid diets run back to back with beer commercials during televised football games. Beyond athletic events, the television viewer is bombarded throughout the week with weight-loss-program advertisements and individual case histories of weight loss. Multiple weight-loss-program endorsements from different companies seemingly occur with a greater frequency than any other type or category of advertisement. Society is also familiar with the problem of maintenance of weight loss and relapse experienced by the majority of dieters who fail to exercise and seem to eat unconsciously in response to negative emotions (Kayman, Bruvold, & Stern, 1990).

The difficulty Oprah Winfrey reports in maintaining weight loss and her admission that her eating behavior involves many factors—such as childhood and adolescent sexual abuse—serve to further educate the public on the complexities of compulsive overeating (*People*, 1991). The willingness of people to recognize the impact of this kind of childhood trauma and of childhood development in alcoholic and dysfunctional families (Wallace, 1990) also constitutes a societal movement of sorts. A resulting obsession with self-help groups, educational books, and workshop programs on dysfunctional families effectively teaches individuals about the roots of codependent behavior, addictions, and compulsive behavior.

The current emphasis on encouraging cigarette smokers to quit and the advent of programs to assist them (Carmody, 1990; Borland, 1990; Brandon, Tiffany, Obremski, & Baker, 1990) have also resulted in the spread of knowledge about relapse. We have all learned that smokers typically try to stop smoking several times and experience numerous relapses before, and if, they achieve final success. In this way, society has become increasingly sophisticated about addictions, the problem of relapse, and how childhood trauma in a dysfunctional family can create a susceptibility to addiction and relapse (Bollerud, 1990; Young, 1990; Rohsenow, Corbett, & Devine, 1988; Wallace, 1990). Talk shows have played a role in educating the public on the problems of shopaholism, gambling, workaholism, addictive love, and compulsive sexual behavior. So even within a discussion of the chemically dependent, our domain includes compulsive behavior of any kind that may serve to ward off anxiety or negative affect or can be engaged in as symptom substitution once a chemical addiction is treated (Washton, 1989; Corless & Dickerson, 1989; Fitzgibbon & Kirschenbaum, 1990; Wallace, 1991a).

THE ROLE AND POTENTIAL OF AN EVOLVING FIELD

These societal trends, together with the cocaine, crack, and AIDS epidemics, suggest the potential for the field of chemical dependency and addiction treatment increasingly to play a valuable role in combating problematic behavior. Society is perhaps more aware now of the problems posed by addictions and compulsions than at any other time in history. The need to address intravenous drug use by potential AIDS carriers, the continuing problems of cocaine and crack users, the still-significant challenge created by alcohol and heroin, and the need to be prepared for the introduction of the next designer drug create a compelling treatment challenge to be countered in the 1990s and beyond.

A key purpose of this book is to provide treatment practitioners and researchers with a handbook that attempts to contribute to the foundation of knowledge necessary to facilitate the continuing evolution of the field of chemical dependency. The development, growing sophistication, and improved long-term treatment outcome of the addictions field require a sound, integrated theory to guide clinical practice and research. This book attempts to move the field toward the creation of integrated theory. It also aspires, in the process, to serve as balm and counsel for standing disputes between (1) the alcoholism and the drug treatment fields, (2) the psychodynamic and cognitive-behavioral theoretical camps, and (3) disease-model proponents and those who find this concept inappropriate.

The field of chemical-dependency treatment represents one of the few fields in psychology in which an integration of diverse theoretical perspectives is both feasible and necessary in order to improve long-term treatment efficacy. Through presentation of contemporary perspectives and developments in several areas—psychodynamic theory and technique, cognitive-behavioral and self-help interventions, selected research, and issues that arise when working with special populations—the authors attempt to help build an integrated theory to guide treatment. An integrated theory may foster the utilization, within an overall long-term treatment plan, of practical clinical interventions that technically derive their rationale for implementation from diverse theoretical perspectives. Biological neuronutrients, cognitive-behavioral interventions essential to effective relapse prevention, self-help groups, and long-term psychodynamic individual and group therapy all have a place in such long-term treatment plans.

The purpose of an integrated theory guiding the implementation of diverse treatment interventions is to improve long-term treatment outcome for a large body of chemically dependent persons. The refinement and amalgamation of today's best, even though diverse, addiction treatment approaches into efficacious actions on behalf of the field of chemical dependency are crucial and timely. Individuals today may be more willing than at any other time in history to seek help for a range of addictive and compulsive behaviors. The mental health field might indeed find that the subspecialization of chemical-dependency treatment, or addictive behaviors, and the intimately interrelated work with adult children from alcoholic and other dysfunctional families represent one of its most vital branches. This branch not only may realize its potential to address a wide range of problematic behaviors, but may find itself bombarded with willing consumers of treatment if the trend of the late 1980s and early 1990s continues. More and more people in contemporary society—not requiring emergency psychiatric treatment for severe mental illness such as mood disorders or psychosis—may be motivated to seek out their first lifetime contact with a mental health professional. This trend will likely continue because of the growing awareness of the availability and role of treatment for chemical dependency, addictive or compulsive behavior, and the closely related problems stemming from dysfunctional-family childhood histories.

In order for the field of chemical dependency to realize its potential to provide efficacious treatment to these new consumers of mental health services, a foundation of knowledge relevant to the task is needed. Outcome-evaluation research in the field has produced knowledge of factors important to successful long-term treatment outcome (Wallace, 1991), but also has been flawed methodologically. This book presents selected research suggestive of needed modifications in treatment and future research trends that might clarify what will be effective in improving treatment outcome with the chemically dependent.

Theory can inform research, and research findings, in turn, can direct modified stances on the part of those practitioners who may rigidly embrace theoretical or conceptual positions. Just as rigid marital partners do during family disputes, partners in the field of chemical-dependency treatment must eventually surrender rigid stances and begin to work hard in partnership toward solutions for the sake of all family members—especially the chemically dependent.

Research findings in this book may also assist in the evolution of an integrated theory that partly resolves "standoffs" among disease-model proponents, those who rigidly oppose the disease view, and social-learning advocates of controlled drinking (Blum & Trachtenberg, 1988; Peele, 1990; Gorman, 1989; Heather, 1990; "Comments on . . . ," 1990). Findings may also suggest a role for valued beliefs held within psychobiological, psychodynamic, and cognitive-behavioral camps. These camps cannot remain divided if the critical needs of the chemically dependent and compulsive behaviorally are to be met effectively. And, since multiple addictions affect our primary alcoholics and heavy-drinking drug addicts, the resolution of theoretical and conceptual disputes can only help front-line treatment practitioners increase their effectiveness—even as they await the next designer drug or creative chemical cocktail to be described when they take drug-use histories.

THE CONCEPT OF PHASES OF TREATMENT AND RECOVERY

Perhaps most important, the book provides a novel approach to the chemically dependent population by discussing issues in the context of phases of treatment and recovery. Emphasis on the notion of such phases rests in the conviction that specific kinds of clinical interventions derive the rationale for their implementation depending on the phase of recovery a client is in. Phases of treatment in which certain interventions are delivered thereby correspond to the phase of recovery a client currently negotiates. The phase of recovery is defined in terms of the specific amount of time since the last use of a chemical substance. (See Table 1-1).

Although authors are free to interpret phases of recovery according to their own perspective, this author's (Wallace, 1991a) phases of recovery help to clarify this concept: From day 1 to day 14 since the last chemical use, clients negotiate an early initial phase of abstinence called the withdrawal phase. Thereafter, and for the first six months, the client attempts to prolong the period of abstinence, and avoid the high risk of relapse associated with this phase, during a phase called prolonging abstinence. Beyond six months of having achieved a phase of stable abstinence, clients continue to pursue an abstinent life-style or a path of lifetime recovery—which is most difficult to sustain during the first several years of recovery—called the phase of lifetime recovery.

A strong rationale exists for embracing the notion of phases of treatment and recovery as a critical concept that should guide the evolution and refinement of the field of chemical dependency. Clinicians from various perspectives—psychodynamic, cognitive-behavioral, physiological—have recognized the validity

Table 1-1
Phases of Recovery and Professionals' Tasks During Phases of Treatment

Phase	Time Period	Clinicians' Task	Researchers' Task
Phase I: The Withdrawal Phase	Days 1–14 of initial abstinence	* assessment * stabilization * retain in treatment * prevent relapse * enhance motivation	* determine utility of neuronutrients, chemotherapy * determine ideal client-to-intervention matching strategies.
Phase II: Prolonging Abstinence	First 6 months of abstinence	* continuing assessment * reduce risk of relapse, which is high * sustain motivation * support ego functioning * improve self-regulation	* determine utility of neuronutrients, chemotherapy * determine ideal and cost-effective client-to-intervention matching strategies
Phase III: Pursuing Lifetime Recovery	Six months onward (first few years of recovery are most difficult)	* continuing assessment * foster stable drug-free lifestyle * prevent relapse * address other psychopathology * improve self-regulation	* same as above * long-term follow-up in outcome evaluation * operationalize in research self & object relation theory

of implementing specific treatment strategies depending on the client's phase of recovery. This book presents the perspectives of such diverse practitioners and researchers, highlighting developmental trends in the field of chemical dependency that rest on the premise that the phase of recovery dictates the timing of delivery of treatment interventions. The intervention to be delivered may involve medically supervised provision of a neuronutrient to ease intense cravings during withdrawal, the teaching of relapse prevention strategies to permit prolonging the period of abstinence, or the provision of individual and group psychotherapy to facilitate the successful pursuit of lifetime recovery.

Appreciation of the phase of recovery a client is negotiating also permits the clinician to engage in a thoughtful client-to-treatment matching strategy. Therapists need to conclude thorough individualized assessments of clients with a strategy of matching clients to treatments of appropriate intensity (Marlatt, 1988; Wallace, 1991a). Another way of conceptualizing when inpatient, versus outpatient, versus long-term residential therapeutic community treatment is the appropriate treatment recommendation involves the concept of phases of treatment and recovery. As a potential handbook for clinicians and researchers working with the chemically dependent, this book asserts the importance of assessing the client's unique characteristics which may (1) predict the ability to successfully negotiate a specific phase of recovery—withdrawal, prolonging abstinence, pursuing lifetime recovery—and (2) dictate specific client-to-treatment or client-to-intervention matching strategies. For example, assessment might reveal such high-dose and high-frequency chemical use by a client that one can anticipate severe difficulty negotiating the withdrawal phase and consider the wisdom of matching this client to medically supervised inpatient treatment (Wallace, 1991a). Assessment might also reveal that a client possesses a high potential for relapse that suggests the need for intensive outpatient treatment, therapeutic support in negotiating the first six months of recovery in which relapse is most common, and the provision of psychoeducation on relapse prevention. Client characteristics and assessment findings may further dictate matching a client to a long-term residential therapeutic community that spans both the initial six-month period, in which relapse is most likely, and the first and second year of recovery, in which a drug-free functional lifestyle must be established. In sum, the concept of phases of treatment and recovery can serve as an important guide in client-to-treatment matching strategies both in research and in clinical practice, as Table 1-1 suggests.

A BIOPSYCHOSOCIAL APPROACH

The book also attempts to integrate psychodynamic, cognitive-behavioral, and physiological perspectives by utilizing a biopsychosocial approach to chemical dependency. Such an approach permits the development of an integrated theory that recognizes the value of biologically, psychologically, and socially-environmentally based interventions (Wallace, 1991a). Within biopsychosocial approaches, an individualized assessment focusing on all of these factors further permits matching patients to specific treatment modalities (Donovan & Marlatt, 1988; Wallace, 1991a) as a part of a cost-effective treatment strategy. In this way, any state-of-the-art treatment approach rightly arises from a biopsychosocial model of addiction. This book will attempt to draw on the work and perspectives of various clinicians and researchers in order to utilize further a biopsychosocial approach toward the development of an integrated theory.

Relapse prevention has also been a prime focus of biopsychosocial model proponents (Marlatt & Gordon, 1985; Marlatt, 1988; Wallace, 1991a). This book expands this view and links relapse prevention to phases of treatment and recovery. This author goes so far as to advocate a multidimensional approach to relapse prevention that subsumes diverse interventions to be implemented within every phase of recovery. Within this view, relapse prevention includes interventions as seemingly diverse as providing neuronutrients, teaching cognitive-behavioral coping skills, and insuring that clients have therapeutic and self-help group support. These kinds of relapse-prevention activities should take place as early as a phase of early initial abstinence, or withdrawal, and especially throughout the phase of prolonging abstinence. The kind of long-term professional individual therapy, group therapy, and 12-step program involvement advocated in the book also constitutes relapse prevention, even when occurring from one to three years since the last drug use. Relapse prevention thereby addresses the biological, psychological, and social-etiological roots of addiction (Wallace, 1991a). The value of implementing varied forms of relapse prevention within every phase of treatment and recovery finds support throughout the book. In fact, the essence of working with the chemically dependent and behaviorally compulsive may rest on this broad conceptualization of relapse prevention.

CONCLUSION

This chapter has reviewed the historical developments in the 1980s that have created the need for a field of chemical dependency capable of an efficacious response to varied addictions and compulsions. Key developments include the cocaine, crack, and AIDS epidemics and a growing public willingness to seek mental health treatment for the addictions, compulsions, and interrelated histories of childhood development in alcoholic and dysfunctional families. The book draws on the expertise of seasoned clinicians and the findings of high-caliber researchers in an attempt to elevate the chemical-dependency field to a level where clinical interventions are grounded in a sound theoretical rationale supported by research findings. The book strives to provide both treatment practitioners and clinical researchers with a handbook that can inform clinical practice, treatment design, and future research directions. The notion that practice need be grounded in a theoretical rationale, that treatment models must be repeatedly refined in light of research findings, and that the special characteristics of patient populations must be considered in treatment design all emerge through the thrust and focus of the book as principles to guide the field of chemical dependency as it continues to evolve.

Toward this end, the concept of phases of treatment and recovery, a biopsychosocial approach, and emphasis on relapse prevention shall be brought to bear in examining the challenge presented by a large body of chemically dependent persons. As a possible outcome, the author aspires to integrate seemingly diverse points of view that are all critical to the evolution of the field of chemical dependency.

REFERENCES

Bagnall, G. (1990). Alcohol education for 13 year olds—does it work? Results from a controlled evaluation. *British Journal of Addiction*, 85, 89–96.

Blum, K.,& Trachtenberg, M. C. (1988). Alcoholism: Scientific basis of a neuropsychogenetic disease. *International Journal of the Addictions*, 23, 781–796.

Bollerud, K. (1990). A model for the treatment of trauma-related syndromes among chemically dependent inpatient women. *Journal of Substance Abuse Treatment*, 7, 83–87.

Borland, R. (1990) Slip-ups and relapse in attempts to quit smoking. *Addictive Behaviors*, 15, 235–245.

Botvin, G. J., Baker, E., Filazzola, A. D., & Botvin, E. M. (1990). A cognitive-behavioral approach to substance abuse prevention: One year follow-up. *Addictive Behaviors*, 15, 47–63.

Brandon, T. H., Tiffany, S. T., Obremski, K. M., & Baker, T. B. (1990). Postcessation cigarette use: The process of relapse. *Addictive Behaviors*, 15, 105–114.

Bruvold, W. H. (1990). A meta-analysis of the California school-based risk reduction program. *Journal of Drug Education*, 20, 139–152.

Carmody, T. P. (1990). Preventing relapse in the treatment of nicotine addiction: Current issues and future directions. *Journal of Psychoactive Drugs*, 22, 211–238.

Caudill, B. D., Kantor, G. K., & Ungerleider, S. (1990). Project Impact: A national study of high school substance abuse intervention training. *Journal of Alcohol and Drug Education*, 35, 61–74.

Comments on Gorman's "Is the 'new' problem drinking concept of Heather & Robertson more helpful in advancing our scientific knowledge that the 'old' disease concept?" (1990). *British Journal of Addiction*, 84, 847–852.

Corless, T., & Dickerson, M. (1989). Gamblers' self-perceptions of the determinants of impaired control. *British Journal of Addiction*, 84, 1527–1537.

De Leon, G. (1989). Therapeutic communities for substance abuse: Overview of approach and effectiveness. *Psychology of Addictive Behaviors*, 3, 140–147.

Des Jarlais, D., & Friedman, S. (1990). Shooting galleries and AIDS: Infection probabilities and "tough" policies. *American Journal of Public Health, 80,* 142–144.

Donovan, D. M., & Marlatt, G. A. (Eds.) (1988). *Assessment of addictive behaviors.* New York: Guilford.

Fitzgibbon, M. L., & Kirschenbaum, D. S. (1990). Heterogeneity of clinical presentation among obese individuals seeking treatment. *Addictive Behaviors, 15,* 291–295.

Gorman, D. M. (1989). Is the "new" problem drinking concept of Heather & Robertson more useful in advancing scientific knowledge than the "old" disease concept? *British Journal of Addiction, 84,* 843–845.

Heather, N. (1990). Problem drinking as a form of learned behaviour: A final rejoinder to Gorman and Edwards. *British Journal of Addiction, 85,* 617–620.

Kayman, S., Bruvold, W., & Stern, J. (1990). Maintenance and relapse after weight loss in women: Behavioral aspects. *American Journal of Clinical Nutrition, 52,* 800–807.

Klitzner, M., Bamberger, E., & Gruenewald, P. J. (1990). The assessment of parent-led prevention programs: A national descriptive study. *Journal of Drug Education, 20,* 111–125.

Klitzner, M., Gruenewald, P. J., & Bamberger, E. (1990). The assessment of parent-led prevention programs: A preliminary assessment of impact. *Journal of Drug Education, 20,* 77–94.

Kolar, A. F., Brown, B., Weddington, W., & Ball, J. C. (1990). A treatment crisis: Cocaine use by clients in methadone maintenance programs. *Journal of Substance Abuse Treatment, 7,* 101–107.

Marlatt, G. A. (1988). Matching client to treatment: Treatment models and stages of change. In D. M. Donovan & G. A. Marlatt (Eds.), *Assessment of addictive behaviors.* New York: Guilford.

Marlatt, G. A., & Gordon, J. R. (1985). *Relapse prevention.* New York: Guilford.

Massey, R. F., & Neidigh, L. W. (1990). Evaluating and improving the functioning of a peer-based alcohol abuse prevention organization. *Journal of Alcohol and Drug Education, 35,* 24–35.

Peele, S. (1990). Why and by whom the American alcoholism treatment industry is under siege. *Journal of Psychoactive Drugs, 22,* 1–13.

Rawson, R. A. (1990). Cut the crack: The policymaker's guide to cocaine treatment. *Policy Review, 51,* 10–20.

Rohsenow, D. J., Corbett, R., & Devine, D. (1988). Molested as children: A hidden contribution to substance abuse? *Journal of Substance Abuse Treatment, 5,* 13–18.

Schilling, R. F., Schinke, S. P., Nichols, S. E., Zayas, L. H., Miller, S. O., Orlandi, M. A., & Botvin, G. (1989). Developing strategies for AIDS prevention research with Black and Hispanic drug users. *Public Health Reports, 104,* 2–12.

Sorenson, J. L., Batki, S. L., Good, P., & Wilkinson, K. (1989). Methadone maintenance program for AIDS-affective opiate addicts. *Journal of Substance Abuse Treatment, 6,* 87–94.

Van Meter, W., & Rioux, D. (1990). The case for shorter residential alcohol and other drug abuse treatment of adolescents. *Journal of Psychoactive Drugs, 22,* 87–88.

Wallace, B. C. (1990). Crack cocaine smokers as adult children of alcoholics: The dysfunctional family link. *Journal of Substance Abuse Treatment, 7*, 89–100.

Wallace, B. C. (1991a). *Crack cocaine: A practical treatment approach for the chemically dependent.* New York: Brunner/Mazel.

Wallace, B. C. (1991b). Chemical dependency treatment for the pregnant crack addict: Beyond the criminal sanctions perspective. *Psychology of Addictive Behaviors, 5.*

Washton, A. M. (1989 December). Cocaine abuse and compulsive sexuality. *Medical Aspects of Human Sexuality,* 32–39.

Washton, A. M., & Stone-Washton, N. (1990). Abstinence and relapse in outpatient cocaine addicts. *Journal of Psychoactive Drugs, 22,* 135–147.

Young, E. B. (1990). The role of incest issues in relapse. *Journal of Psychoactive Drugs, 22,* 249–258.

2

Inpatient Treatment for the First Phase of Withdrawal

Barbara C. Wallace, Ph.D.

While authors argue that intensive outpatient rehabilitation treatment (Chapter 3) or comprehensive and intensive outpatient treatment (Rawson, 1990) can effectively meet the treatment needs of a majority of chemically dependent clients, the question remains as to for whom and under what conditions an inpatient stay remains appropriate. This chapter will attempt to answer this question by drawing primarily on the author's experiences in working with severely dependent crack cocaine patients in Interfaith Medical Center's inpatient detoxification units.

THE VALUE OF OUTPATIENT TREATMENT

As we shall see in Chapter 3, a compelling argument can be made for the utility of an intensive outpatient treatment model. Tatarsky and Washton draw upon their clinical experience in witnessing the efficacy of a highly structured, intensive outpatient program that works very well with crack addicts, alcoholics, heroin addicts, and other chemically dependent patients. These authors note that this general success was seen in a context in which most professionals might routinely assume that these clients needed inpatient care; however, many of their clients also had histories of having relapsed shortly after discharge from one or more residential programs. Tatarsky and Washton correctly assert several key points that can guide our discussion of inpatient treatment in this chapter: (1) it is not sufficient to lock clients away for a month or longer, but it is imperative to give them tools that permit them to stay clean/sober in a real world full of drugs and triggers to use them; and (2) the attainment of self-knowledge regarding problems, typically acquired in an inpatient

15

stay, is less important than the critical task of delivering interventions that can prevent relapse after discharge. These criticisms of traditional inpatient or residential programs are on target.

In addition, our discussion of inpatient treatment in this chapter can be informed by Tatarsky and Washton's highlighting of some of the strengths of an intensive outpatient treatment model. These involve (1) a heavy emphasis on psychoeducation through workbooks, films, and frequent psychoeducational groups with a structured educational format that insures that key issues are covered; (2) an appreciation of the fact that such education provides a cognitive framework in which clients can organize and understand their experience; (3) the value of cognitive interventions that explore clients' faulty or addictive thinking—which can lead to relapse—and increase their awareness of internal and external triggers of relapse; (4) the need to improve clients' coping ability in face of stress, challenging feelings, and high-risk situations; and (5) the value of combined individual and group therapy with the same therapist, which permits work on intimate personal problems and the utilization of insight-oriented techniques in addition to cognitive interventions.

These timely and on-target criticisms of inpatient treatment, and my summary of some of the strengths of the outpatient model to be described in depth in Chapter 3, provide an excellent foundation for our discussion. We start from a foundation suggesting that clinicians learn from the patients "what works," while bringing their training and a theoretical rationale to bear on the treatment process. What strikes me as most fascinating comes out of my own experiences on an inpatient detoxification unit that serve to validate what Tatarsky and Washton indeed discovered, implemented, and articulate as the essence of "what works" with today's chemically dependent clients, although from their vantage point in an outpatient setting. From my vantage point in an inpatient setting, I perceived the metaphorical elephant of chemical dependence in much the same way; however, somewhat different perspectives while viewing the same elephant are inevitable, given our different vantage points.

A MODEL OF INPATIENT TREATMENT

From my vantage point, I saw that mere residence in our inpatient detoxification units (two weeks for those dependent on crack cocaine and up to 21 days for heroin addicts) was useless unless the tools to stay clean postdetoxification were given to clients. Similarly, the self-knowledge and insight into problems we strove to stimulate while clients were on our units did not seem nearly as important in my mind as did the provision of relapse prevention. I came to realize that psychoeducation (Wallace, 1989b) containing a specific educational content/curriculum needed to be given to every addict. Also, education did provide clients with a new and sorely needed cognitive and intellectual framework (Wallace, 1991) in which they could organize and understand their experience, as well as the challenge of avoiding relapse. To my surprise as a psychodynamically trained clinician, cognitive interventions emerged as critical in providing clients with new ways of thinking, and I felt compelled to transform and replace their very dangerous cognitions, which seemed certain to lead them down the road toward relapse. As a psychodynamically trained clinician, I had to become an active educator who, in effect, relied heavily on cognitive reframing (Wallace, 1991).

Similar to Tatarsky and Washton, I also came to appreciate the importance of improving clients' coping skills in the face of stress, challenging feelings, and other high-risk situations (Wallace, 1989a) likely to trigger a relapse. However, not having been trained in graduate school as a behaviorist, and being less than enthusiastic about the behavioral stress-reduction techniques I did learn to teach clients on internship, I chose not to deliver behavioral interventions. Nonetheless, within psychoeducation I found it imperative to teach clients about classical conditioning, the process of extinction, and the danger of performing automatic conditioned responses when confronted with conditioned stimuli postdetoxification (Wallace, 1991). In this way, psychoeducation expanded on 12-step-program admonitions to "avoid people, places, and things" by breaking down complex behavioral principles of conditioning and extinction into terms clients could understand.

What seemed to work in accomplishing the goals of psychoeducation with clients during the two-week detoxification period became my treatment arsenal. The use of metaphorical forms of communication that conveyed graphic and visual information held clients' attention and seemed to work most effectively (Wallace, 1989b, 1991) in educating them about complex behavioral principles and accomplishing cognitive reframing. Metaphors, analogies, and stories most effectively described numerous high-risk situations and the appropriate alternative behavioral response to avoid relapse. The microanalysis in group of individuals' experiences in encountering real-life high-risk situations and the mistaken behaviors that led to relapse evolved into graphic storytelling interventions to be retold in all groups.

Also, the combined provision of individual and group therapy by the same therapist was most effective in facilitating acceptance of the need for aftercare treatment—our primary goal. Individual therapy permitted the attainment of detailed assessment data that allowed the matching of clients to aftercare treatment appropriate to their needs (Wallace, 1991). Both individual and group sessions served as opportunities for me to be an active educator who cognitively reframed and interpreted the varied impact on clients of their unique experience of childhood trauma or development in a dysfunctional family that they reported as part of their histories. For other clients, a discussion of social and environmental factors, the highly reinforcing nature of crack cocaine, the drug's neurochemical actions, and/or feelings of emptiness and boredom were high-lighted as possible etiological factors in their drug addiction. Psychologists work-ing with clients over a two-week inpatient detoxification period attempted to put together for all individuals the pieces of the puzzle that might provide clients with a cognitive and intellectual framework in which to understand how their drug dependence came about. In effect, an active multifaceted clinical tech-nique, utilizing educational, psychodynamic, cognitive-behavioral, and meta-phorical elements, was necessary to achieve clinical efficacy.

Diverse, but overwhelmingly dysfunctional, family histories (alcoholism, domes-tic violence, parental separation, physical abuse, incest, sexual abuse, emotional abuse, overstimulation, spoiling) were cognitively reframed as possible etiological variables in a client's low self-esteem, interpersonal problems, deficient self-care and the major deficit of an inability to identify and process feelings. My ability to attune empathically to clients' inner experiences, empathically mirror the pain har-bored by split-off aspects of the self, label affects for them, and effectively interpret the effect of childhood trauma on their lives motivated initially ambivalent addicts to accept aftercare treatment referrals (see Wallace [1991] for a detailed discussion of these interventions), but no outcome data are available on actual entrance into aftercare.

Aftercare treatment was advanced as imperative in order to begin to address a patient's underlying problems, permit receipt of therapeutic support while clients are most vulnerable to relapse (the first three to six months of recovery), and insure that clients learn better coping and self-management skills. The combined use of 12-step groups (with a sponsor) and outpatient treatment providing individual and group therapy was recommended to clients. Depending on assessment findings, treatment might be tailored to include a referral to a residential therapeutic com-munity (TC). The numerous factors influencing referrals have been reviewed in detail elsewhere (Wallace, 1991; see Chapter 4 also). But in the ideal situation, we aspired to link clients to the kind of outpatient treatment described in the next chap-ter. Unfortunately, this was an ever-illusive goal since most of our patients lacked private medical insurance.

Because of the compelling description of outpatient treatment in Chapter 3, the future of inpatient treatment rests on its ability to show an efficacy equal or superior to that of outpatient treatment. Ironically, inpatient treatment can probably only prove equal or superior if it is directly followed by some kind of intensive and com-prehensive outpatient treatment, one that emphasizes relapse prevention (Washton & Stone-Washton, 1990; Schiffer, 1988). At least the matching of clients to indi-vidual and/or group therapy with professionals skilled in treating the chemically dependent, as well as to 12-step programs, needs to follow inpatient treatment. Given this inevitable set of confounding variables that may prevent our arriving at a clear consensus as to whether inpatient or outpatient treatment is preferable, a rationale for inpatient treatment must exist.

RATIONALE FOR INPATIENT TREATMENT

Prior to the crack and cocaine epidemic of the 1980s, which challenged outpatient treatment to evolve into models that could compete with and threaten to replace inpatient treatment, an unsound rationale for the latter prevailed. Marlatt (1988) correctly points out that the ubiquitous 28- or 30-day inpatient hospital treatment stay that prevails in the field may not be appropriate for all patients. In the past, many of these programs may have erred in the widespread use of the 28- or 30-day hospital stay for all patients and in assigning clients to the same set of interventions, without paying attention to the distinct characteristics of the chemicals used or the distinct characteristics of the clients. These practices suggested that all patients were treated in the same manner, leaving little room for today's preferred strategy of letting detailed assessment findings guide the matching of clients to treatments tailored to individual needs and predicaments.

The future of inpatient treatment may rest on programs moving away from extending the same methods and disease models/12-step programs to all clients. The efficacy of interventions is strained in being extended with little modification to all clients regardless of their characteristics and chemicals of abuse. Conflict between proponents of the disease model ("one drink leads to a drunk") and social-learning theory advocates of controlled drinking (Gorman, 1989; Heather, 1990) need not bar inpatient programs from taking something of value from the cognitive-behavioral area. Cognitive-behavioral contributions to our understanding of relapse (Marlatt & Gordon, 1985) suggest the need to augment disease model and 12-step-program models with solid relapse-prevention interventions (Gorski, 1990; Annis, 1990; Wallace, 1991). Similarly, biopsychosocial approaches (Donovan & Marlatt, 1988; Wallace, 1991) need to be embraced as the state-of-the-art treatment models that emphasize individualized assessment and client-to-treatment matching, despite one's primary affiliation with a disease model or cognitive-behavioral camp.

The result is an integrated treatment approach utilizing a multifaceted technique or a multimodal set of treatment interventions. If a sound rationale for the use of inpatient treatment programs is to emerge, it may mean the movement toward more thorough clinical assessments, client-to-intervention matching, and provision of relapse prevention. Both Tatarsky and Washton's perspective and my view of the chemical-dependence elephant suggest this kind of movement; both views advance the provision of psychoeducation integrating cognitive-behavioral and psychodynamic approaches, as well as relapse prevention.

Some argue that not only are these standard 28-day inpatient programs ineffective, but some are actually closing because outpatient treatment—such as that offered through health maintenance organizations (HMOs)—is becoming the dominant route by which chemically dependent clients are being treated (Schwabb, 1991). If this trend continues, and since treatment to be received can only be derived via the options for which insurance will pay, inpatient treatment may be in jeopardy. Perhaps substantially restructured inpatient treatment of a varying and shorter length than the traditional programs may have a role in chemical dependency treatment worth fighting with the insurance companies to preserve. The strongest rationale for inpatient treatment is that there are progressive models (Wallace, 1991) and that modifications can be instituted in other existing models so that, within a continuum of care, inpatient interventions continue to play a role. That role may involve stabilizing those with the most severe chemical dependency who may possess certain characteristics (to be discussed shortly). The way in which they should be stabilized before connection with outpatient treatment—or residential TC treatment—may involve a variable-length inpatient detoxification during a withdrawal phase.

A ROLE FOR INPATIENT DETOXIFICATION DURING WITHDRAWAL

Inpatient detoxification may need to be reserved for those clients who are very debilitated and severely addicted, but often ambivalent about treatment. This state best characterizes compulsive crack cocaine smokers negotiating a withdrawal phase. Tatarsky and Washton recognize in Chapter 3 that there are indeed clients lacking in motivation who may not be ready for outpatient treatment. Rawson (1990) suggests that the "hard core" crack addict similarly may not be able to achieve recovery through his intensive and comprehensive outpatient treatment model. In my experience, many truly hard-core crack-cocaine–dependent clients only entered treatment because of the threatened loss of employment, of a spouse, of child custody, or of their very lives by a drug dealer to whom they owed money. Invariably there were individuals for whom this kind of crisis failed to provide genuine motivation to pursue recovery, and treatment could easily be labeled a manipulation to prevent some negative crisis. These inflated, grandiose, and resistant clients, who could easily end up perceiving treatment as a joke, represented my most challenging brand of client. However, I refined techniques of empathic mirroring that reflected to clients the part of themselves that was in tremendous pain, against which the inflated grandiose self tried to defend. Empathic mirroring served to motivate ambivalent and difficult clients to engage in the treatment process. (See Wallace [1991] for a detailed discussion of this technique.)

For compulsive crack cocaine clients, an inpatient detoxification structured to provide these and other kinds of psychological interventions (described earlier) may be critical for several reasons. During a period of withdrawal, clients experience intense neurochemically based cravings for more crack. They seek to remedy craving, dysphoria, anxiety, and irritability through repeated self-administration of more crack, fueling hours and days of compulsive crack smoking. Clients also exhibit psychopathology caused by the addiction, such as a striking narcissism as a consequence of the trauma of hitting rock bottom (Wallace, 1991; Bean-Bayog, 1986). Many hard-core crack addicts are so debilitated medically that they look anorexic, are malnourished, cough up black phlegm, have high rates of syphilis/gonorrhea/ vaginal warts, and are at risk for the acquired immunodeficiency syndrome (AIDS) as a result of exchanging sex for crack or the promiscuity related to the aphrodisiac effects of cocaine (Washton, 1989). Typically, clients presenting with severe chemical dependency show significant psychosocial deterioration and negotiate environments saturated with classically conditioned stimuli that may fuel repetitive cycles of relapse in response to classically conditioned triggers. Many clients enter inpatient settings not only in need of medical interventions for their debilitated state, but also in need of psychiatric and psychological interventions for the depression and feelings of hopelessness that accompany hitting rock bottom and the experience of repeated relapse. Inpatient detoxification is a critical intervention for many crack-cocaine–dependent patients and other chemically dependent clients. A thorough and proper assessment determines which patients require this most intensive treatment intervention.

Wallace (1991) reports that in a sample of 245 largely African-American compulsive crack-cocaine smokers, 72% used crack daily or three to five times per week. Half (50%) of the daily crack smokers use an average daily dose of over $100 per day of crack. A full 20% of daily crack smokers use between $200 and $500 worth per day. These represent quite severe addictions indeed. The higher the dose and the more frequent the use of crack, the greater is the difficulty in discontinuing compulsive crack smoking. For these severely addicted, high-dose, high-frequency compulsive crack smokers, the intervention of inpatient detoxification remains crucial as a first step in treating their addiction. Aftercare treatment is the next essential step postdetoxification, along a difficult path of recovery.

Within a continuum of care, the next treatment intervention may be either outpatient or residential TC treatment. Inpatient detoxification during a withdrawal phase is a necessary prelude to placement in a residential TC. The trauma of hitting rock bottom involves severe psychosocial deterioration brought about by the total disruption of one's life when one pursues compulsive drug use. Psychosocial deterioration, such as loss of family support, being asked to leave one's household, or ending up homeless, indicates the need for a TC stay. Such patients literally get off the streets and enter inpatient detoxification. After detoxification, they require placement in a residential TC.

Beyond the needs of the severely addicted compulsive crack-cocaine smoker, intravenous heroin user, or alcoholic, other, less severely addicted clients who are psychotic, suicidal, or homicidal may end up in an inpatient setting. The problems of effectively treating the dually diagnosed (see Chapter 17) may suggest that even within an inpatient setting, specialized drug treatment services for these patients can best be delivered on a specialized drug detoxification unit. At Interfaith Medical Center (IMC), on each drug detoxification unit we averaged the treatment of one or two dually diagnosed clients per month presenting with schizophrenia, bipolar disorder, or major depression with suicidality.

MAXIMIZING THE UTILITY OF INPATIENT DETOXIFICATION

Drug detoxification units must not be merely warehouses for the medically supervised provision of progressively lower doses of methadone to heroin addicts or vitamins and pharmacological adjuncts to the crack dependent. At IMC, psychologists were expected to provide psychological interventions in individual and group psychotherapy and to perform thorough individualized assessments in order to match clients to appropriate aftercare treatment. Inpatient detoxification must maximize this brief opportunity—a 10- to 14-day detoxification—to have an impact on patients' consciousness. Clinicians must furnish interventions that reduce the likelihood of a "slip" or full-blown relapse (Marlatt, 1985) and the chances that patients will disregard recommendations for aftercare treatment.

Interventions that reduce the likelihood of relapse are based on a treatment rationale that arises from a biopsychosocial model (Donovan & Marlatt, 1988) of crack addiction (Wallace, 1991). The treatment of crack-cocaine dependence during inpatient detoxification should follow from an appreciation of the interaction of biological, psychological, and social factors that play a role in the development and maintenance of addiction (Donovan & Marlatt, 1988). Biological factors requiring consideration involve the neurochemical disruptions in the brain caused by chronic crack-cocaine smoking. Cocaine has been reconceptualized as our most addicting drug and crack is viewed as the most addicting form of cocaine; this reconceptualization of cocaine arises from an appreciation of cocaine's pharmacological actions and the neurochemical disruptions it produces in brain function (Rosecan & Spitz, 1987). A resulting critical intervention involves the provision of medications and amino acids in an attempt to replenish the precursors of the depleted neurotransmitters. The IMC medical regimen includes L-tyrosine, L-tryptophan, lecithin, choline chloride, and vitamins. Biologically based interventions such as the provision of neuronutrients discussed in Chapter 12 may be important to alleviate the cravings that cocaine, crack, and heroin addicts and alcoholics experience.

Once crack smokers are receptive to treatment, a multifaceted clinical technique is utilized in psychoeducational groups held twice a week on the unit further to maximize the efficacy of inpatient detoxification. A multifaceted technique includes the use of education and metaphor and draws upon clinicians' knowledge of psychodynamic and cognitive-behavioral theory. These interventions recognize the role of psychological and social-environmental factors in the development and maintenance of addiction and seek to address them therapeutically so as to facilitate successful negotiation of the withdrawal phase, the phase of prolonging abstinence, and the pursuit of lifetime recovery.

In sum, what maximizes inpatient detoxification's efficacy may involve the following. Clinicians freely intersperse interventions during psychoeducational groups that involve providing (1) education on "mini topics" (crack's pharmacology, crack cravings, crack dreams, emotional and psychological consequences of development in a dysfunctional family); (2) multiple metaphors (stories of old patients' experiences, actual metaphors on the treatment process and defenses); and (3) interventions that teach psychodynamic and behavioral principles that explain patients' susceptibility to developing an addiction, the propensity to relapse, conditioned responses to conditioned stimuli, and how extinction of these responses occur. Wallace (1989b, 1991) describes 29 clinical interventions in psychoeducational groups that exemplify this multifaceted clinical technique.

THE CRITICAL ROLE OF RELAPSE-PREVENTION EDUCATION

The main goal of treatment in many respects is relapse prevention. Contrary to the beliefs of many clinicians, relapse prevention should begin on day 1 of treatment, finding a critical place in inpatient detoxification settings. Preparing patients for the challenge of avoiding a slip or relapse may be the clinician's most important function. However, a broadened conceptualization of relapse prevention is recommended as discussed by Wallace in Chapter 10. By sharing stories of patients' relapse episodes, actually eliciting in group sessions descriptions of such episodes and explaining triggers of relapse, psychoeducation delivered twice weekly in one-hour groups attempts to prevent patients from experiencing a relapse. Patients are encouraged to engage in alternative preventative behaviors; most important among these are engaging in aftercare treatment and learning how to utilize the support of psychotherapists, Narcotics Anonymous sponsors, and drug-free family members and friends, and to talk about feelings and drug cravings.

Contrary to the practice of many programs that offer different program tracks for patients who have experienced a relapse and those who are new in recovery, those "new" to addiction treatment and recovery also need extensive training in relapse prevention (Gorski, 1990; Kelley, 1991). Groups combining so-called old clients who have had a prior relapse and are returning to treatment with those "new" to recovery permits a microanalysis (Marlatt & Gordon, 1985; Wallace, 1991) within groups of old clients' relapse episodes. In such groups new clients learn how to analyze real-life "slips" and relapses for the role of multiple determinants and high-risk situations in the process of relapse. Also, by virtue of meeting diagnostic criteria for chemical dependence (American Psychiatric Association, 1987; Wallace, 1991), most clients entering treatment for the first time have had repeated experiences of trying to stop or reduce chemical use on their own without success.

Thus, even clients who are new to the treatment and recovery process can learn to examine their past drug-use patterns for determinants of chemical-use episodes and personal high-risk situations so they can anticipate and prepare to alter their behavior in future high-risk situations. Old clients can readily identify with new clients' overconfidence, poor reality testing, and misconceptions about addiction and recovery. The combination of new and old clients in relapse prevention groups permits old clients to realize their growth and to appreciate the knowledge gained from a meaningful relapse experience that is transformed into a powerful learning experience. Also, new clients gain a more realistic understanding of the importance of acquiring "tools," skills, and adequate aftercare treatment to facilitate a recovery without repeated relapse. Individual sessions permit clinicians to acquire more extensive information about a particular client's unique predisposition to relapse in light of his or her particular drug-use pattern, idiosyncratic high-risk situations, personality, defensive functioning, and general life problems. Individualized treatment plans for aftercare and personalized strategies for avoiding relapse should be further delineated in individual sessions.

Treatment interventions that address the emotional and psychological impact of childhood developmental experiences may be necessary components of effective crack-treatment models, constituting a form of relapse prevention. During detoxification, psychoeducation in a group context covers the meaning and impact of childhood experiences in dysfunctional family systems. Wanck (1985) reports that alcoholics who are adult children of alcoholics relapse at higher rates than do alcoholics without that status. Hence crack smokers who are adult children of alcoholics (and adult children of dysfunctional families) may be more likely to relapse. They may require treatments, such as long-term individual and group psychotherapy (see Part V and Chapter 4), that address the consequences of their childhood experiences. Psychoeducational relapse prevention strives to prepare patients for the process of engaging in individual psychotherapy and group therapy. Education explains the effect of poor-quality object relations with parents in childhood; the impact of narcissistic injuries; the goal of learning how to label, identify, feel, and process emotions; the task of learning how to avoid the defense of inflation in response to painfully low self-esteem; and the process of long-term therapy that can remedy these deficits in self- and egofunctioning. Metaphors are particularly effective in explaining deficits patients possess and the process of healing they must take responsibility for seeking in order to reduce the chances of relapse. Since 40% of relapse episodes involve poor management of painful feelings (Wallace, 1991), the remediation of deficits in regulating feelings and self-esteem constitutes essential relapse prevention.

CONCLUSION

Even though inpatient treatment programs have justly deserved criticism, this chapter has outlined key modifications in clinical technique and program structure necessary to make the use of inpatient treatment programs rational and viable. Inpatient detoxification represents an important intervention for the most severely chemically dependent, as embodied in the circumstance of the crack cocaine addict. Following the dictates of a biopsychosocial approach, inpatient detoxification begins with a thorough assessment in which data are gathered on the frequency and dose of crack smoking, crack-related psychosocial deterioration, and childhood experiences suggesting psychological roots of a susceptibility to developing an addiction. Inpatient detoxification is also a time to impress patients with the crucial role of aftercare treatment and to prepare them for the challenge of preventing relapse and for meaningfully engaging in individual and group therapy postdetoxification.

Through the use of education, metaphor, and our knowledge of psychodynamic and behavioral theory, clinicians on inpatient units can use a multifaceted clinical technique with newly abstinent patients and our capacity for empathy to help debilitated patients successfully recover from severe addictions. The multifaceted clinical technique described is also a very active clinical stance. An active technique is appropriate during inpatient detoxification and with newly abstinent patients in general.

Patients are very vulnerable to painful emotions that emerge when they are newly abstinent—feelings that were medicated with crack for years or months during continuous crack smoking. Taking a psychosocial history of childhood experiences in dysfunctional families and of recent crack-related psychosocial deterioration usually does not, and should not, induce a regression or promote fragmentation. In fact, education on how and why patients may have ended up in a hospital for severe crack addiction and on their deficits in affect and self-esteem regulation actually provides them with a cognitive and intellectual framework in which to understand their crack addiction and vulnerability to relapse. Psychoeducation that gives a detailed prescription of how patients can avoid relapse, how they can recover from crack addiction, and how they can take responsibility for healing their underlying injuries to the self empowers patients. By being active and providing extensive education on psychological processes, the clinician need not fear metaphorically "opening up a can of worms" or harming psychologically vulnerable patients. Clinicians should assess individual patients' defensive and ego functioning, but should usually be able to proceed in linking childhood history to current crack addiction. In the process, clinicians build a strong argument for patients' engagement in aftercare treatment as relapse prevention.

As we shall see in subsequent chapters, during different phases of treatment and patient recovery, clinicians may need to adjust the level of their activity and the nature of their clinical technique in order to meet the needs of the chemically dependent patient. This chapter has suggested that the narcissism, grandiosity, and inflation characterizing the newly abstinent crack patient necessitates modifications in clinical technique as briefly described. (See Wallace, 1991, for further discussion of this issue.) This chapter has also sought to emphasize that, when working with the chemically dependent, clinicians achieve greater efficacy by paying attention to the distinct characteristics of particular classes of drugs— such as stimulants—and to the distinct characteristics of patients (Zweben, 1986). This chapter, it is hoped, has highlighted crack's unique addictive potential as a stimulant with certain pharmacological actions, as well as those distinct characteristics of compulsive crack-cocaine smokers that justify the continued utilization and availability of inpatient treatment modalities. However, only through the kind of improvements in inpatient treatment programs recommended in this chapter, will inpatient modalities find a continuing role in the treatment of the chemically dependent.

REFERENCES

American Psychiatric Association. (1987). *Diagnostic and Statistical Manual of Mental Disorders*. Third Edition-Revised. Washington, DC.

Annis, H. M. (1990). Relapse to substance abuse: Empirical findings within a cognitive-social learning approach. *Journal of Psychoactive Drugs, 22*, 2, 117–124.

Bean-Bayog, M. (1986). Psychopathology produced by alcoholism. In R. E. Meyers (Ed.), *Psychopathology and Addictive Disorders*. New York: Guilford Press.

Donovan, D. M., & Marlatt, G. A. (Eds.). (1988). *Assessment of Addictive Behaviors*. New York: Guilford Press.

Gorman, D. M. (1989). Is the "new" problem drinking concept of Heather & Robertson more useful in advancing scientific knowledge than the "old" disease concept? *British Journal of Addiction, 84*, 843–845.

Gorski, T. T. (1990). The Cenaps model of relapse prevention: Basic principles and procedures. *Journal of Psychoactive Drugs, 22*, 2, 125–133.

Heather, N. (1990). Problem drinking as a form of learned behaviour: A final rejoinder to Gorman and Edwards. *British Journal of Addiction, 85*, 617–620.

Kelley, J. M. (1991). Extended stabilization: The future of inpatient treatment. *Addiction and Recovery, 11*, 3, 4–43.

Marlatt, G. A. (1985). Relapse prevention: Theoretical rationale and overview of the model. In G. A. Marlatt & J. R. Gordon (Eds.), *Relapse Prevention*. New York: Guilford Press.

Marlatt, G. A. (1988). Matching clients to treatment: Treatment models and stages of change. In D. M. Donovan, & G. A. Marlatt (Eds.), *Assessment of Addictive Behaviors*. New York: Guilford Press.

Marlatt, G. A., & Gordon, J. R. (1985). *Relapse Prevention*. New York: Guilford Press.

Rawson, R. A. (1990). Cut the crack: The policymaker's guide to cocaine treatment. *Policy Review, 51*, 10–20.

Rosecan, J. S., & Spitz, H. I. (1987). Cocaine reconceptualized: Historical overview. In H. I. Spitz & J. J. Rosecan (Eds.), *Cocaine Abuse: New Directions in Treatment and Research*. New York: Brunner/Mazel.

Schiffer, F. (1988). Psychotherapy of nine successfully treated cocaine abusers: Techniques and dynamics. *Journal of Substance Abuse Treatment, 5*, 131–137.

Schwabb, E. (1991). Personal communication.

Wallace, B. C. (1989a). Psychological and environmental determinants of relapse in crack cocaine smokers. *Journal of Substance Abuse Treatment, 6*, 95–106.

Wallace, B. C. (1989b). Relapse prevention in psychoeducational groups for compulsive crack cocaine smokers. *Journal of Substance Abuse Treatment, 6*, 229–239.

Wallace, B. C. (1991). *Crack Cocaine: A Practical Treatment Approach for the Chemically Dependent.* New York: Brunner/Mazel.

Wanck, B. (1985). Treatment of adult children of alcoholics. *Carrier Foundation Letter, 109*, 6.

Washton, A. M. (1989). Cocaine abuse and compulsive sexuality. *Medical Aspects of Human Sexuality*, December, 32–39.

Washton, A. M., & Stone-Washton, N. (1990). Abstinence and relapse in outpatient cocaine addicts. *Journal of Psychoactive Drugs, 22*. 135–147.

Zweben, J. E. (1986). Treating cocaine dependence: New challenges for the therapeutic community. *Journal of Psychoactive Drugs, 18*, 36–49.

3

Intensive Outpatient Treatment: A Psychological Perspective

Andrew Tatarsky, Ph.D.

Arnold M. Washton, Ph.D.

Our clinical experience indicates that intensive outpatient treatment is an effective alternative to traditional inpatient care for many, if not most, addicts and alcoholics who seek professional help. Contrary to traditional thinking, it appears that most of what goes on in treatment can be done effectively on an outpatient basis. Justifying residential treatment because it offers a controlled, drug-free environment is not very convincing to clinicians such as ourselves who daily see that a highly structured, intensive outpatient program works very well with crack addicts, alcoholics, heroin addicts, and other chemically dependent patients who are routinely thought to need inpatient care. Most of our patients have been through one or more residential programs and have relapsed shortly after discharge.

Outpatient treatment is not for everyone, especially for those who are physically or psychologically unable to participate in an ambulatory program. But while locking addicts away for a month or longer may give them a temporary respite from the consequences of active addiction, it will not necessarily give them the tools they need to stay clean and sober in the real world when they are again faced with easy access to drugs and ubiquitous drug triggers. While in the safe environment of the inpatient rehab away from drugs and the stress of daily life, most addicts experience little or no drug cravings. This may contribute to the inpatient's illusion of being cured or the denial that the addiction exists at all. Addicts often learn a great deal about themselves and their problems in inpatient programs, but in many cases, this knowledge does not prevent them from relapsing after discharge.

We are not claiming that outpatient treatment is the "answer." No currently available treatment option, including intensive outpatient programs, can rightfully claim superiority. And no single modality is nearly as effective as professionals or patients would like it to be. The current and growing interest in outpatient care stems from a combination of economic and clinical factors. Faced with the difficult challenge of providing reasonably effective treatment for larger numbers of addicts at lower cost, treatment providers and third-party payers are turning more and more to outpatient care as an alternative to expensive residential treatment. In the past few years, in particular, cocaine and crack addicts have been flooding the treatment system, many of whom cannot afford inpatient care or strongly prefer to be treated as outpatients.

In this chapter, we describe the philosophy, indications, and some of the clinical techniques of intensive outpatient treatment. Due to space limitations, we can provide only a very general description of our work in the outpatient setting. The interested reader is referred to other publications for further details (Washton, 1988, 1990; Washton & Stone-Washton, 1990).

TREATMENT PHILOSOPHY

The goals of our outpatient program are to support the addict in establishing abstinence from *all* mood-changing chemicals and to lay a foundation for long-term recovery. The focus of recovery is learning to live a reasonably satisfying life without the need for mood-altering chemicals. Addiction is approached as a primary addictive disease that takes on a life of its own and gives rise to a broad range of negative psychological and psychosocial problems. These problems intensify the desire to use and, in conjunction with conditioning and specific neurophysiological changes that result from chronic drug use, give rise to an increased desire to use—and thus the vicious cycle of addiction. However, addiction manifests in the context of personality dynamics and a social context that are unique for each patient. The treatment of addicted patients must begin by directly addressing the drug use and associated negative consequences, while concurrently identifying the broader psychological and environmental context within which the person's drug use occurs. Only after total abstinence has been firmly established and major crises are resolved, can work on these broader issues begin. Certain of the addict's psychological difficulties predate the onset of compulsive drug use and may have contributed to his or her vulnerability to addiction. Other of these difficulties result from the compulsive drug use itself, which drastically alters personality, values, life-style, communication skills, and ego functioning (coping abilities). The treatment process must address these issues, with an appreciation of sequence and timing as the recovery process unfolds.

INDICATIONS FOR OUTPATIENT TREATMENT

It has long been thought that outpatient treatment is only for functional, highly motivated patients in the early stages of addiction who have supportive non–drug-using families. Today, very few people who appear for treatment come even close to fitting this description. Moreover, with the recent appearance of intensive outpatient programs, these highly restrictive notions about the appropriateness of outpatient care are no longer applicable. By "intensive" we mean a program that offers a full range of treatment services, such as those normally found only in inpatient programs (including individual counseling, group counseling, drug education, self-help, medical and psychiatric evaluation, urine testing, and family treatment), and provides actively addicted patients with a structured programmatic course of treatment that requires four to five visits per week at the beginning of treatment and then tapers off to once or twice per week over several months. This type of program is obviously much better able to serve a more heterogeneous population of addicts as a primary treatment modality than is the traditional loosely structured once-per-week outpatient aftercare program. A good, solid, intensive outpatient program should be able to treat just about any addict who wants treatment, except those with serious psychiatric problems (e.g., psychosis or suicidal depression) or dangerous physical dependencies (e.g., high-dose sedative-hypnotic dependence) who are best managed in a hospital.

THE TREATMENT PROCESS

The initial task of recovery, breaking the cycle of addiction and establishing abstinence, is a tall order for several reasons. By the time most patients come for treatment, the structure of their lives is supporting active drug use. Treatment must interrupt this addictive life-style and facilitate the rapid substitution of an alternative structure that supports abstinence. Also, the patient's coping abilities have been impaired by the addiction. That is, the premorbid level of ego functioning has been disrupted and there has generally been some degree of regression that leads to reduced frustration tolerance and poor impulse control. For these reasons, the program must be highly structured and supply the structure that the patient's daily life lacks. However, within this structured context, the treatment approach must be flexible enough to address the personality and psychosocial issues that are unique to each individual.

Assessment

A thorough clinical assessment is the first step in the treatment process. This may be completed in one session or may extend for several weeks, involving a combination of individual and family or couple sessions along with supervised urine testing for drugs. The first goal is to determine the nature of the patient's involvement with mood-altering substances and to assess his or her psychological status, psychosocial functioning, social supports, medical status, attitudes toward drug use, and motivation for initial abstinence. The ultimate goal of the assessment is to enlist the patient's cooperation in formulating a specific treatment plan.

Particular sensitivity is required at this early stage of clinical intervention. Most addicts feel intensely guilty and ashamed of their drug-related behavior and are concerned about being misunderstood, criticized, or punished. These concerns are usually psychodynamically rooted, in addition to having some clear basis in reality. Addicts tend to defend themselves against guilt and shame by projecting their own harsh, self-critical attitudes onto others and experiencing the threat as being outside themselves. Nonetheless, we must realize that historically addicts have been stigmatized and punished in our culture and, despite contemporary notions of addiction as "disease," many professionals and lay people alike still regard addicts as irresponsible criminals. It is especially important that the clinician operate from a nonjudgmental vantage point and make special efforts to convey to the patient a solid understanding of drug addiction and recovery, thus, it is hoped, alleviating the patient's fear of being misunderstood and promoting openness.

Addicts typically resist being controlled by others. Rather than assaulting the patient's resistance, which often leads to no-win power struggles and early dropout from treatment, it is important to join with the patient around common goals; that is truly to "start where the patient is." The patient should be given a clearly stated rationale for why and how the recommended treatment approach is expected to address his or her individual needs. Conveying understanding, empathy, and respect for the patient is the only reliable way to make clear that treatment is a safe place where the difficult work of recovery can begin. In spite of addictive denial and ambivalence, these considerations will speak to the part of the addict that feels isolated and hopelessly trapped in a deteriorating addictive cycle and wants to change.

The evaluation may identify certain practical issues, such as financial problems and scheduling conflicts, or clinical problems, such as motivational conflicts about initial abstinence, which must be resolved before the patient can participate meaningfully in the treatment program. In these cases, the assessment phase of treatment may imperceptibly blend into motivational counseling aimed at removing early obstacles to further treatment.

Getting Started

At the end of the evaluation process, major obstacles to treatment will have been at least temporarily removed so that the patient can make his or her "best efforts" to achieve stable abstinence from all mood-altering drugs (including alcohol). The patient will be asked to sign a written treatment contract that outlines the basic treatment plan, goals of treatment, and program requirements. The treatment plan is a clinical tool that functions as a road map for successful recovery. It is a good reference for pointing out to patients discrepancies that arise (as they almost inevitably do) between their originally stated intentions and subsequent behavior regarding such things as program attendance and drug use.

Patients are introduced to the program's requirement for total abstinence. The rationale is explained, but many patients enter treatment with ambivalence about giving up all mood-altering drugs, particularly marijuana and alcohol. Often, patients initially are asked to accept the need for total abstinence on "blind faith" until they have a chance to learn why it is so essential to their recovery. Thus patients are asked to make a commitment to total abstinence for the duration of their treatment and are continuously helped along the way to assess this strategy from an abstinent rather than a drug-using point of view. Approaching the issue of total abstinence in this way avoids unnecessary power struggles and helps to engage the patient's curiosity about the recovery process. It is better to allow decisions about long-term abstinence to emerge from the patient's experience than to try to force the patient into submission on this issue and sacrifice the therapeutic relationship in the process of doing so.

PHASES OF TREATMENT

Our 20-week program is divided into two phases: Phase 1 (initial abstinence) for the first 12 weeks and Phase 2 (relapse prevention) for the next eight weeks. Patients who complete this program are eligible to enter an open-ended aftercare support group or a recovery-oriented psychotherapy group, combined, in some cases, with individual psychotherapy or counseling. The aftercare counseling groups focus on basic day-to-day issues of staying clean and sober. The recovery-oriented psychotherapy groups do the same, but also address more in-depth psychological issues concerning self-esteem, sexuality, and relationships. It almost goes without saying, however, that issues concerning drug cravings or potential relapse always get priority in the psychotherapy group no matter what other issues are being discussed. Patients who continue in treatment beyond the 20-week program decide whether they prefer basic aftercare or recovery-oriented psychotherapy. They receive recommendations but no pressure from their counselor to choose one over the other.

Phase 1: Initial Abstinence

In Phase 1, patients attend four group sessions every week and also receive one individual counseling session and two supervised urine tests. The group sessions primarily deal with day-to-day issues of getting through each weekday and weekend without using alcohol or drugs. At least two group sessions per week have a structured educational format to insure that key issues are reliably addressed. A series of workbooks (Washton, 1990) and films (Washton, 1987) are utilized to structure the content of these psychoeducational groups throughout the 20-week program. These groups cover such topics as avoiding high-risk situations, getting rid of drug supplies and paraphernalia, establishing a support network, structuring free time to support abstinence, managing cravings, understanding addictive disease, managing stress, and handling sexual triggers for drug use (especially cocaine use). Education provides a cognitive framework in which patients can organize their experience in a way that makes the addiction less mysterious and gives them alternatives to drug use. The group immediately supplies the outpatient addict with a recovering peer group and social support system to replace his or her network of drug-using peers. The frequent group meetings help to create structure in the patient's daily life, and the relationships that develop with other group members provide an incentive to stay drug-free and to keep coming back. Groups help addicts with their painful sense of shame and isolation through opportunities for peer identification that allow patients to see that they are not unusually bad or pathetic and can be accepted by others despite their addiction. Our groups are supportive, but afford many opportunities to confront the patient's resistance to change. The group is a learning laboratory where patients can practice abstinent behaviors and develop adaptive coping skills.

The beginning of recovery is a time of crisis in the addict's life and ability to function. He or she is usually having significant problems in all areas of life because of the addiction. To compound this, when the patient confronts the fact that he or she has lost control over drug use to the point of suffering serious psychosocial consequences, it is often a major narcissistic blow. In an effort to prop up a failing self-esteem, the patient tends to deny the need for help and the severity of the distress (Tatarsky, 1986). It is important at the outset of treatment to intervene in ways that do not further threaten the patient's self-esteem since the narcissistic crisis can be a major contributor to continued drug use (Wurmser, 1978). This may be facilitated by avoiding (or postponing) the exploration of unconscious motives for drug use and, instead, presenting treatment as a learning process in which the patient will learn about his or her addictive disease and how to apply a specific set of skills for establishing and maintaining abstinence. Efforts to uncover the deeper roots of the patient's drug use are likely to increase narcissistic vulnerability, anxiety, and cravings to use drugs.

The focus of early treatment must be on establishing abstinence, managing crises, stabilizing the patient's life, and supporting the patient in coping effectively with the challenges of early recovery. Patients are given specific behavioral guidelines for getting rid of remaining drug supplies and paraphernalia, avoiding drug users and high-risk places, structuring free time, and limiting access to money (Washton, 1988, 1990). They must also be taught specific problem-solving skills for dealing with job, family, financial, and legal problems that have been created or compounded by drug use. Patients are asked to put major problems on the "back burner" during early recovery. The task of achieving stable abstinence is all-consuming and the newly abstinent person typically has little or no energy left over to tackle other long-standing or deep-seated problems.

Cognitive interventions are a way to explore the patient's problem in a relatively nonthreatening way. Patients are asked to examine their attitudes toward and beliefs about drug use and whether they conform to the reality of their recent experience with drugs. Unrealistic ideas about drug use are reality-tested and the patient achieves a more realistic view of such use. The discrepancy between attitudes toward use and actual use illustrates the functioning of denial and patients begin to recognize that their addiction is supported by self-defeating defenses. "Stinking thinking" or addictive thinking refers to those attitudes that support continued drug use. This is a cognitive way of looking at the second line of addictive defenses that may be used when denial is threatened. Examples of this are externalization ("I got high because my wife is a bitch") and devaluation ("I'm not going to AA meetings; they're for fanatics and robots who don't think for themselves or losers who are much worse off than I am"). Patients are asked to notice specific moments when drug craving is greater and to identify the internal and external triggers that preceded or were associated with the urge to get high. Patients discover, through a careful examination of their experience, how their desire to get high is meaningfully associated with specific factors. Some of these can be dealt with by avoidance strategies, such as avoiding the people, places, and things formerly associated with drug use. The exploration of internal drug cues leads the patient to an understanding of how he or she uses drugs in an effort to medicate uncomfortable feelings or to satisfy a need or wish symbolically. However, at this point in treatment, the focus is on identifying these factors to whatever extent is possible (and it varies depending on the psychological-mindedness of the patient) and developing alternative ways of managing, coping, or responding.

Stress management, relaxation training, and assertiveness training strengthen the patient's ability to cope with uncomfortable feelings and situations. This increase in coping ability diminishes the patient's need for chemical coping. It also bolsters the patient's self-esteem and self-confidence, both of which are usually damaged by active addiction.

The focus of individual counseling depends, of course, on the individual needs of the patient, but issues pertaining to drug use are always given top priority. In the privacy and safety of individual sessions, many patients reveal intimate personal problems that they are unable or unwilling to discuss in a group setting, such as sexual, family, or self-esteem problems. Whenever possible, the patient's individual therapist is also his or her group leader. We have found that this arrangement maximizes the therapeutic power of combined individual and group therapy.

Supervised urine testing is conducted twice weekly and is an extremely important clinical tool. The prospect of regularly giving a urine sample often helps patients to overcome an impulsive desire to get high. Since most addicts tend to hide or minimize their use out of shame and fear, this insures that we know what is happening and can work on it. An instance of drug use, or "slip," in treatment is viewed as an opportunity for patients to learn about the factors that set it up and to make changes in their thinking or behavior that they may have been unable or unwilling to make before. Continued drug use is a cause for a reexamination of the appropriateness of this approach—it is dangerous for the patients, and it may be indicative of a lack of motivation and willingness to make the changes necessary to attain abstinence. For some patients, it becomes clear that residential treatment is indicated, while others may need to be out of treatment for a while because of a lack of interest in getting sober.

Patients are taught the value of 12-step programs such as Cocaine Anonymous, Alcoholics Anonymous, and Narcotics Anonymous at the outset of treatment and encouraged to attend meetings regularly. Self-help is not a substitute for professional therapy (and vice versa), but it does provide a dimension and continuity to recovery that professional treatment cannot provide. There is no reason why 12-step programs cannot be effectively integrated with any type of professional treatment program.

Phase 2: Relapse Prevention

In the eight-week Phase 2 of our program, patients attend one group each week while individual counseling and urine testing continue as in Phase 1. The primary treatment goal of this phase is to teach patients how to prevent relapse and to move them from an intellectual understanding of the addiction to an emotional acceptance of the need for inner change in order to achieve a comfortable existence without drugs. This important shift in the addict's awareness is what results in an increase in internal motivation for lifelong recovery.

Patients learn that relapse, or a return to drug use after a period of abstinence, is often the result of a process. Patients work on identifying what this process is for them in terms of behavioral, attitudinal, and emotional "early warning signs" of movement toward relapse. This leads to an exploration of specific "addictive" attitudes and behaviors that supported the addiction and need to be exchanged for new ones supporting sobriety. In some cases, these attitudes and behaviors predated the addiction and set the stage for its emergence. In others, they were developed by the addict's personality as adaptations to the addiction as it developed or as defenses against the guilt, shame, and anxiety caused by the addict's conflict about drug use and associated activities. This constellation of traits can be described as the "addicted self." This "self," or aspect of the self, is often disowned or split off from the consciousness and keeps the addict vulnerable to relapse unless it is recognized and addressed in treatment.

Unlike the specific behavioral and cognitive changes that are necessary for establishing abstinence in Phase 1, these attitudes and behaviors are more characterological in nature. They are often not accessible to treatment until the patient has established some stability in abstinence from drugs. Then they often emerge as resistance to further change or as a regression to ways of being that were previously associated with drug use. These traits may emerge when the acute addictive crisis abates and the premorbid personality reconstitutes, or they may become reactivated in response to a threat to the patient's psychological equilibrium, such as disappointment at work or intense feelings of anger. Common behavioral examples are the tendency to be secretive or withdrawn when upset, a difficulty with asking for help, and a tendency toward taking impulsive action to handle emotional discomfort. These are often associated with conscious or unconscious grandiosity ("I don't have to do what other recovering addicts do because I'm different"), devaluation of others ("I don't have to take this counselor's suggestion because he can't understand me; he's not an addict himself"), feelings of omnipotence ("I feel so good about how my recovery is going that I'm going to visit my old friends to show them how well I'm doing; and I'm absolutely sure that I won't use drugs"), and minimizing or denying that there was ever a serious drug problem. It is essential to teach patients how to identify these relapse attitudes and behaviors, how to short-circuit them, and how to practice alternative behaviors before relapse becomes inevitable.

Recovery at this stage must also focus on the patient's quality of life. With the crises and mask of active drug use now gone, areas of dissatisfaction often begin to surface in the patient's relationships, work, social life, moods, and self-concept. Unless these issues are addressed, the patient may remain stuck in a "dry drunk"— not using alcohol or drugs, but still thinking and acting like an active addict who is immersed in problems and doing nothing to improve his or her life. This underscores the fact that recovery requires much more than just not using alcohol or drugs. It requires fundamental changes in attitudes, values, self-concept, and behaviors. Without significant change in each of these areas, abstinence is likely to be temporary and short-lived. The process of recovery is a process of psychological and behavioral change. As we often say to patients: "Don't try to go back to being the person you were *before* you got addicted: *that* person became an addict!!"

Phase 3: Aftercare or Advanced Recovery

Before completing the 20-week program, patients are helped to develop a coherent plan for maintaining the gains they have made in treatment and for addressing unresolved issues. By the time they complete the program, many of our patients are strongly linked into 12-step programs as their primary ongoing support system. Whether involved in self-help or not, many of our program graduates elect to enter either our aftercare or a recovery-oriented psychotherapy group. With active drug use in remission and the ongoing support of both professionals and peers, the recovering addict can face the inevitable task of learning how to deal with expected and unexpected life problems without resorting to drugs or alcohol. The impulse or craving to get high will reemerge at some point to be sure, especially in response to severe stress and heartache, but through consistent feedback and reassurance, patients eventually learn how to get through the boobytraps and minefields of daily living. In group and/or individual therapy, they deal with problems of intimacy, such as failure to differentiate between sex and love; with the tendency to become trapped in substitute addictions, such as compulsive eating, shopping, or gambling; with unrealistic expectations of others; with how to recognize, label, and express genuine feelings, whether positive or negative; and with their impulsiveness and inability to "sit" with feelings that are often the driving forces behind the need for immediate gratification.

FINAL COMMENT

Working with seriously addicted people in outpatient settings for many years, we have come to appreciate the extreme diversity of the addict population and the fact that there is no single pathway to change that is best for everyone. Our professional training, experience, and personal inclinations lead us to favor an intensive outpatient treatment approach that is psychotherapeutic, psychoeducational, and consistent with the disease model of 12-step programs. Our approach emphasizes structure, intensity, and behavioral focus in early recovery and gradually shifts toward more cognitive, insight-oriented techniques in subsequent stages.

We are very clear with our patients about the vital importance of total abstinence from all mood-altering substances, about the fact that addicts cannot be successfully taught how to "control" their drug use, and about the need for clear limits and program structure. We are not, however, advocates of the rigid, hard-line approach that justifies an all-out assault on the patient's defenses and drives out of treatment addicts who are in the early stages of change and predictably ambivalent about giving up drugs. The goal of addiction treatment is to retain the patient in treatment long enough to have a positive impact on his or her behavior. An admittedly rigid aspect of our treatment approach is our dogged determination to "start where the patient is."

REFERENCES

Tatarsky, A. (1986). Cocaine abuse and psychological functioning: An exploratory comparison of recreational and compulsive cocaine users. Unpublished doctoral dissertation, City University of New York.

Washton, A. M. (1987). Staying off cocaine (video). Treating cocaine addiction successfully (Parts 1 and 2). Woodstock, NY: Reelizations.

Washton, A. M. (1988). *Cocaine addiction: Treatment, recovery, and relapse prevention.* New York: Norton.

Washton, A. M. (1990). *Cocaine recovery workbooks.* Center City, MN: Hazelden.

Washton, A. M., & Stone-Washton, N. (1991). Outpatient treatment of cocaine addiction: Strategies to increase its effectiveness. *International Journal of the Addictions, 25,* 1421–1429.

Wurmser, L. (1978). *The hidden dimension: Psychoanalysis in compulsive drug use.* New York: Jason Aronson.

4

The Therapeutic Community as a Treatment Modality and the Role of the Professional Consultant: Spotlight on Damon House

Barbara C. Wallace, Ph.D.

The rationale for delivering specific treatment interventions within long-term residential therapeutic communities (TCs) and for matching certain chemically dependent clients to the TC is presented in this chapter. In order to elucidate the functioning of the TC as the third major contemporary treatment modality, Damon House New York Inc. is spotlighted as an example of a progressive TC. Reflective of progressive developments within Damon House, this chapter describes my experiences as a consulting clinical psychologist who sought to deliver staff training and group psychotherapy to improve treatment outcome.

In Chapter 3, Tatarsky and Washton present a model of intensive outpatient treatment that spans a phase of initial abstinence (defined by the authors as 12 weeks), a phase of relapse prevention (an 8-week phase), and a third phase called aftercare or advanced recovery in which a professional and peers provide group support for continued growth and abstinence as clients move from month 6 to month 12 of being drug free. Tatarsky and Washton emphasize that as clients enter into advanced recovery, professionally led group work in assisting clients in successfully managing life problems without resorting to chemical use, achieving intimacy, avoiding symptom substitution with other compulsive behaviors, and in learning how to improve regulation of affects and impulses. Although Tatarsky and Washton define phases of treatment and recovery in a manner that differs from my conceptualization (Chapter 1), similarities emerge in emphasizing the utility of specific treatment interventions delivered during specific phases of recovery. Consistent with the work of Tatarsky and Washton (Chapter 3), professionally led group therapy will be underscored in this chapter as a powerful treatment modality that can both provide support for clients and furnish them with tools needed to negotiate the first year of recovery. Clients desperately need to improve regulation of affect, impulses, self-esteem, and interpersonal behavior (Khantzian, 1985) if they are to successfully pursue lifetime recovery.

A long-term stay in a residential TC covers for most clients what I call the second phase of prolonging abstinence—spanning the first six months of recovery—as well as my third phase of pursuing lifetime recovery, which spans the first to second year of abstinence for those who remain in a TC for up to two years on average. Occasionally a client is admitted to a TC without an immediately prior detoxification. Therefore, in some instances TC residents also negotiate the first phase of early initial abstinence or withdrawal while in the TC setting. The interventions described in this chapter reflect my attempt to assist chemically dependent clients in effectively negotiating these various stages of recovery within the context of a TC environment.

THE TC AS A TREATMENT MODALITY

The TC has a relatively short but interesting history which has been covered elsewhere (Frye, 1986a; Mandelbrote, 1979). Also, the nature of TC treatment, techniques, recent trends in programs, staff issues, population characteristics, and treatment outcomes have been discussed in detail by numerous authors (Winick, 1990; DeLeon, 1989a, 1989b; Zweben, 1986; Zweben & Smith, 1986; Frye, 1986b; Indianer, 1986; Freudenberger, 1986; Yohay & Winick, 1986; Jainchill, DeLeon, & Pinkham, 1986; DeLeon & Jainchill, 1986; Rothschild, 1986). As a treatment modality, the TC remains the treatment of choice for many clients.

For Whom Is a TC Stay Indicated?

The kind of thorough assessment that is part and parcel of a biopsychosocial approach (Donovan & Marlatt, 1988; Wallace, 1991) is critical to the process of matching clients to treatment modalities. When assessment reveals that a client is a high-dose and high-frequency chemical user, has experienced severe drug-related psychosocial deterioration, is pregnant, or is homeless, then a TC begins to emerge as a proper referral. After inpatient detoxification (see Chapter 2), many individuals require direct entrance into residential TCs. When assessment reveals that a client is unemployed, or lacks medical insurance or the funds typically required to benefit from state-of-the-art intensive outpatient rehabilitation (see Chapter 3), a residential TC stay may be the best alternative treatment of choice.

For some clients, even if an outpatient option were available, a residential TC might be preferable. Those with the most severe chemical dependency not only require inpatient detoxification to handle a significant withdrawal syndrome, but also may be more vulnerable to classically conditioned stimuli in the environment as a consequence of possessing deeply ingrained chemical-user patterns. Cravings and negative reinforcement frequently lock individuals into a cycle of chronic self-administration in response to the dysphoria of withdrawal—necessitating detoxification with pharmacological interventions, often in a safe inpatient environment. Similarly, beyond withdrawal into a second phase of prolonging abstinence, the TC can be a critical intervention for our most vulnerable and severely addicted clients who still need a safe and therapeutic treatment environment. The TC provides this kind of treatment setting.

Vulnerable clients who begin to experience painful feelings when newly abstinent and might ordinarily respond to them with chemical use receive the support of a community. The TC helps clients to learn how to manage feelings. Problematic attitudes, defensive armor, poor impulse control, unconscious tendencies to engender conflictual interpersonal relations, and difficulties in self-care (Khantzian, Halliday, & McAuliffe, 1990) might also contribute to relapse episodes. These client characteristics similarly can be effectively managed in the supportive TC environment. The TC assists individuals in remediating problematic attitudes and behaviors.

The most severely chemically dependent frequently have to cope with several challenging factors that indicate the need for TC treatment. These factors include family members who openly abuse chemicals, a crack-saturated neighborhood heavily populated with drug peddlers, an abundance of classically conditioned stimuli in the immediate housing environment, and drug-related losses of family support, housing, employment, or infant/child custody. Thus, given the reality that many recovering clients must cope with multiple stressors, the best chances of prolonging their newly abstinent state may lie in receiving treatment within a TC environment.

Although some might rightly argue that intensive outpatient rehabilitation models (Chapter 3) might still meet the needs of many severely addicted clients with general life problems, other factors militate against the utilization of outpatient treatment. The client's lack of medical insurance, and of funds to pay for treatment, and the dearth of publicly funded programs that are emulating intensive and comprehensive outpatient clinic models necessitate the continued use of the TC model by a large group of chemically dependent persons.

NEEDED IMPROVEMENTS IN TCs

The TC has been the object of balanced and sensitive critiques, suggesting areas in which it needs to improve (Carroll & Sobel, 1986). One of the major suggestions advanced involves the need for more training for recovering counselors and the greater incorporation of mental health professionals into TC staffs; preferably, mental health consultants who join a TC staff should possess some training and experience in working with the chemically dependent (Carroll & Sobel, 1986).

Among the issues that need to be addressed when mental health professionals and recovering counselors work side by side are the harboring of feelings of mutual suspicion and distrust and the waging of territorial or turf battles; evincing conflicting claims of superiority based on each group's background and experiences; and allowing patients to become aware of each group's contempt for the other so that the patients can divide and manipulate staff members. These potential complications that can arise from attempts to integrate mental health professionals into the TC staff structure can sabotage efforts to realize the overall goal of improving the quality of treatment clients receive.

As a clinical psychologist with chemical-dependency training and treatment experiences, I fit the "bill" from the perspective of Damon House staff as the kind of mental health professional deemed desirable for integration within the TC structure as a consultant. The remaining sections of this chapter describe the TC into which I sought successful integration as a valued and respected consulting staff member, my experiences as a consultant, and my attempts to avoid the potential pitfalls described above.

DAMON HOUSE NEW YORK INC.

Damon House New York Inc. opened in 1984 as a relatively small TC composed of roughly 70 members, of which approximately 15 were women. Damon House is located in the Williamsburg section of Brooklyn, New York. Prior to his departure, a former program director, Keven Frawley, identified the ways in which Damon House is different from the older, more traditional TCs.

First, Damon House is located in an inner-city drug environment, whereas many TCs are located in rural or isolated communities where there is little drug use. At Damon House, one literally might look out of the window and view phenomena suggestive of active drug use in the area. An advantage of this kind of location is that "if you can cope, it makes you stronger" (Frawley, 1990). (Chapter 10 also notes this TC advantage in terms of opportunities to experience natural processes of extinction of classically conditioned responses to drug-related conditioned stimuli.)

Second, Damon House has a shorter treatment program than many TCs—15–18 months as compared with the more traditional 18–24 month TC program. The goal of the TC experience still entails saving $3,000 in the bank, getting a job, and living independently in an apartment. The reason why this goal is achievable in less time at Damon House actually relates to the TC's location in a drug environment. Residents are exposed to that environment throughout treatment and reentry does not have the same effect on them as it does on TC residents returning from a rural environment. Thus Damon House does not have to allow for a three-month period to readjust to the city. In fact, pass requests are also accommodated earlier in the TC stay and residents attend outside Narcotics Anonymous (NA) and Alcoholics Anonymous (AA) meetings. Thus, since they never left the environment and so need not take three months to adjust, the overall TC stay is shorter here (Frawley, 1990).

Damon House also distinguishes itself from other TCs via a third practice. Just as the use of NA and AA is encouraged, so is involvement in other forms of support. A large number of clients are encouraged to pursue outside individual or group therapy, for which they pay through Medicaid. Those who test positive for the AIDS virus attend Positive Anonymous (PA) groups. Others attend outside classes in parenting skills. Both through the introduction to NA and AA and as a result of permitting contact with outside sources of support, Damon House prepares clients to survive if they leave the facility before treatment ends. Also, Damon House will help clients preparing to "split" to get into a different treatment facility or to connect with aftercare treatment. In sum, Damon House does not ostracize those who leave the TC prematurely, and sometimes has even permitted such individuals to join the Damon House aftercare group for clients in reentry living outside the facility. This exhibits a real flexibility and willingness to meet client needs, while evaluating a client's possible manipulativeness in trying to alter program structure.

The integration of residents who are negotiating different phases of the program also distinguishes Damon House. Both new residents and those who are working or going to school on the outside live together in the same setting. There are some positive implications to this practice, as Frawley (1990) explains, including the fact that "younger" residents are exposed to role models so they can set their sights on concrete and visible goals embodied in these "older" residents' lives. Among the drawbacks are that the reentry activities of residents who have been in the program for seven months create a critical treatment period. Such "older" residents need to focus on issues involving the outside world, such as searching for jobs and apartments, socializing, and coping with the stresses characteristic of this phase. On the other hand, residents who have been in the facility only three months tend to focus on local conflicts, such as those occurring while working in the kitchen. Thus, at this point, reentries (seven months and longer in the facility) attend a separate group. Separate groups permit a focus on the different kinds of issues affecting individuals at different times in the TC program.

Also, unlike most other TCs, Damon House has incorporated the 12 steps into the TC and clients attend 12-step-program meetings three times a week; one of these meetings is outside the facility. Clients are exposed to both NA and AA meetings. The 12 steps are discussed as a topic, literature is made available, and relevant visual displays can be seen on walls (Frawley, 1990).

The integration of the 12 steps into the TC structure is becoming more popular in TCs as a whole, but such integration can be both conflicting and exasperating. As Frawley (1990) explains, within the old TC, treatment was not discussed but familiarity with NA treatment can cause the client to question TC treatment. Philosophical differences between NA and the TC help to create these problems. For example, in the TC, if you use drugs, you are severely reprimanded or dismissed, whereas in NA, if you relapse, you are welcomed back. Also, some people may decide to leave the TC once they hear success stories of those who recovered via NA. On the other hand, those who leave the TC for whatever reason at least have recourse to NA by virtue of having established NA connections while in the TC (Frawley, 1990).

Frawley (1990) points out yet another way in which Damon House is different from other TCs. He found that Damon House staff members are not as critical of residents as staff members in his prior TC experiences. The program is less regimented and less discipline oriented; there is no screaming at clients and no stripping away of a client's "image" or "ego." The discipline administered at Damon House does not involve "corporeal discipline," according to Frawley. For example, there are no physical "learning experiences," such as having special haircuts or the wearing of signs. In sum, Damon House utilizes "a kinder, gentler treatment approach," explains Frawley. Damon House tries to treat residents with respect and to "build them up." When discipline is invoked, it is designed to reinforce the learning experiences via such techniques as reprimands, assignment to cleanup crews, and stripping of one's job function.

Frawley describes the rationale for this "kinder, gentler treatment approach" as follows: Today's primarily crack-cocaine-using clients enter the TC with less ego strength than did the heroin addicts with whom he worked years ago in traditional TCs. These observations of less ego strength seem to be related, at least in part, to the nature of the residents' family systems; clients enter treatment with a lack of support from anywhere. Clients also seem to lack a strong belief system and enter treatment "scattered." Moreover, some crack users do not seem to last very long "drugging" in the street and are entering treatment at a younger age, particularly since to do so is perceived as "okay," and even fashionable. As a consequence, a kinder and gentler treatment approach has been invoked that means "trying to help them regain or even gain dignity, perhaps for the first time," according to Frawley (1990). Also, a strict behavior-modification setup does not exist at Damon House. In fact, in carrying out this approach, the program has relinquished some control over residents' behavior and they are not forced to do things (Frawley, 1990).

Bailey (1990), a program counselor, notes another modification in counseling technique implemented in a group designed to permit residents to confront each other and express anger over negative behavior. Bailey feels strongly that the real issue is the pain and not the anger. For him, clients have a more primary need to address and express their underlying pain by talking about what went on within the family of origin. Thus, he frequently finds himself reorienting the focus of these groups so that clients begin to talk about their pain and traumatic experiences in dysfunctional families of origin.

A change that Damon House initiated in January 1990 followed the request of another counselor, Boones (1990), who expressed astonishment at the high rates of childhood molestation, incest, and abuse among clients—especially the women. Boones approached the executive director, Irwin Scheintaub, and suggested securing professional assistance for the counselor and the women clients.

As a clinical psychologist with training and experience working with the chemically dependent, my consultation work with Damon House thus was initiated. The staff and I agreed upon several objectives: (1) to assist the women's program in its development; (2) to help staff members manage some of the "heavy issues" arising from female clients' histories of incest, molestation, and childhood trauma; and (3) to provide training to increase the effectiveness of counselors. An additional objective mentioned as a possible outcome was to decrease departures of residents from treatment. The remaining sections of this chapter describe my consultation experiences at Damon House over the initial one-year period.

PROFESSIONAL CONSULTATION EXPERIENCE AT DAMON HOUSE

We pursued our goals by my utilizing a three-hour, once-a-week consultation period in the following way: a 1½-hour group for all women in the facility at that time (ranging from seven to 14 women, with an average attendance of 10), followed by an hour of staff training, and finally a half hour of individual therapy with any woman seen in group that day who seemed to require individual therapeutic support.

Staff Training

The original model of staff training involved two female counselors working as cotherapists in the women's group. We discussed group dynamics with three additional, male counselors within the context of a one-hour staff training session, also designed for seminar discussion of various issues. Initially, at the one-hour staff training seminars, attendees discussed assigned readings on dysfunctional families, crack cocaine smokers' characteristics, relapse prevention, and how to improve clinical interviewing and assessment techniques (Wallace, 1991). I introduced useful concepts, such as their need to be "consistent" and to avoid re-creating a dysfunctional family dynamic reminiscent of the clients' backgrounds. Reinforcement was also provided for the counselors' feelings that the family and the issues that transpired there should be a primary focus of their counseling work. In fact, for most of these seasoned recovering counselors, the training sessions served primarily as validation that they had been doing some good and appropriate things. They also commented that they received ideas from the readings regarding additional questions they might ask clients in assessment, things they might say to clients within their counseling interventions, and techniques they might add to their counseling repertoire.

Gradually, over the course of six weeks, staff training evolved into a case-consultation process. Obstacles to female staff members consistently attending the women's group also contributed to a change in the staff training seminar format. Eventually, it seemed logical to utilize less time in staff seminars and to give more time to the women clients. Thus a beneficial change occurred after about four months of consultation whereby the women's group was extended to a two-hour format and staff seminars tended to involve a half hour of case consultation.

In retrospect, I regard staff training as having played a critical function. Not only did I validate staff members' competency as counselors, but I gained credibility as someone with whom they would feel comfortable as a staff consultant. As they got to know me, they found it easier to talk with me informally. In this way, staff training underwent a transition from being a formal teaching activity and seminar discussion of group therapy process to focusing on problem patients they wanted to consult me about. Staff training, perhaps most important, permitted the development of a working alliance between myself and the staff. When they need support in a crisis, counselors feel comfortable in discussing the issue with me and, where appropriate, allowing me to intervene clinically—whether the crisis involved a male or a female resident. At present, informal case consultations ranging from 15 to 30 minutes long take place with staff members permitting a two-hour group and, at times, as much as 45 minutes for one or two individual therapy sessions with selected women. Interventions with male clients in crisis average one per month.

Evolution of a Four-Level Group Process

Consistent with the psychodynamic perspectives presented in Part II of this book, the chemically dependent person possesses poor self-regulatory capacities, especially an inability to identify, regulate, and process feelings. Regulation of self-esteem is also problematic, as is the management of impulses and interpersonal behavior. From the perspective of Hawkins' (Chapter 8) stress-coping theory within a life-contextual viewpoint, the management of emotions, as well as effective coping in an environmental context, is an important goal. From both a psychodynamic and a cognitive-behavioral viewpoint, the successful long-term recovery of the chemically dependent requires clinical interventions designed in light of the client's deficient self-regulatory capacities and coping skills in real-world environments.

The model of group therapy that evolved in my work at Damon House attempted to enhance patients' self-regulatory capacities and improve their coping in order to facilitate successful long-term recovery. Coping both within the TC environment and in the real world after TC treatment may be facilitated when an enhanced ability to regulate painful affective states, manage aggressive and sexual impulses, and relate interpersonally is achieved through professional therapy. Whether women were in the first month of recovery and struggling to prolong the period of abstinence or had been abstinent for twelve months and were seeking to pursue lifetime recovery, participation in the women's group was geared toward enhancing self-regulatory capacities and coping.

The four levels, phases, or categories of group work involve (1) providing psychoeducation; (2) carrying out therapeutic work geared toward the articulation of personal memories of trauma, connection with painful affects felt at the time of trauma, and integration of the trauma; (3) assisting clients in gaining conscious knowledge of transference states, behavioral dramas, and problematic attitudes through "here and now" analysis of unconscious behavior rooted in trauma; and (4) complementing TC techniques and assignments and punishments given to residents by TC staff through interpretations linking a knowledge of a client's trauma and unique pattern of deficits, with how the TC interventions serve to strengthen these deficits and to improve coping.

As a consultant, I found myself—to my surprise and pleasure—repeatedly pointing out how TC techniques, punishments, and assignments provided an invaluable opportunity and training ground for the improvement of clients' self-regulatory capacities and stress coping. In this way, the four-level group process that evolved included interventions that effectively reinforced the value and utility of TC techniques that existed long before I arrived, but seem effectively designed to strengthen residents' deficient self-regulatory capacities and stress-coping abilities.

The nature of the group process is such that therapeutic work involves movement back and forth among these four levels. Psychoeducation might be interspersed at any time, as might an opportunity for a woman to describe a trauma from childhood or the crack street culture. Or at any moment I might deliver here-and-now or genetic interpretations linking present behavior to past trauma or events. Similarly, on any given day or at any point in a group session, a member might report losing a TC job function, being assigned to a new job function, or having received a work-crew punishment in response to a behavior performed. A better sense of this four-level group process can be conveyed through a more detailed description of work on each level.

LEVEL 1: PSYCHOEDUCATION

The first level of group work involves the provision of psychoeducation on several topics: the nature of the status of being an adult child of a dysfunctional family; the impact on children of alcoholic, chemically dependent, or otherwise dysfunctional parenting; the defenses of denial and narcissistic inflation; defending against pain with anger; relapse prevention (Wallace, 1989); learning how to identify, process, and better regulate affective states; managing sexual and aggressive impulses; regulating and managing one's interpersonal behavior; characteristic client attitudes as a crystallized defense in response to trauma; and anorexia, bulimia, and compulsive overeating as problems involving poor regulation and expression of affective states. Each time a new woman enters the group, some repetition of fundamental psychoeducation occurs on topics such as the effect of childhood trauma in dysfunctional homes, the importance of learning how to express and process emotions, and the probable link between chemical dependency and these kinds of issues.

Psychoeducation on relapse prevention and how to cope with situations offering a high risk for relapse also occurs when women anticipate going on a first pass outside the TC, attending school, or pursuing job training. We begin to see that movement back and forth from one level of group work to another takes place throughout the group process, particularly as new members join the group and older members reenter the outside world.

The refreshing results of psychoeducation are that seasoned group members can educate new members—serving as cotherapists at times and reflecting basic principles of self-help modalities—regarding how important it is to talk about childhood or family trauma, for example. These older group members can explain how anger is only a defense against pain; they can identify defensive stances in each other and some are able to analyze "mental" slips or "near miss" relapse episodes for their determinants. Psychoeducation also helps all clients understand how children in chaotic households may turn off their feelings in a defensive maneuver, which permits a child's survival, but compromises later adult development and an ability to function effectively. They understand the need to learn what they feel at all times, and to be able to label, identify, and process feelings. In addition, patients understand that they may suffer from low self-esteem and feelings of never having been adequately loved or mirrored or from not having had their needs attended to in a dysfunctional family—a family marked by alcoholism, violence, incest, physical abuse, emotional abuse, and spoiling. This understanding permits clients to participate meaningfully in the next level of group work.

LEVEL 2: ARTICULATION AND INTEGRATION OF TRAUMA

A second level of group intervention attempts to assist patients therapeutically in the rather difficult process of (1) identifying one's personal and significant traumas, (2) verbalizing the traumas, (3) expressing painful affects experienced at the time of the traumas, and (4) integrating repressed and split-off memories of the traumas. The ego is therapeutically supported in this process through empathic interpretations, affect labeling, and positive cognitive reframing (Wallace, 1991). Group members may embrace, hold, touch, or comfort a group member engaged in this very painful and difficult work. Traumas described typically involve exposure to alcoholic and drug-abusing parents, domestic violence, early death of parents, abandonment by parents, incest, and repeated sexual molestation. Combinations of several of these negative dynamics are common in the women's backgrounds. Residents also discuss crack and street-related traumas associated with hitting rock bottom— such as rapes by "Johns," abuse by partners, battering by men, informal exchange of sex for drugs, and prostitution.

Not only are memories, images, or "motion pictures in the mind" described verbally, but the feelings associated with traumatic events are felt and expressed. Bodies tense up, shake, and produce deep sobs. In this way, soul injuries or injuries to the self of a vulnerable child or wife are gradually healed. Some describe painful events more than once, exhibiting more calm with each repetition. Each time memories are shared, the working-through process aims to produce greater integration into consciousness, acceptance of events without self-blame or guilt, and a more balanced perspective. This hard work is cognitively reframed as the way in which the women must take responsibility for their own healing. Within this working-through process, anger may first be expressed as the trauma is described. A second time around, the deeper pain associated with events may be expressed. Others begin blankly and without affect to describe traumatic events. With the exploration of how they felt and how events affected them, the women are guided toward the processing of affects associated with the trauma. Interpretations are critical at such points and affect labeling may occur to assist in the expression and processing of affect.

Some clients have no idea of how they felt at the time of significant events or feel as they describe a trauma, but, with more individual or group work, may begin to connect with feelings split off or repressed from the ideational content of the memory. Others with very early trauma may come to understand their sarcastic or angry attitude as a crystallized defense in response to trauma. Some of these women have difficulty processing affects. They present well-hidden inhibitions and phobias (see Chapter 6) that block the expression of feeling, prevent intimacy, and spare them the danger of ever trusting human beings again. A much longer group and individual therapy process is needed for these women for remediation of these deficits to take place. Empathy for their characterological defensive stances remains easy to express and maintain—even though these are the most challenging cases—in light of the nature of their experience of multiple trauma at key points in their development.

For the most part, the articulation of trauma has been very important and has resulted in clients' working through feelings of shame, guilt, anger, and sadness. Another result involves the effective integration of trauma. What was overwhelming and confusing to a young child is better managed by an adult ego—therapeutically supported—and the adult is able to integrate and make sense out of old chaos and trauma. A reduction in the feelings of shame, guilt, anger, and pain, as well as the integration of formerly split-off or repressed memories, permits clients to function more effectively. Increased self-knowledge also enhances self-esteem. Without a certain amount of self-knowledge regarding one's history and the impact of childhood trauma, work on level 3 of the group process would be impossible.

LEVEL 3: HERE-AND-NOW ANALYSIS OF UNCONSCIOUS BEHAVIOR

Not only does the client possess self-knowledge as a consequence of group work on level 2, but perhaps even more important, the therapist—and other group members—now have fundamental facts about a client that serve as keys to unlock mysteries about who the client is today and why the client functions in such a way. Information on an individual's childhood and other traumas permits, on level 3 of the group process, an analysis of the woman's here-and-now behavioral and emotional problems. These here-and-now issues and difficulties include both problems within the TC and manifestations within the group. This dimension of group work involves identifying how transference states, behavioral dramas, characteristic patterns of behavior, characteristic attitudes, and typical patient reactions in interpersonal situations are rooted in that woman's personal experiences of childhood trauma (and frequently adult trauma, as well).

Repeated discussion of clients' unconscious dramas, which they repeatedly play out and are based on their traumatic experiences, is particularly helpful. These dramas are essentially transference manifestations derived from interpersonal interactions at the time of the trauma. Some clients describe contemporary interpersonal problems that reflect the recurrence of the entire behavioral drama straight from the script of the original events. Others describe more diffuse behavioral scenarios in which they may unconsciously act out only the anger or aggression (or a related attitude) split off from the ideational content of the trauma. An attitude colored by certain affects may be repeatedly presented to others. More easily identifiable are actual behavioral dramas that involve others. A trauma or behavioral pattern out of childhood is enacted over and over again. In this way, patients reveal how they are not conscious actors creating reality, but are unconscious victims of their personal histories. They unconsciously assign roles to others with prewritten scripts based on how parents or other adults abused, neglected, and mistreated them as children.

These behavioral dramas or transference states also involve powerful expectations regarding how others will treat or respond to them. This permits "unwitting others" to join with the women in replicating and re-creating key dynamics from traumatic childhood interactions. Some dramas have a new outcome that unconsciously permits mastering the trauma. But this is typically maladaptive and abusive to the recipients of massive amounts of rage and aggression intended for the original molester or violator of that woman's inner child. Usually we observe intense interpersonal conflict and mysterious tension seemingly coming out of nowhere. A woman might then begin to express to the "unwitting other" her historical anger or aggression, which harms innocent people today who are left wondering, "What is this person's problem?" Frequently, the therapist interrupts these transference dramas of anger and tension being acted out in the group and cuts through the tension with a depth interpretation. Suddenly, the woman at the center of the storm begins to see that this is "her garbage" based on "her trauma," her expectations from others, and her historical affects and impulses from the time of the traumatic event. Other women who became embroiled in the conflict end up seeing that they might have been the "unwitting other" drawn into the conflict because they identify with the woman's problem. I hear time and again, "That's my problem too," expressed by these unwitting others when ideal objects for that woman's projective identification drew them into the unconscious scenario. Other women who merely wondered, "Why is she so angry?" or "What is this really about?" can now understand that they witnessed a transference drama from a woman's past. They gain a sophistication in being able to detect when a person's personal "garbage" is creating interpersonal conflict and tension.

Thus clients' attitudinal, interpersonal, and other behavioral problems reflect the lasting impact of childhood dysfunctional family dynamics or of crack-related trauma such as battering or rape. Clients are very much like Vietnam veterans who keep reexperiencing the trauma, sometimes with and sometimes without vivid flashbacks. We achieve our therapeutic goals when women see in here-and-now situations the shadow of past events. Today's actors emerge cloaked in the here and now with old expectations and scripts. Through well-timed depth interpretations and metaphoric analogies, group members can see and understand what has just happened and emerge from a group a little more conscious and self-aware.

We cognitively reframe these women's contemporary problematic attitudes and behaviors as merely playing out again and again what happened at the time of trauma. We assist clients in understanding that now, in the TC, with other women and men with whom they interact daily, as well as outside the TC facility, they unconsciously act out old behaviors and attitudes from the time of trauma. Through interpretations of behavior and detailed explanations of recurrent projections, transference dramas, and repetition compulsions based in trauma, clients gain conscious knowledge of what they are doing. As a consequence of this new awareness, they gradually gain the freedom to observe themselves, retract projections when they occur, avoid repeating old dramas, and attempt behaviors not derived from old scripts. Clients literally gain the freedom to act and create behaviors, often for the first time in their lives, as truly conscious beings.

When patients tentatively attempt new behaviors and do not unconsciously repeat an old behavior, they receive a great deal of positive reinforcement for the new, positive behavior. For example, a client may defend herself instead of acting out for the 3,000th time how she is unworthy. Or a patient may try a new behavior, not assuming that everyone is against her and will attack her. Another client may articulate a feeling and act appropriately instead of acting out aggressively. The receipt of positive reinforcement for reflecting growth, a greater conscious control of impulses, the enhanced ability to regulate and modulate feelings or self-esteem, an ability to get along with others interpersonally, and a greater degree of self-efficacy help to sustain these positive developments. The rewards inherent in performing a healthy behavior that feels "good" (i.e., not demeaning, or without negative interpersonal consequences) also help to sustain a positive behavior and increase the chances of generalization of the adaptive behavior to other circumstances. Just as a mother might clap in joy and praise an infant taking its first steps, I and other group members clap loudly and praise raucously when group members take their first adaptive steps reflecting enhanced self-regulatory capacities. We then clearly articulate, as well, the growth we see after praise and celebration.

I say "we" because some seasoned group members are very effective in pointing out dynamics and patterns of behavior, in addition to improvements in behavior. The women practice and attempt new, healthier behaviors within the TC, on outside passes, and with family and friends. Tentative attempts to change, regressive movement to old patterns, and negative experiences with family/friends are discussed and appropriate behavioral strategies are brainstormed by group members. In this way, an attempt is made to assist group members to expand adaptive behavioral patterns to the real world to improve coping. First attempts at intimacy are also important opportunities to detect the nature of internalized object relations that they act out with contemporary love partners. We commonly observe a difficulty with trusting, problematic transference dramas unfolding with partners, and tendencies to pursue lust to avoid true intimacy—which is feared.

Thus, through this very important work on level 3 of group work, members experience and gain higher levels of self-esteem, greater self-efficacy, an improved ability to regulate sexual and aggressive impulses, better regulation of affects, and substantially improved interpersonal relationships. In this way, group work can substantially improve those poor self-regulatory capacities and deficient coping skills that are rooted in poor object relations in dysfunctional families and probably left individuals vulnerable to experiencing chemicals as extra-reinforcing (Wallace, 1991). Chemicals are experienced in this way when they serve to assist clients in regulating affects, self-esteem, impulses, and interpersonal behavior.

Six- to nine-month participation in the women's group constitutes a form of relapse prevention, insofar as poor self-regulatory capacities undergo substantial remediation. The result is an individual who is less susceptible to relapse or engagement in some other destructive, compulsive behavior. To avoid engagement in alternative compulsive or destructive behaviors, recent group work has focused on several women's anorexia, bulimia, and compulsive overeating. Eating disorders are repeatedly interpreted as an inability adequately to express and process painful affective states or to cope with stress. As a result of this work, women are becoming more open emotionally and are struggling to express such states. The group accepts that some women who are very deficient in the ability to express affects will occasionally and metaphorically vomit on us; we celebrate this as preferable to the toilet.

LEVEL 4: COMPLEMENTING TC TECHNIQUES

A fourth level of group work involves, at every opportunity, attempting to complement in a positive and supportive way the TC's techniques, punishments, tasks, and assignments. In some cases, an empathic response to "where patients are" emotionally requires that the clinician primarily provide support and understanding. Usually within the first three months of treatment in the TC, and sometimes at any point in the TC stay, clients angrily resist and protest assignments and punishments, and they even find some TC staff members' technical interventions with them to be humiliating, infuriating, and totally unfair. At such times, it is important to attempt to achieve empathic attunement and to help them cope with their extreme sensitivity to slights and insults, as well as with a low tolerance for perceived humiliations and embarrassment. The therapist and other group members make supportive comments and encourage clients to accept a punishment and not leave the facility. Additional interventions attempt to help the client to see her role in creating the situation or provoking the punishment. Ideally, the woman can take responsibility for an inappropriate comment, an angry reaction, a nasty attitude, or even some clearly outrageous behavior, such as violence or threats of violence. Inevitably, we are essentially asking the woman to take responsibility for poor self-regulatory capacities that played a role in bringing about the situation—whether an incident arising from low self-esteem, difficulty with regulating and modulating affects and impulses, or problems interpersonally involving her characteristic transference dramas and projections.

In this way, fragile egos and vulnerable selves receive essential support in managing painful affective states and assistance in avoiding a defensive stance of denial or narcissistic inflation. These defensive stances need to be quickly diffused so that clients will not act out further aggression or leave the facility in an inflated and self-righteous state. Acting out in response to the humiliation and narcissistic injury to the self involved in receiving certain punishments can potentially include depression and the possibility of suicidal gestures. As an aside, two interventions with males in crisis involved such reactions to a punishment rendered in response to some inappropriate behavior in which they engaged. So our supportive and empathic responses to women in crisis in the group when they have received a punishment are critical to their ego's ability to cope.

However, a part of enhancing an individual's ability to cope effectively with limits in the real world, unfair events surely to arise throughout their lifetime, and inevitable bad days rests on the delivery of other interventions. Whether accomplished within five minutes or within two weeks of a woman's reporting a humiliating or infuriating punishment/assignment, we strive to do the following: (1) clearly explain to the woman her problematic attitude, behavioral drama, or specific areas in which her self-regulation is deficient (self-esteem, affective states, impulses, interpersonal behavior); (2) clarify how her "garbage" played a role in bringing about the incident; (3) point out to her that the punishment/assignment represents a wonderful opportunity to strengthen her deficient self-regulatory capacities; and (4) emphasize how the punishment/assignment will prepare her to cope with future negative events in the real world without resorting to the use of drugs.

Humor is also utilized. A patient might be told that given how much she needs to improve self-regulation in a specific area, perhaps the punishment/assignment should be provided for an even longer time than originally prescribed by the TC staff. Or when a patient tries to manipulate me and asks me to speak to the TC staff, I respond jokingly that I would only recommend a longer period of punishment. At other times, I might respond, when told about a recent punishment, "That's good for you," or "You need it." However, such humorous interventions can only be utilized with those clients who have already gained considerable insight into their poor self-regulatory capacities. Humorous teasing increases awareness regarding idiosyncratic behavior and strengthens the individual. But this level of interaction is far down the road from initial reactions of severe narcissistic injury and real crisis typical in most patients with less than seven months of abstinence.

The results of the fourth level of group work involving complementing TC techniques are several. First, clients learn that they cannot manipulate me, although some repeatedly try, and at times I do discuss punishments with staff. Clients also discover that I will not collude with them in acting out anger or hostility toward the TC structure. I also establish myself as someone who recognizes the strengths of the TC model, even though I may provide a different kind of group-therapy experience. However, I empathically discuss TC weaknesses. I might offer the view that staff members are human, may make mistakes, or may make the best possible decisions in private for reasons residents may never know. Clients are encouraged to consider and understand the staff's position and to think about what they will do when they have the responsibility of making decisions in their future jobs.

In sum, (1) psychoeducation, (2) articulation and integration of trauma, (3) here-and-now analysis of unconscious behavior rooted in trauma, and (4) complementing TC techniques/punishments/assignments constitute four levels of group work that evolved in my consultation work at Damon House. The results have been favorable for the women and for the TC in terms of less unconscious acting-out behavior and fewer departures as a consequence of refusing punishments. Of course, not all of these results have been or could easily be quantified, but they do seem important and valuable.

INDIVIDUAL PSYCHOTHERAPY

After the group session and staff case consultation, 45 minutes or a half hour remains for the provision of individual sessions. Individual psychotherapy takes place with selected women who appear in most distress in group sessions, with women who approach me before or after group and request a session, and with those seen merely on a random rotation basis. Individual sessions permit the further development of trusting therapeutic alliances. They also permit the identification, articulation, and integration of trauma within sessions, while providing me with information with which to form interpretations in later group sessions. Often, individual sessions present an opportunity for women to discuss some behavior or history about which they feel great shame or to discuss some fact that they have never before verbalized.

Sometimes, I encourage women, with and without success, to share this information in group. But, most important, I empathically attune to experiences about which clients feel the greatest shame and work hard to facilitate self-acceptance and to alleviate feelings of guilt.

CONCLUSION

This chapter has described Damon House New York Inc. and its practices, which suggest that it is a progressive and evolving TC. The consultation work of a clinical psychologist (the author) who initiated staff training and group therapy with female clients, and provided individual psychotherapy has been described. However, no formal outcome measures suggest the ways in which professional consultation work that attempted to improve clients' self-regulatory capacities and enhance their coping was effective.

As one qualitative outcome, the women in group report that those older "sisters" who have had more professional therapy or have done more therapeutic work in the group act out less and act more responsibly. Clients compare women from the group with those who have had less group therapy work. Some state that they resent having to respect and obey other older sisters whose behavior they are now able to analyze themselves as reflecting unresolved trauma. Negative attitudes, anger, and power trips on the part of older sisters who have not had much group therapy seem to indicate that they have not worked sufficiently on their personal issues.

Female, as well as male, TC residents can benefit substantially from the provision of professional group and individual therapy, which may increase their chances of successful long-term recovery. Group therapy, which is more cost-effective, or even the kind of time-limited three-hour-per-week use of a professional consultant, represents a significant addition to the TC treatment regime. My complimenting of TC techniques, in particular, pleases the TC staff members, and legitimizes and validates their work. In order for successful recovery to be accomplished, both TC interventions and professional therapeutic interventions must improve clients' deficient self-regulatory capacities and coping skills, which created the original susceptibility to addiction and constitute a vulnerability to relapse.

Unless they are helped, clients remain prone to living life with problematic attitudes that turn people off and with interpersonal problems that prevent the ability to love and work. Recovering chemically dependent individuals continue to be inhibited, phobic, rigid, and compulsive unless they receive treatment that sufficiently remediates their underlying psychopathology. Without therapy, they may never achieve the ability to function effectively and are in danger of being plagued by cycles of relapse to chemicals and indulgence in drug-free, compulsive, destructive behaviors. In this way, the interventions described in this chapter aspire to facilitate chemically dependent clients' successful negotiation of various phases of recovery, leading to the pursuit of lifetime recovery without repeated relapse and symptom substitution.

Whether this model of a four-level group therapy process, or that recently advanced by Khantzian, Halliday, and McAuliffe (1990), is employed, the implementation of group therapy offered by professional consultants in TCs and outpatient programs may provide the most cost-effective way to help addicts to solve their psychological problems. At the same time, such group therapy constitutes an essential form of prevention against relapse to chemicals, codependent behavior, and various types of compulsive behavior.

REFERENCES

Bailey, C. (1990). Personal communication. August.

Boones, D. (1990). Personal communication. January.

Carroll, J. F. & Sobel, B. S. (1986). Integrating mental health personnel and practices into a therapeutic community. In G. DeLeon and J. T. Ziegenfus (Eds.), Therapeutic Communities for Addictions. Springfield, IL: Charles C. Thomas.

DeLeon, G. (1989a). Therapeutic Communities for substance abuse: Overview of approach and effectiveness. *Psychology of Addictive Behaviors, 3*, 140–147.

DeLeon, G. (1989b). Psychopathology and substance abuse: What is being learned from research in therapeutic communities. *Journal of Psychoactive Drugs, 21*, 177–178.

DeLeon, G., & Jainchill, N. (1986). Circumstance, motivation, readiness and suitability as correlates of treatment tenure. *Journal of Psychoactive Drugs, 18*, 203–208.

DeLeon, G., & Ziegenfus, J. T. (Eds.). (1986). *Therapeutic communities for addictions.* Springfield, Ill: Charles C. Thomas.

Donovan, D. M., & Marlatt, G. A. (Eds.). (1988). *Assessment of Addictive Behaviors.* New York: Guilford Press.

Frawley, K. (1990). Interview by author, August, 1990, Damon House New York Inc., Brooklyn, New York.

Freudenberger, H. J. (1986) The issues of staff burnout in therapeutic communities. *Journal of Psychoactive Drugs, 18*, 247–251.

Frye, R. V. (1986a). Editor's introduction. *Journal of Psychoactive Drugs, 18*, 191–197.

Frye, R. V. (1986b). To fill the void: Heterodox programming in drug-free residential treatment for addiction—utilizing a theoretical position from evolutionary biology. *Journal of Psychoactive Drugs, 18*, 267–275.

Indianer, M. W. (1986). On empathy: Confronting the confrontation ward, a personal account. *Journal of Psychoactive Drugs, 18*, 277–281.

Jainchill, N., DeLeon, G., & Pinkham, L. (1986). Psychiatric diagnoses among substance abusers in therapeutic community treatment. *Journal of Psychoactive Drugs, 18*, 209–213.

Khantzian, E. J. (1985). On the psychological predisposition for opiate and stimulant dependence. *Psychiatry Letter, III*, 1.

Khantzian, E. J., Halliday, K. S., & McAuliffe, W. E. (1990). *Addiction and the vulnerable self: Modified dynamic group therapy for substance abusers.* New York: Guilford.

Mandelbrote, B. (1979). The therapeutic community. *British Journal of Psychiatry, 135,* 369–371.

Rothschild, B. H. (1986). The use of rational-emotive therapy techniques in the drug-free therapeutic community. *Journal of Psychoactive Drugs, 18,* 261–266.

Wallace, B. C. (1989). Relapse prevention in psychoeducational groups for crack cocaine smokers. *Journal of Substance Abuse Treatment, 6.*

Wallace, B. C. (1991). *Crack cocaine: A practical treatment approach for the chemically dependent.* New York: Bruner/Mazel.

Winick, C. (1990). Retention and outcome of ACI, a unique therapeutic community. *International Journal of the Addictions. 25,* 1–26.

Yohay, S. J., & Winick, C. (1986). AREBA-Casriel Institute: A third-generation therapeutic community. *Journal of Psychoactive Drugs, 18,* 231–237.

Zweben, J. E. (1986). Treating cocaine dependence: New challenges for the therapeutic community. *Journal of Psychoactive Drugs, 18.*

Zweben, J. E., & Smith, D. E. (1986). Changing attitudes and policies toward alcohol use in the therapeutic community. *Journal of Psychoactive Drugs, 18,* 253–260.

PART II

—————◆—————

THE THEORY AND TECHNIQUE OF INDIVIDUAL PSYCHODYNAMIC THERAPY THROUGH PHASES OF TREATMENT AND RECOVERY

5

Survey of Contemporary Psychoanalytically Oriented Clinicians on the Treatment of the Addictions: A Synthesis

Daniel L. Yalisove, Ph.D., CAC

Since the inception of ego psychology, several analytically oriented therapists have written on addiction. Before that time, instinct theory prevailed, and articles on addiction from that point of view have been adequately reviewed. This chapter aims to survey the relatively contemporary views of alcoholism from the psychoanalytic perspective and provide a synthesis. More ambitiously, it will spell out what remains to be done from this perspective, to correct the misplaced emphases and neglected aspects of addiction.

Addiction is viewed as a symptom that compensates for deficits in ego functioning. There are several deficits cited by analytic writers: deficits in superego functioning, self-care functioning, affect tolerance, and self-object differentiation. These will be fully discussed in the chapter. It is important to establish the relationships among narcissistic disorder, borderline condition, and addiction; which I will set out in this chapter. The analytic therapists in the addiction field suggest significant modifications in psychoanalytic technique to treat addicts. These include an initial didactic supportive phase of treatment, reduced frequency of treatment sessions, a more active role for the analyst, and/or minimized transference and interpretation. The rationale for these and other modifications will be discussed.

Finally, I will summarize the contributions of analytic theory in the treatment of addicts and lacunae of psychoanalytically oriented writings on addiction. Primarily, my view of the latter is that analysts seriously underestimate the effects of drugs on psychological functioning. In addition to the phases of intoxication and acute withdrawal, there is prolonged withdrawal syndrome (documented for alcohol) lasting up to a year that affects thinking, emotions, sleep, and other important functions. While there is little dispute that abstinence must be established early in treatment, there has been insufficient discussion of a second phase of treatment, which is helping the addict gain or regain an adjustment in the community and take into account prolonged withdrawal syndrome. It is here that Alcoholics Anonymous (AA) and Narcotics Anonymous (NA) are invaluable. Analytic writers have given insufficient attention to AA and NA. The role of AA in treatment will be discussed briefly from a psychoanalytic point of view. Only after this second phase of treatment is completed can a more typically psychoanalytic treatment be profitably undertaken. The contribution of analytic theory to addiction treatment permits the understanding and use of the concepts of the treatment alliance, transference, and countertransference; it permits the treatment of underlying problems once the addict is stabilized. These contributions will be spelled out in the following.

DIFFERENT SUBSTANCES

A problem in reviewing any work on addiction is that authors tend to focus on different substances. In fact, clinics in many states are separately licensed to treat addicts addicted to alcohol and to illicit drugs. Analysts have traditionally viewed addiction as a relatively unitary phenomenon, yet current writers are divided in their views. There is no strong evidence of large differences among addicts who use different substances, although some differences in personality and ego functioning have been shown between heroin users and amphetamine users. One would suspect that users of illicit drugs would be more prone to antisocial personality traits as well. However, this aside, for the most part, I will refer to addicts rather than "alcoholics," "heroin addicts," or "cocaine addicts," unless specific research is being cited.

EARLY FORMULATIONS

Early formulations focus on the regressive act of drug taking and oral pathology (Blum, 1966; Crowley, 1939; Rosenfeld, 1965). There are contradictory points of view regarding diagnosis (Yourke, 1970) and treatment (Lorand, 1945). Some early writers felt that the addiction masked an underlying psychosis (Blatt et al., 1984a; Rosenfeld, 1965). While Blum (1966) notes that the early analysts report great difficulties in treating addicts, the early articles do reinforce the idea that addiction is a preverbal disorder (Chafetz, 1959). In discussing technique in treating addictions, it is wise to recall that in a preverbal disorder, language does not serve its usual functions (Chafetz, 1959). With the advent of ego psychology, such disorders have become more amenable to psychoanalytic treatment.

DIAGNOSTIC ISSUES

Analytic writers have noted the oral nature of the symptom (Chafetz, 1959; Forrest, 1984; Krystal, 1978; Silber, 1967). Though analysts call addiction a symptom, it should be viewed as a very special one (Silber, 1974, 1982), because it gradually dominates the addict's life to an inordinate degree and no constructive work can be accomplished until it is faced. In one way or another, analysts have focused on the premorbid personality of the addict to explain the addiction (Ghaffari, 1987). By and large, the analysts feel that the premorbid personality is some form of personality disorder: borderline (Kernberg, 1975; Hellman, 1981; Wurmser, 1974, 1977; Davidson, 1977; Kaplan, 1977), narcissistic (Kohut, 1971; Levin, 1987; Adams, 1978), or antisocial personality (Wurmser, 1977). Most of the ego psychologists focus on developmental deficits in the addict's ego formation rather than on a specific diagnostic entity. This will be discussed later.

Can it be said that the addict is primarily borderline or has narcissistic character pathology? The research indicates otherwise for the borderline condition. In both the alcoholic (Nance, Saxon & Shore, 1983) and the heroin addict (Blatt et al., 1984a), only a minority of treated patients appear to fall into the borderline condition. Although similar research has not been done with narcissistic pathology, it appears that addicts manifest it (Levin, 1987; Khantzian, 1985; Wurmser, 1984). But as Levin points out (1987), it is not clear whether the addiction caused the narcissistic problems or vice versa.

Another point of view, represented by Silber (1967, 1974), Chafetz (1970), and Khantzian (1980), is that though underlying pathology is implicated in the cause of addiction, almost all types of underlying disorders are found in addicts. A third view is that addiction causes the "personality problems" (Vailliant, 1981, 1983; Zinberg, 1975; Brickman, 1988). Bean (1981), for example, states that the effects of addiction can be viewed as a trauma to the personality. Suffering loss of control over drinking, dangerous situations, being stigmatized, damaged interpersonal relations, negative health consequences, and thinking problems can cumulatively cause shame, guilt, and narcissistic injury and foster denial, and thus negatively affect personality functioning.

There are, however, addicts who are borderline (or borderlines who abuse substances) (Hellman, 1981; Forrest, 1984). Borderline addicts appear to require a different treatment than the typical addict (Forrest, 1984), and their addiction often takes a different form (Forrest, 1984). Hellman (1981) suggests that addicts be treated as borderlines until it is clear that they are not. Forrest (1984) suggests that treating the underlying psychopathology results in amelioration of the addiction. In other cases, they may require addiction counseling as well as treatment for the underlying psychopathology (Forrest, 1984). (See Chapter 8 for a discussion of addiction in characterological disturbances.)

Depression should be mentioned in any discussion of diagnostic considerations of addicts. While it is difficult to ascertain the cause, addicts often manifest depressive symptoms (heroin: Blatt et al., 1984b; Meissner, 1980; Wishnie, 1974; Rounsaville & Kleber, 1986; and alcohol: Chordokoff, 1964; Khantzian, 1987; Forrest, 1984; Chafetz, 1959; Jaffe & Ciraulo, 1986). Female alcoholics are more likely to have an underlying depression than males (Jaffe & Ciraulo, 1986; Allen & Frances, 1986). Does the addict medicate the depression, which leads to addiction? Does addiction cause such great problems that a depression ensues? Are there drug effects that cause depression? The answer probably lies in a combination of the three. While there is evidence that depression remits with abstinence (Jaffe & Ciraulo, 1986; DeSoto, O'Donnell, Allred & Lopes, 1985), it appears that a significant proportion of addicts do have an underlying depression beyond drug effects and effect of the addictive life-style (documented for heroin by Blatt et al., 1984b).

Before leaving the topic of diagnosis, I would like to make note of a problem in diagnosing addicts. Addicts may appear to have more underlying disturbances than are actually present. Analysts (or other clinicians) may be confused by the presentation of addicts in the active phase of their addiction or early in the abstinent state. These individuals appear quite disorganized and pathological. Many analysts, however, seem to ignore the impact of the drug on the brain, which accounts for many of the symptoms that are acute (Gallant, 1987; Washton, 1989; Kornetsky, 1976; Khantzian, 1980; Jaffe & Ciraulo, 1986; Allen & Frances, 1986; Mirin, 1986). On the other hand, as early writers noted, the addiction can mask severe pathology (Blatt et al., 1984b; Rosenfeld, 1965). The clinician must be sensitive to both of these factors in making a proper diagnostic assessment.

Even after considerable abstinence, personality traits associated with narcissism and borderline remain: grandiosity, self-centeredness, a sense of entitlement, lack of empathy, lack of frustration tolerance, impulsive behavior. Do these traits reflect underlying borderline or narcissistic pathology of addicts? The answer is probably "yes" in many cases. However, it is also possible that subtle brain impairment as a result of using the drug may be responsible for at least some of these traits. This is documented for alcohol (Gallant, 1987; Gorski, 1986; Bean, 1981; Becker & Kaplan, 1986). As addicts remain increasingly abstinent, without deep dynamic therapy, these traits frequently abate, often dramatically (DeSoto, et al., 1985). This idea relates to the concept of prolonged withdrawal syndrome in alcoholics, where long after the acute effects of alcohol withdrawal subside, subtle problems in brain functioning presumably persist for up to one year (Gallant, 1987; Gorski, 1986; Bean, 1981; Becker & Kaplan, 1986). These authors and others have referred to effects on mental and emotional functioning after acute withdrawal from alcohol. This phenomenon has been called prolonged withdrawal syndrome, protracted withdrawal, and postacute withdrawal. Becker and Kaplan (1986) summarize the research on deficit mental functioning evident in long-term alcoholics. For this chapter, the term "prolonged withdrawal syndrome" will be used.

EGO DEFICITS

Lack of Affect Tolerance

Krystal and Raskin (1970) and Krystal (1975) have postulated that because of poor parenting, addicts do not learn as children to develop signal anxiety or to label or tolerate affects. Hence as adolescents, and later as adults, when somatic sensations arise that normals can tolerate, potential addicts become terrified by undifferentiated and unlabeled affects and seek relief through drugs. It is obvious that this would be a primary reason for addiction. Krystal (1975) outlines the normal development of affect tolerance in childhood and adolescence. Cumulative traumata in childhood and adolescence cause children to dedifferentiate, deverbalize, and resomatize affects (Krystal, 1978). This will leave them vulnerable to affects because they are experienced as self-alien somatic attacks and under the sway of unconscious fantasies (Krystal, 1978). These individuals become vulnerable to addiction, using drugs to obliterate, manage, or otherwise control affects. Krystal has developed a theory of affect development that is a much-needed addition to psychoanalytic theory. Moreover, I have found it useful in understanding affect problems for addicts in treatment.

Lack of Self-Care Functioning

Krystal (1978) states that typically addicts' parents were unable to provide sufficient care. Addicts are then not able to identify with the caring function of the parent and thus do not learn to care for themselves (Krystal, 1978). Instead, they manifest precocious maturity, recklessness, a blatant disregard for reality, a lack of safety, and impulsivity. Khantzian (1986, 1978, 1981) supports a similar notion. He notes that the self-destructive dynamic does not completely explain this phenomenon (1978).

Poor Self-Object Differentiation

Krystal and Raskin (1970) feel that addicts have problems with self and object representation. To them, because the early love object was too frustrating or seductive, it became ambivalent. As infants, they could not successfully resolve their aggression with the love object. As a result, they have an inability to own the contents of their minds, keeping self and object representations rigidly separated. This also explains why addicts are only capable of narcissistic types of object relations. Addicts need to be given, and demand constant reassurance by their love objects. Addicts are often depressed because of the inevitable loss of these objects (Krystal & Raskin, 1970).

Deficits in Superego Functioning

Several authors refer to the primitive superegos of addicts (Berggren, 1984; Krystal, 1978; Wurmser, 1974; Silber, 1967, 1974, 1982). The harshness, punitiveness, and self-critical aspects of addicts' superegos are noted. Addicts will often alternate between self-blame and externalizing blame (Wallace, 1978). They will seek to "create" a persecutor in order to externalize and then fight against this aspect of themselves (Berggren, 1984). The reasons for such problems are not sufficiently discussed in the literature. It is my impression that neglect and abuse in childhood, as well as a lack of appropriate figures with which to identify, combine to create these problems.

A related issue for addicts is that they have often failed to establish a useful set of personal values (Adams, 1974). Without having learned a reasonable and useful value system from parental figures, they are left to devise a hedonistic, exploitative, and shallow way of life. The addictive process may, in addition, cause a healthy value system to disintegrate or exacerbate a weak one.

Failure of Neutralization

Meissner (1980) notes problems in the growth of autonomous ego functions in addicts. He relates this difficulty to the absence of nonconflicted ego identifications. I call it a failure of neutralization. Wurmser (1984), Krystal & Raskin (1970), Simmel (1948), and Silber (1982) refer to a common problem of overstimulation during the addict's childhood. The child is overstimulated and never reaches latency with the ability to concentrate in a neutral manner. This accounts for the sexually or aggressively overly charged atmosphere in some patients' reaction to treatment.

Wurmser (1985) feels that addiction is conflict based, which takes issue with the basic premise of the ego psychologists that ego deficits are the result of developmental deficits.

DYNAMICS

Addicts have a range of dynamics that encompasses all human conditions. The addiction may be driven by any number of issues. Clearly, many of the cited ego psychologists feel that developmental deficits provide the impetus to make affects tolerable or to moderate a severe superego. Though this is true for many addicts, some are more purely neurotic, and every addict attaches specific dynamic meaning to drug taking. In addiction, they use drugs defensively to deal with some conflict or difficult situation. Taking drugs may permit sexual, homosexual, aggressive, or assertive acts. It may also be used to blot these feelings out or to avoid guilt feelings about behavior or fantasies.

Chafetz (1970) indicates several motives for excessive drinking: to self-medicate for depression, to blur perceptions, to sustain psychological systems of defense, to function well while heavily under the influence, to break down barriers, to seek oblivion, to become more tolerable to his or her spouse. In my experience, fear of insanity is a common dynamic in addicted individuals. Often parents or siblings have severe psychopathology (Silver, 1967, 1970, 1974, 1982), and this can remain a significant secret fear. Other dynamics include grief reactions (Khantzian, 1985) and pathological mourning reactions.

Much has been written about the symbolic meaning of the drug (Yourke, 1970; Crowley, 1939; Rosenfeld, 1965; Meissner, 1980; Chafetz, 1959). Consider the following two examples. The alcoholic becomes intoxicated to return symbolically to a state of infantile bliss (Chafetz, 1959). The drug is experienced ambivalently, as was the mother during the addict's infancy (Krystal & Raskin, 1970). While there is some truth in these formulations, I have never had occasion to make such an interpretation, or even found it useful in thinking about a treatment. For most of these patients, exploration of archaic material is so threatening that it mobilizes intense anxiety and precipitates a return to the drug, termination of treatment, or other dire consequence (see quote from Khantzian [1980] under "Treatment Modifications").

I would like to emphasize a point of technique here. Before exploring the patient's dynamics, the addict ought to be stably abstinent. Once this has been achieved, which may take considerable time, an exploration of the dynamics is possible. As in any good clinical treatment, the therapist must be alert to any possible hidden dynamics. There may be sexual-identity conflict or shame over a lack of knowledge or skills, illiteracy, or a learning disability. The addict may have spent considerable effort disguising and compensating for these problems. (See Chapter 6 for further discussion of addicts' dynamics.)

CHILDHOOD FAMILY PATTERN

Childhood sexual abuse is very common in addicts, particularly women. Rohsenow, Corbett, and Devine (1988) report that up to 75% of women and 16% of men in an inpatient treatment center for addiction reported sexual-abuse experiences during childhood or adolescence. This obviously would account for the failure of neutralization in these addicts.

Alcoholism and drug addiction are common in parents of alcoholics (Goodwin, 1978). While it is still unclear as to what degree a genetic factor applies, one can readily see how an alcoholic parent could severely disrupt the family's functioning and negatively affect the child's development.

Psychosis or other serious mental illness is common among members of addicts' families (Silber, 1967, 1970, 1974, 1982). Several authors report severe difficulties in an addict's early mother–infant relationship (Krystal, 1978; Silber, 1967, 1970, 1974, 1982; Chafetz, 1959; Simmel, 1948), while others point to significant object loss during the addict's childhood or adolescence (Chordokoff, 1964; Krystal & Raskin, 1970; Chafetz, 1959).

TREATMENT MODIFICATIONS

Almost all writers now agree that psychoanalytic treatment must be modified for the addict (Silber, 1967, 1970, 1974, 1982; Khantzian, 1980; Levin, 1978; Krystal & Raskin, 1970; Berggren, 1984; Brickman, 1988). In my review of Wallerstein's 42 lives in treatment (Yalisove, 1988), I note that almost half of the subjects in psychoanalysis or psychoanalytic therapy were addicts and that most fared poorly in treatment. The only exceptions were treatments that were highly modified. Knight's (1937, 1938) dramatic modifications of technique in treating addicts many years ago foreshadow many of these current ideas.

Adams (1974) states, "Traditional psychotherapy . . . relies on the mobilization of anxiety to produce change. . . . The addict has not developed the capacity to tolerate anxiety. . . . an alternative to drug taking must be offered." And Khantzian (1980) comments:

We have probably grossly underestimated the degree to which the complicated transferences and "pathologic dependency" so frequently alluded to in working with alcoholics is less a function of the patient and more the result of iatrogeny. In such instances, we have mistakenly used an outmoded, detached, and passive model that stirs up longings and frustration, rather than responding to the real needs and impairments of the alcoholic than can be identified, managed, and understood by the therapist and patient alike.

Silber (1974), writing about his suggestions in treating alcoholics, says:

This approach, based on sound psychoanalytic principles, makes extensive use of suggestion, persuasion, and education to help deal with the many developmental deficits appearing in these patients. Transference meanings or implications are avoided. It becomes very clear that this approach to the psychotherapy of the alcoholic patient is at great variance with the traditional analytic method. The rationale for this different approach, of course, comes from knowledge originally obtained from psychoanalysis and modified to fit our particular objective in psychotherapy.

McDougal (1989) states:

The patient who seeks analysis in order to lose an addictive propensity poses a particular problem, for such an individual is frequently not seeking self-knowledge but power—a power stronger than his/her own which of course we are quite unable to promise. Psychoanalysis or psychoanalytic therapy replaces neither AA nor a drug treatment center. Psychoanalytic treatment is potentially effective only if our addicted patient is eager to discover *why* he/she flies to the soothing substance at the slightest signal of stress.

Particularly emphasized is an introductory phase of treatment. Khantzian (1980, 1985) emphasizes the necessity of stabilization and control over drinking and protecting the safety of the patient. Both Silber (1959) and Krystal and Raskin (1970) advocate an introductory phase of treatment that is more concrete and educational than traditional psychotherapy.

Silber (1959) advocates fostering the positive transference in the beginning of treatment, along with offering guidance, help with judgments, and education regarding affects. Khantzian (1980, 1985), Berggren (1984), and Krystal and Raskin (1970) all advocate an intermediate phase of educating the addict regarding affect. These authors feel a more traditional psychotherapy can then be employed after the first two phases are negotiated.

There are some variations to the above phases. Forrest (1984) begins treatment with a much more alcohol-focused plan, but in the second phase, he moves into transference and resistance analysis. Adams (1978), on the other hand, advocates establishing a narcissistic transference in the first phase of treatment. Most suggest reducing the frequency of sessions to once or twice per week (Silber, 1959; Forrest, 1984; Levin, 1987; Adams, 1978). Only Adams mentions the couch.

Role of Therapist

In almost all cases, particularly at the beginning of treatment, the role of the therapist in treating the addicted patient differs dramatically from a classical approach. The therapist must be more active, offer more of himself or herself, offer practical suggestions, ward off dangers, and be more of a real object because of the crisis nature of the beginning of treatment, the patient's lack of trust and poor judgment, and other issues of safety (Khantzian, 1985). This, of course, affects transference. Because the extraordinary interventions necessary for these patients at the beginning of treatment preclude the traditional unfolding of transference, some authors recommend changing therapists after the patient is stabilized (Mack, 1981; Khantzian, 1986; Wurmser, 1974).

Table 5-1 indicates phases of therapy for addicted patients, as derived from the literature and my own experience.

Affect Training

Several authors cite the development of affect tolerance as an important aspect of addiction treatment (Silber, 1982; Berggren, 1984; Khantzian, 1985; Krystal & Raskin, 1970). This includes teaching the addict to recognize, label, and tolerate the affect and ultimately to understand its meaning. This aspect of treatment is much more educational and practical than found in a traditional setting. In my own work, I offer reassurance, particularly early in abstinence, regarding strong affects. Addicts are prone to powerful affects, which they previously dealt with by drugs. There may also be an organic component to the affect reaction attributed to the prolonged-withdrawal syndrome.

Addicts often report experiencing strong but inappropriate emotional reactions early in abstinence. In these instances, the patient is reassured that this is a common early-abstinence phenomenon, but no effort is made to interpret the emotion. Only after a considerable time in treatment are these reactions discussed from a dynamic

Table 5-1
Phases of Therapy for Addicted Patients

Presentation of Patient	Course of Therapy	Role of Therapist	Therapeutic Goal
Intoxicated, unstable, depressed, angry, desperate, coerced	Assessment; crisis management	Protector, reality guide; provide judgment	Provide for immediate safety; diagnostic impression; referral, if necessary
Abstinent, unstable, confused	Further assessment of addiction; establish need for abstinence	Teacher; supportive of progress	Abstinence; acceptance of addiction
Abstinent, unstable	Behavioral focus, AA, establish rules of treatment	Reassurance; encourage positive transference	Stable abstinence
Stable abstinence	Education; assessment of strengths and weakness	Parental, teacher role	Adapt to reality without drugs or acting out
Abstinent, stable adjustment to reality	Insight into cause of addiction, symptoms, character	Supportive; traditional therapeutic role	Self-knowledge, resolve conflict, alleviate symptoms

point of view. By this time, however, such reactions are often greatly attenuated and more under the sway of the strengthened ego of the patient.

Confrontation

While not discussed by analytic writers, denial and confrontation are emphasized by addiction specialists (Forrest, 1984; Bean, 1981; Adams, 1974). Denial is used somewhat differently in addiction treatment than in traditional usage (Bean, 1981). In addiction treatment, it refers to a turning away from reality in a variety of ways. This also includes avoidance, externalization, and rationalization, which permit addicts to continue to drink or to ignore dangerous behaviors (Brown, 1985).

Addicts generally need to be confronted first about the addiction problem and the difficulties it is causing, which is generally reflected in a chaotic life-style. As treatment progresses, acting-out behavior, denial of self-responsibility, magical thinking, grandiosity, and lack of reflectiveness may all need to be confronted.

Addicts generally experience life as happening directly, uniquely to them. They do not feel they have an "inside" or sense of self. Projection is rampant. If, for addicts, we are to follow the psychoanalytic principle of starting at the psychic surface before going deeper, we must remain in the phase of confronting denials for a very long time.

It should be emphasized that addicts are prone to acting out. After giving up the addiction, this may be the only means available for modulating affect. One must encourage addicts to develop the capacity to delay impulses to act out, while at the same time helping them to understand the specific reasons for their acting out. Firm limits must be established, however, when the safety of the addict or other persons is threatened.

Therapeutic Compact and the Working Alliance

Silber (1970) suggests that the addict cannot sustain the normal "working alliance." He suggests a modification, which he calls the "therapeutic compact." He feels that the addict requires "a more rapid and concrete depiction of the structure of the therapeutic situation to ward off the anxiety that would otherwise accrue from being subjected to a more abstinent, slowly evolving, gradually structured, analytical situation." He also feels that the addict requires an implied promise of relief if he or she cooperates in the treatment.

TRANSFERENCE

At the beginning of treatment with addicts, there is a danger of a psychotic transference developing (Yalisove, 1988; Davidson, 1977). Krystal (1978) speaks of an early aggressive transference and several other phenomena that resemble a psychotic transference. Such a transference at the beginning of treatment bodes disaster, as there is no therapeutic relationship to bear this strain. This is one reason why transference interpretations are avoided at the beginning of treatment (Silber, 1982). Why addicts are prone to such reactions is not entirely clear. The above quote from Khantzian (1980) suggests it is iatrogenic. This is my view as well. The addict early in treatment may be suffering intoxication, withdrawal, and panic. To subject such a patient to the rigors of psychodynamic therapy is to place too great a strain on a weakened ego. Krystal (1978) feels that addicts may panic at the potential for a good object. He feels that they often experience the transference as a life-and-death struggle. For these reasons, particularly at the beginning of treatment, some authors recommend that transferences be diluted among staff members (Krystal & Raskin 1970; Krystal, 1978; Vailiant, 1981; Chafetz, 1970) and other patients in group therapy (Krystal, 1978), and in AA through sponsorship and other AA members (Moore, 1965). Those patients who suffer failure in neutralization require therapy firmly based in reality until some basic trust is developed. They often have fears of panic proportion about therapy.

Three other reasons to delay transference interpretations, as well as to delay fostering transference reactions, are brain impairment caused by alcohol withdrawal (Gallant, 1987; Gorski, 1986; Bean, 1981; Becker & Kaplan, 1986), the prolonged-withdrawal syndrome (Gorski, 1986; Gallant, 1987; Bean, 1981; Becker & Kaplan, 1986), and the chaotic life-style of addicts.

An example of focusing on a transference too early in the treatment of an addict is given by Gustafson (1976). Though a mirroring transference did occur and was interpreted, the patient was not stably abstinent and had at least one nearly fatal accident during the treatment. Gustafson failed to focus on the patient's dangerous drinking behavior, confront it, and help the patient become stably abstinent before attempting to interpret the transference.

It is common to see narcissistic transference reactions in addicts (Levin, 1987), of both the grandiose and the mirroring type. One also sees a great deal of splitting transferences (Krystal, 1978), which pertain to "borderline" transference. Once the patient is stably abstinent, these can be addressed. Adams (1978) considers it important to begin interpretation of narcissistic transference relatively early in treatment. In my experience, it rarely becomes the focus in treatment because of the need to deal with "practical" reality-oriented problems, such as earning a living and curtailing acting out.

COUNTERTRANSFERENCE

Moore (1961), Seltzer (1967), and Steiner (1971) comment on the traits of addicts, which therapists may respond to in less than therapeutic manner. Seltzer (1967) states that addicts may be openly dependent, demanding that the therapist take care of them; they may be very egocentric and not show any concern for others; they may be depressed and hopeless; or they may be very hostile, often in a covert manner, which may be a way to provoke anger in the therapist. Examples are premature termination, missing appointments, coming to sessions intoxicated, denial of drinking problems, not controlling acting out, and obstinacy.

Moore (1965) points out that the addict is not grateful; the therapist can never give enough. Similarly, Krystal (1975) states that the addict "will insist in the transference that the therapist take care of him, relieve his bad feelings, prevent their future development and, like an idealized mother, guarantee his comfort and safety from his bad feelings." Seltzer (1957) and Moore (1961) note that alcoholics openly indulge in infantile oral gratification. Moore (1965) similarly comments that the alcoholic often manifests a refusal to grow up. Bean (1981) observes that the alcoholic makes use of avoidance, minimization, projection, and rationalization. Krystal (1978) comments on the great rage of these patients, and Krystal and Raskin (1970) indicate that the addict's aggression can present problems for treatment. Davidson (1977) notes that patients in a methadone clinic manifested extreme affects, expected to be treated unfairly, and denied the importance of their methadone treatment. Forrest (1984) emphasizes that authority problems become manifest in the transference.

Steiner (1971) points out that some alcoholics are coerced into treatment and this affects the treatment relationship. In our clinic, a majority of addicts seeking treatment are coerced in some manner, which will affect transference. Steiner also notes that many alcoholics present themselves in a chronic physically ill, helpless state.

Seltzer (1967) raises a very important point: there are limits to what therapists can hear without becoming angry. The patient may abuse the therapist. These patients do not know proper limits or respect them. Therapists, as an important part of their stance, must properly protect themselves. In addition, in my work with addicts, I have observer that they often have a chaotic and dangerous life-style. Because the addict often begins treatment in a desperate state, full of denial and poor judgment, great pressure can be felt by the therapist. The addict may have sociopathic traits, be lacking in values, and demand to be an exception to the rules, all of which places a strain on the therapist.

A somewhat different issue is mentioned by Seltzer (1957), who points out that the therapist's esteem rests on whether the patient stops drinking. The patient's refusal to do what is "good for you," and indirectly what is good for the therapist, may cause frustration. This may lead to an over- or underemphasis on the drug-taking or acting-out behavior.

Any or all of the above factors may cause difficulties for the therapist. Steiner (1971) indicates there are two common responses to the coerced patient. The therapist may become a "patsy" and fall for the patient's rationalizations, externalizations, denials, and prevarications, aligning in a nontherapeutic way with the corrupted ego of the patient. The therapist may make excuses for the addict rather than providing treatment. Alternatively, the therapist may become a persecutor, falling into alignment with the complaining source—spouse, boss, criminal-justice system, etc. The helpless, chronic alcoholic may bring out a "rescuer" response, where one's limitations in one's job are forgotten.

Therapists may respond with outright hostility to some combination of these factors (Seltzer, 1957, 1967; Moore, 1961, 1965; Brown, 1950). They may then make unfairly harsh demands on the patient. More socially acceptable is seeming to care, disguising the underlying unresolved hostility in a reaction formation (Moore, 1961, 1965; Chafetz, 1959). The therapist may react with reaction formation by becoming overly kind, permissive, and indulging, unable to deny any request. With reaction formation, the therapist will accept at face value what the patient says about his or her drinking patterns and other aspects of life about which the patient may not be candid.

Another response is distancing oneself. Gustafson (1976) reports taking a cool distance from an alcoholic patient. Silber (1967, 1970, 1974, 1982) has noted that many addicts have severe familial pathology. In supervision, he has found that residents have a tendency to deny this pathology. Obviously, in treating these patients, therapists must be aware of their own internal affect states. Adams (1978) states that the addict will often "induce" feelings into the therapist, which then can be interpreted and properly "owned" by the patient. Krystal and Raskin (1970) feel the aggression they have causes therapists to give too much or too little. As they point out, "Because [these] patients are very demanding, expressing insatiable, 'endless' oral fantasies, the analyst has to deal with their fears of being devoured or destroyed, and often becomes overly concerned with 'giving' too much or too little to them."

Brown (1950) and Silber (1959) refer to the importance of the positive transference. Chafetz (1959) refers to the importance of the relationship between the therapist and patient. Combined with the view that addicts often do not derive much benefit from insight (Brown, 1950; Silber, 1982), it may be that the primary curative factor in addiction treatment is a form of "transference cure."

Spelling out all of the potential countertransference pitfalls may give the appearance that treating the addict is daunting. It is. However, in my own experience, it is extremely rewarding; a large number of addicts respond well to proper technique.

AA AND THERAPY

Many psychoanalytic authors advocate AA or NA in the treatment of addicts (Khantzian, 1959, 1986, 1985, 1987; Hellman, 1981; Levin, 1987; Forrest, 1984; Mack, 1981; Moore, 1965; Dodes, 1988). Simmel (1948), Mack (1981), and Dodes

(1988) have written about AA from a psychoanalytic perspective, and Spiegal and Mulder (1986) have written on ego functioning and AA. As do Brickman (1988) and Dodes (1988), I have found that AA complements treatment. Having an AA sponsor has advantages for advancing the treatment process. It produces less strain on the transference and therapeutic relationship. It allows the patient to have two separate figures on which to depend. The patient will often have a transference on AA itself (Dodes, 1988). This can be analyzed. The practical advice and help of AA and NA cannot be emphasized enough. The AA philosophy of recovery is detailed in the "12 steps." Each of the 12 steps has relevance to the treatment process. The point is that not only should AA or NA be encouraged, but the therapist must be very familiar with the 12-step program and integrate treatment with it. Issues around split transference or conflicts between therapy and AA are rare; when they occur, they can generally be worked with. In those instances where they cannot, the problem is attributable to the resistances of the patient, which would take a similar course elsewhere. Dodes (1988) notes that "alcoholic patients often engage in both dynamic psychotherapy and AA with surprisingly little difficulty living in both worlds." (Chapter 10 in this volume details the use of AA in the therapeutic process.)

LIMITS OF TREATMENT

Several authors have commented on the necessity for maintaining realistic treatment goals for these patients that are less ambitious than those of psychoanalysis (Berggren, 1984; Adams, 1974; Shea, 1954; Chafetz, 1959; Brown, 1950; Khantzian, 1978). Utilizing a very demanding, more traditional psychoanalytic treatment, Wurmser (1984) notes that he rarely sees a course of treatment reach a successful conclusion with addicts. Krystal (1978) discusses the rarity of working through intransigent transferences. It would be better to end a treatment with mutual consent when a reasonable amount of progress has been made. Alcoholics tend to leave treatment at positive life transitions, such as finding employment or getting married. They may return to treatment at some future time. For treatments that are not progressing or that are too chaotic from the onset, it might be best to curtail them as their impact is likely to be minimal, or even negative.

CONCLUSIONS

It appears clear from the survey done here that many modifications of psychoanalytic therapy are required to treat addicts successfully. These modifications, which make use of psychoanalytic principles (Silber, 1974), include reduced frequency of sessions, a more active approach on the part of the therapist, a preliminary phase of treatment, a more didactic therapy, minimization of transference reactions early in treatment, and the use of AA. The goals of treatment are often more modest for these patients.

During the early phase of treatment, psychoanalytic theory helps one to understand transference–countertransference dilemmas as outlined. Once the patient is stably abstinent and has made a good adjustment to the community, he or she may choose to, or need to, explore such dynamic issues as sexual identity, severe inhibition, phobias, and object loss. A clinician who knows addiction and psychoanalytic theory will have an understanding of what is essential to be worked through and what is better left as it is.

As I have indicated, few analytical writers address the effect of the drug in the active phase of addiction, acute withdrawal, or the prolonged-withdrawal syndrome. Not enough attention has been paid to the limited ego resources of addicted or newly abstinent patients, although this is noted by Silber (1974, 1982) and Zinberg (1950). A nondemanding, supportive treatment is needed in this phase of treatment. Another criticism of analytical writers is that they focus excessively on the active, addicted state rather than the phases of amelioration of the condition.

There are some theoretical controversies that remain. While most analytical writers ascribe addiction to the premorbid character of the alcoholic, addiction specialists focus on the effect of the drug and drug experience on the personality (Bean, 1981; Brickman, 1988; Vaillant, 1981, 1983). Khantzian (1987) notes the possible relationships between the premorbid character and addiction. Clearly, some addicts have premorbid character problems. On the other hand, addiction will have some negative consequences on personality functioning. It remains for research to show conclusively the relative importance of the two factors, although the research done by Vaillant (1981, 1983) favors the notion that addiction is the primary factor.

If one accepts the notion of acute withdrawal and the prolonged-withdrawal syndrome, and the fact that severe addiction can act like a trauma and that addiction can mask psychopathology, it seems good clinical sense not to assume severe character pathology at the outset of treatment. It would be the wiser course to treat the "symptom" or "addiction" or "disease." When stability in mental function and adaptation is achieved, or has progressed to its limit, one can evaluate ego pathology.

Though analysts call addiction a symptom, it should be viewed as a very special one (Silber, 1974, 1982), because it gradually dominates the addict's life to an inordinate degree and no constructive work can be accomplished until it is faced. Of the analytical writers, only Brickman (1988) and Dodes (1988) refer to addiction as a disease.

Because psychoanalytic theory focuses on the personality and dynamics of the individual, one could mistakenly conclude that the addict's personality alone causes the addiction, rather than including other factors. Of current analytical writers, Zinberg (1950) counters this possible bias. He notes that the set and the setting of the drug must also be taken into account (i.e., environmental factors). Conditions of severe stress and deprivations of various sorts can take precedence over character structure. As cited by Crowly (1939), Fenichel noted the connection between drug addiction and social conditions many years ago. Finally, genetic factors must not be forgotten.

PERSONAL NOTE

It has been a challenge for me to integrate the views of addiction specialists and analysts in my clinical work. I have found the writings of the addiction specialists helpful in areas of confrontation, the effects of the drug, and use of AA. Moreover, the work of Silber has been very helpful in developing a therapeutic relationship with patients. Krystal and Raskin have been helpful in addressing problems of affect in addicts, and Khantzian has been useful in framing practical suggestions within an analytical framework.

REFERENCES

Adams, J. W. (1974). A philosophy of psychotherapy with the drug-dependent person: Six basic imperatives. *Drug Forum, 4,* 53–63.

Adams, J. W. (1978). *Psychoanalysis of drug dependence. The understanding and treatment of a particular form of pathological narcissism.* New York: Grune & Stratton.

Allen, M. H., & Frances, R. J. (1986). Varieties of psychopathology found in patients with addictive disorders: A review. In R. E. Meyer (Ed.), *Psychopathology and addictive disorders.* (pp. 17–38). New York: Guilford.

Bean, M. H. (1981). Denial and the psychological complications of alcoholism. In M. H. Bean, & N. E. Zinberg (Eds.), *Dynamic approaches to the understanding and treatment of alcoholism* (pp. 53–96). New York: Free Press.

Becker, J. T., & Kaplan, R. F. (1986). Neurophysiological and neuropsychological concomitants of brain dysfunction in alcoholics. In R. E. Meyer (Ed.), *Psychopathology and addictive disorders* (pp. 263–292). New York: Guilford.

Berggren, B. (1984). Alcohol abuse and super-ego conflicts. *International Journal of Psychoanalytic Therapy, 10,* 215–225.

Blatt, S. J., McDonald, C., Sugarman, A., & Wilber, C. (1984a). Psychodynamic theories of opiate addiction: New directions for research. *Clinical Psychology Review, 4,* 159–189.

Blatt, S. J., Rounsaville, B., Eyre, S. L., & Wilber, C. (1984b). The psychodynamics of opiate addiction. *Journal of Nervous and Mental Disease, 172,* 342–352.

Blum, E. M. (1966). Psychoanalytic views of alcoholism. A review. *Quarterly Journal of Studies on Alcohol, 27,* 259–299.

Brickman, B. (1988). Psychoanalysis and substance abuse: Toward a more effective approach. *Journal of the American Academy of Psychoanalysis, 16,* 359–379.

Brown, C. L., (1950). A transference phenomenon in alcoholics. *Quarterly Journal of Studies on Alcohol, 11*, 403–409.

Brown, S. (1985). *Treating the alcoholic. A developmental model of recovery.* New York: Wiley.

Chafetz, M. E. (1959). Practical and theoretical considerations in the psychotherapy of alcoholism. *Quarterly Journal of Studies on Alcohol, 20*, 281–291.

Chafetz, M. E., Blane, H. T. & Hill, M. J. (1970). *Frontiers of alcoholism.* New York: Science House.

Chodorkoff, B. (1964). Alcoholism and ego function. *Quarterly Journal of Studies on Alcohol, 25*, 292–299.

Crowley, R. M. (1939). Psychoanalytic literature on drug addiction and alcoholism. *Psychoanalytic Review, 26*, 39–54.

Davidson, V. (1977). Transference phenomena in the treatment of addictive illness: Love and hate in methadone maintenance. *NIDA Research Monographs, 12*, 118–125.

DeSoto, C. B., O'Donnell, W. E., Allred, L. J., & Lopes, C. E. (1985). Symptomatology in alcoholics at various stages of abstinence. *Alcoholism, 9*, 505–512.

Dodes, L. M. (1988). The psychology of combining dynamic psychotherapy and Alcoholics Anonymous. *Bulletin of the Menninger Clinic, 52*, 283–293.

Forrest, G. G. (1984). *Intensive psychotherapy of alcoholism.* Springfield, IL: Charles C. Thomas.

Gallant, D. M. (1987). *Alcoholism: A Guide to Diagnosis, Intervention and Treatment.* New York: W. W. Norton.

Ghaffari, K. (1987). Psychoanalytic theories on drug dependence: A critical review. *Psychoanalytic Psychotherapy, 3*, 39–51.

Goodwin, D. W. (1978). Hereditary factors in alcoholism. *Hospital Practice, 13*, 121–130.

Gorski, T. A. (1986). Relapse prevention planning. *Alcohol Health and Research World, 11* (1), 6–11, 63.

Gustafson, J. (1976). The mirror transference in the psychoanalytic psychotherapy of alcoholism: A case report. *International Journal of Psychoanalytic Psychotherapy, 5*, 65–85.

Hellman, J. M. (1981). Alcohol abuse and the borderline client. *Psychiatry, 44*, 307–317.

Jaffe, J. H., & Ciraulo, D. A. (1986). Alcoholism and depression. In R. E. Meyer (Ed.), *Psychopathology and addictive disorders* (pp. 293–320). New York: Guilford.

Kaplan, E. H. (1977). Implications of psychodynamics of therapy in heroin use: Borderline case. *NIDA Research Monographs, 12*, 126–141.

Kernberg, O. F. (1975). *Borderline conditions and pathological narcissism.* New York: Jason Aronson.

Khantzian, E. J. (1978). The ego, the self, and opiate addiction: Theoretical and treatment considerations. *International Review of Psychoanalysis, 5*, 189–198.

Khantzian, E. J. (1980). The alcoholic patient: An overview and perspective. *American Journal of Psychotherapy, 34*, 4–19.

Khantzian, E. J. (1981). Some treatment implication of the ego and self disturbances in alcoholism. In M. H. Bean, & N. E. Zinberg (Eds.), *Dynamic approaches to the understanding and treatment of alcoholism* (pp. 163–188). New York: Free Press.

Khantzian, E. J. (1985). Psychotherapeutic interventions with substance abusers—the clinical context. *Journal of Substance Abuse Treatment, 2,* 83–88.

Khantzian, E. J. (1986). A contemporary psychodynamic approach to drug abuse treatment. *American Journal of Drug and Alcohol Abuse, 15,* 213–222.

Khantzian, E. J. (1987). A clinical perspective of the cause–consequence controversy in alcoholic and addiction suffering. *Journal of the American Academy of Psychoanalysis, 15,* 521–537.

Knight, R. P. (1937). Dynamics and treatment of chronic alcohol addicts. *Bulletin of the Menninger Clinic, 1,* 233–250.

Knight, R. P. (1938). The psychoanalytic treatment in a sanatorium of chronic addiction to alcohol. *Journal of the American Psychoanalytic Association, 3,* 1443–1448.

Kohut, H. (1971). *The analysis of the self.* New York: International Universities Press.

Kornetsky, C. (1976). *Pharmacology; Drugs affecting behavior.* New York: Wiley.

Krystal, H. (1974). The genetic development of affects and affect regression. *Annual of Psychoanalysis, 2,* 98–126.

Krystal, H. (1975). Affect tolerance. *Annual of Psychoanalysis, 3,* 179–219.

Krystal, H. (1977). Self and object representations in alcoholism and other drug dependence: Implications for therapy. *NIDA Research Monographs, 12,* 88–100.

Krystal, H. (1978). Self representation and the capacity for self care. *Annual of Psychoanalysis, 6,* 209–246.

Krystal, H., & Raskin, H. A. (1970). *Drug dependence: Aspects of ego function.* Detroit: Wayne State University Press.

Levin, J. D. (1987). *Treatment of alcoholism and other addictions. A self-psychology approach.* New York: Jason Aronson.

Lorand, S. (1945). Survey of psychoanalytic literature on problems of alcohol. *Yearbook of Psychoanalysis, 1,* 359–370.

Mack, J. E. (1981). Alcoholism, AA., and the governance of the self. In M. H. Bean, & N. E. Zinberg (Eds.), *Dynamic approaches to the understanding and treatment of alcoholism* (pp. 128–162). New York: Free Press.

McDougal, J. (1989). *Theaters of the body.* New York: Norton.

Meissner, W. W. (1980). Addiction and paranoid process: Psychoanalytic perspectives. *International Journal of Psychoanalytic Therapy, 8,* 273–310.

Mirin, S. M. (1986). The relevance of laboratory studies in animals and humans to an understanding of the relationships between addictive disorders and psychopathology. In R. E. Meyer (Ed.), *Psychopathology and addictive disorders* (pp. 199–237). New York: Guilford.

Moore, R. A. (1961). Reaction formation as a countertransference phenomenon in the treatment of alcoholism. *Quarterly Journal of Studies on Alcohol, 22,* 481–486.

Moore, R. A. (1965). Some countertransference reactions in the treatment of alcoholism. *Psychiatry Digest, 26,* 35–43.

Nance, E. P., Saxon, J. J., & Shore, N. (1983). A comparison of borderline and non-borderline alcoholics. *Archives of General Psychiatry, 40,* 54–56.

Rohsenow, D. J., Corbett, R., & Devine, E. (1988). Molested as children: A hidden contribution to substance abuse. *Journal of Substance Abuse Treatment, 5*, 13–18.

Rosenfeld, H. A. (1965). *Psychotic states.* London: Hogarth Press.

Rounsaville, B. J., Glazer, W., Wilber, C. H., Weissman, M. M., & Kleber, H. D. (1983). Short-term interpersonal psychotherapy in methadone-maintained opiate addicts. *Archives of General Psychiatry, 40*, 629–636.

Rounsaville, B. J., & Kleber, H. D. (1986). Psychiatric disorders in opiate addicts: Preliminary findings on the course and interaction with program type. In R. E. Meyer (Ed.), *Psychopathology and addictive disorders* (pp. 140–168). New York: Guilford.

Selzer, M. L. (1957). Hostility as a barrier to therapy in alcoholism. *Psychiatric Quarterly, 31*, 301–305.

Selzer, M. L. (1967). The personality of the alcoholic as an impediment to psychotherapy. *Psychiatric Quarterly, 41*, 38–45.

Shea, J. E. (1954). Psychoanalytic therapy and alcoholism. *Quarterly Journal of Studies on Alcohol, 15*, 595–605.

Silber, A. (1959). Psychotherapy with alcoholics. *Journal of Nervous and Mental Diseases, 129*, 477–485.

Silber, A. (1967). Psychodynamic therapy in alcoholism. In R. Fox (Ed.), *Alcoholism: Behavioral research and therapeutic approaches* (pp. 145–151). New York: Springer.

Silber, A. (1970). An addendum to the technique of psychotherapy with alcoholics. *Journal of Nervous and Mental Diseases, 150*, 423–437.

Silber, A. (1974). Rationale for the technique of psychotherapy with alcoholics. *International Journal of Psychoanalytic Psychotherapy, 3*, 28–47.

Silber, A. (1982). The contribution of psychoanalysis to the treatment of alcoholism. In J. Soloman (Ed.), *Alcoholism and clinical psychiatry* (pp 195–211). New York: Plenum.

Simmel, E. (1948). Alcoholism and addiction. *Psychoanalytic Quarterly, 17*, 6–31.

Spiegel, E., & Mulder, E. A. (1986). The anonymous program and ego functioning. *Issues in Ego Psychology, 9*, 34–42.

Steiner, C. (1971). *Games alcoholics play.* New York: Grove Press.

Vaillant, G. E. (1981). Dangers of psychotherapy in the treatment of alcoholism. In M. H. Bean, & N. E. Zinberg (Eds.), *Dynamic approaches to the understanding and treatment of alcoholism* (pp. 36–54). New York: Free Press.

Vaillant, G. E. (1983). *The natural history of alcoholism.* Cambridge, MA: Harvard University Press.

Wallace, J. (1978). Critical issues in alcoholism therapy. In S. Zimberg, J. Wallace, and S. B. Blume (Eds.), *Approaches to alcoholism psychotherapy* (pp. 31–43). New York: Plenum.

Washton, A. M. (1989). *Cocaine addiction.* New York: Norton.

Weider, H., & Kaplan, E. H. (1969). Drug use in adolescents. Psychodynamic meaning and pharmacogenic effect. *Psychoanalytic Study of the Child, 24*, 399–431.

Wishnie, H. (1974). Opioid addiction as a masked depression. In S. Lesse, (Ed.), *Masked Depression* (pp. 350–367). New York: Jason Aronson.

Wurmser, L. (1974). Psychoanalytic considerations of the etiology of compulsive drug use. *Journal of the American Psychoanalytic Association, 22,* 820–843.

Wurmser, L. (1977). Mr. Pecksniffs horse? (Psychodynamics in compulsive drug use.) *NIDA Research Monographs, 12,* 36–72.

Wurmser, L. (1984). More respect for the neurotic process: Comments on the problem of narcissism in severe pathology, especially in addictions. *Journal of Substance Abuse Treatment, 1,* 37–45.

Wurmser, L. (1984). The role of super-ego conflicts in substance abuse and their treatment. *International Journal of Psychoanalytic Psychotherapy, 10,* 227–258.

Wurmser, L. (1985). Denial and split identity: Timely issues in the psychoanalytic therapy of compulsive drug users. *Journal of Substance Abuse Treatment, 2,* 89–96.

Yalisove, D. L. (1988). Review of 42 lives in treatment: A study of psychoanalysis and psychotherapy. R. W. Wallerstein. (1986). New York: Guilford. *Journal of Nervous and Mental Diseases, 176,* 696–697.

Yourke, C. (1970). A critical review of some psychoanalytic literature on drug addiction. *British Journal of Medical Psychiatry, 43,* 141–159.

Zinberg, N. E. (1975). Addiction and ego-function. *Psychoanalytic Study of the Child, 30,* 567–588.

6

Treating the Substance Abuser: Psychotherapy Throughout the Recovery Process

Debra E. Rothschild, Ph.D., CAC

There are many stereotypes concerning drug addicts and many beliefs about their treatability. This chapter will address these issues, dispel several of the commonly held generalizations, and present some alternative approaches.

Drug addiction crosses all social classes, professional levels, ethnicities, and diagnostic categories, regardless of the drug used. Addicts are varied as human beings are varied. Yet there are certain dynamics and specific ego deficits that appear to be common among most people who are addicted. Whether these characteristics preceded the addiction, are consequent to it, or, as is likely the case, are maintained and exacerbated by it, can be debated, but is largely irrelevant here. The case is that these people will present for treatment, and understanding the things that they have in common can help in the engagement and treatment process.

This chapter will focus on individual psychotherapy with chemically dependent patients. It is to be assumed that this therapy will take place in a context of abstinence, and often in conjunction with other modalities and supports—group and/or family therapy, psychoeducation, and, almost always, a 12-step program such as Narcotics Anonymous (NA) or Alcoholics Anonymous (AA). Sobriety is, of course, a primary goal of any substance-abuse treatment. It is not, however, sufficient as a goal in itself. Rather, it is a necessary first step in order that effective psychotherapy and growth may follow. It is this author's belief that although drug use may cease, without psychotherapy, the internal changes necessary to reduce the probability of relapse and to create more comfortable living for the addict will be difficult at best to achieve.

82

"DIFFICULT PATIENTS"

Drug addicts are, by reputation, notoriously "difficult patients." Some even call them untreatable. It is this author's belief that these impressions stem from a basic misunderstanding, or even a kind of fear of the addicted person. Drug addicts tend to be people living in pain, suffering some very fundamental psychological deficits. Contrary to popular belief, they are not all sociopaths. Nor are they simply irresponsible hedonists who cannot give up the pleasure of getting high. Those who maintain that addicts are untreatable with traditional (psychodynamic) psychotherapy because they are unable to form the necessary interpersonal relationships frequently misunderstand the phenomenology of addiction. A common cause of failure to engage addicts into treatment is the clinician's tendency to ignore the adaptive value that drug taking is serving for that individual. The tendency is to focus merely on the maladaptive, or apparently immature, hedonistic aspects of the substance abuse.

The early psychoanalytic literature about addiction (e.g., Freud, 1962/1905; Abraham, 1974/1908) emphasized the regressive aspects of drug taking. These writers conceptualized it as a libidinal or oral-erotic phenomenon. However, today the prevailing view is one of adaptation, or, as Glover (1956/1932) put it, it is a "progressive" rather than a regressive phenomenon. In other words, drug use is seen as an adaptive attempt by the user to cope with, or compensate for, particular psychological deficits. "The dominant conscious motive for drug use is not the seeking of 'kicks,' but the wish to produce pharmacologically a reduction in distress that the individual cannot achieve by his own psychic efforts" (Wieder & Kaplan, 1969, p. 403). Addicts are generally believed to have difficulties with a few specific areas of ego functioning. Those ego functions most commonly identified as impaired in addicts are regulation and control of affect, object relations, judgment, and self-care (Wurmser, 1974; Khantzian, 1975; Treece, 1984).

IMPAIRMENT OF EGO FUNCTIONS

Judgment and self-care deficits are fairly obvious in their meaning and implications. Their psychodynamics and etiology are, of course a bit more complex, and are not necessarily alike for all addicts. They may be related to issues of low self-esteem, an inability to use anxiety as a signal to avoid danger, an overriding need for thrill and adventure seeking (Zuckerman, 1979), masochistic tendencies, or other consequences of narcissistic disturbance. The implications for treatment are that early in therapy the clinician may find himself or herself having to provide specific guidance or education, pointing out what appear to be obvious consequences of proposed behaviors. For example, many addicts, when they first get sober, decide to announce their drug abuse to the entire world, including their co-workers and bosses. This is not always a necessary or wise decision. It is the clinician's role then to explore with the patient what the results of such exposure might be.

The object-relations deficits affect all areas of the individual's life, including forming and participating in a therapeutic relationship. These impairments in addicts are similar to those of many patients with borderline or narcissistic character disturbance. Many clinicians who willingly treat other such patients refuse to work with addicts. The object-relations impairments of addicts and their impact on transference and countertransference phenomena are discussed in depth in Chapter 7 in this volume.

Recognizing and addressing the deficits in affect management are critical in the early phases of the treatment of addicts. This ego function comprises at least two separate abilities (Kantrowitz, Paolitto, Sashin, Solomon, & Katz, 1986)—the ability to identify and label different affective experiences, the absence of which is called alexythymia, and the ability to tolerate, modulate, and express affect in an appropriate and constructive manner. Addicts tend to have deficits in both. Wurmser (1974) describes drug addicts as suffering from what he calls "hyposymbolization," or a curtailed ability to symbolize, especially the inner life, emotions, and self-references. Krystal and Raskin (1970) explain that addicts live in dread of being overwhelmed by an affect that they cannot distinguish or define, but that is intolerably dysphoric. The discomfort is preverbal, like the primitive emotion of an infant before anxiety and depression become differentiated. It can be so threatening that the desire to exclude it from consciousness in whatever way possible overwhelms. So one of the initial tasks of therapy once abstinence has been achieved is to help the addict learn how to recognize and label emotions. Characteristically, addicts early in treatment tend to somaticize extensively or to locate their distress in the environment rather than in themselves. For example, a heroin addict spent most of the first six months of therapy complaining about the dirt and crowds in his city, his neighborhood, the streets, and the subway trains. Only gradually did this man come to recognize and begin to "own" his emotions. As this occurred, his complaints about the city diminished considerably.

A woman cocaine addict who had been sober and in treatment for about a year spoke at an AA meeting. During her next session, she described the experience and said, "I didn't know I was nervous until I saw my hands shake, felt my stomach go tight, and then I knew, this is anxiety." A young male attorney, addicted to opiates and sober for a few months, described in his individual therapy a scene from his therapy group. A woman was talking. He was incredibly bored. The next thing he said he addressed to her, intending to be kind. Instead, it came out so cutting that she burst into tears. When asked how he had been feeling at the time, he said that he had no idea. It was then suggested that his reaction appeared to be one of anger and that perhaps we should examine what she had been talking about and his possible feelings about it. This led to a series of associations and a sudden and very clear awareness of the anger he had, in fact, experienced at the time. He was surprised, but also relieved to discover the reason for his behavior, and to understand that such anger has not only a cause but a consequence when directed at others.

Of course, alexythymia does not exist only in addicts. Many patients, addicted or not, are not aware that they are angry or sad, or know what to call how they feel. And often one goal of the psychotherapy process is to help them figure that out. The fact of not knowing can lead to inappropriate emotional expression or acting out. The process is a slow one. These people have been experiencing ills in the environment or in their bodies for a long time, and it takes constant repetition of recognition before they can truly identify, own, and express their emotions. Along the way, a person may say, as a heroin addict with nine months of treatment once did, "It was a feeling. I don't know what it's called, but I can make a sound." And he made a roaring-like sound. Or consider the alcoholic, rather new to sobriety, who had to put his body in postures to express how he felt.

SIGNIFICANCE OF THE DRUG OF CHOICE

Another consideration when treating an addict is the significance of the drug of choice. There is controversy in the literature today about exactly what meaning this has. It is known that most addicts do have a preference for a specific drug effect, and most experts believe that the one preferred has some psychological significance (i.e., Milkman & Frosch, 1973; Khantzian, 1985). Of course, most substance abusers go through periods of multidrug experimentation, but almost all eventually find one that is most relieving and most comfortable for them. Some authors, such as Wieder and Kaplan (1969), who subscribe to this self-medication hypothesis, explain it in developmental or hierarchical terms, with, for example, addiction to opiates representing an earlier developmental level in terms of defenses and other ego functions than amphetamine or cocaine addiction. Specifically, narcotics induce withdrawal, or a nodding out, like the tuning out or sleep of an infant—a more primitive response to distress than the hypomanic or grandiose denial induced by amphetamines. Intuitively, this seems to make sense, and research by Milkman and Frosch (1973, 1977) found that addicts do prefer drugs that support their characteristic styles of defense.

When working clinically with cocaine and opiate addicts, one realizes that they obviously "feel" different. However, recent research by this author (Rothschild, 1989) found no significant differences in levels of defensive functioning or regulation and control of drive, affect, and impulse between groups of highly functional opiate abusers and cocaine abusers. Similarly, Derby (1989) found no difference on a measure of object relations with a similar group of addicts. In both studies, the notable finding was that the heroin addicts' scores were not unexpectedly high, but the cocaine addicts scored surprisingly low on all measures. In other words, despite their apparent social and vocational success, these addicts revealed themselves as markedly deficient in the areas of defensive functioning, affect management, and object relations. For the clinician, then, the important point is that these patients can be very deceptive. Superficially, they often appear far more intact than they actually are. It is an easy pitfall, therefore, to view drug use as a self-indulgent pleasure rather than as the attempt to self-medicate, to escape from distress, or to adapt to deficits that it so often is. Clinicians can fail to recognize the absolute terror the idea of living drug-free can evoke in an addict. Therefore, one of the early tasks when engaging a drug addict into treatment is to explore the patient's belief about what life will be like without the drugs and to make clear one's understanding and support.

Similarly, it is crucial that the clinician not make assumptions about the function that the drugs serve for any individual addict. Not all same-drug abusers are alike. For example, a small percentage of cocaine addicts use their drug to medicate an attention-deficit disorder. They find that with cocaine they can concentrate and function at work. When this is noted to be the case, it is up to the addiction therapist to address it and, if necessary, refer the patient for appropriate medical intervention. (For a review of the subtypes of cocaine abusers, see Weiss & Mirin, 1986.)

GRIEF AND DENIAL

Related to, but separate from, the fear of giving up the drug is the grief over its loss that must be processed early in treatment. Often this grief involves not only loss of the drug, but separation from friends and companions and a change in lifestyle, familiar locations, and activities, as well as a loss of a fundamental sense of identity, that is, "I am a person who uses these drugs." The phases of grief are similar to those of any life change or loss, except that they are perhaps complicated by additional factors. The addict has, albeit ambivalently, chosen this change. And the first phase of grief, denial, is a primary defense characteristic of almost all addicted individuals. It is a delicate task, therefore, for the clinician to help the addict work through this difficult phase.

Denial can mean an addict's assertion, "I didn't get high," when, in fact, the person did. Or, more commonly, "I am not an addict," when it is pretty obvious that the person is one. For addicts, as for many patients, denial is a defense against fear, and a rather primitive one. The fear is of admitting that they have the disease, of the implications of that admission, and of the knowledge that, once they admit it, they will be pressured to stop using. The denial can be so potent that, in the face of all evidence, they do not see what is obvious. Rationalizations abound: "I don't drink before breakfast." "I don't drink every day." "I'm working; I'm not a Bowery bum."

This kind of denial can be especially infuriating for the helping professional and almost inevitably will be an issue in treatment. Sometimes the denial can look like actual lying. Or addicts can be so convincing that even the therapist is confused. When this occurs, it is easy either to be seduced and collude with the denial, to become frustrated and angry, or to decide that the patient is a sociopath. Understanding that denial is a normal part of the addictive condition can help the clinician to be alert to its presence and to break through it in a systematic, yet supportive, manner.

Consistent with the denial and the fear of losing the drug is the addict's characteristic resistance to treatment. Though it happens, it is rare for someone to come in voluntarily simply because he or she is using too much. Usually a job, health, a relationship, or something else important is being threatened or the addict is unhappy, has marital problems, is in financial difficulties, or has some other complaint, and presents for help with that particular problem. An astute clinician will discover the substance abuse. Often at this point the patient denies that the issue is addiction and insists it is someone or something else that is at fault and causing the distress. As with any resistant patient, joining the resistance, rather than battling directly against it, is the most effective way to overcome it and engage the patient in therapy. "Maybe you're right. Maybe you don't have a problem. Let's find out together."

RISKS FOR RELAPSE

As the addict gains time in sobriety, of course, life will go on. The time varies, but in this author's experience, usually in about three to six months, and then at about a year, many of these patients become angry, frustrated, or sad. They have done it. They have abstained from using their drug. But life is still tough. By being prepared for these feelings, being involved in an effective psychotherapy and in a 12-step program such as AA, and learning to recognize and express emotions rather than to act them out or experience them as somatic or environmental distress, addicts are better able to cope with these down periods.

Another common experience, and a frequent cause of relapse, is the boredom that sets in. This is a complex phenomenon, and will only be touched upon briefly at this point. Addicts describe the excitement and pleasure derived from the ritual of obtaining their drug, "skirting the edge" of getting caught and ruining their professional or personal lives. Research found that addicts, particularly cocaine abusers, tended to be greater sensation seekers when compared with nonaddicted controls (Zuckerman, 1979). In addition, the sense of boredom probably relates to the fact that many, perhaps even most, cocaine and other drug addicts suffer the sense of emptiness, or nothing inside, or the shaky sense of self that characterizes people with narcissistic disturbance. Levin (1987) states that addicts and alcoholics are either fixated at or regressed to pathological narcissism. According to him, the structurally deficient self characteristic of pathological narcissism is experienced as an empty depression that can be manifested by a lack of interest in people, activities, and goals. Once the drug effect clears and sobriety becomes stabilized, these feelings often emerge.

Related to this concept is the addict's frequent belief that without drugs there is no way to have fun or to play in any sense of the word. Addicts perceive and experience many phases of life in black-and-white terms, including the responsibility/ irresponsibility or maturity/childishness dimension. Drug use, of course, reinforces this split. Many addicts when sober are ultraresponsible or suffer from extremely harsh superego controls. This may be related to their dysfunctional, often alcoholic, family backgrounds and to the role they assumed in that system. In addition, a difficulty with modulating and expressing emotions and a fear of being overwhelmed by them inhibits any ability to relax or "let go." For addicts, then, the only avenue to relinquishing responsibility and becoming playful is through use of their drug. It appears that yet another ego function should be added to the list of those in which addicts have deficits—adaptive regression in the service of the ego. When Milkman and Frosch (1973, 1977) did their research on substance abusers and ego functions, this was the only one of the 12 Bellak scales for which results could not be reported because of the unreliability of the data. To my knowledge, no other research has specifically measured this trait. In doing treatment, however, it becomes clear that this is an area of trouble for most substance abusers. They have no idea that it is even possible to have fun without drugs, not to mention how to do so. Sobriety, therefore, can be seen as extremely depriving, and frequently there is a desire on the part of addicts to be able to use occasionally. It is the only way that they can conceive of abandoning control or behaving even for a moment in a childlike manner. This is a significant relapse risk and must be considered in the therapy of sober addicts.

An ophthalmologist with many years of practice was in treatment for opiate addiction. Once sobriety was stabilized, the therapy quickly deepened. A full range of emotions was expressed and experienced in most sessions. About a year and a half into treatment, the sessions became especially playful, with much laughter and joking on the parts of both the therapist and the patient. One day after several weeks of this, the patient said that he had had a wonderful insight. He could be "human"—that is, he could have fun and laugh with his patients and be a good doctor to them at the same time. It was a great revelation to this man that he could integrate playfulness and moderate, appropriate regression and a serious, responsible position.

Implied throughout this chapter is the notion that as the patient grows in sobriety, the nature of the therapy changes. The patient becomes increasingly able to identify and use affective experience to introspect and to explore. The therapist must monitor these changes and recognize that, as they occur, the treatment can progress from one that is primarily supportive in nature to one that is exploratory and insight-oriented.

FUNCTIONS OF THE THERAPIST

Early in treatment, the clinician must provide for the patient some of what that person was seeking with drugs. To understand these concepts better, a theory of narcissism, such as that provided by Kohut (1971), can be helpful. Although the affects or sensations that manifestly trouble addicts may differ, it is believed that almost all addicts suffer basic narcissistic conflicts that lead to the impairments in ego functions that have been described and for which the addict, through use of the drug, is attempting to compensate (Wieder & Kaplan, 1969; Kohut, 1971; Treece, 1984; Levin, 1987). The nature of early object relations is hypothesized to relate to these conflicts and consequent deficits. For example, in his discussion of narcissistic disturbance, Kohut explains that very early traumatic disappointments can interfere with the development of a psyche that can maintain, on its own, the narcissistic equilibrium of the personality. This early trauma is most frequently experienced in the form of inadequate parenting, parenting that did not fulfill the functions that the mature psychic apparatus should later be able to perform. This includes functioning as a stimulus barrier, as a provider of stimuli, and as a supplier of tension-relieving gratification. These people remain fixated on aspects of their archaic objects, and many find them in the form of drugs. Similarly, Wieder and Kaplan (1969) explain that during early childhood, an ongoing object relationship is required by the still-incomplete psychic structure in order to maintain psychic homeostasis. The object compensates for the immaturity of the ego until its functions develop. Some adults remain dependent on their objects to supplement ego and superego functions. Others turn to drugs. As Kohut states, "The drug serves not as a substitute for loved or loving objects, or for a relationship with them, but as a replacement for a defect in psychological structure" (p. 46).

Using this model, then, we see what functions the therapist must serve and what reparative work must be done in order successfully to separate the addict from the drug. Drug use that may have begun as a substitute for adequate psychological structure has done nothing but exacerbate the problem. Using a substance to cope has deprived the addict still further of any chance to develop adequate ego strengths for managing affects or impulses. Any potential that may have existed will have atrophied from disuse. The typical character defenses that ordinarily would be used to resolve conflict or subdue dysphoria or pain were replaced by the drug.

A therapist, however, is not the same as a drug. A therapist may supply the needed functions at first, but in a planned and conscious manner and with interaction. In other words, early in treatment, education, structuring and support of sound judgment, and self-care are required. The therapist must be reliably available and empathic and, in addition, must fill the role of expert and teacher. The task of the therapy, however, is to help the patient develop these capacities for himself or herself so that eventually neither a drug nor a separate object will be required. As Levin (1987) puts it, secure sobriety depends on the "building of psychic structure so that the alcoholic can perform the psychic tasks apparently performed by the alcohol" (p. 309).

The addict comes to trust the therapist and, at the same time, to rely on himself or herself to delay gratification, tolerate frustration, self-soothe, and integrate affective experience. As this occurs, an exploratory and introspective psychotherapy becomes not only possible, but useful.

REFERENCES

Abraham, K. (1973). The psychological relations between sexuality and alcoholism. In E. Jones (Ed.), *Selected papers on psycho-analysis* (pp. 80–89). London: Hogarth Press. (Original work published 1908.)

Derby, K. (1989). *Levels of internal representation of the therapist among heroin and cocaine addicts.* Unpublished doctoral dissertation, Teachers College, Columbia University, New York.

Freud, S. (1962). *Three essays on the theory of sexuality.* New York: Basic Books. (Original work published 1905.)

Glover, E. (1956). On the etiology of drug addiction. In *On the early development of mind* (pp. 187–215). New York: International Universities Press. (Original work published 1932.)

Kantrowitz, J. L., Paolitto, F., Sashin, J., Solomon, L., & Katz, A. L. (1986). Affect availability, tolerance, complexity and modulation in psychoanalysis: Followup of a longitudinal prospective study. *Journal of the American Psychoanalytic Association, 3,* 529–559.

Khantzian, E. (1975). Self selection and progression in drug dependence. *Psychiatry Digest, 36,* 19–22.

Khantzian, E. (1985). The self-medication hypothesis of addictive disorders: Focus on heroin and cocaine dependence. *American Journal of Psychiatry, 143,* 1259–1264.

Kohut, H. (1971). *The analysis of the self.* New York: International Universities Press.

Krystal, H., & Raskin, H. A. (1970). *Drug dependence: Aspects of ego function.* Detroit: Wayne State University Press.

Levin, J. D. (1987). *Treatment of alcoholism and other addictions: A self psychology approach.* New York: Jason Aronson.

Milkman, H., & Frosch, W. A. (1973). On the preferential abuse of heroin and amphetamines. *Journal of Nervous and Mental Disease, 156,* 242–248.

Milkman, H., & Frosch, W. A. (1977). The drug of choice. *Journal of Psychedelic Drugs, 9,* 11–23.

Rothschild, D. (1989). *Differentiating cocaine and opiate addicts: Affect management, defen-*

sive functioning, and narrative style. Unpublished doctoral dissertation, New School for Social Research, New York.

Treece, C. (1984). Assessment of ego functioning in studies of narcotic addiction. In L. Bellak & L. A. Goldsmith (Eds.), *The broad scope of ego function assessment* (pp. 268–289). New York: Wiley.

Weiss, R. D., & Mirin, S. M. (1986). Subtypes of cocaine abusers. *Psychiatric Clinics of North America, 9,* 491–501.

Wieder, H., & Kaplan, E. H. (1969). Drug use in adolescents: Psychodynamic meaning and pharmocogenic effect. *Psychoanalytic Study of the Child, 24,* 399–431.

Wurmser, L. (1974). Psychoanalytic considerations of the etiology of compulsive drug use. *Journal of the American Psychoanalytic Association, 22,* 820–843.

Zuckerman, M. (1979). *Sensation seeking: Beyond the optimal level of arousal.* New York: Wiley.

7

Psychology of
Compulsive Drug Use

Leon Wurmser, M.D.

So often in science it is not one perspective, one method of access, one model of understanding, that gives true insight, but the complementarity of opposite ways of looking at, and inquiring into, the phenomena. One version of this dialectic germane to substance abuse is the primary versus the secondary view. In the primary view, the focus is strictly on the phenomenon of the compulsive use of some mind-altering substance and its medical and psychological sequels. The focus on the specific concrete abuse dictates the treatment philosophy: "Drug abuse or alcoholism is the disease. Our main task is to remove the misuse of this noxious agent: everything else is diversion." The secondary view sees substance abuse of any kind only as a symptom, an expression of a hidden agenda of great complexity, usually involving not just the abuser, but the immediate environment as well, and reflecting not only conscious cognition and feeling, but also the intricate layers of deeper strata. The trickiness lies in the fact that one of these views alone does not suffice. If one explores the unconscious depths, but fails to see and to treat the surface phenomena, one is bound not even to get started in effective treatment. In turn, one who just focuses on the dependency may obtain striking first success, but unless he or she goes beyond the immediately visible problem of substance abuse and studies the underlying psychopathology, will hardly be effective in the long run. The difference between these two viewpoints is a matter of method, not one of more or less truth.

If there is any truth to the view that compulsive substance abuse is not simply an event of happenstance, but that there must be some imminent readiness in the individual to succumb to such ever-present dangers, then we are immediately faced with the question: What specifically prepares the personality to acquire this illness and not any other?

92

Intensive as well as extensive work, informed by the psychoanalytic way of ordering experience, allows us to single out certain regularities and specificities.

Psychoanalysis is defined as a consistently applied model of understanding centered on the conflict of motives—external and internal (mostly internal), conscious and unconscious. Utilizing this one perspective as a method of understanding cannot exhaustively explain mental life, but, if consistently applied, psychoanalysis still proves to be an approach offering astonishing richness and depth.

The following presents the main psychological features on three levels: clinical observation, the psychoanalytic study of three major forms of defenses, and a more theoretical consideration of the type of conflict solution.

CLINICAL OBSERVATION

1. Drugs uniformly are used as an artificial affect defense, that is, they are taken compulsively to bring about relief from overwhelming feelings. Specifically, drug use is, in the final analysis, only a pharmacologically reinforced denial—an attempt to get rid of feelings and thus of undesirable inner and outer reality. This presupposes not only a particular proneness for this particular defense, but also an inclination for what has been described as affect regression—the global, undifferentiated nature of emotions that often can be difficult to describe in words and other symbolic forms, and instead are partly converted into somatic sensations. The choice of drugs shows some fairly typical correlations with such otherwise unmanageable and deeply terrifying affects: narcotics and hypnotics are deployed against rage, shame, and jealousy; stimulants against depression and weakness; psychedelics against boredom and disillusionment; and alcohol against guilt, loneliness, and related anxiety.

2. In many addicts, one can detect phobic features, typically fears about, but also wishes for, being closed in, captured, and trapped by structures and limitations, commitments, and any type of closeness.

It is striking how the compulsive search of the addict is almost a mirror image of the compulsive avoidance of the phobic. Whereas the latter condenses all dangers into one object or one situation, thus directing all his or her anxieties toward this one threat and arranging all of life around its avoidance, the addict does exactly the reverse: his or her life's entire content and pursuit, that which he or she seeks above everything else and depends on, has also become condensed in one object or situation.

3. Where there are phobias, there are protective fantasies—fantasies of personal protective figures or of impersonal protective systems, specifically counterpoised to the threats. This search for a protector against the phobic object and the anxiety situation almost inevitably leads to a compelling dependency once such a factor is found. Protectors are highly overvalued; they are "narcissistic objects" expected

to be all-powerful, all-absolving, and all-giving, and yet also feared as all-destructive, all-condemning, and all-depriving.

4. The helplessness of the state of primary phobia, especially the pain of having been repeatedly and uncontrollably overwhelmed, is defended against by a thick crust of narcissism. Grandiosity and haughty arrogance, more or less extensive and deep withdrawal of feelings from the painful environment, and hence coldness and ruthlessness, are typical.

5. Torn between fears of the condemning and humiliating powers on the outside and these narcissistic needs of a defensive nature from within, the personality assumes a strikingly unstable, unreliable quality. Periods of high integrity and honesty suddenly give way to episodes of ruthless coldness and criminality. The alternation may go so far that we actually encounter split or multiple personalities.

6. Acute narcissistic crises (feared or real disappointments in others and the self) usually trigger the overwhelming affects described and launch the patients into compulsive drug use.

Case History

Jason had entered intensive treatment because of the severe anxiety underlying his massive, recurrently addictive abuse of narcotics, sedatives, and cocaine. He was an only child. His parents' marriage had fallen apart when he was less than 5 years old. His anxiety attacks and ensuing use of heroin increased greatly after his separation from his wife. The attack was described as resembling acute withdrawal: "a rush, chills, restless tossing and turning." He could not sleep and banged his hand against the bed in anger and frustration. He traced the terror back to similar fits of extreme, nearly murderous, rage when he felt betrayed and rejected. "I am almost swollen inside, so full of steam, flushed. My heart would beat faster, I get 'starey' eyed, a look of danger around me, like another force taking over, the strangest feeling . . ." He was reminded of the many instances when he was left alone at home by his mother to whom he was excessively close, but whose presence was unreliable: "It was furious rage, feeling choked—and utter helplessness, when I kept screaming out of the window for her—deep into the night." When recounting these episodes, he was puzzled: "What do I do with these bits and fragments of information?" He felt, in his rage turned into panic, a dissolution of inner continuity and cohesion, a repetition of the traumatic state. The sedative drug assuaged the affect storm and almost instantaneously began reconstituting this inner continuity.

As for the claustrophobia, there was a pervasive dread of being trapped by any closeness or limitation. In his dreams, he was smothered, pulled into a hole or under the water by some monster, with his screaming going unheard. He enjoyed sex, as long as it was not confined by marriage. He had to break all limitations by transgressing whatever rules were in place, thus inviting mortal danger and social ostracism (including imprisonment). He engaged in motorcycle jumping, gambling, and climbing along facades of buildings or jumping from roof to roof, and in the illegal trafficking of drugs.

His fear of shame and his provocation of humiliation and seeking for forgiveness through contrite self-debasement were compulsively repeated time and again. With each drug-taking episode, he expected to hear, "Now, you have had your chance. You should be ashamed for having abused my patience. Get the hell out of here!"

THE MAIN DEFENSES

Denial

Drug use, in the final analysis, is only a pharmacologically reinforced denial, an attempt to get rid of feelings and thus of undesirable inner and outer reality. Denial has been defined as the failure to appreciate emotionally the significance of what is being perceived.

Not only are painful reality and painful feelings denied, but so is the awareness of any inner conflict: "There is really nothing wrong with me. I take drugs only to have some fun, to feel relaxed, and to enjoy the company of my friends," "That I am an alcoholic has nothing to do with deeper inner problems. Psychotherapy is ineffective." Such disclaimers are only momentarily successful and may be followed by the admission: "You are right, I do not feel well. There is something wrong with me." The feelings denied are perceived, repudiated, and then again acknowledged.

Again our patient, Jason: "I let my bills pile up. I let things go. I just deny their existence. I am shutting my eyes. It's the same as when I was driving around with several pounds of pot in my car. I was sure I would not be caught. All along I never faced up to the possibility that I ever would have to go to jail. Somehow, I thought, I'll be bailed out." When rejected, or even just mildly rebuked, it feels "as if I had been hit with a knife." He feels crushed by shame and loneliness and then finds refuge in a system of fantasies that have to be made real by lies and drug taking.

Reversal

A number of drive reversals are generally of much greater significance as defenses than the literature indicates—turning active into passive, turning passive into active, the turning against the self. It appears to me more and more persuasive to see in the defense of turning passive into active a cardinal type of defense in severe psychopathology, and especially against aggression, much as with repression in the more typical neurotics, and particularly against libido.

Just as it is a main theme of their lives that these patients suffer and fear disappointment and helplessness, they do everything possible to enlist help, but then turn the tables and try to prove their therapists helpless and defeated. Thus they want to inflict the same helplessness, defeatedness, and humiliation on others—family, the therapist, the treatment or penal system—that they have suffered. These patients want to defeat *them*, because they themselves feel defeated; they want to make *them* feel as helpless, weak, and ashamed, as they do; they try to scare *them*, because they themselves are scared. They try to box others in because they feel so confined, and want to break out. In Jason's case: "Everybody I get close to will betray me—so I must betray her [or him] first." This preemptive betrayal, deceiving, and lying, and his anticipatory disappointment in and disillusionment with the other is an attempt to turn passive into active, to be the one who inflicts it on the other instead of suffering it passively and helplessly: "Instead of being passively fooled and feeling humiliated for it, I am fooling everyone else." In his life's experience, "I trusted my mother—yet how much has she cheated on me and has made me feel an absolute fool . . .?"

Externalization

"The whole internal battle ground is changed into an external one," according to Anna Freud. To paraphrase, externalization is the defensive effort to resort to external action in order to support the denial of inner conflict. For example, ridicule, rejection, and punishment are provoked from (not just suspected of) the outside world—a frequent response by no means restricted to compulsive drug users. Or limit setting is invited and demanded from the therapist, but then fought against. Or oral and narcissistic "supplies" are sought from spouses and friends, and their limitation is responded to with envy and rage. Much of the "acting out," the "impulsiveness," is just such a defensive use of action, an action with the aim of taking magical, omnipotent control over the uncontrollable or risking the ultimate threats (separation, humiliation, castration, dismemberment), and yet, counterphobically, proving that these terrors are unfounded, that fate can be propitiated and forced to protect. It may be action by gambling or motorcycle racing; by lying, manipulating, and cheating; by violent acts and acts of revenge. Or it may be by drugs: "I have the power, with the help of this magical substance, to master the unbearable."

TYPE OF CONFLICT SOLUTION

Our patient said: "For so long I have thought it was impossible to let anybody know what my fantasies were because they were so different from what reality is and what the laws would allow. I was afraid I would be called down, so I concealed them . . . I hid them but enacted them at the same time . . ."

This brief statement reflects what his defenses are most intensely directed against, not sexual wishes or urges of aggression, dominance, or revenge, but, as he puts it, reality and the law. Thus the psychodynamic specificity for this form of psychopathology is singled out.

It is well known from Freud's writings, especially from *Neurosis and Psychosis* (1924), that in neurosis the ego stands on the side of the superego and outer reality and directs its main defenses against the id. In contrast to it, it allies itself in schizophrenic psychosis with the archaic drives and the equally regressive superego demands and exerts its defensive efforts, mostly in the form of denial and withdrawal of investment ("decathexis"), against outer reality (Waelder, 1951). In severe depressions the ego is almost completely submerged in the archaic superego. Its mirror image is "sociopathy" and Rangell's (1974, 1976, 1980) "syndrome of the compromise of integrity," where the ego battles mainly against the superego. While it certainly also makes "inoperative" crucial elements of outer reality, the latter is, by and large, enlisted against the main enemy. In compulsive substance abuse, the defensive endeavor is very similar to that in "sociopathy": the ego also deploys much defensive action against the superego, but it does so hardly less against external reality, including the body's reality. Not only is "the world" attacked insofar as it is bearer of limits, authority, responsibility, and commitment (that is to some extent true for sociopathy as well), but this fencing off is much more general, particularly where it directly has to do with self-preservation, anticipation of consequences, delay and later gratification, and basic contradictions and logical impossibilities. In other words, in compulsive drug use, the ego eventually not only tries to invalidate values, authority, and responsibility (i.e., the superego), but also the lines drawn between objects, the boundaries between time, and between inside and outside, the borders between social entities, the limits between concepts. It is an attack on the syllogistic basis of rationality, somewhat similar to that in psychoses (Wurmser, 1978).

Commonly, these conflicts are transient and easily shift. Kubie used to say: "No one is psychotic or neurotic 24 hours a day." There are steady changes in equilibrium, alliance, and defense. Neither are any of these schematic relations total. In the following schema (Figure 7-1) these correlations are presented diagrammatically whereby "alliance" is symbolized by the equal sign ($=$) and "defense against" by the crossed arrow ($\nleftrightarrow$). The structural relations are ordered in three pairs; each pair is made up of two mirroring configurations. I have presented this synopsis in greater detail elsewhere (Wurmser, 1981a, 1981b, 1981c, 1982, 1983).

Although blatantly anthropomorphic, the description I am going to employ is most useful to organize a great many observations and lower-level theoretical inferences that otherwise could not be seen in any comprehensive and logical order.

In the case of toxicomania, the main anxieties and depressive affects straddle the "borders" of the ego toward the superego and the outside world. In particular, the defenses—mainly, turning passive into active, externalization, and denial—are directed not only against such superego related affects as guilt, shame, and depression, but, more important, against the superego's admonishing, observing, con-

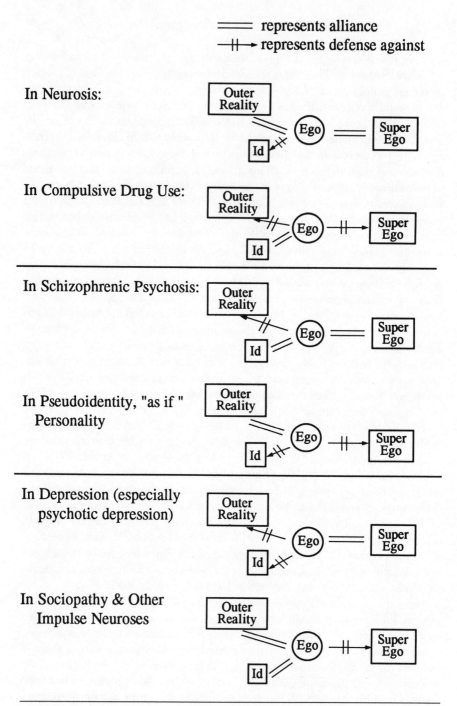

Figure 7-1. *Three pairs of conflict solution.*

demning functions and against many ideals posited by that important part of the self. When Waelder (1951) writes with regard to psychosis, "Emancipated from reality, the ego creates for itself a new world which is set up in accordance with the desires of the id" (p. 214), this may actually be more true for drug abuse than for psychosis, though in a time-limited way, since at least the claims of the superego against the id are usually retained, and even become particularly prominent in psychosis, while they are repudiated specifically and on a broad front during the states of self-alteration brought about by acute intoxication.

To be even more precise, ultimately, it may still be the terror of the id—mostly of rage engendered by severe early helplessness—that underlies the conflict at hand. However, the toxicomanic's ego joins with broad segments of the id, mostly its libidinous drives, and chooses the superego as its main enemy, which can be, at least momentarily, vanquished by denial and supplanted by the countervailing, largely narcissistic fantasies. Originally, those underlying aggressions that are central to the basic conflict were a direct response to an overwhelmingly traumatizing outer reality. Very early in life, these aggressions already were directed against external structure, against any form of authority—in brief spasms of spite and rebellious destruction or in a chronic attitude of provocativeness and defiance. Already, then, the superego and its external prototypes were treated as the main enemy.

Eventually, important parts of the id, particularly many forms of libido, are recruited in this fight against superego and outer reality—fusion fantasies, masturbatory forms of excitement (masturbation was called by Freud the primary addiction), anal-sadistic forms of pleasure. But then, as well as later on when drugs serve as the conflict solution, it is not pleasure as such that is sought, but as a defense against the superego and outside world and the severely fearsome rage involved in this battle—as a sign of victory over the anxiety involved in the conflict.

When we have such a solution, however, it usually is not more than a precarious attempt at one. This at least holds true in the cases we see in the sociocultural circumstances in which we work. Its precariousness is spelled out by the famous "return of the repressed or denied"—that what should have been warded off in that solution reappears in a distorted but mighty form and in a more primitive shape than when it was fended off originally. If the conflict solution that is typical for compulsive drug users consists in defending against crucial aspects of the superego and related aspects of outer reality ("limitations"), we can expect to find a return of its disowned functions, but in distorted and archaic form.

The superego has six major functions: (1) the ego ideal; that is an ideal image and code of ideal actions; (2) self-criticism and self-punishment; (3) stabilization of mood and affects; (4) self-observation; (5) the protection of outer reality's boundaries; and (6) self-approval, self-care, and self-protection.

1. *The return of the denied ego ideal.* This can be found primarily in that narcissism that has been vested in the ego ideal, but now returns as narcissistic gratification reclaimed in the drug-induced intoxication. Specifically, it can be stated:

"I am as good, as grand, as full, rich and strong as my wishes bid me to feel because I am protected. My inner judge has been silenced. I am close to an ideal state because I am one with the protector and thus have eliminated the voice of my conscience and of every limit-setting authority." This topic has been covered in detail elsewhere (cf. Wurmser 1978, 1981a).

2. *Self-punishment.* The second part of this "return to the denied superego" lies in the fact that criticism, retaliation, and punishment are invited by provocative action externally and usually accepted. The "protector" thus changes into "the monkey on my back"—into the confining, enslaving, imprisoning master. The superego, denied, reasserts its claims in the form of social ostracism, evoked scorn, severe penalties, imprisonment, and even death.

3. *Discontinuities of ego states.* In my book ("The Hidden Dimension"), I kept coming back to the strange flip-flop phenomena, those peculiar switches from one extreme to the other, the utter emotional unreliability of substance abusers. It can now be assumed that it is above all the defense against the superego-induced affects that is ultimately accountable for this multiplicity of self. The superego is known to act as the mood and affect stabilizer (Jacobson, 1957/1971, pp. 77-78). If it is temporarily and recurrently made "inoperative," all life, but behavior and attitudes in particular, takes on that especially disrupted, chaotic quality that is so bewildering in these personalities even if they are abstinent—and the more so when they are under the influence of mind-altering drugs.

Strictly speaking, it thus falls outside the argument being pursued here: "the return of the warded-off superego aspects."

There is much talk today about "splitting" and "fragmentation." The prevalence of archaic conflicts, with their radical forms of anxiety and defenses, mostly of the reversal type, leads phenomenologically to a perceived discontinuity of the inner sense of self as well as to outward manifestation of "split" and "multiple" personalties, of sudden flip-flops, and of that unreliability that is so characteristic of these and other severely ill patients ("borderline," schizophrenic, manic-depressive): One moment they give honest pledges, make grand plans, engage in ambitious, often idealistic enterprises, and show love and affection, considerateness, and caring: the next moment, all promises are angrily broken, the plans forsaken, the commitments forgotten, and anger, contempt, and arrogance rule.

This phenomenological "split" is not a defense, but a functional disparity and contradictoriness between conflicting ego parts. It seems to me that this important symptom is in fact due, to a very large extent, to the defensive efforts against the superego: ideals and loyalties are suddenly replaced by narcissistic pursuits, inner prohibitions being betrayed under the onslaught of desire and dread. By deploying various protective systems, the effort is made to ward off this bewildering discontinuity and fragmentation to cover it up. Such a cover-up is not so much made by the provision of specific "narcissistic supplies" or by any direct counteraction to a supposed defense by splitting, but by a temporary elimination of the pervasive and globally threatening anxieties and the direct soothing of the related affective storms, whether by substitute ideals and substitute consciences, or by the magical effect of the drug. Any protective person (drug dealer, peer group, sponsor) or protective system (drug culture, Synanon, Alcoholics Anonymous) is a reexternalized version of the archaic superego, one established to guarantee power, continuity, and mastery for an ego that is faced by traumatic anxiety and depression. The protector is set up to oppose the opposite version of the archaic superego, the harshly condemning, but easily externalized authority that has become the repository of the severe traumatization and operates almost exclusively with shame rather than guilt.

4. *The return of repressed self-observation.* This brings us to the issue of the vast prevalence of shame over guilt. Here I give only a few excerpts from a much larger work (Wurmser, 1981c). It is striking how important various shame affects are in much of psychopathology, particularly in compulsive drug use. And it is more the hidden, denied, unconscious shame than the conscious one that lurks behind much of symptomatology. It is the more surprising that, despite the study of narcissism, one finds not much thought given to either overt or to hidden shame and its vicissitudes—or, for that matter, to its opposites, the sense of pride and dignity.

Since shame is a form of contempt for oneself, it is understandable that contempt for others is frequently a form of reversal: "Instead of my despising myself, I direct withering ridicule or cold scorn against others." Arrogance and haughtiness may be understood as masks for the feeling of shame.

What is the affect of shame? It comes down to seeing one's weakness and failure exposed to the eyes of someone else or to the "inner eye" of one's conscience, to seeing oneself looked at with cold disregard, and contempt. It is followed by a wish either to wipe out the disgrace by a furious counterattack or to hide oneself, actually or symbolically, by disappearing or by freezing up and "turning into stone." It is less known that shame is also the fear to look. One wishes not to know and covers one's eyes.

Chronic severe depersonalization is another mask of shame: "I observe myself and I am not myself anymore—not this disgusting, weak being." The correlation of continuous estrangement with shame is so regular that chronic severe states of depersonalization can be seen as reflecting underlying unconscious shame just as chronic depression is "caused" by underlying unconscious guilt. For many patients, drug use is an artificial form of such self-estrangement.

Spite, paranoid fears, a compulsion to want to be mysterious and to mystify others, grandiose ambitions, and hiding one's feelings behind a mask of coldness and lack of emotion—all may be characteristic ways of dealing with shame. Anyone who works with alcoholics and drug addicts knows how typical all these character attitudes are—quite independent of the drug use itself.

5. *Limitations.* It has been repeatedly mentioned that the addict specifically fights against limits and limitations. It appears that an important symbol for the superego is precisely such limits, enclosures, and confining structures: the claustrum. It thus

should not be surprising that we encounter in many compulsive drug users a more or less severe claustrophobia, although one must add that this symptom is not specific for these patients. It is also significant that this claustrophobia usually is displaced further to metaphorical enclosures. Many feel stifled, smothered, and uncomfortably hemmed in by human warmth and physical or emotional closeness (including intensive psychotherapy) and either have to beat a frightened or angry retreat or "burst out" when someone gets too close. ("Close" comes from the Latin *clausus*—closed in, from the same stem as claustrum.) Any gesture of closeness is experienced as a concrete threat of being engulfed by the other.

Another symbolic variant is manifested by procrastination and indecision: every deadline, every chore or task, becomes a confining limit, and thus represents a claustrum, evoking both fear and anger.

Yet another character variation can often be traced back to a hidden claustrophobia (cf. Arlow, 1966). These patients have to escape any commitment (e.g., school, marriage), do not persevere in tasks, and are perpetually running away, avoiding, playing hooky, or, later on, traveling compulsively.

One can easily imagine how this claustrophobia results in a particularly intense resistance against the very structure of therapy, and hence the recurrent interruptions and undermining. I remember very few patients with serious drug problems who ever really terminated their therapy; most of them broke it off or at least missed many appointments.

The oral meaning of such a claustrum is easily recognizable, but it is equally easily overlooked what cardinal importance the equation of such a "devouring claustrum" with the superego and all its representations and representatives really has, especially for these patients. It appears that this equation forms part of a central fantasy of great specificity for such patients. The superego is limitation par excellence, and hence the main referent for a claustrum.

On all levels, anxiety is accompanied by a series of usually aggressive actions that would liberate the self from these various concentric bounds. Yet this liberation and bursting out raise many new specters: condemnation in the form of guilt and shame and aloneness because of the separation from the enclosing, protective, shielding claustrum, and the fear of fragmentation and self-loss. With this original closeness of anxiety and claustrum, one can see in claustrophobia the primary phobia (Wurmser, 1980).

Nothing has yet been said about the true origin of this equation of several factors of inner life. As mentioned, Freud saw it in the act of birth, but this seems too speculative, Instead, the essential *fons et origo* may be found in the massive overstimulation, mostly of an aggressive, but occasionally of a libidinal or combined nature, that is so typical for compulsive drug users. Such traumatic overstimulation can be found in the history of nearly all compulsive drug users seen in intensive exploratory psychotherapy or analysis and in many others more whom one gets to know only in more superficial therapy.

Theoretically, one could speculate that overstimulated children would later become compulsive seekers of sedatives, including narcotic drugs, whereas understimulated, deprived children would fill the emptiness with stimulants (particularly amphetamines) or psychedelics—but this has not been borne out by the observations. Most addicts of all varieties have quite uniformly gone through severely traumatic periods from early childhood through adolescence; that is, traumatic in the sense of unusually severe real exposure to violence, sexual seduction, and brutal abandonment; of severe real unreliability, mendacity, betrayal, and abandonment; or for real parental intrusiveness or secretiveness (Wurmser, 1981a). This overstimulation is experienced as traumatic anxiety, typically in the form of helpless confusion and a loss of felt controls, a vague aimless tension. Probably because of the physiological concomitants of internally, somatically felt narrowness and stricture, this severe anxiety becomes concretized in, and attached to, the general idea of confinement, entrapment, and enclosure, and projected on to all external structures lending themselves to being viewed as claustra (see for this also Shengold, 1989). Relief from such anxiety can only come from protection, and yet this protection would be sought primarily in external structures, in outside controls and limitations, in the hope that somebody else will take over and constrain, and thus shield, him or her against this dark overwhelming part within. The tragic paradox, of course, is that all such protection is bound to become once more just a new claustrum and, therefore, a renewed source of terror.

The battle against "claustrum = limits = superego = confining external world" is thus an indispensable psychodynamic factor in the battle, with the help of drugs, against all those indomitable affects that refer to the conflict with the superego.

6. *The "loving and beloved superego."* It is well known that the superego is not solely the ideal-setting, self-observing, and self-condemning part of one's inner life, but is also the approving and protecting inner agency (Waelder, 1930; Schafer, 1960). This implies that the defense against the superego may prominently involve its aspect as protector, soother, and caregiver; the consequence would be that there is a constant sense of unprotectedness and hurt leading to the frantic search for other "protectors and forgivers" (the drugs being but one example), to undo the narcissistic injury and chronic shame and forgive the guilt.

Several leading explorers of this area have recently stressed the deficit in the self-caring function in these patients (Krystal, 1977; Khantzian, 1978). We may assume that what they refer to is just this protective, assuring, approving side of the superego that falls victim to the general defensive effort directed against it and by its ensuing regression, splintering, and projection. Thus we should not be surprised to encounter concomitantly an overriding need for a quite specific system to protect solidly and concretely against the overwhelming general and more phobically focused anxieties. To put it simply, the system of phobic fears is opposed by a protective system in the form of protective figures and protective fantasies. This "antiphobic" system prominently encompasses the drugs, but is never limited to them. What would be the characteristics of such a magical "protector" who is just as compulsively sought as the phobic object is avoided? Most of all the phobic and the antiphobic objects would need to be very closely related to each other. If the phobic equation is "over-stimulation and anxiety = claustrum = superego = all limitations," the protective system must resemble this archaic "syllogism." In fact, we know this well from all those substitute protectors: harshly confronting therapists; groups slashingly aggressive while seeming supportive; tightly knit, overbearing systems, such as therapeutic communities, AA and Narcotics Anonymous, Black Muslims—any kind of highly limiting external structure. This protective system serves in large part as a superego substitute in its many facets—sought for, fought against, submitted to.

This countervailing fantasy of protective objects, which have to be split off from the hated and frightening anxiety object but share in the power of the latter, are the direct counterpart to the underlying phobia. As stated initially, the addiction is the photographic negative of a phobia and so are its most effective forms of therapy.

Incidentally, there may be parallels to sexual perversion. Again, it appears that the perverse act is not primarily dictated by the goal of pleasure, but by that of protection against otherwise overwhelming anxiety, although we probably would not find the same centrality of the defense against the superego and the return of its repressed aspects.

More specifically, the drug effects themselves can be seen as various types of counterphobic fantasies that validate the attempted and hoped-for protection against the main anxieties and thus also against the major phobias: "I am strong, not vulnerable" (with stimulants, mostly amphetamines and cocaine, but to a lesser degree also nicotine); "I am blissful, not enraged" (with narcotics and other sedative drugs); "I am trustful, not disillusioned" (with psychedelics); "I am accepted, approved, and belonging, not isolated and guilty" (with alcohol). More generally for all drug use: "I am intact, protected, and know and control myself; I am not fragmented, helpless, and directionless."

It also does not appear so farfetched to see in this sixth function, the search for an external magical protector against a specific anxiety, the factor that almost solely accounts for those addictive phenomena usually not encompassed under "compulsive drug use": food addiction ("sugar high"), compulsive smoking, compulsive reading, perhaps even compulsive television watching, and especially "love addiction" (in the sense of masochistic bondage).

The parallel of addiction and phobia goes even further, to the central use of condensation.

Drug dependency and all its accoutrements thus reenact this countervailing fantasy of protectors and protective systems with all its implied anxieties and rages; this reenactment shows to various degrees the six aspects of the superego I described as being partly or fully defended against, but as returning now from denial and repression.

FAMILY DYNAMIC

No comprehensive study of the specific features (dynamic, attentional, communicational) of the families of various types of compulsive drug users exists as yet, in contrast to what especially Lidz and co-workers and Wynne and Singer have done for schizophrenia. What we know does not appear specific enough.

The best studies to date are those of Stanton and his group (1977, 1978) based on the incisive work of Boszormenyi-Nagy. They see the drug addict's life in antithesis. Overtly, the addict breaks all the rules and commitments (described above as part of the claustrophobia) in order to show his or her independence and forceful breaking away from home, but ultimately the reverse is attained: a cementing of his or her dependency on the family and thus a saving of the family cohesion. Were the addict to forsake the career of addiction, he or she would risk the dissolution of the family. Even the addict's death may be a sacrificial move to keep the family together. In turn, the family needs the addict as the scapegoat, the attacking of whom holds them together. "He is a loyal son who denies himself and rescues his family. He is a savior." "Not only did the addict fear separation from the family, but the family felt likewise toward him . . . this was an interdependent process in which his failure served a protective function of maintaining family closeness."

I have little question now that this is generally true—but perhaps too generally so. All neurotics and psychotics show similar hidden loyalty conflicts in their family systems. It may be granted, though, that these families place an excessive emphasis on such covert dependency and loyalty, while the front of the stage is ruled by treason and breach of faith.

It seems to me that we can discern four types of families, marked by massive traumatization, deception, intrusiveness, and inconsistency, respectively. A fifth feature would be parental alcoholism or drug abuse, which is often mentioned. I omit it here, not because it is not important, but rather because it is itself the expression of dynamically more important processes. Excluded is that not inconsiderable group where organic factors, mainly in the form of "minimal brain damage" or "limbic system disorders" outweigh psychodynamic ones in relevance and where family pathology plays no significant role.

1. Corresponding to the traumatic intensity of anxiety, including the phobic core, and, more generally, to the cardinal feature of all compulsive drug use, profound affect regression or primitivity of affects, we should expect severe and real external traumatization. We do find this in most, though not all, cases.

Danny, a patient described by Dr. Richard Anderson, is a polydrug user and an alcoholic. He is a homosexual in his 20s. "The mother was extremely overprotective and intrusive with Danny, always interested in his every activity. She insisted on absolute obedience, and when he failed to do exactly as she wanted, she administered harsh physical punishment, such as beatings with a belt and putting his head under water. Punishments were for such things as being a few minutes late for a meal or not practicing his piano lessons. Additionally, Danny was invited into his parents' bed when frightened at night, and he recalls that they always slept in the nude."

A second case: "My mother tried to kill herself when she was pregnant with me. I was always taught that sex is a bad thing. She now keeps me at home all the time and locks me up. . . . She said if I did not shape up—with sex or drugs—she would shoot me and herself. She cut up my clothes so that I cannot leave the house." Her father tried to rape her. "My mother threatened to kill him. . . . They always yelled at each other. He used to whip us with a belt. If he tried to sleep with me again, I'd kill him with a butcher knife. . . . My mother already has bought three burial plots." All this was confirmed to me by the mother. The girl, a barbiturates and narcotics addict, soon thereafter killed herself by an overdose.

Case 16 in my book: "When I was 12 or 13, I stole some money from my father and gave it to friends. When it was discovered, my father beat me with a stick and made me eat a pack of cigarettes. My mother is just crazy. She steals and sells furniture and pictures of my stepfather. They scream at each other all the time. She is either raving about a person or feels persecuted." Again, I found external corroboration for much of this.

Case 23: "There were many fistfights between my mother and father and my grandfather and father. When I was about 5, my father tried to kill himself with iodine. He told me what he had done. . . ." Later, when the parents were separated, the mother had a coterie of lovers: "I slept in my mother's bed and was often awakened by her intercourse [with a lover]—with me in the same bed. Often she would leave me alone in our second-story apartment to go out with one of her lovers. I remember how once they slammed the door and locked me in. I climbed out of the window and jumped onto the roof of the car so that they would not leave me alone. They brought me back, gave me a beating, and left me at home anyway."

Let me stress again that this is not the case in all instances of compulsive drug use. I see severe parental violence and intense exposure to sexual activities as an amazingly frequent family factor—playing a role in over 50% of the cases I have seen over the years. I would like to single it out as one prominent group—that of traumatization by family violence, brutality, and overt, continued involvement of the child in sexual activities, including sexual abuse and incest.

Based on the extent of profound anxiety, I would, however, postulate that other, more subtle, more veiled forms of external traumatization would have to have occurred in many other addicts—unmanageable overstimulation of aggression and libido, yet I am not entirely sure where to look for it without unduly stretching the concept of trauma. I am also quite certain that such traumatization would have originated in early childhood, but would not have remained confined to it.

2. In a second group and corresponding to the defense by externalization, intru-

siveness is the prominent feature. It is similar to what has been described for families of schizophrenics and results in the same curious mixture of pseudoidentity and pervasive shame in the children. If anything, the abuse of the child for the parents' grandiose expectations and their disregard for the child's age-appropriate needs often is even more pronounced, than in the families of schizophrenics. This includes the crossing of intergenerational boundaries, the parentification of the child and the sexualization of the parent–child relationship. I am puzzled, however, as to why this symptom choice and not schizophrenia? Might it have a much lesser impact on the cognitive and linguistic functions in the transactions? I hope that further studies of shared focal attention and communication will provide some clues.

It needs to be emphasized how much such intrusive running of the lives of the children, this exploiting and "busy-body" behavior, evokes both rage and shame in the child. The intrusive family breeds a child who is, though manifestly compliant, secretly, then overtly rebellious and profoundly shame prone. There is nothing of which the child feels proud and confident, and everywhere he or she senses impending put-downs and humiliation. Some neurotics with strong phobic inclinations show milder forms of this correlation; severer versions are found among many compulsive drug users of various types. Why this prevalence of shame in the child? The steady intrusions into the child's emotional and physical intimacy leave him or her exposed, without control over the most private concerns. The child has to assume a masklike pseudoidentity in order to shield the nucleus of something very much his or her own from the possessive, overbearing invasions—a refuge of privacy protected by the walls of shame. The "drug therapy" of shame is then a method of choice, as one form of affect defense. Not only does the drug dampen the shame anxiety, but it safeguards by an additional curtain the real self while simultaneously guarding the dependency on the parent.

3. The next group is almost a counterpart to the second one—here it is not intrusiveness, but secretiveness and unavailability on the parent's part. It is the pendant, the corresponding family defense, to denial as one of the leading defenses in the individual. It is they, the parents, who live their "life lie" (Ibsen's "livsløgnen" behind a facade of propriety and respectability. A barbiturate addict, for example, was not informed when her older brother had to get married; she was 9 years old at the time. She found out when the rest of the family came home from church in festive clothes. It was a screen for much else that had remained hidden from her, veiled by a thick curtain of decorum and religious piety. Like the intrusive family, the secretive family promotes a profound depersonalization, a pervasive sense of unrealness and lack of authenticity; this estrangement is re-created or combated by various drugs (barbiturates and narcotics deepening it, amphetamines and cocaine piercing the veil, and psychedelics variably doing both).

4. A fourth type is represented by a family of utter inconsistency and unreliability, reflecting the overall prevalence of archaic defenses and ensuing ego and superego "splits." Again, any narcissistic whim dictates what should be real, what should

be right and proper. Today's sin is tomorrow's merit. The mother's reward is the father's penalty. Very often, there is only a rudiment of a family—a grandmother or an aunt, an older sibling, no parent at all. The dissolution of hierarchy, and with that of stable superego structures, is, to some extent, present in all compulsive drug users and may well be one of the most specific family hallmarks. However, we are probably justified to single out a fourth group in which such a dissolution of boundaries and limitations is particularly remarkable, where anything goes, where the law of the day is lawlessness. Characteristically, such patients do not stay in treatment, coming perhaps at best to a first interview; therefore, they have been quite insufficiently studied.

In looking back, I believe we can discern these four major types of families predisposing somewhat selectively to drug use without distinguishing more precisely what type of drug abuse may correspond to which kind of family. I do not think we can distinguish these types too sharply; much overlapping occurs. Still there may be some heuristic value in starting more systematic and controllable research with such clinical types.

In addition, these family types exemplify some of the central dynamic features of the individual patients: defective affect defense and phobic core ("traumatizing families"); defense against superego, the flip-flop syndrome ("inconsistent, antihierarchical, anarchical families"); denial and prevalence of shame ("deceptive and secretive families"), externalization, separation anxiety, clinging demandingness and possessiveness ("intrusive families"). Since in most cases we see a combination of types, it may be legitimate to talk about a *tetrad of family characteristics* in compulsive drug use of *aggressive and sexual overstimulation, inconsistency, deceptiveness,* and *intrusiveness.*

Drug use is a pharmacologically induced denial of affect. We have seen that denial is an especially prominent aspect of these personalities. Might it be equally prominent in the makeup of their families? I am reminded of a strikingly beautiful and pertinent passage in Thomas Mann's *Joseph and His Brothers.* "Carelessness toward the inner life of people and ignorance about it result in a totally false (distorted) relationship to reality; they generate self-deception (self-blinding). . . . The power of imagination and the art of guessing in regard to the feelings of others, i.e., feeling oneself into them, is not merely laudable, insofar as it breaks through the barriers of the self, but it is also an indispensable tool of self preservation." I believe that our patients give up this vitally important tool towards themselves—they cannot allow themselves to feel themselves into their own affective world (Krystal's work)—and hence towards others—out of devastating anxiety. This giving up is denial. Moreover, they pick up an external means to cement such denial—the pharmacon. The defenses of denial and externalization bring about the characteristic *Verblendung,* the self-deception and blinding. They "learned," however, from their parents how and why not to use "empathy into feelings," not to accept emotions and conflicts, and how to cover them up. The sharing of such crucial anxieties, defenses, and fantasy systems constructed around them as most prominent parts of the life-style may be one of the most convincingly solid bridges between individual and family.

THOUGHTS ABOUT TREATMENT

Many of the conflicts described and the severely traumatizing family disturbances underlying them lead to massive, manifest, and almost untreatable deficits: lack of operative conscience and ideals; self-care deficit; loss of protection against overwhelming, often preverbal and somatized affects; lack of self-constancy and object constancy; and extreme narcissistic prepossession.

Taking one tack and correcting one deficit or dealing with one conflict may force us to choose a method that contradicts to other needs and necessities. Hence we see the proliferation of, yet dissatisfaction with, a multiplicity of methods and controversy among adherents of various therapeutic schools. Where one harbors a deep uncertainty, one tends to indulge in fanaticism. In my experience, the answer lies not in one method, or in one method for a given patient, but in a combination of several, at times almost contradictory, methods. The psychodynamic paradoxes may require paradoxes in treatment. I believe it is this combination of what follows that ultimately is the answer. This includes pharmacological approaches, which I am not going to discuss.

1. One may move horizontally and simply substitute one protector—the drug—with a socially more acceptable one. The more powerful and "ideal" the protector, the more likely the displacement from the drug onto it will be. Programs of whatever kind—psychotherapeutic bonds to an idealized therapist, causes like Islam or Christian fundamentalism, groups of intense solidarity dedicated to shared and captivating idealization, mainly of the nature of AA—all can be mighty protectors, making drug use unnecessary. The closer, however, such a protective system moves toward the original and fought-off threatening superego figure, the more what is sought is also combated, rebelled against, and defeated—a delicate balance that is more often disrupted than preserved. For example, according to a number of studies, AA has proved effective only in 14–18% of all the cases involved, including all the dropouts at the beginning (Fingarette, 1988; Fridell, 1990) (Mats Fridell). How to resolve this intrinsic ambivalence is an open question, which is answered in many individual cases by art and skill rather than by real understanding. It is still amazing to me how often this group of approaches really succeeds, how often, in other words, the rebellion against and wish to defeat authority is outweighed by idealization. We may call this approach "displacement of idealization." Fenichel called it the "repressive–inspirational" form of treatment (1945, p. 258).

2. A vertical approach is the in-depth exploration mainly of the anxieties, of their history, and of the underlying conflicts—the psychotherapeutic access either as focal

psychotherapy, as intensive exploratory psychotherapy, or as somewhat modified psychoanalysis. In all such approaches, particular attention needs to be paid to the defenses against the superego and against reality, rather than mainly to the defenses against drives. Obviously, this approach is restricted as to numbers and selection. This is the "insight-oriented approach," relying on clarification and, to a considerable extent, on abreaction, on catharsis. Optimally, true in-depth insight is obtained.

Psychotherapy appears to succeed only if the protective fantasy presented before is reexperienced in the transference. This aspect of transference is far more difficult to deal with and more resistant to recognition and working through than the negative transference. As mentioned, the therapist has to replace the drug as an object to depend upon, as Anna Freud proposed. Anxiety and anger directed at the psychotherapist then become so intense that many patients cannot tolerate it and interrupt therapy. There is as yet no generally applicable way to make this transition safer. Still it appears that a consistent attention from the beginning to the twin problems of claustrophobia and the fear of feeling guilty or ashamed as mobilized in the therapy and witnessed in countless situations of current and past life may reduce the likelihood of this flight from therapy.

3. The most common, and least successful, method is deterrence. The externalization by the patient of the denied conscience in the form of provoked punishment is responded to with affirmation of such punishment. Every invitation for retaliation is met with retaliation; every evocation of humiliation is met with such humiliation. This is indeed society's response. By and large, this tit-for-tat method has proven to be disastrous.

In modest terms, however, I observed that neither displacement of idealization nor insight therapy alone can entirely work without using some sanctions or threats of sanctions. The most rational version of this is, I found, civil commitment—the authoritatively enforced, compulsory treatment in lieu of imprisonment, yet with the background threat of such jailing.

A final word with regard to the political implications of what I have presented.

If the substance abuser's attitude is: "I use a concrete but magically potent means—the drug—to deny inner conflict, and, more specifically, to combat the functions of inner authority, but invite its retaliation," society plays beautifully along. First, it accepts the demonic power of that drug. Second, it accepts the negation of inner conflict; the hostility against a psychological, especially psychodynamic, understanding of compulsive substance abuse, including alcoholism, has remained astounding, and simplistic solutions (AA, Synanon, methadone as exclusive approaches of comprehension and treatment) are propagated with religious fervor and at the cost of any rational weighing of the merits of an intrapsychic understanding.

And third, it accepts the drug addict's invitation to play punisher, scorner, castrator, executioner—and secret ally!

REFERENCES

Abend, S. M., Porder, M. S., & Willick, M. S. (1983). *Borderline patients: Psychoanalytic perspectives*. New York: International Universities Press.

Arlow, J. A. (1966). Character and conflict. *Journal of Hillside Hospital, 15*, 139–151.

Böszörmenyi-Nagy, I. & Framo, J. L. (1965). *Intensive family therapy: Theoretical and practical aspects*. New York: Harper & Row.

Böszörmenyi-Nagy, I. & Spark, G. M. (1973). *Invisible loyalties*. New York: Harper & Row.

Brenner, C. (1982). *The mind in conflict*. New York: International Universities Press.

Fenichel, O. (1941). Problems of psychoanalytic technique. D. Brunswick. *Psychoanalytic Quarterly.*

Fenichel, O. (1945). *Psychoanalytic theory of neurosis*. New York: Norton.

Fenichel, O. (1954). *Collected papers*. New York: Norton.

Fingarette, H. (1988). *Heavy drinking: The myth of alcoholism as a disease*. Berkeley, CA: University of California Press.

Fraiberg, S. (1982). Pathological defenses in infancy. *Psychoanalytic Quarterly, 51*, 612–635.

Freud, A. (1936/1971). *The ego and the mechanisms of defense*. New York: International Universities Press.

Freud, A. (1965). *Normality and pathology in childhood: Assessments of development. The Writings of Anna Freud, 6*. New York: International Universities Press.

Freud, A. (1974). Problems of technique in adult analysis. *Journal of Philadelphia Association of Psychoanalysis, 1*, 60–101.

Freud, S. (1924). *Neurosis and psychosis*. Standard edition. pp. 149–156.

Fridell, M. (1990). *Kvalitetsstyrning i psykiatrisk narkomanvård. Effekter på personal och patienter*. Stockholm: Almqvist & Wiksell.

Jacobson, E. (1957a). On normal and pathological moods: Their nature and functions. *Psychoanalytic Study of the Child, 12*, 73–113.

Jacobson, E. (1957b). Denial and repression. *Journal of the American Psychoanalytic Association, 5*, 61–92.

Jacobson, E. (1959). Depersonalization. *Journal of the American Psychoanalytic Association, 7*, 581–610.

Jacobson, E. (1964). *The self and the object world*. New York: International Universities Press.

Jacobson, E. (1971/1957). *Depression: Comparative studies of normal, neurotic and psychotic conditions*. New York: International Universities Press.

Kernberg, O. F. (1975). *Borderline conditions and pathological narcissism*. New York: Jason Aronson.

Kernberg, O. F. (1976). *Object-relations theory and clinical psychoanalysis*. New York: Jason Aronson.

Kernberg, O. F. (1984). *Severe personality disorders*. New Haven, CT: Yale University Press.

Khantzian, E. J. (1974). Opiate addiction: A critique of theory and some implications for treatment. *American Journal of Psychotherapy, 28*, 59–70.

Khantzian, E. J. (1978). The ego, the self and opiate addiction: Theoretical and treatment considerations. *International Review of Psycho-Analysis, 5,* 189–198.

Khantzian, E. J. (1987). *Substance dependence, repetition and the nature of addictive suffering.* Unpublished Manuscript.

Khantzian, E. J. & Mack, J. E. (1983). Self-preservation and the care of the self: Ego instincts reconsidered. *Psychoanalytic Study of the Child, 38,* 209–232.

Kohut, H. (1971). *The analysis of the self.* New York: International Universities Press.

Kohut, H. (1972). Thoughts on narcissism and narcissistic rage. *Psychoanalytic Study of the Child, 27,* 360–400.

Krystal, H. (1974/1975). The genetic development of affects and affect regression. *Annual Psychoanalysis, 2,* 98–126; *3,* 179–219.

Krystal, H. (1977). Self- and object-representation in alcoholism and other drug dependence: Implications for therapy. In *Psychodynamics of drug dependence* (pp. 88–100). NIDA Research Monograph 12. Washington, DC, U.S. Government Printing Office.

Krystal, H. (1978a) Trauma and affect. *Psychoanalytic Study of the Child, 36,* 81–116.

Krystal, H. (1978b). Self representation and the capacity for self care. *Annual Psychoanalysis, 6,* 209–246.

Krystal, H. (1982). Adolescence and the tendencies to develop substance dependence. *Psychoanalytic Inquiry, 2,* 581–617.

Krystal, H. (1988). *Integration and self-healing: Affect, trauma, alexithymia.* Hillsdale, NJ: Analytic Press.

Kubie, L. S. (1937). The fantasy of dirt. *Psychoanalytic Quarterly, 6,* 338–425.

Kubie, L. S. (1947). The fallacious use of quantitative concepts in dynamic psychology. *Psychoanalytic Quarterly, 16,* 507–518.

Kubie, L. S. (1954). The fundamental nature of the distinction between normality and neurosis. *Psychoanalytic Quarterly, 23,* 167–204.

Kubie, L. S. (1978). Symbol and neurosis. Selected papers. Ed. H. J. Schlesinger. *Psychological Issues,* Monograph 44. New York: International Universities Press.

Lidz, T. Cornelison, A., & Fleck, S. (1965). *Schizophrenia and the family.* New York: International Universities Press.

Mann, T. (1933). *Joseph und seine Brüder.* Berlin: S. Fischer.

Rangell, L. (1963a). The scope of intrapsychic conflict: Microscopic and macroscopic considerations. *Psychoanalytic Study of the Child, 18,* 75–102.

Rangell, L. (1963b). Structural problems in intrapsychic conflict. *Psychoanalytic Study of the Child, 18,* 103–138.

Rangell, L. (1974). A psychoanalytic perspective leading currently to the syndrome of the compromise of integrity. *International Journal of Psychoanalysis, 55,* 3–12.

Rangell, L. (1980). *The mind of Watergate.* New York: Norton.

Rangell, L. (1981). Psychoanalysis and dynamic psychotherapy: Similarities and differences twenty-five years later. *Psychoanalytic Quarterly, 50,* 665–693.

Rangell, L. (1982). The self in psychoanalytic theory. *Journal of the American Psychoanalytic Association, 30,* 863–892.

Rangell, L. (1986). The executive functions of the ego: An extension of the concept of ego autonomy. *Psychoanalytic Study of the Child, 41,* 1–40.

Rangell, L. (1987). A core process in psychoanalytic treatment. *Psychoanalytic Quarterly, 56,* 222–249.

Schafer, R. (1960). The loving and the beloved superego. *Psychoanalytic Study of the Child, 15,* 163–188.

Shengold, L. (1989). *Soul murder: The effects of childhood abuse and deprivation.* New Haven: Yale University Press.

Stanton, D. M. (1977). The addict as savior: Heroin, death, and the family. *Family Process, 16,* 191–197.

Stanton, D. M., & Todd, T. C., et al. (1978). Heroin addiction as a family phenomenon. *American Journal of Drug & Alcohol Abuse, 5,* 125–150.

Waelder, R. (1930). The principle of multiple function. In *Psychoanalysis: Observation, theory, application* (pp. 207–228). New York: International Universities Press.

Waelder, R. (1951). The structure of paranoid ideas. In *Psychoanalysis: Observation, theory, application.* New York: International Universities Press.

Waelder, R. (1976). *Psychoanalysis: Observation, theory, application.* Ed. S. A. Guttman. New York: International Universities Press.

Wurmser, L. (1974). Psychoanalytic considerations of the etiology of compulsive drug use. *Journal of the American Psychoanalytic Association, 22,* 820–843.

Wurmser, L. (1978). *The hidden dimension: Psychodynamics in compulsive drug use.* New York: Jason Aronson.

Wurmser, L. (1980). Phobic core in the addictions and the addictive process. *International Journal of Psychoanalytic Psychotherapy. 8,* 311–337.

Wurmser, L. (1981a). *The mask of shame.* Baltimore: Johns Hopkins University Press.

Wurmser, L. (1981b). The question of specific psychopathology in compulsive drug use. *Annals of the New York Academy of Sciences* (pp. 33–43).

Wurmser, L. (1981c). Addictive disorders. In J. R. Lion (Ed.), *Personality disorders* (pp. 221–268). Baltimore: Williams & Wilkins.

Wurmser, L. (1984a). More respect for the neurotic process. *Journal of Substance Abuse Treatment, 1,* 37–45.

Wurmser, L. (1984b). The role of superego conflicts in substance abuse and their treatment. *International Journal of Psychoanalytic Psychotherapy, 10,* 227–258.

Wurmser, L. (1987a). Shame: The veiled companion of narcissism. In D. L. Nathanson (Ed.), *The many faces of shame* (pp. 64–92). New York: Guilford.

Wurmser, L. (1987b). *Flucht vor dem Gewissen. Analyse von über-Ich und Abwehr bei schweren Neurosen.* Heidelberg: Springer.

Wurmser, L. (1988). *Die zerbrochene Wirklichkeit. Psychoanalyse als das Studium von Konflikt und Komplementarität.* Heidelberg: Springer.

Wurmser, L., & Zients, A. (1982). The "return of the denied superego"—A psychoanalytic study of adolescent substance abuse. *Psychoanalytic Inquiry, 2,* 539–580.

Wynne, L. C., Cromwell, R. L., & Matthysse, S. T. (1978). *The nature of schizophrenia.* New York: Wiley.

Wynne, L. C., Ryckoff, I. M., Day, J., & Hirsch, S. J. (1958). Pseudomutuality in the family relations of schizophrenics. *Psychiatry, 21,* 205–220.

Wynne, L. C. & Singer, M. T. (1963, 1965). Thought disorder and family relations of schizophrenics. *Archives of General Psychiatry, 9,* 191–206; *12,* 187–212.

8

Some Difficulties in the Treatment of Character-Disordered Addicts

Karen Derby, Ph.D., CAC

Many varied and powerful treatment options are available to the practitioner who treats addicts, but many clinicians continue to have the impression that addicts are untreatable by psychotherapy. Although most no longer regard drug addiction as merely a sociolegal problem that is best dealt with as a criminal matter, there are therapists who still consider addicts to be "sociopathic." However, I believe that many addicted patients are labeled sociopathic when, in fact, the nature of the disturbance may be pathological narcissism or a borderline condition. Thus it is the confusion surrounding the character diagnosis—and, therefore, the integrity of the underlying ego and self structures—that makes these patients difficult to treat.

This chapter will briefly address the problem of differentiating between the truly sociopathic patient and the addict whose underlying disturbance is more precisely classified as pathological narcissism, followed by a discussion of two key areas of ego-function disturbance typically presented by these narcissistic patients: object relations and defensive functioning. Finally, it considers feelings that arise in the therapist when working with the narcissistically disturbed addict.

SOCIOPATHY VERSUS PATHOLOGICAL NARCISSISM

Some clinicians believe that patients meeting the diagnostic criteria for antisocial personality disorder have too little energy available to become involved in a relationship with the therapist: they do not care about the therapist's approval and do not need the therapist's support. In such cases, in order to engage the patient in therapy long enough to have some kind of benevolent influence, the therapist's task

115

is to enter into a kind of contract with the patient. For example, the patient agrees to attend all scheduled individual and group therapy sessions and to provide five random urinalyses per month, in exchange for which the therapist provides the relevant reports to the probation officer. Through experience, however, one finds that even with such arrangements, sociopathic patients do not stay in treatment long, often because they are unable to live up to the terms of the contracts to which they have agreed. The very activity that brought them to the attention of the drug-treatment setting generally does them in. In other words, "good" (i.e., successful) sociopaths do not become drug addicts.

The interpersonal exploitativeness, grandiosity, and lack of empathy that characterize a narcissistically disturbed person can appear at first to be sociopathic. Careful attention to the stories of these individuals will reveal their vulnerable self states (vulnerability to criticism, with responses of rage, inadequacy, shame, emptiness), their alternating idealization and devaluing of those around them, their sense of entitlement. Often, these patients will not be able to find words to describe what they are feeling, sometimes because of hyposymbolization and isolation of affect (see Chapter 5 of this volume), but at times also because the affect state that the patient is attempting to identify had its origins in the preverbal part of life. In such cases, the rage, shame, and other feelings can only be inferred through the awareness of the types of early object-relations disturbance that characterize the lives of these patients and through feelings experienced by the therapist in the treatment.

ETIOLOGY OF PATHOLOGICAL NARCISSISM

A complete review of theories of the development of pathological narcissism is beyond the scope of this chapter; readers are directed to the works of Kohut (1971) and Kernberg (1975) for detailed overviews of the two prevailing psychoanalytic schools of thought regarding narcissistic personality disorder. In this chapter, I will describe the ways in which these theoretical approaches can be used to understand the phenomena that emerge in the therapeutic situation.

What clinicians seem to be describing in their work with many of these addicts are the consequences of failures in the mother–infant relationship, which are replayed in the relationships that these individuals have throughout their lives. Krystal and Raskin (1970), Weider and Kaplan (1969), Winnicott (1960), and other theorists have alluded to the ways in which, in the early months of life, the mother provides the function of stimulus barrier for the infant, protecting the baby from experiences too agitating to neutralize on his or her own. Gradually, she also helps the infant differentiate among feeling states and assists the child in managing dysphoric affect. If this function is not provided well enough by the mother in the individual's early months and years, then he or she must discover another means of self-soothing. Addicts have turned to drugs to provide this missing function.

Kohut (1971), Winnicott (1960), and others believe that the development of the self-representation is determined by how well the child was nurtured and soothed. A stable sense of self-in-relation-to-others, that is, a cohesive self-representation, provides the individual with a sense of security and stable self-esteem that will not falter in the face of disappointment, rejection, and other assaults on the shelf. The cohesiveness of the self-representation is also reflected in the development and continuity of object relations. Drug addicts invariably exhibit marked disturbances in the object-relations realm.

It is believed that the stable, well-boundaried self evolves from a relatively nontraumatic maternal–infant environment. The individual will not develop a cohesive self-representation if he or she has been used by the maternal figure to soothe herself or to contain unwanted (i.e., "bad") parts of her self. In these cases, the mother places the child in her own sphere of omnipotent control, her "self" space. In this way, she can feel protected from anxiety and from the demands of the child, and she renders the child safe and helpless (dependent). Later in their lives, the patients described here discovered how to maintain this helpless, dependent state by becoming dependent on drugs.

Of course, the actual damage to their development may appear later in life in some of these patients; in those cases, self states become metaphoric for the individual's experience in ensuing object relations.

OBJECT-RELATIONS DISTURBANCE

In the previously cited literature of narcissistic personality disorder, two ways of managing the object relation between patient and therapist are described. Kohut (1971) believed that the therapist should accept the patient's idealizing feelings without interpreting the negative transference. Kernberg (1975) stressed the importance of aggression, especially oral aggression, in the narcissistic personality configuration. Kernberg believed that interpretation of both the positive and negative aspects of the transference was essential.

More recently, Khantzian (1985) has articulated how, in the treatment of addicts, the expression of a true negative transference is difficult, since these patients cannot allow themselves to experience the person who "saved their lives" (the therapist) as disappointing. This view is in agreement with Kohut's approach to the treatment.

Khantzian (personal communication, 1990) also has agreed that some of these patients communicate their negative feelings indirectly, if they are unable directly to express their rage at the therapist. They may mildly convey their devaluing of the therapist by compliantly attending sessions and "yes, buting" the therapy. They may form stubborn resistances to understanding or accepting interpretations, all the while projecting intolerable feelings onto the therapist. They may frustrate the therapist by continuing to drink or use drugs. In the early phases of treatment, the therapist must be aware of the temptation to react to the patient's rage non-therapeutically (to be discussed later).

As has been suggested, the individual has probably never known the maternal sensitivity that defines an optimal nurturing and soothing relationship. As a result, in infancy, the person does not form a soothing introject. As adult patients, such people often use others in their interpersonal world as self-objects (Kohut, 1971); the patients discussed here soon discovered that drugs can function as better self-objects than any of their friends: drugs do not talk back, or make demands, they simply do the job. Drugs calm the chronic agitation and they stimulate productivity when apathy strikes; a drug can be found to provide relief for any defect in the psychological structure (Kohut, 1971) that is experienced by the individual. The drug then becomes, in a sense, a primary object related to by the individual. The continual, soothing presence of the drug prevents the person from learning to identify and manage his or her own affective experience, and the self becomes more and more impoverished and empty.

I believe that the drug is initially used to fill the emptiness and relieve the boredom that are the consequences of the developmental deficits just described. Then, with its sustained presence, the drug prevents the individual from developing areas of interest and activity that typically would become identified with the "self."

DEFENSE MECHANISMS

Addicted patients present us with a fairly consistent picture relative to defensive operations. This section will describe three mechanisms that commonly appear in the treatment of these patients: denial, splitting, and projective mechanisms.

Denial

Addicted patients deny many things: the fact of their drug (and alcohol) use, the amount of drug used, the awareness of the concomitants of drug use, and the damaging effects of drug use. The patient may deny feelings moments before they are expressed. The therapist must juxtapose the stark contradictions of the reality of the patient's life with the patient's view of that reality. This can be done gently, although technically it is a "confrontation." The patient must be helped to examine critically the ways in which he or she continues to act to bring about his or her own destruction ("self"-destruction). From the perspective of advocacy for the patient, the therapist can position himself or herself in such a way as to avoid defensive rejection of the interpretive exploration of the patient's experience. It is a frequent misunderstanding in the treatment of addiction that confrontation must involve battering away at the patient's defenses. This usually causes either (1) rejecting maneuvers in the service of self-protection or (2) superficial compliance with treatment, whereby the patient learns the proper things to say and the proper ways to act with the therapist. In either case, the needed and appropriate internalizations derived from the therapist's soothing presence do not occur.

Splitting

The patients described here are those who have developed a "grandiose self" (Kernberg, 1975; Kohut, 1971) that is used to protect them from becoming aware of the intolerable terrifying emptiness and psychic void. In their perceptions of themselves, they typically vacillate between these two opposites: grandiose all or worthless nothing. This self-perception is then projected outward, with the result that many aspects of the world are also experienced as "all" or "nothing." Addicts expect their experiences to be all highs and lows, nothing in between. This view is, of course, confirmed by the experience of drug taking—of euphorias and crashes.

These patients commonly hold the belief that perfection is not an ideal to be aimed for, but is an attainable goal. This example serves to illustrate well the distorted world view typically held by these individuals. Addicts believe that if they were only good enough, they could achieve perfection in some realm—in business, in relationships—and they set off after the unattainable. Often this striving for perfection exhausts the patient, who then crumbles in a heap, feeling worthless. This leaves the person with a permanent sense of not measuring up, confirming the belief in his or her own sense of worthlessness, which, of course, becomes part of the addict's identity. At these times, drug taking often is used to restore the grandiose self.

The process of internalizing frustration tolerance that is necessary in order to cope in a world of gray areas requires the investment of a great deal of time and patience on the part of both therapist and patient.

Projection

Projection describes a mechanism by which discrete impulses and parts of the self are moved outward from the psyche onto an external object. As a consequence, the targeted object is likely to experience emotional states that originated in the projecting person. Volkan (1987) articulates the distinction between the various types of projective mechanisms. He characterizes projective identification as a rather stable defense in those with borderline personality organization who maintain obligatory contact with the object onto which they project their intrapsychic experiences, and then try to control it as though to keep from having to take back what has been projected (p. 10).

In the therapy, especially in the early phases, the therapist is the recipient of these "intrapsychic experiences" (intolerable-feelings states) that the addict cannot manage. As addicts typically do not place themselves in a very sympathetic light through the actions that attend the drug use, it is tempting for the therapist to respond to the patient in a nonsoothing, nonnurturing way. This will confirm for the addict that the treatment experience is no safer than any other object relationship, and if the failure occurs often enough, the addict will flee therapy. Therefore, the therapist must not abandon the position of advocacy for the patient: one of understanding the patient's emotional life, not reacting to it.

Volkan (1987) described externalization as "an earlier defense mechanism, one pertaining to aspects of the self as well as to internalized objects" (p. 60). Summarizing Novick and Kelly (1970), he stated that "[w]hen the child faces the very difficult task of integrating the various dissonant components of his developing self-representations as well as the internalized object world," then the child is faced with potential humiliation when dealing with aspects of the self that are not valued (by the child or by the parents). In such a case, the child may "externalize" that aspect of himself or herself. Volkan believed that "all patients of the purely preoedipal type, once they are in treatment, initially include their analyst in their constant effort to externalize and reinternalize, making their analyst one split-off image after another, and so on" (pp. 60–61).

In this article, externalization refers to the ego's attempt to create an outer world or to construct a reality that is a replica of internal experience. Often, these patients replay their chaotic inner object-relations world by suffusing the environment with their feelings of inner disruption, creating external chaos and thereby gaining relief of their inner tension. By having the addict carefully clarify the confusion in the events and emotional states he or she describes, the therapist helps to minimize the anxiety attendant to the chaos and helps to teach the individual how to begin to structure and quiet his or her disrupted internal life.

FEELINGS IN THE THERAPIST

By understanding the etiology of the deficits that accompany addiction, the therapist can remain mindful of the potential for responding to the patient in such a way as to make the patient feel unsafe or rejected. Often such responses are classified as "countertransference." Since the term "countertransference" has come to have a number of different meanings in the psychotherapy literature, I have chosen to discuss instead the problem of "feelings in the therapist." I will refer to countertransference using a narrower rather than broader definition.

Transferences to the Patient

In this chapter, the addict has been depicted as psychologically fragile, even though exhibiting a tough exterior. Because of this fragility, I suggest that the holding environment that is the treatment situation has to be constructed so as to demonstrate explicitly that the therapist is there to provide soothing and nurturing, which are not expected from the rest of the environment.

This attitude on the part of the therapist is impossible if he or she carries into the treatment preconceived notions about addicts. Preset attitudes must be abandoned by the therapist, not only because we are tempted to be judgmental about drug use and all its attendant damage, but also because each patient is unique and has his or her own phenomenology.

Prejudice about addiction, enforced by lack of information and education, prevents the therapist from acknowledging that the disorder has completely stripped addicts of their self-control and ability to delay gratification. These deficits lead to irresponsibility on the part of the addict, and the uninformed clinician, as a result, may have unrealistic expectations about what the patient can accomplish. The therapist may see the patient as self-indulgent, with little self-control and without empathy. Under these circumstances, it is easy to forget that these deficits are a result of the pathology.

The addict/patient expects angry and critical remarks from the therapist. Neutral remarks are experienced as critical. The therapist must be able to interpret the patient's distortion of the therapist's comments, but cannot do so if he or she is angry with or judgmental about the patient.

Countertransference

Volkan (1987) distinguished between countertransference as the response on the part of the therapist to the patient's transference and

> a totalistic form of countertransference (Kernberg, 1965) that includes the analyst's total emotional reaction to the patient. There are other factors over and beyond a response to the patient's transference that influence how we feel about our patients. It should be remembered that countertransference is unconscious; we know of its existence through self-analysis of its derivatives, by naming our feeling state, examining our fantasies as they appear in our sessions, observing our nonverbal gestures or bodily reactions, and so on. (p. 66)

Many theorists (Giovacchini, 1979; Racker, 1968; Searles, 1979) have suggested that the therapist's emotional responses can be useful in assessing the patient's ego state and developmental level as the patient reproduces these in the transference. With addicts, if the therapist fails to recognize the patient's need to treat the therapist as a self-object (i.e., as the patient has used the drug), or if the therapist mishandles the anger the patient feels about being perceived as able to function at a higher developmental level than that of which he or she actually is capable, then one may expect to have disruptive countertransference reactions that could lead to impasses in the treatment.

It is easy for the therapist to lapse into believing that these articulate, superficially insightful patients are able to identify and understand feeling states that, to the therapist, are obvious. Similarly, these patients have often revealed to us that there is no underlying content to the agitation and anxiety (i.e., conflict) that produces these feeling states. The clinician must be careful not to attempt to fit the patient into a construct that assumes a higher level of psychic integration of ego than the patient is capable of attaining.

Often these patients form an attachment to the therapist but cannot acknowledge it. As a result, the patient may express devaluing feelings about the treatment, although truly valuing it. In addition, the addict often depicts himself or herself as fully independent, not needing anybody (certainly not needing the help of the therapist). This pseudoindependence masks the patient's fear that he or she is tremendously needy, fully dependent (on drugs, for example, as well as other people), which signifies to the patient that he or she is a failure. This situation illustrates the all-or-nothing perception that addicts maintain about their emotional lives. They cannot imagine being dependent on some people for some things, and being independent in other areas, as having a mixture of relative independence/dependence. If they perceive that they cannot fully provide everything they need for themselves, they experience a catastrophic drop in self-esteem. These situations may leave the therapist feeling angry, frustrated, or tempted to rescue.

At times, these patients' neediness tempts us to help them, to show them the way, rescue them, save them. At other times, their stubborn rejection of our therapeutic efforts causes us to feel angry—a feeling that we would rather not confront with the patient. However, understanding anger is a great part of the treatment of these individuals; failing to confront anger in the therapeutic relationship can be countertransference avoidance.

CONCLUSION

The very fact that the drug has been withdrawn before or during therapy is going to make the patient anxious. In most cases, the patient has no idea how to manage anxiety, and often does not even know what the feeling is. He or she may react to this internal state by projecting these feelings outward, as would an infant; however, the patient is no longer an infant and signals of distress may be more difficult to interpret than those of a baby.

Without awareness, the therapist can succumb to the temptation to repeat the pattern of early failures, thereby confirming for the patient that no one is safe to trust. When the therapist observes the patient struggling with the experience of rage, through isolation of affect, projection, or disavowal, the therapist must take an educative role, not only pointing out the struggle, but also supplying the missing awareness of feelings. The therapist must not, as a result of being the unwitting container of unwanted feelings, fail to soothe the patient (and in the later stages of therapy, as the benign aspects of the therapist are internalized by the patient [transmuting internalization, Kohut, 1971], remind the patient how to soothe himself or herself). It is the failure to recognize and properly respect the power of rage and anxiety that typically causes the therapist to influence the treatment such that it may come to a premature end (Boyer, 1961).

"Being with" these patients means surviving the rage and chaos. Clinicians who work with addicts must recognize that, unlike other symptoms, drug use presents a special problem: drugs produce their effects from the "inside," that is, physiologically. We must investigate how the addict's drug of choice was internally experienced as providing needed compensation for defective psychological structure. Then the patient and therapist together can proceed to reconstruct aspects of ego and self structure previously unrecognized as defective.

REFERENCES

Boyer, L. B. (1961). Provisional evaluation of psycho-analysis with few parameters in the treatment of schizophrenia. *International Journal of Psycho-Analysis, 42,* 389–403.

Giovacchini, P. L. (1979). *Treatment of primitive mental states.* New York: Jason Aronson.

Kernberg, O. F. (1965). Notes on countertransference. *Journal of the American Psychoanalytic Association, 13,* 38–56.

Kernberg, O. F. (1975). *Borderline conditions and pathological narcissism.* New York: Jason Aronson.

Khantzian, E. J. (1985). The self-medication hypothesis of addictive disorders: Focus on heroin and cocaine dependence. *American Journal of Psychiatry, 142,* 11.

Khantzian, E. J. (1990). Personal communication.

Kohut, H. (1971). *The analysis of the self.* New York: International Universities Press.

Krystal, J., & Raskin, H. A. (1970). *Drug dependence: Aspects of ego functions.* Detroit: Wayne State University Press.

Novick, J., & Kelly, K. (1970). Projection and externalization. *Psychoanalytic Study of the Child, 25,* 69–95.

Racker, H. (1968). *Transference and countertransference.* New York: International Universities Press.

Searles, H. F. (1979). *Countertransference and related subjects.* New York: International Universities Press.

Volkan, V. D. (1987). *Six steps in the treatment of borderline personality organization.* Northvale, NJ: Jason Aronson.

Wieder, H., & Kaplan, E. H. (1969). Drug use in adolescents: Psychodynamic meaning and pharmacogenic effect. *Psychoanalytic Study of the Child, 24*, 399–431.

Winnicott, D. W. (1960). The theory of the parent-infant relationship. In *The maturational process and the facilitating environment* (pp. 37–55). New York: International Universities Press.

PART III

---◆---

COGNITIVE-BEHAVIORAL, SELF-HELP, AND RELAPSE-PREVENTION: INTERVENTIONS TO FACILITATE RECOVERY

9

Substance Abuse and Stress-Coping Resources: A Life-Contextual Clinical Viewpoint

Raymond C. Hawkins II, Ph.D.

INTRODUCTION

The purpose of this chapter is to describe substance use and abuse from a clinical, theoretical perspective elaborated from stress-coping theory (SCT) (Shiffman & Wills, 1985; Wills, 1990; Monti, Abrams, Kadden & Cooney, 1989), the social ecological "life contextual process" model of Rudolph Moos and colleagues (Moos & Finney, 1983; Moos, 1984, 1988), and cognitive constructivist, systemic theory (Brown, 1985, 1987, 1991; Steinglass, 1987).

Essentially, from this vantage point, substance use represents a habitual maladaptive coping response to decrease temporarily life stress. In the case of abuse or chemical dependence, however, there may be adverse consequences on physical and mental health and social and occupational functioning (American Psychiatric Association, 1987). The contention of SCT is that substance use or abuse is an adaptive process involving cognitive social learning mechanisms. A psychosocial skills deficit is often assumed (e.g., Monti et al., 1989), such that alternative coping strategies must be acquired by the individual prior to his or her relinquishing of a maladaptive coping response such as substance use.

According to SCT, substance abuse is a multifactorial biopsychosocial process. Biopsychosocial models are among the most prevalent conceptualizations for the cognitive-behavioral assessment and treatment of alcohol abuse/dependence (Monti et al., 1989; Moos, 1985), as well as for related addictive behaviors such as eating disorders (Hawkins & Clement, 1984; Weiss, Katzman, & Wolchik, 1986). Such a framework allows for biological factors (genetic vulnerability or psychopharmacological effects of drugs) and early environmental trauma; however, the current

127

psychosocial context mediates the final common pathway of the expression of the addictive behavior. Thus the vulnerability ("diathesis") is triggered by an environmental "stress."

There are two important assumptions to be stated at this juncture: (1) there is a commonality of processes of substance use or abuse (Shiffman & Wills, 1985; Schubert, Wolf, Patterson, Grande, & Pendleton, 1988; Diclemente & Prochaska, 1985), and (2) substance use can be ordered along a continuum of severity ranging from nonaddictive experimentation, or "normal" social use, through continuous use or "abuse" (Shiffman & Wills, 1985), to chemical dependency (Vaillant, 1983; Robins, West, & Murphy, 1977, as cited by Steinglass, 1987; Piazza & Wise, 1988). The timing and sequence across addictive substances are not invariant, of course.

These two assumptions are highly important for the consideration of substance use as a response for coping with life's stresses or strains. There would appear to be a trade-off for both the individual and the larger family or social network between an individual's choice of substance use to increase positive affect or temporarily decrease negative affect from stress (Wills & Shiffman, 1985), and chemical dependency, in which case the consequences for the individual and the family are extreme and dysregulatory (Steinglass, 1987).

Peele (1985) has defined the "addictive experience" as an extreme, dysfunctional attachment to an experience that is acutely harmful, but which is an essential part of a person's ecology and that the person cannot relinquish. This state is the result of a dynamic social learning process in which the person finds an experience rewarding because it ameliorates urgently felt needs, although, in the long run, it damages the person's capacity to cope and ability to generate stable sources of environmental gratification (p. 97).

At the boundary where stress-coping resources are threatened by losses or stress (Hobfoll, 1989), a reformulated stress-coping theory, life-contextual viewpoint (SCT-LCV) is needed to account for the processes of the addictive experience and "recovery." According to cognitive constructivist and systemic theory (Brown, 1985, 1987, 1991; Steinglass, 1987), chemical dependency becomes the "central organizing principle" for the individual and family. The deep regulatory structures involved in the unfolding of normal growth-enhancing functions for the person and his or her life context are "invaded" by chemical dependency and the system accommodates with narrowing and increasingly rigid behaviors and loss of growth-sustaining routines and rituals (Steinglass, 1987).

THE STRESS-COPING THEORY OF SUBSTANCE USE, ABUSE, AND CHEMICAL DEPENDENCE

Only recently have substance abuse and chemical dependency been viewed from the SCT perspective (Shiffman & Wills, 1985; Monti et al., 1989). According to

SCT, substance abuse represents a habitual maladaptive attempt to cope with stress and strain. The SCT viewpoint toward substance abuse reflects an adaptive orientation (Marlatt, 1985), an extension of social learning theory within the cognitive-behavioral framework. While SCT may postulate psychosocial skills deficits that would contribute to substance use, abuse, or dependence (Monti et al., 1989), it is a compensatory model with emphasis placed on social-skills training and the acquisition of social competencies (Marlatt, 1985).

Application of SCT to substance use/abuse is most clearly specified in the volume edited by Shiffman and Wills (1985). Shiffman and Wills operationally defined psychosocial stress as occurring at three levels: major life events (e.g., divorce, loss of employment), enduring life strains (e.g., difficulties in societal and interpersonal relationships that are chronic and not easily resolved) (Pearlin & Schooler, 1978), and everyday "hassles" (e.g., losing one's keys, having an argument) (Lazarus & Folkman, 1984). They defined coping as "activities or behaviors a person uses in the attempt to maintain a balance between demands from the environment and resources currently available to meet those demands" (Wills & Shiffman, 1985, p. 6).

Wills and Shiffman (1985) have applied SCT to the initiation, maintenance, and cessation of substance use. They distinguish alternative responses used for coping with generalized stresses and responses used to cope with the temptation to reuse substances.

The stress-coping theory of substance use may be expressed in three propositions: (1) psychosocial stress increases the likelihood of substance use; (2) substance use reduces psychosocial stress (i.e., it serves as a temporarily effective coping response); and (3) deployment of alternative coping responses (acquired through skills training) serves to buffer the relationship between stress and substance use.

Wills (1990) has reviewed stress and coping factors in the epidemiology of substance use. His review may be summarized by stating that concurrent cross-sectional studies of substance abuse and SCT support the first proposition (i.e., stress increases the likelihood of substance use); however, more prospective studies are needed—especially field-naturalistic studies of the dynamic interactions among stressful life events, coping, and ongoing substance use on a day-to-day basis.

The second proposition (i.e., substance use decreases stress) is also supported by concurrent and prospective studies, insofar as perceived short-term stress is concerned (Wills, 1990). An important caveat was raised by Pentz (1985) in what she called the "stress response model." According to this model, substance use may actually increase stress rather than reduce it, thus establishing some boundary conditions for the SCT of substance use. In her prospective study of 254 sixth- through ninth-grade students who composed the control group for a two-year, drug-abuse-prevention study, Pentz (1985) observed that high levels of initial drug use led to reductions in social competence and to increases in drug use over time. Similarly, Kaplan and colleagues' (Kaplan, Martin, & Robbins, 1982, 1984) prospective studies of composite indices of drug use revealed indications of a reciprocal process in which early substance use predicted more rejection by family and school, which, in turn, increased the risk for subsequent increased substance use (as cited by Wills, 1990).

Finally, Newcomb and Bentler (1988) reported some findings from their prospective longitudinal study of 654 individuals who were repeatedly tested over an eight-year period from early adolescence to early adulthood. They found evidence that high drug use in adolescence (which included alcohol) was associated with a variety of negative consequences in young adulthood, including continued problems with drugs, health problems, and family problems. These studies, consistent with the stress-response model, cast doubt on the assertion that substance use is an effective coping mechanism in the long term.

THE STRESS-BUFFERING EFFECTS OF ALTERNATIVE COPING MECHANISMS

While the first two propositions are merely of academic and theoretical interest, certainly for the practicing clinician the stress-buffering effects of coping attributes and/or intrapersonal or interpersonal skills training would be particularly relevant for treatment applications. Wills (1990) has summarized much of this literature, which may be divided into prospective epidemiological studies and interventions.

Epidemiological Studies

Wills and colleagues (Wills, 1985, 1986; Wills & Vaughn, 1989) conducted a longitudinal prospective study of the relationship between stress coping and cigarette and alcohol abuse in early adolescence. They adapted the "Response Profile" from the Coping Assessment Battery (CAB), a multifactorial measure developed by Bugen and Hawkins (1981). The CAB measures active behavioral coping, cognitive coping, general social support, physical exercise, relaxation, and avoidant emotionally based coping (e.g., distraction and denial). Students in three New York City (mid-Manhattan) junior high schools were surveyed at the beginning and end of each school year (i.e., four waves with two each year). The first cohort comprised 675 students and the second cohort contained 901 students. Prospectively, for the first cohort, the use of behavioral coping at wave 1 was related to decreased smoking at wave 2 and at wave 3. Relaxation coping at wave 1 was inversely related to alcohol use at wave 4. Avoidance coping (i.e., the distraction measure) was positively associated with substance use in waves 1, 2, and 3. For the second cohort, there was an inverse prospective relationships between the use of cognitive coping and both smoking and alcohol use, and a replication of the inverse relationship between behavioral coping and substance use. There was also an inverse relationship between relaxation coping and smoking. Use of religious coping was inversely related to substance use. Peer support, aggression, and distraction predicted increased use over several waves. Finally, as Wills (1986) has stated, there were significant stress-coping interactions in support of a "buffer" effect for the coping-response categories of behavioral coping, cognitive coping, and adult support.

As summarized by Wills (1990), Kaplan, Martin, and Robbins (1986) provided a prospective long-term analysis of marijuana use by seventh graders in Houston, Texas, with a 10-year follow-up. For those students who had not tried marijuana at time 1, escalated marijuana use at follow-up was associated with avoidant coping style, along with family and school problems.

In a more recent study, Needle, Lavee, Su, Brown, and Doherty (1988) used a retrospective case control design and a prospective longitudinal design in their study of family functioning and adolescent substance abuse over a three-year period. A variety of measures of family cohesion, stress, alcohol and marijuana use, and coping were prospectively administered to three groups of teenagers and their families, matched demographically within a health maintenance organization (HMO) population: 25 clinically treated drug abusers, 25 nonclinical drug abusers, and 25 nonclinical controls. Needle et al. (1988) found few differences between the clinical and nonclinical drug-abusing adolescents and their families. The non–drug-using control teens and families, however, showed higher levels of family cohesion and flexibility, better use of problem solving and other adaptive coping mechanisms, and an increased capacity to communicate and share feelings.

In summary, the evidence from these epidemiological studies suggests that substance use was inversely proportional to the availability and effective deployment of active behavioral and cognitive coping responses and directly related to a predominance of avoidant coping. This conclusion is also consistent with the literature from relapse prevention (e.g., Shiffman, 1985), which found that the use of any active coping response was associated with a decreased probability of relapse.

Intervention Studies

Given the overall finding that individuals who reportedly make more use of active behavioral or cognitive coping strategies are less likely to initiate substance use, less likely to escalate ongoing substance use, and more resistant to relapse after cessation of substance use, the obvious question to consider is whether coping-skills training would further amplify the efficacy of alcohol- and drug-abuse treatment interventions. The following is a selective review of some of these studies.

The general rationale for coping-skills training is best illustrated in a program recently developed by Peter Monti and his colleagues at Brown University for treating alcohol dependence. Coping-skills strategies covered by Monti et al. (1989) include skills for coping with specific intrapersonal problem situations (e.g., problem solving, increasing pleasant activities, relaxation training, anger management, awareness of negative thinking, and managing thoughts) and acquiring interpersonal skills (e.g., how to initiate conversations, give and receive compliments, engage in "feeling talk" and active listening, be assertive, and give and receive criticism, as well as drink-refusal skills).

Monti, Abrams, Binkoff, and Zwick (1990) randomly assigned 69 inpatient males with alcohol dependence to a standard treatment program combined with either interpersonal communication-skills training, communication-skills training with family members present, or intrapersonal cognitive-behavioral "mood management" training. Each of these supplemental training conditions comprised 12 hours of group coping-skills training. All patients were assessed before and after treatment on the Alcoholic Specific Role Play Test (ASRPT), and measures of drinking were obtained at six months' follow-up. The results were that the alcoholics receiving communications-skills training, with or without family involvement, drank significantly less alcohol relative to alcoholics who received the cognitive-behavioral mood-management training. A limitation of this study was the failure to include a control group not receiving any coping-skills training.

Hawkins, Catalano, and Wells (1986) reported the results of supplemental skills training and a social network aftercare program administered to 130 adult drug abusers (mostly males) from residential therapeutic communities. The subjects were randomly assigned to a supplemental 10-week skills intervention that included initiating social behavior, assertiveness, giving and receiving praise and criticism, problem solving, stress management, social network formation, and drug- and alcohol-refusal training, or to a control group that did not receive this training. The dependent measure was the Problem Situations Inventory (PSI), which assessed drug abusers' skills in dealing with a range of high-risk situations for relapse. This measure was administered before entry in the skills-training component and 12 weeks later. The results were that patients who received the supplemental skills training had significantly higher mean scores on avoiding drugs and alcohol, relapse coping, and awareness of consequences of substance reuse, as well as social problem solving and stress coping, compared with the control group.

Hawkins, Catalano, Gilmore, and Wells (1989) provided follow-up data from this same study. The PSI was administered again at six and 12 months posttreatment, along with a measure of drug and alcohol use. At follow-up, although there was some decay over time, the patients who had received social-skills training continued to show significantly higher skill scores compared with the controls. Unfortunately, however, the skills-training intervention did not differentially affect the patients' substance-use relapse rates during the year after treatment, with the exception of clinically small effects on amphetamine and marijuana use in favor of the experimental group. Wells, Catalano, Plotnick, Hawkins, and Brattesani (1989) recently reported that the PSI subscales tapping specific skills for coping with temptation did predict the number of drug- and alcohol-free weeks at six months' follow-up for the whole sample, but that the general social, stress-management, and problem-solving skills did not.

In summary, the coping-skills intervention training results were equivocal but promising. Particularly with younger individuals in the initiation stage of substance use, general stress-coping and social-skills training appear to have demonstrable effects on subsequent substance use and increased utilization of alternative active coping skills (Wills, 1985; Pentz, 1985). In the case of patients with alcohol or drug dependence, there were indications of generalization and persistence of coping-skills training effects on process measures, but no clear-cut clinically significant decrease in posttreatment relapse rates and/or substance usage.

SCT: A LIFE-CONTEXTUAL VIEWPOINT

Moos and his colleagues (Billings & Moos, 1983; Cronkite & Moos, 1980; Moos & Finney, 1983; Moos, 1984, 1988) have emphasized the importance of "extratreatment" factors (e.g., life-contextual measures of stress, family, and work environment) to the outcome of alcoholics at follow-up. Knowing these social ecological extratreatment factors more than doubled the variance explainable at follow-up, as shown in Figure 9-1 from Moos and Finney (1983).

Wills and Shiffman (1985), and especially Monti et al. (1989), have acknowledged the importance of such life-contextual factors in moderating the effects of stress-

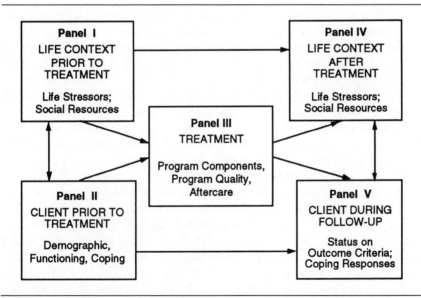

Figure 9-1. *A process-oriented framework for the evaluation of alcoholism treatment, emphasizing life-contextual "extratreatment" factors (Reprinted by permission of Oxford University Press from Moos, Finney, & Cronkite's* Alcoholism Treatment: Context, Process, and Outcome. *Copyright © 1990 by Oxford University Press.)*

coping training. However, in the intervention studies reviewed in the previous section, the contributions of these contextual factors to substance use have not been explictly measured. For example, in the Hawkins et al. (1986, 1989) skills-training study with adult drug-dependent clients, one might hypothesize that the decay in the process measures of social skills and stress-coping-response utilization at one year follow-up, as well as the lack of a clinically significant impact on substance use or relapse proneness, might have been due to the failure to measure extratreatment factors.

Even concurrent or prospective studies that demonstrate that stressful life events are associated with increased substance use or abuse may be interpreted within the framework of the indirect effects of life-contextual variables. When inventories of life changes are "unpacked," many of the negative events are related to social ecological losses. Moos and colleagues' life-contextual "process" view of substance abuse and chemical-dependence treatment differs from that of SCT in that it is explicitly a systems perspective (Billings & Moos, 1983). An intervention is merely one temporary part of multiple environmental "microsystems," or specific settings in which the client is embedded (Moos & Finney, 1983). This contextual approach is thus a framework that "enables clinicians and evaluators to consider an individual's overall life situation in planning and evaluating interventions" (Moos & Finney, 1983, p. 1037).

One illustration of the application of this perspective is Billings and Moos' (1983) description of a study comparing two groups of treated alcoholics two years after treatment. Patients in the "recovered" group, who were essentially abstinent and well functioning, were compared with patients from a "relapsed" group who either had been rehospitalized for treatment of alcoholism or were drinking heavily and having problems. Matched community controls of families were also studied. Several self-report measures were administered to assess social environmental stresses and resources (Health and Daily Living Form, Family Environment Scale, Work Environment Scale). Not only were the recovered alcoholics not having problems with alcohol, but their personal, familial, and occupational functioning in general was superior to that of the relapsed alcoholics and equal to that of the controls.

Moreover, the spouses and children of the recovered alcoholics were functioning as well as the control family members from the matched community sample. The relapsed alcoholics were having poorer personal, familial, and occupational functioning; their spouses displayed more mood disorders and had higher levels of alcohol consumption; and their children had more health and physical problems. The recovered alcoholics and controls reported that they were more likely to use active behavioral and cognitive coping strategies. In contrast, the relapsed patients and their spouses were more likely to use avoidant coping responses that served to discharge emotion (e.g., eating or smoking more, blaming others) or ignoring the problem.

As Billings and Moos (1983) have suggested, this systems perspective implies a reciprocal or bidirectional relationship between alcoholics' environments and functioning. Accordingly, a key consideration is whether posttreatment factors were causally related to recovery status independently of the alcoholics' prior level of functioning. In some short-term longitudinal studies (cited by Billings & Moos, 1983), there were indications that stresses and social resources were significantly related to alcoholics' functioning at follow-up even after controlling for prior levels of these stresses and resources.

THE ALCOHOLIC FAMILY SYSTEM

While there have been several earlier attempts to conceptualize stress and coping within the context of the family life cycle (e.g., McCubbin & Figley, 1983), the life-contextual, systemic viewpoint is seen most clearly in the recent clinical research of Steinglass (1987) and his colleagues on the alcoholic family. The reciprocal and transactional relationship between the alcoholic and his or her family is seen in Steinglass' distinction between the "alcoholic family" and the "family with an alcoholic member." In the latter case, the basic deep regulatory structures of the family are not compromised by the alcoholic's drinking and dysfunctional behavior, and family routines and rituals remain intact. In the case of the alcoholic family system, there is an "invasion" of routines and rituals as the family accommodates to the alcoholic's increasingly dysfunctional drinking and behavior. Thus two alcoholics with an equivalent amount of alcohol consumption might experience considerably different life courses depending on the moderating effects of the family context.

Stanton, and associates (1982) have postulated that in drug-abusing families there is an enmeshment between parents and a particular offspring who abuses drugs. Cancrini, Cingolani, Compagnoli, Constantini, and Mazzoni (1988) have suggested that this viewpoint is too simplistic. Instead, they categorize several distinctive types of interaction patterns between juvenile heroin addicts and their families. One hypothesis for further study is that the distinction between these family types may involve varying manifestations and degrees of breakdown in life-contextual levels. The most extreme case would be the complete disengagement or disintegration of the family structure, as seen recently in families in the inner city invaded by crack cocaine abuse (Wallace, 1987, 1989).

ADVANTAGES AND LIMITATIONS OF SCT

The view of substance abuse as a maladaptive habitual coping response to psychosocial stress has several advantages for the practicing clinician. This theory provides a compensatory-based, optimistic framework for intervention. Emphasis is placed on acquisition of personal and social skills for coping with problems. Thus the acquisition of alternative coping skills is emphasized, above and beyond "just saying no" to alcohol or drugs. When SCT is contextualized within Moos' social ecological framework (i.e., SCT-LCV), the complex interplay of stresses and personal and social coping resources is seen even more clearly. More explicit theorizing and pro- spective research studies are needed to specify those cases in which substance use is stress reducing or produces no adverse consequences as compared with cases where substance use or abuse increases stress (Pentz's [1985], "stress response model").

Furthermore, individual differences in stress-coping responses are not specified; SCT-LCV has not been conceptualized within a longitudinal, developmental frame- work of the natural course of alcoholism and drug addiction (Vaillant, 1983). Only recently have very important aspects such as cultural differences and acculturation pro- cesses been addressed in SCT models of substance use and abuse (e.g., Schinke, Moncher, Palleja, Zayas, & Schilling, 1988). The existence of gender differences has not been considered by SCT-LCV; indeed, the data for females with chemical- dependency problems were rarely analyzed separately from the males' data.

CONSERVATION OF COPING RESOURCES MODEL

In his more recent publications, Moos (1984, 1988) has addressed an overarching question: "How can we understand the processes by which human contexts and coping resources promote human adaptation and growth?" (Moos, 1984, p. 6). Within the life-contextual perspective, "feedback loops indicate that one important function of social network and coping resources is to prevent stresses prior to their occurrence, or when stress is inevitable, to forestall a continuing sequence of strain that is ultimately debilitating" (Moos, 1984, p. 13).

Hobfoll's (1989) recent conservation-of-resources model may constitute a new conceptualization of stress and coping that may be of value in integrating what has been said so far about SCT and substance abuse. It may suggest new directions for research and clinical practice for treatment of chemical dependency within the cognitive-behavioral framework.

Hobfoll has criticized SCT because stress either has been defined or treated (1) as analogous to the process in physics in which some force impacts on an object that has previously been at rest, but now must respond; (2) as a stimulus, without clearly specifying the context of stressful events over time for individuals; or (3) as a homeostatic "imbalance" where environmental demand exceeds the organism's capabilities. The third definition, most commonly accepted currently, is problematic in that stress and coping resources are not often independently defined (for excep- tions, see Moos [1988] and Moos, Fenn, Billings, & Moos, [1989]), or the imbal- ance is defined after the fact. Furthermore, the assumption is still that after a stressor is managed, the organism is in some neutral or quiescent state—until the next stressor occurs (Hobfoll, 1989).

Hobfoll's (1989) basic tenet is that "people strive to obtain, protect, and build resources, and that what is threatening to them is the potential or actual loss of these resources" (p. 516). He defines stress as "a reaction to the environment in which there is a threat or actual net loss of resources, or a lack of resource gain following investment of resources" (p. 516). He defines resources as "those objects (e.g., a home), personal characteristics (e.g., hardiness), conditions (e.g., marriage, tenure), or energies (e.g., time, money, and knowledge) that are valued by the individual, or that serve as a means of the attainment of these objects, personal characteristics, conditions, or energies" (p. 516).

With respect to substance abuse and chemical dependency, a particular case Hobfoll (1989) describes is the "loss spiral" (p. 519), which may develop because coping resources cannot be allocated in such a fashion as to offset loss. The opposite case would be that when individuals develop resource surpluses, they may be more likely to experience positive well-being (p. 517).

Thus Hobfoll's model substitutes an economic "investment" metaphor for the coping process, or it might also be viewed organismically as an active accumulation of life resources or energies. Either metaphor would be quite compatible with Moos' emphasis on the systems perspective of stress coping: the assumption of the person as actively accumulating diverse resources both individually and within social networks.

With reference to the continuum of severity of substance use as it affects individuals and families, Hobfoll's conservation-of-resources model could be applied to measure what might be termed the "functional adaptive state" of the individual and his or her life context with respect to coping. The clinical assumption has been that individuals who have reached or surpassed Jellinek's (1952, 1960) "crucial" stage of the "disease" process have depleted their resources for coping, that they are experiencing very adverse consequences, and that their social networks are deteriorating. (See, for example, Carroll's [1984] social ecological use of his instrument, the Substance Abuse Problem Checklist.)

Bugen and Hawkins (1981) have developed a Likert scale measure called the Quality of Life Indicators (QLI), which provides a brief, simple self-report measure of coping resources in six areas: job satisfaction, leisure activities, love relationships, health, financial status, and spirituality. In comparison with normative adult controls, patients with alcohol dependence (in either inpatient or outpatient settings) experienced a generalized depletion of self-perceived resources for coping: their mean scores on all six areas of the QLI were lower (Table 9-1).

Moos (1988) and Moos et al. (1989) recently developed more sophisticated tools for measuring life stresses and social resources independently (i.e., the Life Stresses and Social Resources Inventory). Moos (1988) has also reported the Coping Responses Inventory (CRI), a new measure of coping resources. A description of the functional adaptive status of an alcoholic individual or family member can be measured at a given time using these instruments as a guide to clinical interventions.

FUTURE DIRECTIONS

Two aspects of Moos' (1988) recent formulations of the life-contextual process perspective are important to the correction of limitations in the stress-coping theory of substance abuse: (1) his emphasis on the person–environment interaction (Moos, 1984) and (2) the dynamic systems orientation to the complex interplay among individual and contextual factors. These two aspects will be addressed in this section since they are more conjectural, with limited data available for validation.

Specifying the "Person Variable"

In Figure 9-1, from Moos and Finney (1983), the cell entitled "client pretreatment factors," including individual personality, was relatively deemphasized in comparison with extratreatment factors influencing posttreatment adaptation. Moos and colleagues' proposals for "integrated" assessment using the LISRES and CRI tools reflect a recent effort to map the person–environment match.

The history of alcoholism treatment models reflects a gradual disinclination to postulate theories of a monolithic or unitary "alcoholic personality" (Wills & Shiffman, 1985). It is important that the personological tradition be maintained in that alcoholism affects individuals, not "variables," regardless of whether these are measured more sophisticatedly and reliably within the SCT-LCV framework. Monti et al. (1989) have posed the challenge of screening individuals to improve patient-to-treatment matching strategies. Hobfoll's (1989) conservation-of-coping-resources model specifies "personal characteristics" as among these resources. How

Table 9-1

Coping Assessment Battery (Bugen & Hawkins, 1981). Quality of Life Indicators Means and Standard Deviations for an Adult Normative Sample (137 females, 57 males), an Inpatient Alcholic Sample (11 females, 24 males), and an Outpatient Alcoholic Sample (10 females, 23 males). Gender differences were not significant.

QLI	Normal Adults		Inpatient Alcoholics		Outpatient Alcoholics	
	Mean	SD	Mean	SD	Mean	SD
Job	3.9[a]	0.6	3.5[b]	1.0	3.5[b]	1.0
Leisure	3.7[a]	0.8	2.5[b]	0.8	2.8[b]	0.8
Love	3.8[a]	1.1	2.3[b]	1.4	2.7[b]	1.2
Health	4.0[a]	0.8	3.3[b]	1.1	3.3[b]	0.9
Finances	3.3[a]	1.0	2.1[b]	1.0	2.9[a]	0.9
Spirituality	—	—	—	—	3.0	1.0

Notes. The higher the mean score, the more satisfaction on the five-point Likert QLI scales. Means with different superscripts differ ($p < 0.01$, two-tailed t test for independent groups).

are an individual's choices for coping (or conservation of resources) channeled by the person's personality?

Kunce and Newton (1989) recently reported an interesting study of normal and nonpsychopathological personality characteristics of 72 male alcoholics who were being treated in an inpatient Veterans Administration hospital setting. These investigators administered the MMPI along with their own nonpathological measure, the Personal Styles Inventory (PSI), and examined the correspondence between these two measures. The PSI is a complex measure containing a total of 24 scales purporting to measure human behavior in three domains: emotional, physical, and cognitive. For the purposes of this study, however, the PSI was used to sort the alcoholic patients into the four categories produced by the bipolar dimensions of extraversion–introversion and stability–change. Most (77%) of the alcoholics were categorized as introversive on the PSI. Most interestingly, Kunce and Newton found a correspondence between the Alfano, Nerviano, and Thurstin (1987) MMPI-based subtypes for alcoholism and the fourfold grouping on the PSI. The majority of the alcoholics ($n = 41$) were categorized as of the introvert stable type, which corresponded to the "guilty drinker" MMPI profile type. Fifteen of the alcoholics were of the introvert change type, which corresponded to the "bright, unrealistic" MMPI type with elevations on scales 2, 4, 7, and 8. Eleven alcoholics were of the extravert stable type, called passive-dependent on the MMPI. Only five of the alcoholics were found to be of the extravert change type, corresponding to Alfano et al.'s (1987) MMPI compulsive drinker type.

There are several important implications in Kunce and Newton's findings. If replicated in other samples of alcoholics, this categorization of personality types may be of relevance for matching specific alcoholics or addicts to appropriate treatments (e.g., a more group-oriented approach for extraverted individuals, and for introverted clients, training in alternative stress-reduction methods). Although not discussed by Kunce and Newton, within the framework of the life-contextual approach of Moos, there is the question of the correspondence between individual normal adaptive personality types and social environmental contexts that maintain or accentuate these individual characteristics. Finally, of course, there is the intriguing question of whether these normative personality types may be antecedent rather than consequent to alcohol dependence, and thus measurable in longitudinal studies of the natural course of the development of alcoholism (Vaillant, 1983) that might reveal different paths of substance use or abuse.

In my own clinical research (Hawkins, 1989a, 1989b, 1990a), I have used the Myers-Briggs Type Indicator (MBTI) (Myers & McCaulley, 1985), in a fashion analogous to Kunce and Newton's use of the PSI, to assess the distribution of "psychological types" for various Diagnostic and Statistical Manual of Mental Disorders (third revised edition) (DSM-III-R) clinical diagnostic groups, including males and females with alcohol abuse or dependence. Like the PSI, the MBTI is a nonpathological personality instrument. It is widely used and has satisfactory reliability and validity (Myers & McCaulley, 1985). The MBTI consists of four dichotomous dimensions: extraversion–introversion, sensing–intuition, thinking–feeling, and judging–perceiving. Recently, McCrae and Costa (1989) found that the MBTI dimensions correspond to four of the five primary dimensions of personality: extraversion–introversion, openness to experience, agreeableness, and conscientiousness respectively. Only the fifth dimension, neuroticism, was uncorrelated with the MBTI dimensions, as would be expected since the MBTI is a nonpathological personality measure. Hammer (1989) recently reported that individuals' coping responses appear to differ as a function of their psychological type as revealed by the MBTI. An important caveat to note here is that neither Kunce and Newton (1989) nor clinicians using the MBTI have reported any treatment-outcome studies showing that these nonpathological personality test measures significantly predict differential treatment outcome for alcohol or drug abuse. Clinically, as I shall describe in two case studies subsequently in this chapter, the MBTI appears to be useful in that clients find the holistic personality "portrait" of their psychological type encouraging and enhancing to self-esteem, suggesting moreover a path for good type development guiding recovery and acquisition of new stress-coping resources. Of relevance to the life-contextual viewpoint, either the MBTI or the PSI as a conceptual framework could be applied not only to the chemically dependent individual, but also in the extratreatment context, facilitating exploration of the person–environment match or mismatch.

Dynamics and Natural Course of Substance Use, Abuse, and Dependence

A limitation of SCT as applied to substance use and abuse even when augmented by the Moos' life-contextual process model is that it represents a rather static, nondevelopmental perspective. Although Wills and Shiffman (1985) have implied that stress-coping interactions may differ at transitional points (initiation of substance use, continuous use or abuse, chemical dependency, cessation, and relapse prevention), the dynamics of these interactions are not specified clearly. A life-contextual model surely does suggest in its systemic aspect that a dynamic reciprocal transaction process would be found; however, this assumption is not explicit either.

In particular, as noted earlier, SCT-LCV does not address the phases of the Jellinek (1952, 1960) progressive disease concept of alcoholism and chemical dependency. Although the progressive-disease notion is somewhat of an oversimplification, there is no doubt that in chemical dependency the aversive social, occupational, and health consequences outweigh any stress-coping functions. I wish to argue that Hobfoll's (1989) conservation-of-coping-resources model might predict that during crucial and chronic stages of chemical dependency (i.e., the bottom portion of the Jellinek curve), the individual's coping resources would be depleted. At this transitional point, as Peele (1985) states in his definition of the addictive experience, the drug or the addictive object supplants "functional, realistic action" and alternative coping efforts are abandoned. Thus the course of addiction can be monitored by the increased focus on the addictive experience and the narrowing of other interests, relationships, and activities.

It is precisely the dynamics of each phase that Brown (1985, 1987, 1991) emphasizes in her developmental model of alcoholism and the recovery process. As shown in Figure 9-2, Brown has distinguished four phases in her model: the drinking phase, the transition phase, early recovery, and ongoing recovery. Her conceptualization is transtheoretical, incorporating the Alcoholics Anonymous (AA) 12 steps and reformulating them within the Piagetian, object-relational, and cognitive constructivist framework (Brown, 1991).

Brown's (1985) central notion is that for the alcoholic, the chemical dependency becomes the central organizing principle. There is a progressive narrowing of environmental interaction and a corresponding narrowing interpretation of self and others. Thus, during the drinking stage, the alcoholic's increasing isolation, constriction, and narrowing of interest to the focus on alcohol involve a struggle for control and denial of a problem: "I am not an alcoholic." During the transition stage, the individual "hits bottom," acknowledges loss of control (powerlessness), and begins to accept the support and help of others. Brown emphasizes the importance of the change in epistemology that occurs during the transition stage, during which a significant shift in object attachment occurs: "Bateson (1971) describes this conversion as a shift from a symmetric, competitive relationship with the world

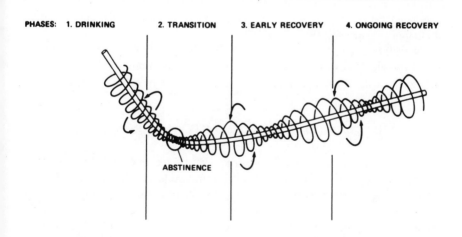

Figure 9-2. Brown's (1985) developmental model of alcoholism stages (Reprinted by permission of John Wiley & Sons, Inc. from Brown's Treating the Alcoholic: A Developmental Model of Recovery. Copyright © 1985 by John Wiley & Sons, Inc.).

to a complementary stance in which the individual sees himself or herself as part of a larger whole" (p. 34).

During early recovery, the individual's denial is broached and he or she admits to being alcoholic or chemically dependent. As Brown (1985) puts it: "New attitudes and new values dictate new directions and a different way of evaluating oneself and one's experiences . . . this movement into abstinence is a new journey both exciting and frightening, sustained by feelings of identification and belonging" (p. 35).

Periodically there may be a return to the alcohol focus, but progressively the individual enters the ongoing recovery stage, which is characterized by increased environmental interaction and integration, in an expanding awareness:

> Interpersonal relationships and environmental concerns become more important as the individual begins to integrate internal needs with external demands. During this time growing self-awareness, enhanced by positive experience and achievement of sobriety, contributes to an adaptive spiral, moving the individual in a forward momentum similar to that described for the downward progression . . . recovery is the interactive flow of a network of experiences, new ideas, and new behaviors reinforcing, reshaping, and building on one another on the base of a new belief system about the self in relation to alcohol and to the world. (p. 37)

Brown (1985) has described the therapeutic task of early recovery as a process of reciprocal determinism (Mahoney, 1977). More recently, she expanded her developmental model of recovery beyond various forms of chemical dependency to describe the recovery process for other family members, particularly "adult children of alcoholics" (Brown, 1987, 1991).

The shift to a cognitive constructivist position is seen clearly in a quotation from one of the alcoholics in Brown's (1985) study: "If I say I am an alcoholic, I will have to reconstruct the meaning I have given to my whole life" (p. 142).

THE COGNITIVE CONSTRUCTIVIST PERSPECTIVE

I shall describe the cognitive constructivist perspective and then seek to reoperationalize the SCT-LCV within this framework. Perhaps the clearest presentation of the constructivist epistemology for the human change process is that of Mahoney (1981): "(1) Personal experience is extensively embedded in an individual context of meaning; and (2) we are active participants in the creation and change of our meaningful contexts" (p. 80).

Mahoney (Mahoney, 1981; Guidano & Liotti, 1983; Mahoney & Lyddon, 1988) refers to a process called autopoeisis, the self-renewing function of open systems or of the human knowing system. According to this viewpoint, each individual has tacit self-knowledge structures in which formative events, particularly from early caregiver–infant attachment experiences, are enfolded, and from which unfold cognitive-affective structures for actively constructing meaning and behavior. "The constructivist approach to cognition imbues human knowing and the human knower with activity. The dominant constructivist themes are evolutionary, self-organizing, and developmental in nature" (Mahoney & Lyddon, 1988, p. 211).

Within this framework of cognitive constructivism, the stress-coping process may be seen as a reflection of adaptive strategies rather than as the occurrence of mistakes. "Problems provide the individual with powerful opportunities for exploring developmental processes [and] allow for the emergence of higher-order patterns and cognitive structures" (Mahoney & Lyddon, 1988, p. 217). It is precisely this connotation that is represented by Brown (1985, 1987, 1991) in her model of the recovery process for chemically dependent individuals and their families.

Steinglass (1987) presented a systems perspective in which not only for the individual, but also for the alcoholic family, is alcoholism the central organzing principle. As described earlier in this chapter, he utilizes the metaphor of the "invasion" to describe the process by which the central focus on alcoholism is associated with the progressive accommodation by the family to the dysfunctional behavior of the alcoholic member. The result is that vital daily routines and meaningful rituals are destroyed. In Brown's developmental model, this mutuality and meaningful fabric of life are gradually restored during the ongoing-recovery stage.

According to another proponent of constructivist theory, Vittorio Guidano (1987):

> In the course of life each individual will find him/herself proceeding along a unique and irreversible developmental pathway whose trajectory is in turn, the ongoing dynamic product resulting on the one hand from the ideal or normative directionality stemming from the individual's systemic coherence, and on the other hand from his/her integrative ability to articulate it throughout adulthood transitions and significant life events. (pp. 205–206)

In her most recent writings, Brown (1991) provides an even greater challenge for conceptualizing stress-coping processes in substance abuse and the impact on the individual and the family. She describes the central organizing principle as not merely the alcoholism or the chemical dependency, but also the chemically dependent parent, with the result being the children of alcoholism syndrome.

How may we articulate stress-coping theory within the new epistemological framework of cognitive constructivism family systems theory? First, I would argue that Hobfoll's (1989) conservation-of-resources model will point us in the right direction. As in Brown's developmental model of ongoing recovery, the emphasis is placed on the active, ongoing process of accumulation of ample and diverse resources for coping. This adaptive process results in a mutual coevolution (Willi, 1989) or dialogue (Bohm, 1980) involving the person and his or her social ecological context.

Brown (1991) would argue that this reformulated framework must be spatial and relational, rather than linear, in a multilevel interactional process. She emphasizes the importance of clinicians' acknowledging the reality of the traumas experienced by the offspring who have grown up in chemically dependent families.

Guidano and Liotti (1983) have described the tacit self-knowledge structures internalized from real-life dysfunctional and traumatic attachment relationships between infant and caregiver, which, in turn, give rise to irrational beliefs, including eating disorders (Hawkins, 1983), that may be similar in some respects to chemical dependency. Epistemologically, SCT as a form of cognitive social learning theory eschews unconscious mechanisms. Still, cognitive processes such as the interpretation of stressful events (Lazarus & Folkman, 1984) may require acknowledgment of the primacy of strong affects (Zajonc, 1980).

Wills (1990) has indeed speculated within SCT that some individuals appear to self-select negative environments and events. In the oscillating human change process (Guidano, 1987; Mahoney, 1981; Mahoney & Lyddon, 1988) life problems in the constructivist framework are seen as failures of adaptation, in that an individual or life context lacks sufficient complexity and/or integration to assimilate the change event. Bowen's (1978) theory of lack of differentiation in the family of origin as an antecedent to an individual's subsequent psychopathology seems to be an earlier related notion. It would appear necessary for SCT to acknowledge the importance of formative life events. In the positive case, these events, which may include chance encounters (Bandura, 1982), allow the individual and his or her life context to make important choices, a launching into new life trajectories. Thus, in the positive instance, the constructivist framework provides a holistic scaffolding for the individual's organizing and reorganizing "the self" in autopoeitic fashion, within the context of real-world environments and events over time. In the negative instance, however, traumatic formative events may impose constraints on the coevolution (mutual dialogue) process. Steinglass' (1987) alcoholic family, wherein alcoholism has "invaded" deep regulatory structures, would describe such a negative outcome. In terms of SCT, reformulated in this spatial and relational fashion, individuals within the chemically dependent, dysfunctional family system would have fewer social and personal coping resources and would display a repertoire for coping that would be narrower and more rigid, with more emphasis on emotion-based avoidance coping in contrast to more active and effective behavioral and cognitive coping.

THE PROBLEM OF MOTIVATION

Within the context of Brown's (1985) developmental model of recovery from alcoholism, particularly in her reformulation (Brown, 1991) with the emphasis on cognitive constructivism, there is a strong implication that the change process involves a cocreation or coevolution of meaning structures for the individual and his or her life context. This cocreation is teleonomic (Mahoney, 1981) in nature. Teleonomy refers to "inherent ordering processes which serve to direct the maintenance and growth of open systems . . . connoting more of a flexible direction rather than a particular destination" (Mahoney, 1981, p. 112). Such an inference invokes motivational processes. Implicit in Brown's theory (1985, 1987, 1991) is that recovery involves a transition from a state of hopelessness to the restoration of hope (Vaillant, 1983).

Marlatt (1985) has suggested that motivation or volitional aspects represent an area where there is a need for further study within SCT. Marlatt, for example, operationally defined willpower as "the global application of intent in the absence of specific coping skills" (p. 381). Hobfoll's (1989) conservation-of-resources model posits like variables with heavy motivational properties.

Diclemente and Prochaska (1985), in their transtheoretic model for the processes of change, have emphasized self-liberation, helping relationships, and consciousness raising as essential to the process of getting ready to quit any of the addictive substances in common. Samsonowitz and Sjoberg (1981), in their study of a small group of alcoholics who were socially stable, reported that the most frequently utilized technique to resist relapse was "bringing values to mind" (i.e., recalling the positive consequences from maintaining abstinence and the negative consequences of drinking).

Similarly, the intention to reuse an addictive substance or to initiate substance use is a very important predictor variable. Thus Chaney and Roszell (1985) found that most of the relapses experienced by their group of heroin addicts were intentional decisions. Similarly, Newcomb and Bentler (1986, 1988), in a longitudinal study of cocaine use among adolescents, found that intent to use cocaine was strongly predictive of subsequent self-use and the copresence of social context variables (i.e., peer use and adult use).

Although it is difficult to provide an operational definition for such abstract motivational constructs as hopelessness, shame, hope, or joy within the SCT life-contextual view of substance use, the clinical currency of such constructs may provide a strong impetus for continued efforts for so doing. Strack, Carver, and Blaney (1987) found that a self-report measure of dispositional optimism was a statistically significant predictor of success in completing a transition program after treatment for alcoholism. Cook (1987) has developed an experimental scale to measure shame. Fossum and Mason (1986) have argued clinically that chemical dependency, as well as abusive behavior patterns, is rooted in "shame-bound" family systems.

There is an interesting parallel between Fossum and Mason's description of the shame-bound family as "a self-sustaining, multigenerational system of interaction [which] unconsciously instills shame in the family members . . . and binds them to perpetuate the shame in themselves and their kin" (p. 8) and Steinglass' (1987) depiction of the alcoholic family wherein alcohol invades the regulatory rituals to become the central organizing principle. One hypothesis for clinical research is that such a deterioration of deep regulatory structures in the family may leave a residual signature of shame, internalized in the offspring as a vulnerability factor.

In his constructivist theory of coevolution, Willi (1989) has described the importance of circular regulations, essentially mutual feedback interactions on a daily basis between individuals within their social ecological systems. Within the alcoholic, shamebound family, people "feel alone together" (Fossum & Mason, 1986, p. 19). I wish to offer the hypothesis that the recovery process for chemical dependency proceeds from a systemic state phenomenologically characterized by the motivational construct of shame and the deployment of emotionally palliative behavioral and cognitive avoidance coping mechanisms. Next, in early recovery, there would occur an acceptance of "hopelessness" or "powerlessness" characterized by the acceptance of social-support forms of coping through new fellowship groups. As Vaillant (1983) has described, "the first step of treatment would be the restoration of hope" within this social embeddedness and mutuality. With the breaking of the addictive cycle, there would be a restoration of volitional choice (e.g., Samsonowitz & Sjoberg, 1981) and utilization of more active cognitive and behavioral coping behaviors (or what Peele [1985] has characterized as "functional, realistic actions" within the context of "real-life rewards").

One future direction that the SCT of substance use and abuse could take, therefore, would be to track the parallels between the utilization of specific coping resources and the cognitive/affective experiences of the individual (shame, hopelessness, hope, or optimism).

Waterman (1989) has developed a reliable psychometric measure of the Aristotelian concept of "eudaimonia" (i.e., the feeling that an activity is fulfilling, what he or she was "meant to do in life," and thus self-defining and personally expressive of the individual). This construct of well-being may be a useful index of the restoration of personal meaning and mutuality in ongoing recovery as described by Brown (1985, 1987, 1991).

FAMILY RECOVERY PROGRAM

The Family Recovery Program (FRP) identifies the more formal, structured treatment components of an outpatient group program I have coordinated in an HMO setting for the past six years. In essence, the FRP consists of three group sessions per week (7 ½ hours in total duration) over an eight-week period, followed by six months of an aftercare group meeting for 90 minutes once weekly. The program's content has reflected the integration of the AA 12-step philosophy and a mental health viewpoint, more recently emphasizing SCT. The FRP thus is one structured component of a multidisciplinary outpatient mental health clinic, where about 50%

of substance-abuse cases, often displaying dual diagnoses, are treated with an individualized combination of individual, couples, or family treatment, the FRP, and psychiatric medications.

Within the past year, the assessment package for the FRP, which initially comprised the SCL-90 (Derogatis, Lipman, & Covi, 1973)—along with an open-ended paper-and-pencil client self-evaluation of the pattern of substance abuse and health, emotional, social, and legal consequences—was modified in accordance with SCT-LCV.

The QLI (Bugen & Hawkins, 1981) was included as a measure of generalized coping resources. The Substance Abuse Problem Checklist (SAPC) (Carroll, 1984) was added as a self-report measure of the chemically dependent individual's perception of personal and environmental (home, work, neighborhood) problems in living associated with abusing chemicals. An experimental clinical measure, the Adult Children of Alcoholics Test (ACAT) (Hawkins, 1988) has been administered as a measure of this "don't talk, don't trust, don't feel syndrome" (Black, 1981), which is presumably associated with shame-bound family systems. Finally, the MBTI (Myers & McCaulley, 1985) has provided an additional measure of non-pathological psychological type.

Two case studies will illustrate the utilization of some of these assessment tools within the context of our overall outpatient intervention program. Names and other identifying information have been disguised to protect clients' confidentiality.

Case Study 1

Robert was a 45-year-old white male who was referred to the FRP when his chronic pattern of secretive, compulsive binge-drinking episodes was brought to light by his wife's complaint during marital therapy sessions. Robert, an attorney, was a self-described "workaholic." With respect to personal coping resources on the QLI, Robert obtained much satisfaction from his profession, and also considered his health an important resource. In general, his QLI resources were higher financially and spiritually than the norms for the FRP and for the adult normative sample, with two exceptions: love relationships and leisure activities. In these areas, he scored lower. On the SAPC, Robert tended to minimize his alcohol problem, as well as his anger tendencies. He used alcohol to cope with negative feelings and described himself as wanting to be left alone when depressed or hurt. Sensitive to criticism, he described his primary motivation to enter treatment as a fear that his wife would leave him otherwise. He described himself as remorseful, but also resentful.

Robert had difficulty talking in the group sessions, describing his pattern of solitary drinking as being very "different" from the problems of the other FRP members. He denied any history of alcoholism in his family of origin, but characterized his father as strong-willed and dictatorial and his mother as codependent. On the MBTI, Robert was an introverted intuitive (INTJ) type, while his wife was an introverted sensing (ISFJ) type. In comparison with clinical norms from 277 male out-patients in my practice, Robert's MBTI type was significantly underrepresented among male alcoholics, but overrepresented among males presenting for therapy with marital problems (Hawkins, 1989a, 1990). The INTJs are characterized as having "original minds and a great drive for their own ideas and purposes" but also as "skeptical, critical, independent, determined, and often stubborn" (Myers & McCaulley, 1985). My clinical impression of males displaying this alcohol-abuse pattern is that they are solitary, compulsive drinkers who engage in control battles with alcohol and/or use alcohol for avoidant coping with angry feelings and frustrated dependency needs.

The MBTI type portrait for Robert's wife, Sue, an ISFJ, is characterized as "quiet, friendly, responsible, and conscientious" (Myers & McCaulley, 1985). Having devotedly reared the couple's children, now nearly grown, Sue complained that her husband's behavior was controlling and that her identity development had taken a back seat to serving her husband and children. With her memory of her husband's "broken promises," she would verbally criticize him and threaten to leave the marriage.

The MBTI was a particularly useful instrument in the treatment of this patient. Robert strongly identified with his INTJ type, and his isolation and denial decreased as he accepted more social support and dialogue within the FRP and at AA meetings. He also accepted more responsibility for his controlling behaviors vis-à-vis his wife, and his wife reported that this acknowledgment was a "breakthrough" in attempts to solve the marital problem. Robert's excessive-drinking episodes stopped and his wife began to pursue individual and group psychotherapy to further her individuation efforts.

Case Study 2

This case provides a further illustration of the use of the MBTI as a tool for assessing the relational potential of family members, as well as for reframing trans-action patterns, encouraging more active prosocial coping behaviors. Billie, the identified patient, was a 17-year-old white female, the daughter of Richard, an optometrist, and Mary, a legal secretary. The presenting problem, according to her parents, was Billie's escalating alcohol and nicotine use, her "lying," and her "borrowing" of her mother's possessions without permission. Billie, a high school senior, was an extraverted sensing (ESTP) type, while her father's type was ESTJ and her mother was an INFJ. Although she was still attending school fairly regularly, Billie's grades had begun to drop. Her interactions with her mother and father were increasingly characterized by aggressive denial of any problems and her parents' accusations.

According to Wills' (1985) list of adolescents' coping responses, Billie increasingly was engaging in accepting peer support (from the partying and drug-using crowd) and turning to social entertainment excessively so that she was seldom at home in the evening. In response to his daughter, Richard began escalating his own aggressive and controlling behavior, while Mary alternated between verbal aggression, cognitive avoidance, and withdrawal (depression) and appeasement efforts. Using the MBTI results, the following interventions were made.

1. The similarity between Billie's ESTP type and her father's ESTJ profile was pointed out and positively reframed as a healthy adolescent-stage combat for control. Billie's manipulativeness and disinclination to show remorse were reframed in terms of the ESTP's preference for action and adventure, with less use for small talk. Billie strongly identified with the description of her type, which she considered exciting and self-determining.

2. Billie's manipulativeness was reframed as cleverness, and she was shown some other prosocial communications and assertiveness tactics to use with her parents more effectively. In addition, Billie was shown a list of occupational titles arranged according to MBTI type patterning. From this list, she selected "pathologist" as an occupation of interest. We were able to arrange for her to participate in a high school premed volunteer program at a local hospital, where she received praise for her activities and became involved with a new peer group.

3. The negative mother–daughter relationship was improved by the therapist's assisting Mary with her chronic dysthymia, a pattern characteristic of INFJ females (Hawkins, 1989a), and her obsessive fear that her daughter's future might replicate Mary's mother's alcoholism. When Mary was able to tell Billie about this fear, Billie's empathy with her mother strengthened the mother–daughter bond. The outcome in this case was that Billie's drinking ceased and the frequency of parent–daughter arguments and blaming decreased as well, until Billie was able to leave for college.

INTEGRATIVE SUMMARY: MULTIPLE PATHS FOR THE INITIATION, MAINTENANCE, AND RECOVERY PROCESSES

In this chapter, I have described the stress-coping theoretical model for substance use and abuse. According to SCT, substance abuse represents a habitual maladaptive attempt to cope with life's stresses and strains. This viewpoint toward substance abuse reflects an adaptive orientation with an emphasis on compensatory social-skills training as an extension of social learning theory. I have offered a reformulation of SCT within the life-contextual viewpoint (Moos, 1984, 1988), according to which substance abuse is seen as an alternative coping response contextualized and given meaning within the life span of an individual's choice making regarding resource investments (Hobfoll, 1989), that is, decisions about relationships with other people, about work, and about the real-world environment, including influences of gender, race, class, culture, and formative events. Thematically, this reformulation of SCT has incorporated Peele's (1985) social psychological perspective on the "addictive experience"; Brown's (1985) developmental model of alcoholism recovery with its integration of Piagetian, object-relational, and AA frameworks; and my own clinical research studies on the relationship between an individual's psychological type (as measured by the Myers-Briggs Type Indicator), specific symptomatology, and specific preferences for accumulating resources and deploying coping responses. This life-contextual reformulation is a constructivist framework combining SCT's scientific measurement of substance-abuse patterns and coping behaviors with a nonreductionistic, holistic emphasis on the individual's autopoeitic activities within the context of real-world environments and events over time (Peele, 1985; Vaillant, 1983).

In this section, I conclude by illustrating how this SCT-LCV implies the existence of multiple paths that may be specified for the initiation, maintenance, and

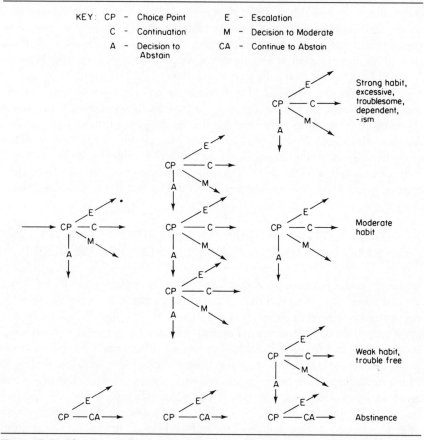

Figure 9-3. *The career of substance use as a series of choice points (Reprinted by permission of John Wiley & Sons, Inc. from Orford's* Excessive Appetites: A Psychological View of Addictions. *Copyright* © *1985 by John Wiley & Sons, Inc.).*

recovery processes of substance use, abuse, and dependence. At the beginning of this chapter, I stated that substance use, abuse, and dependence may be arranged along a continuum of severity—from abstinence to social or nonsocial occasional use; to heavy continuous use (abuse); to binge-type, excessively lengthening and intensifying episodes of abuse; to an end point of the "gamma alcoholic" (Jellinek, 1952, 1960), where the progressive-disease concept is applicable. Vaillant (1983) has estimated that approximately 3% to 5% of white males may fall into this category. The comparable percentages for women and minorities remain unspecified.

Life-span longitudinal studies are required to examine these multiple pathways (Orford, 1985; Vaillant, 1983), since an individual's placement along this continuum will oscillate over time. Vaillant (1983) has found numerous life outcomes in his 40-year longitudinal study. The chronicity of substance use and abuse may predict severity to an extent, but far from perfectly. For example, binge drinkers and heavy, continuous drinkers appear to be separable both in terms of person variables and family environmental contextual variables (Vaillant, 1983; Steinglass, 1987). Gamma alcoholism is not necessarily the "final common pathway" of chemical dependency. Psychological dependence (the "learned habit" view) and the Jellinek (1952, 1960) progressive-disease concept of physical dependence may represent only two paths out of many that can be derived. The complex interplay of person and environment factors in the SCT-LCV can be put into motion over time (the temporal dynamics) in Figures 9-3 and 9-4. Figure 9-3, from Orford (1985), shows the career of substance use as a series of choice points:

> The implications of adopting such a view is that chronic excess is to be seen not as the inevitable result of a progressive disease process, but rather as the end result of a succession of wrong or failed decisions. The model is not one of the unfolding of a process which was latent from the beginning and which could be predicted on the basis of personality or social factors, but rather one of uncertain movements upwards and downwards with the ever present, although perhaps diminishing possibility of removing oneself from the group at risk by making a decision to drastically reduce or perhaps abstain from use or activity. (pp. 276–277)

The salience of volition is thus affirmed in Orford's (1985) dynamic model of choice points. In Figure 9-4, Orford's (1985) "choice point" (CP) is reformulated within SCT-LCV to illustrate the influence of personal and social ecological coping resources and life-stress events on an individual's choice at a given time. The choice point is contained or "embedded" within the context of personal and social environmental coping resources in which the individual's "investments" can be measured at a moment in time (Hobfoll, 1989). To the extent that an individual's coping resources are ample or sufficient, the system will be relatively impermeable to negative stressful life events or losses (buffering effect) and the likelihood of escalation of substance use as avoidant coping will be decreased. While personal and social ecological coping resources are coconstructed, the impinging of stressful life events implies an element of chance encounter (Bandura, 1982). This is not a deterministic system, but it is determinate (Mahoney, 1981) in that it cannot forecast particular outcomes but does specify certain ordered relationships and reciprocal processes, the rules of which may become known. Thus social ecological resources can be estimated through Moos' (1988) Life Stresses and Social Resources Inventory, while personal coping resources can be estimated through various coping batteries, (e.g., the CRI [Moos, 1988], but also including personality dispositional measures, particularly nonpathological measures such as the PSI [Kunce & Newton, 1989] and the MBTI [Hawkins, 1989a, 1989b, 1990a].

At or near equilibrium, when coping resources buffer stressful life events, these operating characteristics of the system may be specified. The outcome of the choice point would be hypothesized to be either a weak trouble-free habit or a moderate

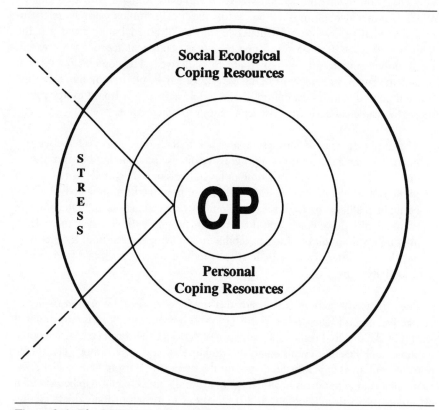

Figure 9-4. *The SCT-LCV reformulation of the choice point model for the path of substance use or abuse.*

habit including possibly continuous heavy drinking (Steinglass' [1987] "alcoholic in the family"). The most interesting question is to consider those escalating paths where substance use is not self-limiting, but where instead a "break-off" point occurs with the system entering "chaos." (Hawkins, 1990b) Does the Jellinek curve of the progressive-disease concept describe the "dissipative structures" (Prigogine & Stengers, 1984) of this path? Perhaps the break-off point may be indexed by the depletion of personal and social environmental resources (as a consequence of chemical dependency) and the emergence of shame and denial characteristics in place of hope (optimism, eudaimonia). In Figure 9-4, this might be pictorially illustrated by the contraction of the concentric spheres around the choice point to the extent that perceived choice or self-determination would vanish and substance use would be determined solely by the opponent processes of addiction (e.g., Solomon & Corbit, 1984), according to physiological and psychological principles of withdrawal, craving, and increased tolerance for drug effects. Even the correlation between stressful life events and substance use would become negligible at this point.

The SCT-LCV should thus be of practical use to clinicians for individualizing chemical-dependency treatment plans. For researchers, the model provides a rationale for new treatment-matching intervention studies. Finney and Moos (1986) have summarized some conceptual and methodological issues for matching patients with treatments. The purpose of this endeavor is that such matching is expected to enhance treatment outcome, in that certain patient characteristics, or characteristics of the extratreatment environment, would interact with treatment variables differentially. Essentially, the SCT-LCV emphasizes the importance of matching patients' coping resources and extratreatment environmental ecology with specific skills-training treatment components. Given the multiplicity of variables that can be matched, one preliminary strategy would be to limit heterogeneity among chemically dependent patients, as suggested by Svanum and McAdoo (1989), to uncover prognostic indicators. The PSI or the MBTI could be used for this purpose.

Morey, Roberts, and Penk (1987), for example, have shown the replicability of the "2-8-7-4" schizoid MMPI subtype among severely alcohol-dependent males. Kunce and Newton (1989) have identified this MMPI subtype with the "introvert change" nonpathological subtype on the PSI. Comparison of pathological or nonpathological subtypes in separate groups of chemically dependent individuals, with concurrent measurement of other personal and social ecological coping resources, might permit testing of the prediction that gamma alcoholism or other end-stage chemical dependencies are the result of a series of failed choices (Orford, 1985) or may represent individuals with some biogenetic predisposition to progress more readily along the substance-use continuum to alcohol dependence. The stress-coping theory, life-contextual viewpoint would thus seem to provide a useful framework both for clinical applications and for furthering research.

REFERENCES

Alfano, A., Nerviano, V. J., & Thurstin, A. H. (1987). An MMPI based clinical typology for inpatient males: Derivation and interpretation. *Journal of Clinical Psychology, 43*, 431–437.

American Psychiatric Association. (1987). Diagnostic and statistical manual of mental disorders (3rd ed.). Washington, DC: Author.

Bandura, A. (1982). The psychology of chance encounters and life paths. *American Psychologist, 37*, 747–755.

Bateson, G. (1971). The cybernetics of self: A theory of alcoholism. *Psychiatry, 34*, 1–18.

Billings, A. G., & Moos, R. H. (1983). Psychosocial processes of recovery among alcoholics and their families: Implications for clinicians and program evaluators. *Addictive Behaviors, 8*, 205–218.

Black, C. (1981). *It will never happen to me.* Denver: MAC.

Bohm, D. (1980). *Wholeness and the implicate order.* New York: Ark.

Bowen, M. (1978). *Family therapy in clinical practice.* New York: Aronson.

Brown, S. (1985). *Treating the alcoholic: A developmental model of recovery.* New York: Wiley.

Brown, S. (1987). *Treating children of alcoholics: A developmental perspective.* New York: Wiley.

Brown, S. (1991). Children of chemically dependent parents: Academic perspectives. In T. M. Rivinus (Ed.), *Children of chemically dependent parents: Academic, clinical, and public policy perspectives.* New York: Brunner/Mazel.

Bugen, L. A., & Hawkins, R. C., II. (1981). The Coping Assessment Battery: Theoretical and empirical foundations. Presented at the meeting of the American Psychological Association, Los Angeles.

Cancrini, L., Cingolani, S., Compagnoli, F., Constantini, D., & Mazzoni, S. (1988). Juvenile drug addiction: A typology of heroin addicts and their families. *Family Process, 27*, 261–271.

Carroll, J. F. X. (1984). The Substance Abuse Problem Checklist: A new clinical aid for drug and/or alcohol dependency treatment. *Journal of Substance Abuse Treatment, 1*, 31–36.

Chaney, E. F., & Roszell, D. K. (1985). Coping in opiate addicts maintained on methadone. In S. Shiffman & T. A. Wills (Eds.), *Coping and substance use* (pp. 267–293). Orlando, FL: Academic Press.

Cook, D. R. (1987). Measuring shame: The Internalized Shame Scale. *Alcohol Treatment Quarterly, 4*, 197–215.

Cronkite, R., & Moos, R. H. (1980). The determinants of posttreatment functioning of alcoholic patients: A conceptual framework. *Journal of Consulting and Clinical Psychology, 48*, 305–316.

Derogatis, L. R., Lipman, R. S., & Covi, L. (1973). The SCL-90: An outpatient psychiatric rating scale. *Psychopharmacology Bulletin, 9*, 13–28.

Diclemente, C. C., & Prochaska, J. O. (1985). Processes and stages of self-change: Coping and competence in smoking behavior change. In S. Shiffman & T. A. Wills (Eds.), *Coping and substance use* (pp. 319–343). Orlando, FL: Academic Press.

Finney, J. W., & Moos, R. H. (1986). Matching patients with treatments: Conceptual and methodological issues. *Journal of Studies on Alcohol, 47*, 122–135.

Fossum, M., & Mason, M. (1986). *Facing the shame: Families in recovery.* New York: Norton.

Guidano, V. F. (1987). *Complexity of the self: A developmental approach to psychopathology and therapy.* New York: Guilford.

Guidano, V. F., & Liotti, G. (1983). *Cognitive processes and emotional disorders: A structural approach to psychotherapy.* New York: Guilford.

Hammer, A. (1989). The relationship between the Coping Resources Inventory and the MBTI. *Proceedings of the Eighth Biennial Conference of the Association for Psychological Type,* Boulder, Col.

Hawkins, J. D., Catalano, R. F., Jr., Gillmore, M. R., & Wells, E. A. (1989). Skills training for drug abusers: Generalization, maintenance, and effects on drug use. *Journal of Consulting and Clinical Psychology, 57,* 559–563.

Hawkins, J. D., Catalano, R. F., & Wells, E. A. (1986). Measuring effects of an experimental skills training intervention on drug abusers' skill acquisition. *Journal of Consulting and Clinical Psychology, 54,* 661–664.

Hawkins, R. C., II. (1983). Cognitive processes in bulimia. Presented at the Special Interest Group meeting on Obesity and Eating Disorders, Association for the Advancement of Behavior Therapy, Washington, D.C.

Hawkins, R. C., II. (1988). Preliminary measure of the ACAT: A self-report measure of the "don't talk, don't trust, don't feel" syndrome. Presented at the annual meeting of the National Association for Children of Alcoholics, New Orleans.

Hawkins, R. C., II. (1989a). In sickness as in health: Type and psychopathology. *Proceedings of the Eighth Biennial Conference of the Association for Psychological Type,* Boulder, Col. (pp. 42–45).

Hawkins, R. C., II. (1989b). Psychological type and anxiety disorders: Preliminary findings. Presented at the annual meeting of the American Psychological Association, New Orleans.

Hawkins, R. C., II. (1990a). Psychological type and the dynamics of substance abuse: A life contextual systems approach. Presented at the Southwest Regional Conference of the Association for Psychological Type, Austin, Tex.

Hawkins, R. C., II. (1990b) Dynamics of substance abuse: Nonlinearities in individual trajectories. *Network (The Newsletter for Psychology Teachers at Two Year Colleges), 8* (3), 9–10.

Hawkins, R. C., II, & Clement, P. F. (1984). Binge eating: Measurement problems and a conceptual model. In R. C. Hawkins, II, W. J. Fremouw, & P. F. Clement (Eds.), *The binge-purge syndrome: Diagnosis, treatment, and research* (pp. 229–253). New York: Springer.

Hobfoll, S. E. (1989). Conservation of resources: A new attempt at conceptualizing stress. *American Psychologist, 44,* 513–524.

Jellinek, E. M. (1952). Phases of alcohol addiction. *Quarterly Journal of Studies on Alcohol, 13,* 673–684.

Jellinek, E. M. (1960). *The disease concept of alcoholism.* New Haven, CT: College and University Press.

Kaplan, H. B., Martin, S. S., & Robbins, C. (1982). Application of a general theory of deviant behavior: Self-derogation and adolescent drug use. *Journal of Health and Social Behavior, 23,* 274–294.

Kaplan, H. B., Martin, S. S., & Robbins, C. (1984). Pathways to adolescent drug use: Self-derogation, peer influence, weakening of social controls, and early substance use. *Journal of Health and Social Behavior, 25,* 270–289.

Kaplan, H. B., Martin, S. S., & Robbins, C. (1986). Escalation of marijuana use. *Journal of Health and Social Behavior, 27,* 44–61.

Kunce, J. T., & Newton, R. M. (1989). Normal and psychopathological personality characteristics of individuals in alcohol rehabilitation. *Journal of Counseling Psychology, 36,* 308–315.

Lazarus, R. S., & Folkman, S. (1984). *Stress, appraisal, and coping.* New York: Springer.

Mahoney, M. J. (1981). Psychotherapy and human change processes. *Master Lecture Series, 1,* 77–122.

Mahoney, M. J., & Lyddon, W. J. (1988). Recent developments in cognitive approaches to counseling and psychotherapy. *Counseling Psychologist, 16,* 190–234.

Marlatt, G. A. (1985). Coping and substance abuse: Implications for research, prevention, and treatment. In S. Shiffman & T. A. Wills (Eds.), *Coping and substance use* (pp. 345–363). Orlando, FL: Academic Press.

McCubbin, H. I., & Figley, C. R. (Eds.). (1983). *Stress and the family: Coping with normative transitions,* Vol. 1. New York: Brunner/Mazel.

McRae, R. R., & Costa, P. T., Jr. (1989). More reasons to adopt the Five-Factor Model. *American Psychologist, 44,* 451–452.

Monti, P. M., Abrams, D. B., Binkoff, J. A., & Zwick, W. R. (1990). Communication training, communications training with family, and cognitive behavioral mood management training for alcoholics. *Journal of Studies on Alcohol, 51*(3), 263–270.

Monti, P. M., Abrams, D. B., Kadden, R. M., & Cooney, N. L. (1989). *Treating alcohol dependence: A coping skills training guide.* New York: Guilford.

Moos, R. H. (1984). Context and coping: Toward a unifying conceptual framework. *American Journal of Community Psychology, 12,* 5–36.

Moos, R. H. (1985). Foreword. In S. Shiffman & T. A. Wills (Eds.), *Coping and substance use* (pp. xiii-xix). Orlando, FL: Academic Press.

Moos, R. H. (1988). Life stressors and coping resources influence health and well being. *Psychological Assessment, 4,* 133–158.

Moos, R. H., Fenn, C. B., Billings, A. G., & Moos, B. S. (1989). Assessing life stressors and social resources: Applications to alcoholic patients. *Journal of Substance Abuse, 1,* 135–152.

Moos, R. H., & Finney, J. W. (1983). The expanding scope of alcoholism treatment evaluation. *American Psychologist, 38,* 1036–1044.

Moos, R. H., Finney, J. W., & Cronkite, R. C. (1990). *Alcoholism treatment: Context, process, and outcome.* New York: Oxford University Press.

Morey, L. C., Roberts, W. R., & Penk, W. (1987). MMPI alcoholic subtypes: Reliability and validity of the 2-8-7-4 subtype. *Journal of Abnormal Psychology*, 96, 164–166.

Myers, I. B., & McCaulley, M. H. (1985). *Manual: A guide to the development and use of the Myers-Briggs Type Indicator.* Palo Alto, CA: Consulting Psychologists Press.

Needle, R., Lavee, Y., Su, S., Brown, P., & Doherty, W. (1988). Familial, interpersonal, and intrapersonal correlates of drug use: A longitudinal comparison of adolescents in treatment, drug-using adolescents not in treatment, and non-drug-using adolescents. *International Journal of the Addictions*, 23, 1211–1240.

Newcomb, M. D., & Bentler, P. M. (1986). Cocaine use among adolescents: Longitudinal associations with social context, psychopathology, and use of other substances. *Addictive Behaviors*, 11, 263–273.

Newcomb, M. D., & Bentler, P. M. (1988). Impact of adolescent drug use and social support on problems of young adults: A longitudinal study. *Journal of Abnormal Psychology*, 97, 64–75.

Orford, J. (1985). *Excessive appetites: A psychological view of addictions.* New York: Wiley.

Pearlin, L. I., & Schooler, C. (1978). The structure of coping. *Journal of Health and Social Behavior*, 19, 2–21.

Peele, S. (1985). *The meaning of addiction: Compulsive experience and its addiction.* Lexington, MA: Lexington Books.

Pentz, M. A. (1985). Social competence and self-efficacy as determinants of substance use in adolescence. In S. Shiffman & T. A. Wills (Eds.), *Coping and substance use* (pp. 117–145). Orlando, FL: Academic Press.

Piazza, N. J., & Wise, S. L. (1988). An order-theoretic analysis of Jellinek's disease model of alcoholism. *International Journal of the Addictions*, 23, 387–397.

Prigogine, I., & Stengers, I. (1984). *Order out of chaos: Man's new dialogue with nature.* New York: Bantam Books.

Robins, L. N., West, T. A., & Murphy, G. E. (1977). The high rate of suicide in older White men: A study testing ten hypotheses. *Social Psychiatry*, 12, 1–20.

Samsonowitz, V., & Sjoberg, L. (1981). Volitional problems of socially adjusted alcoholics. *Addictive Behaviors*, 6, 385–398.

Schinke, S. P., Moncher, M. S., Palleja, J., Zayas, L. H., & Schilling, F. (1988). Hispanic youth, substance abuse, and stress: Implications for prevention research. *International Journal of the Addictions*, 23, 809–826.

Schubert, D. S. P., Wolf, A. W., Patterson, M. B., Grande, T. P., & Pendleton, L. (1988). A statistical evaluation of the literature regarding the associations among alcoholism, drug abuse, and antisocial personality disorder. *International Journal of the Addictions*, 23, 797–808.

Shiffman, S. (1985). Coping with temptations to smoke. In S. Shiffman & T. A. Wills (Eds.), *Coping and substance use* (pp. 223–242). Orlando, FL: Academic Press.

Shiffman, S., & Wills, T. A. (Eds.). (1985). *Coping and substance use.* Orlando, FL: Academic Press.

Solomon, R. L., & Corbit, J. (1984). An opponent process theory of motivation. I: Temporal dynamics of affect. *Psychological Review*, 81, 119–145.

Stanton, M. D., Todd, T. C., et al. (Eds.). (1982). *The family therapy of drug abuse and addiction*. New York: Guilford.

Steinglass, P. (1987). *The alcoholic family*. New York: Basic Books.

Strack, S., Carver, C. S., & Blaney, P. H. (1987). Predicting successful completion of an aftercare program following treatment for alcoholism: The role of dispositional optimism. *Journal of Personality and Social Psychology, 53*, 579–584.

Svanum, S., & McAdoo, W. G. (1989). Predicting rapid relapse following treatment for chemical dependence: A matched-subjects design. *Journal of Consulting and Clinical Psychology, 57*, 222–226.

Vaillant, G. E. (1983). *The natural history of alcoholism: Causes, patterns, and paths to recovery*. Cambridge, MA: Harvard University Press.

Wallace, B. C. (1987). Cocaine dependence treatment on an inpatient detoxification unit. *Journal of Substance Abuse Treatment, 4*, 85–92.

Wallace, B. C. (1989). Psychological and environmental determinants of relapse in crack cocaine smokers. *Journal of Substance Abuse Treatment, 6*, 95–106.

Wallace, B. C. (1990). Crack cocaine smokers as adult children of alcoholics: The dysfunctional family link. *Journal of Substance Abuse Treatment, 7*, 89–100.

Waterman, A. S. (1989). Two conceptions of happiness: Research on eudaimonia and hedonic enjoyment. Presented at a meeting of the American Psychological Association, New Orleans.

Weiss, L., Katzman, M., & Wolchik, S. (1986). *Treating bulimia: A psychoeducational approach*. New York: Pergamon.

Wells, E. A., Catalano, R. F., Jr., Plotnick, R., Hawkins, J. D., & Brattesani, K. A. (1989). General vs. drug-specific coping skills and post-treatment drug use among adults. *Psychology of Addictive Behaviors, 3*(1), 9–21.

Willi, J. (1989). Some principles of an ecological model of the person as a consequence of the therapeutic experience with systems. *Family Process, 26*, 429–436.

Wills, T. A. (1985). Stress, coping, and tobacco and alcohol use in early adolescence. In S. Shiffman & T. A. Wills (Eds.), *Coping and substance use* (pp. 67–94). Orlando, FL: Academic Press.

Wills, T. A. (1986). Stress and coping in early adolescene: Relationships to substance use in urban school samples. *Health Psychology, 5*, 503–530.

Wills, T. A. (1990). Stress and coping factors in the epidemiology of substance use. In L. T. Kozlowski (Ed.), *Research advances in alcohol and drug problems*. New York: Plenum.

Wills, T. A., & Shiffman, S. (1985). Coping and substance use: A conceptual framework. In S. Shiffman & T. A. Wills (Eds.), *Coping and substance use* (pp. 3–24). Orlando, FL: Academic Press.

Wills, T. A., & Vaughn, R. (1989). Social support and substance use in early adolescence. *Journal of Behavioral Medicine, 12*, 321–339.

Zajonc, R. B. (1980). Feeling and thinking: Preferences need no inferences. *American Psychologist, 35*, 151–175.

10

The Role of 12-Step Self-Help Groups in the Treatment of the Chemically Dependent

Karen Derby, Ph.D., CAC

Many psychotherapists and other practitioners are coming to realize the importance of the participation of addicts in self-help groups as they begin to address the problems attendant on chemical abuse and addiction. Although psychotherapists have been addressing the problems of addiction in therapy for years, only recently have there been any systematic attempts by theoretical practitioners to integrate the influence of the self-help systems into psychodynamic thought (Dodes, 1988; Levinson, 1985).

In addition to this lack of integration, there has been some dispute among those in the chemical-dependency treatment community about the efficacy of psychotherapeutic approaches to the problem (Kurtz, 1984). Indeed, there seemed to have been a perception among many of these workers that psychotherapy did not "work" with addicts, and that the only route to recovery was either through the acceptance of the "disease model" of addiction (originally alcoholism, Jellinek, 1960) or through a thorough immersion in the principles of a 12-step program modeled on the original, Alcoholics Anonymous (AA) (Alcoholics Anonymous, 1976).

There is a need for integration on both sides: those workers who favor a self-help or "disease" model approach must understand that a psychodynamic understanding of addiction does not undermine, but rather can enhance, an individual's recovery; those therapists unfamiliar with the contributions of the self-help programs must understand the ways in which this approach assists the individual in rebuilding areas of functioning lost as the result either of the factors predisposing to the drug abuse, of the drug abuse itself, or of both.

THE 12-STEP PROGRAM AND PSYCHOTHERAPY

The history of the 12-step movement began in "June, 1935, during a talk between a New York stockbroker and an Akron physician" (Alcoholics Anonymous, 1976, p. xv). The steps in the evolution of AA, the first and most widespread of the 12-step programs, are well documented in a number of widely used texts on alcoholism (see Alibrandi, 1982; Zimberg, 1982), but nowhere is the story chronicled better than in AA's *Big Book* (i.e., Alcoholics Anonymous, 1976). In the third edition of this universally read book, the worldwide membership of AA was estimated to be more than one million, "with almost 28,000 groups meeting in over 90 countries" (Alcoholics Anonymous, 1976, p. xxii). Zimberg (1982) summarized the therapeutic aspects of the 12 steps of AA, concluding that the program's success is based on an intuitive understanding of the psychological needs of the alcoholic, which include meeting unmet dependency needs through the accepting, nonjudgmental, and nurturing atmosphere of AA meetings and the support of one's peers; the alleviation of guilt through confession of "sins" and making amends; and the sublimation of grandiosity through the helping of other alcoholics (p. 122).

He noted that AA meetings provide needed structure, and that they are available to anyone with a desire to stop drinking. He emphasized the groups' permitting the "sharing of a common life experience, as well as drinking experience" (p. 123), and indicated that since people feel comfortable with their peers, AA groups self-select peers as members, often leading to homogeneity within groups and further enhancing the comfort felt by members. Zimberg believed that the process of the sharing of stories of self-destruction through drinking and recovery through AA allows for guilt to be alleviated and for self-esteem to be restored.

Most authors agree that AA (and later, related groups based on the same 12 steps and traditions, such as Narcotics Anonymous and Gamblers Anonymous) are the "single most effective treatment modality for alcoholism" (Zimberg, 1982, italics in original; see also Mack, 1981). Dodes (1988), Zimberg (1982), and others have pointed out that AA does not help all individuals who try to use this structure to help themselves. Regarding this group's success, however, AA does provide reports of "treatment" outcome; in a published survey (Alcoholics Anonymous, 1972) of 393 members who attended at least 10 meetings, 122 had remained sober for a one-year period. Zimberg (1982) noted that this success rate is comparable to those of other treatment modalities.

Unlike AA, Gamblers Anonymous (GA) maintains books that record the first names of attendees; slips, if any; and individuals' achievement of total abstinence. Although it is difficult to extrapolate from one modality of self-help group to another, data are available from GA that indicate something about early attendance and dropout rates as they relate to outcome/success. One prospective outcome study (Stewart & Brown, 1988) noted that among 232 individuals starting GA, 52 (22.4%)

dropped out after the first meeting, 136 (58.6%) had dropped out after five meetings, and a total of 161 (69.4%) had dropped out after 10 meetings. In another sample of new members (186) who remained in GA for one year, 14 (7.5%) attained a one-year pin (one year's abstinence from gambling), and of 137 who remained in GA for two years, 10 (7.3%) earned a two-year pin. Of interest here is the relatively large number of individuals who drop out before meeting the 10-meeting criterion of the previously mentioned AA outcome study: What happens to those who, for whatever reasons, do not continue as regular AA members? Some of these individuals are treated in individual psychotherapy, and many of those need assistance with using 12-step principles.

Because these programs are anonymous, it is difficult to obtain a clear statistical picture of their success. It is possible, however, to understand how the program works for those who are able to embrace it. Although the AA *Big Book* (Alcoholics Anonymous, 1957) has been criticized on a number of grounds (for example, the language is often deemed archaic), it is probably the best resource available for those who wish to understand how AA works. These words of encouragement referring to following the 12 steps come from those who have suffered the same misery as the alcoholic reader: "At some of these [suggestions] we balked. We thought we could find an easier, softer way. But we could not. With all the earnestness at our command, we beg of you to be fearless and thorough from the very start. Some of us have tried to hold on to our old ideas and the result was nil until we let go absolutely" (p. 58).

The impact of this on the individual who has resisted the same type of exhortations from friends, relatives, and even professionals cannot be underestimated. Similarly, the experience of walking into a 12-step self-help meeting, surrounded by respectable people, all of whom have the same problem, is often more powerful than threats of loss of job, family, or home. An addict or alcoholic who attends a self-help meeting for the first time usually has run out of excuses; the ability to deny the problem is weakening. Often, he* has tried to avoid this confrontation for months, perhaps years. He is usually out of options, and may feel that AA could be his final hope. He is hopeless, ashamed, fearful, and, in his own defense, projects his aggression onto others. At self-help meetings, however, instead of finding what he fears (judgment, condemnation), he finds acceptance, recognition, and a warm welcome. The empathy of other group members allows the individual the chance to hear what is said, to consider whether he can identify with others around him who admit to their problem, to accept, and to learn.

Silber (1974) has described a process similar to this in discussing the rationale for the opening phase of therapy with an alcoholic patient. Referring to the fears that the patient feels about his aggressive impulses, Silber noted:

---

*In this chapter, the masculine pronoun "he" is used to denote the patient; the feminine pronoun "she" is used to denote the therapist.

By interpreting the fear rather than the wish, the therapist operated from the vantage point of the ego and in alliance with the patient's ego. Since this was all initiated early in the therapy, a magical element was introduced: the therapist had a special knowledge about what was going on in the patient's mind, and was thus elevated into the role of a magical, omnipotent figure. (p. 33)

I believe that self-help groups and the individual members in them are elevated to "magical, omnipotent" status through a common dynamic: other sick but recovering alcoholics (and addicts) have a special knowledge about the patient, since they have similar backgrounds pertaining to the substance abuse. This identification with and acceptance by members of AA and other such groups are essential, I believe, to the engagement of the patient in "treatment" with the 12-step program.

Dodes (1988) elaborated on the ways in which AA "offers the opportunity for internalization of specific ego functions and serves as a valuing, idealized object" (p. 287). He believed that aspects of a narcissistic transference are directed toward the AA group, although he suggested that "other elements of this transference may be simultaneously created with the therapist; the balance of attachments will vary with different patients" (p. 287). Dodes suggested that the group's "prescriptive directive stance, its parental omnipotent qualities, and its near omnipresence . . . make AA in reality close to the idealized fantasy sought by some narcissistically deprived patients" (p. 287). He concluded that a split of the narcissistic transference occurs between the therapist and AA in some patients.

Although identification is important, this process has sometimes become too strongly underscored among treatment staff with 12-step/disease-model orientations. The roots of the split between "recovering" helpers and "nonrecovering" or professional helpers can be found in the *Big Book* itself:

It seemed to me that those AA's to whom I talked knew all about me. It is true that the doctors and nurses in the various institutions I attended knew too. But the difference lay in the fact that the AA's knew from their own bitter experience.

In other words, the kindest doctor in the world . . . couldn't help me because I always felt, "You can't know about me—you can't possibly know—you don't even drink!" (pp. 470–471)

also:

An American doctor in Paris said I had an enlarged liver. He also said, "You are an alcoholic and there's nothing I can do for you." This went in one ear and out the other. I did not know what he meant. An alcoholic cannot accept the news that he's an alcoholic unless there is a meaningful explanation given, and an offer of help, such as you get in AA. . . . My first analyst said, "You are becoming more and more of an alcoholic," and sent me to another analyst. This good and gentle man, a brilliant research doctor, got nowhere with me fast. (pp. 406–407)

And finally:

My growing inward unhappiness was a very real thing, however, and I knew that something would have to be done about it. A friend had found help in psychoanalysis. After a particularly ugly one-nighter, my wife suggested I try it, and I agreed. Educated child of the scientific age that I was, I had complete faith in the science of the mind. It would be a sure cure and also an adventure. How exciting to learn the inward mysteries that govern the behavior of people, how wonderful to know, at last, all about myself! To cut a long story short, I spent seven years and ten thousand dollars on my psychiatric adventure, and emerged in worse condition than ever. (p. 434)

Even today, one hears condemnation of some members of the professional community that appears to be based on old-fashioned perceptions on the part of these clinicians. A strong belief that "only a drunk can help a drunk" persists.

Silber (1974) addressed this issue as well. He noted the importance of background factors that will affect the initial contact with the patient. This is of special significance in those instances where it is felt that an ex-member of a particular group who has experienced the situation in question has a unique advantage in dealing with the patient (p. 30). Although initially, the patient may feel more comfortable working with a recovering therapist, it is very important that the therapist be aware of the potential transference/countertransference complications of this situation. For example, the patient may fantasize that the recovering therapist may more easily "understand" his plight, and may not wish to verbalize the more painful aspects of his inner life, feeling that the therapist already "knows" what has happened. In such cases, it is important for the therapist to separate her own experience from that of the patient, allowing the patient to reveal his own experience, thereby coming to understand it. The process of self-revelation is not really different than it would be with a nonrecovering therapist, since the goal of the treatment is that the patient understand himself.

It is important to recognize that the professions have come a long way since the days when the first AAs were putting their stories together. Most professionals now recognize that the achievement of abstinence from all mood-altering chemicals is desirable when working with addicted individuals. It is also widely recognized that the mutative aspects of the psychotherapy begin with the very first visit; the clinician working with addicted patients should not be fooled into thinking that the "real" psychotherapy does not start until months or years later (see Chapter 5, this volume). Because of these points, it is clear that psychotherapists can help addicted individuals establish a mutually beneficial relationship between their therapy and the 12-step program; the two approaches are not mutually exclusive. (Conversely, it is not necessary to rule out the potential efficacy of a psychotherapeutic relationship simply because the therapist's alcohol and drug history does not coincide with that of the patient.)

The 12 Steps and Ego Functioning

Spiegel and Mulder (1986) have detailed the ways in which the 12 steps themselves represent aspects of ego function that are defective in the addicted person. For example, these authors suggested that an individual's relation to reality is enhanced through involvement with step 1, which requires the addicted person to acknowledge powerlessness over the chemical. Denial is gradually diminished, and the addict is able to test reality with increasing accuracy. Steps 4 and 10, which require one honestly to assess one's own strengths and weaknesses, are seen further to enhance reality testing.

The ego function of regulation and control of drive and impulse is understood by Spiegel and Mulder to be strengthened through the working of step 1 (as the chemical use diminishes, thereby freeing the individual to regulate drives). Steps 4 and 5, which involve the development and verbal "sharing" (with another) of a list of strengths and weaknesses (the "moral inventory"), are seen to aid the individual in learning that previously uncontrollable feelings can be understood and controlled. Similarly, step 10 is worked on a daily basis to help the individual maintain control of drives in a manageable time frame.

Spiegel and Mulder suggested that thought processes are transformed from "the magical, self-absorbed thinking of the addict who believes a substance will solve his problems" (p. 37) to a clearer, more focused ego function in which the confusion brought about by absorption in the self and in the chemical dissipates.

The ego function of object relations is demonstrated by these authors to be influenced by the sense of mutuality of the 12-step program: the spiritual influence of the 12 steps, which emphasizes allowing the willingness to accept help from others, interferes with the isolated, often grandiose perspective of the addict. Through the process of accepting help and achieving success that often occurs when an individual makes use of the 12 steps in recovery, the addict begins to develop a more secure sense of trust in others, and therefore begins to develop rudimentary healthy object relations that can be built upon in other areas of life.

Spiegel and Mulder noted a shift in the nature of the defensive functioning of addicted patients as they followed the suggestions in the steps of the program: they articulated the ways in which primitive defense mechanisms such as denial and projection are abandoned in the service of more mature defenses such as rationalization, as when the individual is encouraged to take first things first and not attempt to solve all problems at one time. These authors also noted that the "Fourth Step

Inventory" and the sharing of this personal inventory in step 5 allow individuals to abandon their all-or-nothing, "all bad or all good" views of themselves and begin to integrate previously split-off parts of themselves.

The autonomous and synthetic functions of the ego are recognized and strengthened as the recovering person begins to free the energy previously used to justify the drinking and drugging and to resist the urges to use chemicals (in early recovery). Once the individual establishes the control of impulses, the ego is not as absorbed in defensive functioning and is more able to engage in the so-called "conflict-free" functions, such as motility, perception, memory, judgment, and intention (Spiegel & Mulder, 1986, p. 40). These authors noted that:

> Autonomous functions also are strengthened through the exercise of the observing ego, which in the Fourth, Fifth, and Tenth Steps, is directed toward realistic self-observation. . . . A complete synthesis of the personality takes place when the formerly split self, the tamed drives, and the compassioned yet firm superego come under the guidance of the principles of the program which are outlined in Step Twelve. This translation of the ideals and values of the program into a solution for life situations utilizes the synthetic function of the ego. (pp. 40–41)

Especially in the opening phase of therapy (but even many months or years later), it is incumbent upon the therapist to recognize that these deficits (and later the hidden lacunae) exist, and in the therapy, to supply whatever is necessary to allow the patient to benefit from the treatment. Some authors believe that the most consistently damaged areas that we see are those involving the recognition and management of affective life (see Chapter 5, this volume). Also, Silber (1974) identifies the loss of the autonomous functions of self-observation and verbalization as constituting potential threats to the therapeutic situation. As a result of these deficits, the therapist must be prepared initially to take an educative and directive stance, providing some of the missing functions relating to recognition and verbalization of affect.

Psychodynamics of Resistance to Recovery

Levinson (1985) enumerated several aspects of the addicted person's posture in the early phase of therapy that the clinician must be prepared to understand and, when possible, interpret, so that the work may progress. For example: "The addict's need for control may undermine the treatment to the extent that he cannot admit any problems with alcohol or drugs, for fear of exposing his inner (hidden) loss of control." Levinson identified the patient's denial of dependency needs or omnipotence as the most powerful resistance to the treatment. She believed that the omnipotence protects the adult patient from the awareness that he truly is unable to care for himself, as though he were still a neglected and unprotected child. The therapist's task in establishing a working alliance is to allow the patient to experience trust in her predictable ability to help him to do things that he has not yet learned to do until he can do them himself.

Patients often avoid achieving and maintaining sobriety because they cannot tolerate the guilt that they experience for continuing drinking. The therapist also must recognize that addicted patients experience difficulties with feelings of intimacy. Levinson advocated the establishment of an appropriate feeling of distance in the treatment relationship by using the patient's last name when addressing the patient, for example.

Levinson suggested that the therapist deal with the problem of the patient's impulsiveness by working "to support and build the ego. That is why alternative methods of coping are suggested rather than analyzing what feeling is being acted upon" (p. 17). She noted that these patients are accustomed to taking an action, rather than stopping and discovering what they are feeling, when they are impulsive.

These patients often attempt to externalize responsibility for drinking, drugging, and exhibiting behaviors related to the addiction. Levinson suggested that engagement in a power struggle with the patient is to be avoided; rather, she advocated joining the patient's resistance, requiring the patient to prove that the addictive behavior is truly a problem. By avoiding the struggle, attention can be paid to the patient's thoughts and feelings about being an alcoholic or addict.

These aspects of the patient's feeling life are often, for the most part, unconscious. For this reason, it is important that the therapist be aware of these potential threats to the therapeutic situation and assist the patient in acquiring the abilities to sustain recovery. This is, of course, what self-help members do for the new member of the group. Through identification and support, they supply the needed missing functions (often having to do with verbalization and feeling) that the individual feels incapable of carrying out. If these and other ego functions are impaired, then it is all the better for the patient to make use of the AA group to support those areas of impairment until the functions are restored.

Addicted patients are widely recognized to be extremely dependent and needy. They often experience the self-help group as warm, caring, and giving. The meetings seem to provide "good-enough" (Winnicott, 1951) nurturance, addressing the patient's extreme emotional deprivation. Additionally, the member's sponsor may act as an ever-present (within limits established by the individuals), consistent, mirroring object that the addict in early recovery may use to supply needed nurturance, reality testing, frustration-tolerance education, and other missing affect- and object-related functions.

Regression in Treatment

When the use of AA as a treatment modality fails, often the patient will feel blamed by other group members, as well as by the therapist. At these times, what is needed is an analysis of the resistance to change. In an abstinent context, specific slips and relapses can be understood by the therapist and patient as being linked to specific emotional events or deficits that can be explored in the therapy; in other words, failure to maintain abstinence can be examined as any other regression in the treatment would be. Although members of the AA group may accept the individual's drinking as a manifestation of the "disease," the group will not engage in any type of analysis. It is important, therefore, that the therapist emphasize the necessity of understanding the forces that consciously or unconsciously put pressure on the individual to drink or use drugs. Through this process, a slip can be perceived as something predictable and avoidable, rather than as something that comes out of nowhere to destroy the patient.

Spirituality

One common resistance to AA (or other 12-step group) involvement is the attribution that the program is "religious." Although this particular argument can easily become an extended, philosophical one (for which there is no space here), it should suffice to note that most treatment professionals recognize that the references to "God, as we understood him" in the 12 steps allow a broader philosophical reference so that the AA member does not have to accept a Judeo-Christian interpretation of "God." Indeed, it is widely noted that many alcoholics who have difficulty with this concept use the shared experience of the AA group as the "Higher Power" on which they are encouraged to depend (Zimberg, 1982). The AA program thus differentiates religiosity from "spirituality," a broader concept that involves a relinquishing of the attitude, "I want what I want when I want it (and no one else's needs are important)." This concept emphasizes subjugating one's own impulsive needs to the "needs of the many" and underscores the valuation of the community. Experienced AA members have noted: "We can laugh at those who think spirituality is the way of weakness. Paradoxically, it is the way of strength" (Alcoholics Anonymous, 1976, p. 68).

TOWARD AN INTEGRATION

It is a fact that many addicted individuals are concurrently involved in psychotherapy while they attend AA or other self-help groups. One recent survey showed that 45% of people already in AA had sought psychotherapy, and that of these members, more than 90% had found therapy helpful to them (Brown, 1985).

Levinson (1985) enumerated the ways in which the disease concept of alcoholism can be integrated with psychodynamic understanding. She stated that the individualized psychodynamic formulation is made to help the therapist gear interventions toward the patient's becoming engaged in treatment, developing a working alliance, making the drinking ego dystonic, and getting to AA for help in stopping drinking. The disease concept is used to help the person become interested in maintaining sobriety by adapting behavior to arrest the disease (p. 23).

A number of workers have indicated that clinicians must exercise caution when using a psychotherapeutic approach with addicted patients (Brown, 1985; Rosen, 1981), even to the point of deeming psychotherapy "wasteful" (Vaillant, 1981, p. 49). Dodes (1984, 1988) countered these arguments in pointing out that the patient's manipulative misuse of therapy in order to continue drinking requires the collusion of the therapist. He further suggested that although it is true that continued drinking may be counterproductive to the progress of psychotherapy, so would it be to the progress of self-help participation or any other form of therapeutic endeavor. He concluded that in order for the patient to suffer from the commonly cited perils of psychotherapy with addicted patients, it would require a concomitant failure on the part of the therapist to notice and be appropriately attuned to the patient's needs.

As Levinson (1985) and Spiegel and Mulder (1986) have noted, both the process of psychotherapy and that of self-help involvement address needed restructuring of missing or defective ego functions. Psychotherapy can be used to help the patient identify the ways in which the self-help program rebuilds areas of function previously unidentified as deficient. In order to accomplish this, it is essential that the individual practitioner understand the structure and function of the 12-step program. It may be necessary to help the patient overcome resistances to certain aspects of the program (e.g., the Higher Power concept), or the therapist may be called upon to help the patient release himself from the punitive and self-punitive aspects of his personality that have developed with the acquisition of the addiction and assist in integrating this understanding with the self-help philosophy.

CONCLUSION

As Dodes (1988) has courageously articulated, "Some patients are able to use only psychotherapy, others can use only AA, and there are those who will best be treated by a combination of the two. Accurate prescription of treatment requires individualized clinical judgment" (pp. 283–284). Advocates of each approach must admit that both modalities have proved their efficacy in assisting addicted patients to begin and sustain recovery.

Twelve-step groups provide some types of "holding" that individual psychotherapy cannot; therapy provides some types of holding that the groups cannot. The integration of 12-step and psychodynamic approaches is a challenge and a necessity. Practitioners must develop the clinical acumen to understand the conflicts that patients experience about making use of 12-step programs and help patients to maximize the benefits available in those programs.

REFERENCES

Alcoholics Anonymous. (1972). *Profile of AA meeting*. New York: Alcoholics Anonymous World Services.

Alcoholics Anonymous. (1976). *Alcoholics Anonymous* (3rd ed.). New York: Alcoholics Anonymous World Services, 1939.

Alibrandi, L. A. (1982). The fellowship of Alcoholics Anonymous. In E. M. Pattison & E. Kaufman (Eds.), *Encyclopedic handbook of alcoholism* (pp. 979–986). New York: Gardner Press.

Brown, S. (1985). *Treating the alcoholic: A developmental model of recovery.* New York: Wiley.

Dodes, L. M. (1984). Abstinence from alcohol in long-term individual psychotherapy with alcoholics. *American Journal of Psychotherapy, 38*, 248–256.

Dodes, L. M. (1988). The psychology of combining dynamic psychotherapy and Alcoholics Anonymous. *Bulletin of the Menninger Clinic, 52*, 283–293.

Jellinek, E. M. (1960). *The disease concept of alcoholism*. New Haven, CT: College and University Press.

Kurtz, L. F. (1984). Ideological differences between professionals and AA members. *Alcoholism Treatment Quarterly, 1*, 73–85.

Levinson, V. R. (1985). The compatibility of the disease concept with a psychodynamic approach in the treatment of alcoholism. *Alcoholism Treatment Quarterly, 2*, 7–24.

Mack, J. E. (1981). Alcoholism, AA, and the governance of the self. In M. H. Bean, E. J. Khantzian, J. E. Mack, G. Vaillant, & N. E. Zinberg (Eds.), *Dynamic approaches to the treatment of alcoholism* (pp. 128–162). New York: Free Press.

Rosen, A. (1981). Psychotherapy and Alcoholics Anonymous: Can they be coordinated? *Bulletin of the Menninger Clinic, 45*, 229–246.

Silber, A. (1974). Rationale for the technique of psychotherapy with alcoholics. *International Journal of Psychoanalytic Psychotherapy, 3*, 28–47.

Spiegel, E., & Mulder, E. A. (1986). The anonymous program and ego functioning. *Issues in Ego Psychology, 9*, 34–42.

Stewart, R. M. & Brown, R. I. (1988). An outcome study of Gamblers Anonymous. *British Journal of Psychiatry, 152*, 284–288.

Vaillant, G. E. (1981). Dangers of psychotherapy in the treatment of alcoholism. In M. H. Bean, E. J. Khantzian, J. E. Mack, G. Vaillant, & N. E. Zinberg (Eds.), *Dynamic approaches to the understanding and treatment of alcoholism* (pp. 36–54). New York: Free Press.

Winnicott, D. W. (1951/1971). Transitional objects and transitional phenomena. In *Playing and reality* (pp. 1–25). New York: Basic Books, 1971.

Zimberg, S. (1982). *The clinical management of alcoholism.* New York: Brunner/Mazel.

11

Multidimensional Relapse Prevention from a Biopsychosocial Perspective Across Phases of Recovery

Barbara C. Wallace, Ph.D.

Treatment professionals have recognized the importance of incorporating a relapse-prevention component into any program aspiring to be a viable route by which the chemically dependent can achieve long-term abstinence (Gorski, 1990; Washton & Stone-Washton, 1990; Rawson, Obert, McCann, Smith, & Ling, 1990). In fact, some have argued that relapse prevention may constitute the most criticial component of treatment (Wallace, 1990). Relapse prevention is one of the treatment interventions to be maintained, particularly when cost-effectiveness decisions or staff shortages dictate a decrease in the services delivered.

When working on an inpatient detoxification unit at a struggling inner-city hospital and faced with a staff shortage, I was advised by my unit chief to perform less individual therapy, change the focus of group therapy, and conduct psychoeducational groups. This staff shortage and managerial recommendation coincided with my analysis of data on the process and determinants of relapse in those patients who had returned to the inpatient detoxification unit for a second time (see Wallace, 1991, 1989a). These findings led to the creation of a typology of psychological/personality and environmental/interpersonal determinants of relapse (Wallace, 1991, 1989a). The typology predicted determinants of relapse and directed the creation of clinical interventions I delivered in my new psychoeducational groups. A total of 27 interventions composed the model of relapse prevention I developed (see Wallace, 1991, 1989b). This model of relapse prevention in psychoeducational groups attempted specifically to educate patients to those high-risk situations and multiple determinants of relapse that former patients like those currently in treatment—mostly compulsive crack-cocaine smokers and some intravenous-heroin users—had succumbed to following their release from inpatient detoxification.

171

In this way, my clinical decisions and behavior reflected the belief that when clinical interventions must be streamlined and expedited, if anything should remain, it must be relapse prevention. Or to state it differently, of those things we may aspire to give the chemically dependent, the most important interventions are those that include relapse prevention. However, my concept of relapse prevention is somewhat broader than that of most treatment professionals.

In essence, the view of relapse prevention articulated in this chapter follows a biopsychosocial approach. As I see it, relapse prevention entails the delivery of neuronutrients or pharmacological adjuncts to address neurochemical disruptions in brain function caused by chronic chemical use, and so involves a biological factor that we must address. Relapse prevention also encompasses remediation of underlying problems in self-regulation and treatment of psychopathology as psychological factors to which we must attend. And social factors to be addressed in relapse prevention include interventions that recognize a social environment replete with classically conditioned stimuli, as well as the need for positive reinforcers in recovering individuals' lives that can begin to compete with the memory of chemical-induced euphoria. Moreover, relapse prevention begins in a withdrawal phase, is most intense in the period of prolonging abstinence, and for some clients even continues into the first year or two of pursuing lifetime recovery (see Chapter 1 for an explanation of these phases). Multidimensional relapse prevention from a biopsychosocial view thus extends across all phases of recovery. In the course of presenting a multidimensional approach to relapse prevention, this chapter will demonstrate how utilizing a biopsychosocial model of addiction necessitates drawing upon an integrated theory as we develop a rationale for relapse-prevention interventions.

HISTORY OF RELAPSE PREVENTION

For many workers in the field, the history of contemporary relapse prevention probably is considered to begin with the work of Marlatt and Gordon (1985). However, Marlatt (1985a) cites the earlier important work of Hunt, Barnett, and Branch (1971), who presented the inverted "J" shaped curve as depicting the pattern of relapse for those completing programs for smokers, alcoholics, or heroin addicts. As a summary of multiple treatment-outcome studies, the curves showed that about two thirds of all relapses occurred within the first 90 days following treatment. For Marlatt (1985a), this work suggested the search for the underlying mechanisms involved in addiction to these various substances (p. 35).

The very important research of Cummings, Gordon, and Marlatt (1980) sought to clarify further the underlying mechanisms across several addictive disorders. They analyzed 311 initial relapse episodes in a sample that included recovering problem drinkers, smokers, heroin addicts, overeaters, and compulsive gamblers. This research utilized a microanalysis of relapse episodes via questionnaires to identify high-risk situations or determinants of relapse episodes. Major findings indicated that relapse episodes were determined by negative emotional states (35%), interpersonal conflict (16%), and social pressure (20%).

These findings suggested to Marlatt (1985a) the importance of executing an effective cognitive or behavioral coping response in a high-risk situation. He focused not only on the individual's coping responses, but also on the individual's expectations of a positive outcome when facing high-risk situations. The lack of coping skills or positive outcome expectations increased the possibility of a lapse or relapse.

As this focus on coping skills and cognitive expectations suggests, one of Marlatt's (1985b, 1985c, 1985d) critical contributions to the field was the development of a model of relapse prevention and specific strategies grounded in cognitive-behavioral theory and techniques. Marlatt provided seminal leadership in the field of addictions by advancing the use of cognitive-behavioral interventions and skills training for a range of problem behaviors. Other important contributions include his postulation of the abstinence violation effect (AVE), whereby a lapse or relapse is followed by guilt and self-blame—a reaction to be avoided to prevent a complete relapse from occurring (pp. 41–42).

Marlatt (1985a) also provides an insightful critique of one possible negative consequence of a strictly disease view of addiction, focusing on the disease model's implicit suggestion of an internal causation of chemical dependency and of a possible relapse to chemical use. With this approach, patients may view a relapse as reflecting the fact that they have a disease—an internal cause of their chemical use that is out of their control. For Marlatt, such a view underestimates the degree of responsibility clients can and must assume for avoiding a relapse episode that may be determined by such external factors as classically conditioned stimuli in the environment or caused by ineffective coping skills. Marlatt emphasizes the fact that clients can act effectively to avoid a relapse and can learn from such episodes that do take place about high-risk situations that need to be managed differently in the future.

Marlatt (1985e) also argues the importance of life-style changes if the course of recovery is to be successful. This pioneering work has led to the incorporation of Marlatt and Gordon's (1985) views and recommended procedures into innumerable treatment programs and models for a range of addictive and problem behaviors.

THEORY BEHIND TRADITIONAL RELAPSE-PREVENTION MODELS

The theory and rationale behind Marlatt's (1985) relapse-prevention model, and also behind most Marlatt-derived or traditional relapse-prevention approaches, rest in operant conditioning, classical conditioning, and social learning theory. Most relapse-prevention models derive their rationale for various procedures, as did

Marlatt (1985), from research supporting the development and maintenance of addiction in the positive reinforcement of the chemically induced "high." Also, negative reinforcement explains how the use of the chemical to ease withdrawal symptoms and dysphoria further increases the chances of chemical use when the person is faced again with withdrawal dysphoria. Behavioral principles of classical conditioning draw attention to the role of conditioned stimuli in triggering conditioned responses that lead to chemical use. Social learning theory also dictates the use of role modeling and behavioral rehearsal, for example, as relapse-prevention interventions.

RATIONALE FOR A MULTIDIMENSIONAL MODEL OF RELAPSE PREVENTION

If we follow a biopsychosocial model of addiction as advanced by Donovan and Marlatt (1988), however, then we not only should recognize the etiology of addiction in biological, psychological, and social factors, but we should also create relapse-prevention strategies that address these multiple factors. My recent work (Wallace, 1990) suggests a broad, multidimensional approach to relapse within a biopsychosocial approach to crack cocaine addiction. Similarly, for a range of addictive disorders, we need to recognize how the chemically dependent may require a multidimensional relapse-prevention strategy that addresses the biological, psychological, and social-environmental determinants of relapse.

Biological Factors To Be Addressed

As the work of Blum and his colleagues suggests in Chapter 12, the use of neuronutrients as adjuncts to recovery may be a critical intervention that reduces craving and the chances of relapse. Particularly during a phase of withdrawal or early recovery when cravings and dysphoria may be most severe, the administration of specific neuronutrients that attempt to reverse specific patterns of neurochemical dysfunction caused by the chronic use of a specific chemical can constitute an invaluable relapse-prevention strategy.

The chances of clients signing out of an inpatient detoxification unit or a 28-day inpatient rehabilitation program or failing to comply with an outpatient treatment regime may be reduced by administration of an appropriate neuronutrient. The combined use of neuronutrients and cranial electrical stimulation, described in Chapter 12, may further enhance a biologically based relapse-prevention strategy. The biological basis of compulsive behaviors can be effectively addressed through these kinds of interventions and reduce the chances of relapse once clients begin to pursue recovery. A biopsychosocial approach receives verification as a valid model guiding our approach to addictive disorders if we recognize the value of utilizing these kinds of interventions as one biologically geared component of a multidimensional relapse-prevention program.

Psychological Factors To Be Addressed

Part II of this book examined in depth the kind of difficulties in identifying, labeling, and processing affect that chemically dependent persons typically possess. We saw how individual psychotherapy throughout the different phases of recovery attempts to assist clients in overcoming the critical deficit of poor regulation of affective states (see Chapter 6). Appreciation was gained of how compulsive drug use (see Chapter 7) and character disorders commonly found in the chemically dependent (see Chapter 8) relate to histories of poor object relations and childhood development in dysfunctional families. In sum, Part II established the rationale for and necessity of utilizing psychodynamic and psychoanalytic treatment interventions. As we bring a biopsychosocial model to bear on our design of relapse-prevention strategies, a rationale exists for incorporating strategies that remediate deficits in self-regulatory capacities. A picture emerges from Part II of a diverse group of chemically dependent clients who possess either deficits in the regulation of affect, self-esteem, impulses, or interpersonal behavior or deficits in several, if not all, of these areas.

Essentially, a strong case can be made that the chances of relapse to chemical use are substantially reduced if we remediate underlying deficits in self-regulatory capacities. Only a client who learns to regulate or manage recurrent painful affective states without self-medication has a good chance of avoiding a slip or relapse episode. Similarly, it will probably be that client who begins to make improvements in the regulation of self-esteem who can avoid responding to a plummet in self-esteem or narcissistic injury without resorting to a chemical-induced false bravado and confidence. The client suffering from inhibitions and phobias similarly may find relief from anxiety and greater ease in regulating sexual or aggressive impulses once chemically relaxed. And, in general, interpersonal ease may replace interpersonal conflict and tension when the chemical disinhibits, relaxes, or stimulates the user. Each of these effects demonstrates that chemicals are experienced as extrareinforcing when they serve to regulate feeling states, self-esteem, impulses, and interpersonal behavior. Above and beyond the evidence that alcohol, heroin, and cocaine are powerful positive reinforcers—as shown by laboratory-animal self-administration studies—is the clinical evidence that chemicals are extrareinforcing for those users who experience the added benefit of improved self-regulation (Wallace, 1991).

Wallace (1991) describes in some detail how experimental and recreational users are more likely to advance to abuse and dependence syndromes when they possess certain risk factors. These risk factors include being the adult child of an alcoholic or of a dysfunctional family and childhood trauma. In such cases, experimental or recreational use of chemicals may not be fun, but may be risky. The extrareinforcing effect of these chemicals in temporarily improving self-regulatory capacities or in compensating for deficits in self-regulation can easily lead to movement toward abuse and dependence syndromes.

The point here is that relapse prevention needs to include reducing the risk of relapse to chemical use by remediating the underlying susceptibility or predisposition to abuse and dependence syndromes rooted in poor self-regulatory capacities. In this way, we not only may reduce the risk of relapse to chemical use, but also that of symptom substitution. Without remediation of underlying psychopathology—which may or may not meet criteria for a *Diagnostic and Statistical Manual of Mental Disorders* (DSM-III-R) diagnosis—the chance that one will engage in the abuse of some new designer chemical or in shopaholism, overeating, workaholism, gambling, or any compulsive and destructive behavior remains. Thus relapse prevention may include the delivery of long-term group therapy (see Chapter 4) or long-term individual psychotherapy throughout recovery (Chapter 6). Therapeutic support initially can assist clients in self-regulation and then gradually lead to substantial improvements in self-regulatory capacities. From the perspective of a biopsychosocial model of addiction, those interventions that address critical psychological factors should be viewed as constituting an important and legitimate set of relapse-prevention strategies. As a prelude to psychotherapy, and often as a valid intervention itself, psychoeducation on childhood development in alcoholic and dysfunctional families and the consequent problems in self-regulation can also provide a relapse-prevention strategy, as described in detail elsewhere (Wallace, 1989b, 1991).

Hence, in a biopsychosocial approach to addiction and relapse prevention, psychological factors that may maintain the addictive process and predispose persons to experience a relapse need to be addressed as part of a multidimensional relapse-prevention program.

Social-Environmental Factors To Be Addressed

Experiences in a social-learning and environmental context were discussed in Chapter 9 from Hawkins' cognitive-behavioral perspective. There we saw attention paid to cognitive social-learning mechanisms and psychosocial-skills deficits. Relapse can be prevented, from this perspective, via the kind of cognitive interventions and skills training that Marlatt and Gordon (1985) and Gossop (1989) describe. Interventions in a relapse-prevention program, therefore, might include the practicing of refusal skills, assertiveness training, relaxation training, and rehearsal of cognitive and behavioral strategies to be used in high-risk situations. Such relapse-prevention models place great emphasis on the teaching of cognitive and behavioral techniques likely to produce an effective coping response when faced with a high-risk situation.

From my (Wallace, 1991) perspective, relapse-prevention strategies can also include psychoeducation, which teaches patients about classically conditioned stimuli and responses. Also taught in practical and clear terms is the process of extinction of classically conditioned responses. In teaching these concepts (Wallace, 1989b, 1991), I draw upon the power of metaphorical forms of communications.

Clients are also encouraged to liken strategies used to avoid the police and elaborate behavioral strategies to purchase drugs to the kind of cautious, planned, and controlled behaviors necessary to protect oneself from classically conditioned stimuli early in recovery. Metaphors explain the gradual process of extinction and how, as extinction occurs, individuals gradually gain strength and autonomy in being able to expand their behavioral repertoire beyond an initial rigid avoidance of classically conditioned stimuli. "Hard tests" and "easier tests" that need, respectively, to be delayed and initially attempted are explained via graphic visual metaphors. In this way, psychoeducation, drawing heavily on different metaphorical forms of communication, conveys complex classical conditioning principles that prepare clients for the challenge of relapse. Clients receive an intellectual and cognitive framework in which to understand the risk of relapse, triggers of relapse episodes, and how the risk of relapse may be gradually reduced. The kind of relapse-prevention interventions (Wallace, 1989b, 1991) described can augment the more traditional relapse-prevention strategies arising from the more traditional cognitive-behavioral models discussed above.

Our knowledge of clients' vulnerability in the initial three to six months of recovery when the risk of relapse is greatest also dictates certain "client-to-treatment-modality" matching strategies beyond what Marlatt (1988) suggests. Particular concern can be extended to clients who must return to homes where spouses or family members openly abuse chemicals or to environments saturated with crack houses and crack dealers openly peddling drugs. These circumstances reinforce a rationale for matching such clients to residential therapeutic communities (TCs) (see Chapter 4). In such cases, the TC represents a safe drug-free environment and therapeutic milieu from which classically conditioned stimuli in the environment can be countered via escorted passes out of the facility. Each escorted pass to the outside world constitutes an extinction trial. Those individuals in a TC who must be escorted by a senior TC resident when leaving the facility for the initial three to six months of abstinence receive the kind of support and supervision that maximize their chances of successfully managing classically conditioned responses without relapsing to chemical use. By the time one no longer needs an escort in order to leave the TC on passes, a substantial number of naturally occurring extinction trials have been experienced over a three- to six-month period of escorted outside visits with exposure to conditioned stimuli. Psychoeducation (Wallace, 1989b, 1991) attempts to explain how these kinds of processes occur.

Also, for the most debilitated individuals who are trying to pursue recovery, the TC plays an important role by building into clients' lives sources of positive reinforcement that begin to compete with the recollection of the positive reinforcement of the chemical-induced euphoria. For all recovering clients, positive reinforcers of employment, spouses, family support, savings accounts, child custody, a home, and other rewards provide important sources of positive reinforcement that sustain efforts to maintain abstinence and avoid relapse. In this way, we can interpret chronic relapse in homeless, disaffiliated, chemically dependent clients as understandable when no competing sources of positive reinforcement are available and poorly funded programs and lack of housing fail to permit the systematic addition of sources of positive reinforcement to homeless clients' lives. On the other hand, the levels of motivation of clients who are employed, married, or fear the loss of sources of positive reinforcement can be understood in light of the critical role that alternative sources of reinforcement play in a recovering person's life.

In this section, we have seen how a consideration of social-environmental factors—within a biopsychosocial approach—suggests the need for relapse-prevention interventions that derive from a social learning, operant conditioning, and classical conditioning theoretical base.

CONCLUSION

This chapter has demonstrated that a biopsychosocial model of addictive disorders supports the utilization of a multidimensional approach to relapse prevention that addresses biological, psychological, and social factors likely to contribute to a relapse episode. A broad, multidimensional approach to relapse prevention can be seen as including the provision of neuronutrients, the remediation of poor self-regulatory capacities and underlying psychopathology, and the provision of interventions based on behavioral principles of learning. Another central point involves delivering some form of relapse prevention across all phases of recovery. However, several issues remain worthy of mention as we conclude this chapter.

Toward an Integrated Rationale for Treatment

As a consequence of this kind of broad approach to relapse prevention, utilizing an array of relapse-prevention interventions, we in effect forge an integrated theoretical rationale for relapse-prevention strategies. Physiologically or biologically based theories, psychodynamic or psychoanalytic theory, and cognitive-behavioral or social learning theory achieve integration within a biopsychosocial theory of addiction and relapse prevention.

Recognizing Points of Convergence Across Disparate Approaches

Movement toward an integrated theory also helps us to appreciate how, within certain treatment and relapse approaches, there is an implicit recognition of the value of factors not technically within a particular approach's domain. For example, although there are tremendous conflict and controversy between the advocates of a disease model of alcoholism and the social-learning proponents of controlled drinking (Miller & Giannini, 1990; Peele, 1990; Brochu, 1990; Heather, 1990; Gorman, 1989), the following point is worthy of consideration. Alcoholics Anonymous and 12-step programs have long advocated the avoidance of certain people, places, and things. This is straightforward relapse-prevention education to avoid classically conditioned stimuli. However, an even more elaborate relapse-prevention education program might teach the newly abstinent about processes of extinction and provide the hope for better handling in the future of some people, places, and things that one cannot avoid. Although this might violate the 12-step program admonition to "keep it simple," metaphorical forms of communication convey complex concepts in clear and simple graphic and visual images (see Wallace, 1989b, 1991). We may possess some wisdom in trying to recognize similarities across approaches (disease-model versus social-learning approach) and how movement toward integration of theories can expand our arsenal of relapse-prevention techniques under a biopsychosocial "umbrella" approach.

This may be wise if it means the delivery of more efficacious treatment and greater success in helping clients avoid relapse episodes. A biopsychosocial model provides a scientific, theoretical, and practical clinical foundation upon which we can resolve futile, and often hostile, debate (Heather, 1990; Gorman, 1989). We are forced to recognize such points of convergence across perspectives and can ground some research as valid within a biological domain (see Chapter 12), view other clinical observations and case material as valid within a psychological domain, and appreciate other cognitive-behavioral and social-learning contributions to relapse prevention and the teaching of controlled drinking as valid in a social-environmental domain.

Other seemingly disparate approaches possess points of convergence. Psychodynamic and cognitive-behavioral approaches can, in fact, provide cross-validation for each other. Cognitive-behavioral approaches frequently end up addressing how to improve coping strategies in face of negative emotion (Marlatt & Gordon, 1985; Carmody, 1990). Coping strategies are frequently taught that aim to help clients compensate for what begins to sound like the possession of poor self-regulatory capacities (Carmody, 1990). It seems as though such interventions can be categorized as efforts to compensate for poor self-regulatory capacities from a cognitive-behavioral perspective. In this way, cognitive-behavioral approaches enter into a domain typically seen as belonging to the psychodynamically trained clinician—the improved regulation of affect, self-esteem, impulses, and interpersonal behavior.

On the other hand, I have noted in psychodynamic psychotherapy sessions a phenomenon strongly suggesting the role of cognitions and the validity of cognitive theory. Typically, the point at which patients begin to cry is the point at which they have just delivered to themselves a negative cognitive self-statement. These negative cognitive self-statements also usually express negative outcome expectations; for example, "I'm no good," "I can't do anything right," or, "My father was right, I'll never amount to anything." The straightforward psychodynamic technique I was taught to employ suddenly is a procedure that validates a cognitive theory. Also, few of us can deny that we achieve greater efficacy as clinicians working with the chemically dependent when we draw upon behavioral principles and explain why classically conditioned stimuli are to be avoided, why behavior will not be restricted forever (extinction), and the importance of work and love (positive reinforcers).

In this way, there are more points of convergence across supposedly distinct and disparate clinical approaches than one might initially surmise. A biopsychosocial approach to relapse prevention moves us toward appreciation of the value of an integrated theory that justifies a broad multidimensional approach to relapse prevention, as articulated in this chapter.

Other Issues in Relapse Prevention

Clearly, this chapter cannot cover in a comprehensive way all the issues involved in relapse prevention. The reader is referred elsewhere for a more detailed understanding of the topic and the contemporary approaches (Young, 1990; Weiner, Wallen, & Zankowski, 1990; Gorski, 1990; Shiffman, 1989; Heather & Stallard, 1989; Eiser, 1989; Beridge, 1989; Saunders & Allsop, 1989; Allsop & Saunders, 1989; Rankin, 1989; Sutton, 1989; Marlatt & Gordon, 1989; Brown, 1989; Curry, Marlatt, Peterson, & Lutton, 1988; Marlatt & Gordon, 1985). However, a few issues are worthy of brief mention.

When individuals do experience a slip or relapse episode, we must engage in a clinical relapse interview (see Wallace, 1991) or microanalysis of the lapse or relapse (Marlatt, 1985a) and detect the determinants of that relapse. Our analysis must recognize that relapse is a process and not necessarily a discrete event occurring at a specific time. We must discover the multideterminants of relapse episodes that suggest the role and interplay of psychological/personality determinants and environmental/interpersonal determinants that subtly interact (Wallace, 1989b, 1991). Our microanalysis of relapse episodes must end with concrete recommendations on how treatment must be intensified or modified (add a sponsor, add individual sessions, add couples therapy, send to a TC, try neuronutrients or pharmacological adjuncts) or how a client's behavior must be modified (avoid a mother who makes one angry, talk about feelings) in light of the findings from our analysis of the episode. Relapse must be viewed as a learning opportunity and analyzed in detail as such.

Staff members must not avoid relapse-prevention education for fear that mentioning the word "relapse" will give clients permission to pursue it. We face clients' dismay and rejection of treatment, as well as their wrath, when we fail to educate them and do not arm them with relapse-prevention strategies.

Relapse Prevention Across Phases of Recovery

We must also remember that outcome-evaluation studies (suggesting that, with intensive and comprehensive treatment, up to 64% to 68% of clients have successful outcomes) include over 50% who slipped to some chemical use at least once during the six- to 24-month follow-up period (Washton & Stone-Washton, 1990). In this way, we must realize that the ultimate relapse prevention is providing clients with a continuum of care across phases of recovery—withdrawal phase, phase of prolonging abstinence, and a phase of pursuing lifetime recovery. Only a client in treatment—whether sober one day, one month, or one year—can receive assistance in analyzing a slip and avoiding a full-blown relapse.

It is to be hoped that the treatments in which clients participate are sensitive to the particular biological, psychological, and social-environmental vulnerabilities the clients possess in different phases of recovery. These treatments must also recognize the stresses and risks associated with the various phases. If clients participate in some kind of treatment throughout the different phases of recovery and they do experience a slip, it is hoped that treatment staff members, psychotherapists, sponsors, and 12-step program members will be there to provide the support and assistance necessary in analyzing the return to chemical use to ensure that the slip does not become a full-blown relapse.

SUMMARY OF CHAPTER GOALS

This chapter has aspired to suggest that diverse treatment staff members, the private psychotherapist, and the 12-step program sponsor each needs to take a broader view of relapse, as suggested by a biopsychosocial approach. A treatment perspective brought to bear on the situation of a client in a particular phase of recovery needs to reflect a broad multidimensional view of relapse prevention. Such a treatment perspective can maximize the chances of successful long-term recovery for chemically dependent patients.

If we deliver a biological intervention for what we view as a disease, we must also recognize the value of referring a client to a relapse-prevention group that might even be based on social-learning theory and cognitive-behavioral principles. Also, that same client might need a referral from the relapse-prevention group leader for psychodynamically oriented individual psychotherapy to address underlying psychopathology related, for example, to childhood molestation or physical abuse. If we deliver private individual psychotherapy, we must recognize that referral of chronic chemical users to inpatient treatment or to receive neuronutrient therapy and/or cranial electrical stimulation may be a critical treatment adjunct that will substantially reduce the chances of relapse to chemical use. Beyond the provision of individual psychotherapy, we also need to urge our patients to participate in 12-step programs so they can receive social support and exposure to role models that can further enhance their chances for successful recovery—even if we disagree with the disease concept advocated in such groups. If we are a 12-step program sponsor, we must recognize that a 3:00 A.M. telephone call reporting nightmares and flashbacks of childhood sexual abuse necessitates a recommendation for individual psychotherapy, which may reduce the chances of relapse for that person who has been abstinent for nearly a year. Also, a 12-step program member taking SAAVE, tropamine (see Chapter 12), or naltrexone (Fram, Marmo, & Holden, 1989) early in recovery should be supported and not admonished for utilizing a neuronutrient or pharmacological adjunct for purposes of relapse prevention.

The emergence of this kind of sensitive appreciation on the part of diverse chemical-dependency-treatment professionals and 12-step program sponsors of the value of a multidimensional approach to relapse prevention is the goal of this chapter. A growing population of chemically dependent clients who aspire to successful long-term recovery needs researchers and clinicians to move away from bickering and defensive protection of their "turfs" toward a more integrated treatment field capable of improving long-term-treatment outcomes.

REFERENCES

Allsop, S., & Saunders, B. (1989). Relapse and alcohol problems. In M. Gossop (Ed.), *Relapse and addictive behaviour.* New York: Tavistock/Routledge.

Beridge, V. (1989). The end of optimism: The prehistory of relapse. In M. Gossop (Ed.), *Relapse and addictive behaviour.* New York: Tavistock/Routledge.

Brochu, S. (1990). Abstinence versus nonabstinence: The objectives of alcoholism rehabilitation programs in Quebec. *Journal of Psychoactive Drugs, 22,* 15–21.

Brown, R.I.F. (1989). Relapses from a gambling perspective. In M. Gossop (Ed.), *Relapse and addictive behaviour.* New York: Tavistock/Routledge.

Carmody, T.P. (1990). Preventing relapse in the treatment of nicotine addiction: Current issues and future directions. *Journal of Psychoactive Drugs, 22,* 211–238.

Cummings, C., Gordon, J., & Marlatt, G.A. (1980). Relapse: Strategies of prevention and prediction. In W.R. Miller (Ed.), *The addictive behaviors.* Oxford, U.K.: Pergamon Press.

Curry, S., Marlatt, G.A., Peterson, A.V., & Lutton, J. (1988). Survival analysis and assessment of relapse rates. In D.M. Donovan & G.A. Marlatt (Eds.), *Assessment of addictive behaviors.* New York: Guilford.

Donovan, D.M., & Marlatt, G.A. (Eds.). (1988). *Assessment of addictive behaviors.* New York: Guilford.

Eiser, J.R. (1989). Attitudes and learning in addiction and relapse. In M. Gossop (Ed.), *Relapse and addictive behaviour.* New York: Tavistock/Routledge.

Fram, D.H., Marmo, J., & Holden, R. (1989). Naltrexone treatment—the problem of patient acceptance. *Journal of Substance Abuse Treatment, 6,* 119–122.

Gorman, D.M. (1989). Is the "new" problem drinking concept of Heather & Robertson more useful in advancing scientific knowledge than the "old" disease concept? *British Journal of Addiction, 84,* 843–845.

Gorski, T.T. (1990). The Cenaps model of relapse prevention: Basic principles and procedures. *Journal of Psychoactive Drugs, 22,* 125–133.

Gossop, M. (Ed). (1989). *Relapse and addictive behaviour.* New York: Tavistock/Routledge.

Heather, N. (1990). Problem drinking as a form of learned behaviour: A final rejoinder to Gorman and Edwards. *British Journal of Addiction, 85,* 617–620.

Heather, N., & Stallard, A. (1989). Does the Marlatt model underestimate the importance of conditioned craving in the relapse process? In M. Gossop (Ed.), *Relapse and addictive behaviour.* New York: Tavistock/Routledge.

Hunt, W.A., Barnett, L., & Branch, L. G. (1971). Relapse rates in addiction programs. *Journal of Clinical Psychology, 27,* 455–456.

Marlatt, G.A. (1985a). Relapse prevention: Theoretical rationale and overview of the model. In G.A. Marlatt & J.R. Gordon (Eds.), *Relapse prevention: Maintenance strategies in the treatment of addictive behaviors.* New York: Guilford.

Marlatt, G.A. (1985b). Situational determinants of relapse and skill-training interventions. In G.A. Marlatt & J.R. Gordon (Eds.), *Relapse prevention: Maintenance strategies in the treatment of addictive behaviors.* New York: Guilford.

Marlatt, G.A. (1985c). Cognitive factors in the relapse process. In G.A. Marlatt & J.R. Gordon (Eds.), *Relapse prevention: Maintenance strategies in the treatment of addictive behaviors.* New York: Guilford.

Marlatt, G.A. (1985d). Cognitive assessment and intervention procedures for relapse prevention. In G.A. Marlatt & J.R. Gordon (Eds.), *Relapse prevention: Maintenance strategies in the treatment of addictive behaviors.* New York: Guilford.

Marlatt, G.A. (1985e). Lifestyle modification. In G.A. Marlatt & J.R. Gordon (Eds.), *Relapse prevention: Maintenance strategies in the treatment of addictive behaviors.* New York: Guilford.

Marlatt, G.A. (1988). Matching clients to treatment: Treatment models and stages of change. In D.M. Donovan & G.A. Marlatt (Eds.), *Assessment of addictive behaviors.* New York: Guilford.

Marlatt, G.A., & Gordon, J.R. (Eds.) (1985). *Relapse prevention: Maintenance strategies in the treatment of addictive behaviors.* New York: Guilford.

Marlatt, G.A., & Gordon, J. (1989). Relapse prevention: Future directions. In M. Gossop (Ed.), *Relapse and addictive behaviour.* New York: Tavistock/Routledge.

Miller, N.A., & Giannini, A.J. (1990). The disease model of addiction: A biopsychiatrist's view. *Journal of Psychoactive Drugs, 22,* 83–85.

Peele, S. (1990). Why and by whom the American alcoholism treatment industry is under siege. *Journal of Psychoactive Drugs, 22,* 1–13.

Rankin, H. (1989). Relapse and eating disorders: The recurring illusion. In M. Gossop (Ed.), *Relapse and addictive behaviour.* New York: Tavistock/Routledge.

Saunders, B., & Allsop, S. (1989). Relapse: A critique. In M. Gossop (Ed.), *Relapse and addictive behaviour.* New York: Tavistock/Routledge.

Shiffman, S. (1989). Conceptual issues in the study of relapse. In M. Gossop (Ed.), *Relapse and addictive behaviour.* New York: Tavistock/Routledge.

Sutton, S. (1989). Relapse following smoking cessation: A critical review of current theory and research. In M. Gossop (Ed.), *Relapse and addictive behaviour.* New York: Tavistock/Routledge.

Wallace, B.C. (1989a). Psychological and environmental determinants of relapse in compulsive crack cocaine smokers. *Journal of Substance Abuse Treatment, 6,* 95–106.

Wallace, B.C. (1989b). Relapse prevention in psychoeducational groups. *Journal of Substance Abuse Treatment, 6,* 229–239.

Wallace, B.C. (1990). Treating crack cocaine dependence: The critical role of relapse prevention. *Journal of Psychoactive Drugs, 22,* 149–158.

Wallace, B.C. (1991). *Crack cocaine: A practical treatment approach for the chemically dependent.* New York: Brunner/Mazel.

Washton, A.M., & Stone-Washton, N. (1990). Abstinence and relapse in outpatient cocaine addicts. *Journal of Psychoactive Drugs, 22,* 135–147.

Weiner, H.D., Wallen, M.C., & Zankowski, G.L. (1990). Culture and social class as intervening variables in relapse prevention with chemically dependent women. *Journal of Psychoactive Drugs, 22,* 239–248.

Young, E.B. (1990). The role of incest issues in relapse. *Journal of Psychoactive Drugs, 22,* 249–258.

PART IV

CONTEMPORARY TRENDS IN RESEARCH AND IMPLICATIONS FOR TREATMENT

12

Neurogenetics of Compulsive Disease: Neuronutrients as Adjuncts to Recovery

Kenneth Blum, Ph.D.

Eric Braverman, M.D.

James E. Payne

Olivia Finley, M.D.

Laurel Loeblich-Smith, Ph.D.

Daniel A. Hoffman, M.D.

Compulsive disease, particularly alcoholism, is a major and devastating health problem with an unknown etiological base. Most recently, the question of whether environment or heredity is the prime determinant for the development of compulsive disease continues to receive extensive attention worldwide. In this regard, the United States Supreme Court sided with the notion that alcoholism was not a disease (Traynor v. Turnage, 1988). On the other side, Blum and colleagues found a high association of the dopamine D_2 receptor gene in alcoholism (Blum, et al. & Cook, 1990). This is the first specific gene with such a significant correlation that might confer susceptibility on at least one form of alcoholism. Although more research is required further to confirm these findings, for now this research favors the view that alcoholism is a biogenetic disorder triggered by the environment. However, in terms of treating the neurochemistry

ACKNOWLEDGMENTS. The authors appreciate the grant supplied to Kenneth Blum by NeuroGenesis, Inc. Portions of this chapter are excerpted from *Alcohol and the Addictive Brain: New Hope for Alcoholics from Biogenetic Research* by Kenneth Blum, Ph.D. in collaboration with James E. Payne. Copyright © 1991 by The Free Press, a Division of Macmillan, Inc. Reprinted with permission of the publisher. The authors would like to acknowledge the assistance of their colleagues, Drs. Douglas Cook, Raymond Brown, Michael Trachtenberg, Richard Smayda, E.P. Noble, P.J. Sheridan, and Ray Smith. They also wish to acknowledge the work of Sadie Phillips in typing the manuscript.

of chemically dependent individuals as it relates to certain behavioral anomalies, therapists must begin to understand its complexity.

With this in mind, the purpose of this chapter is to develop a brief but not critical review of the neurogenetics of compulsive disease, providing a blueprint for potential prevention and treatment strategies. Let us briefly and uncritically review the progress that had been made by the beginning of 1990 in our understanding of the genetics of alcohol-craving behavior and the triggering effect of the environment. Although the goal here is to provide a concise understanding of some of the more general research in the field of alcoholism, certain of these findings can be extended to all compulsive diseases, including drug abuse and eating disorders.

PROGRESS TO DATE

Animal Models

McClearn (McClearn & Rodgers, 1959), following up leads suggested by Williams, Berry, and Beerstacher (1949), and Mirone (1957) had developed the C57 strain of mice by 1959 into a model that could be used as a research tool for pharmacogenetics.

In 1977, T. K. Li and his colleagues at the Indiana University School of Medicine developed the P (alcohol-preferring) and NP (nonpreferring) rat strains. The P rats met most of the requirements of an animal model of alcoholism. They voluntarily drank large quantities of an alcohol solution and would actually work to obtain alcohol by pressing a lever. Eventually, they became dependent on alcohol, developed a tolerance to it, and, if it was withdrawn, experienced the symptoms of withdrawal. These mouse and rat strains proved to be powerful tools for genetic research (Lumeng, Hawkins, & Li, 1977).

Li and his associates used these tools in an experiment of classic simplicity to answer some basic questions: Why do alcohol-preferring rats prefer alcohol? Is it the taste or smell—or is it the pharmacological effect of alcohol that the animal craves?

To eliminate the possibility that their alcohol-preferring rat strain sought alcohol because of its taste or smell, the scientists used an apparatus that automatically delivered water or an alcohol solution directly into the stomach of P and NP rats when they consumed one of two flavored-water solutions. If they drank one solution, they automatically received an injection of alcohol into their stomach. If they drank the other solution, they received an injection of plain water. The idea was to see if animals could be trained or conditioned to associate a particular flavor with the presence or absence of the pharmacological effect of alcohol.

The P rats drank up to 14 times more of the flavor linked to alcohol than the NP rats did, indicating that P rats like alcohol because of its euphoric effect on the central nervous system, and not because of taste or smell (Waller, McBride, Gaho, Lumeng, & Li, 1984).

Familial Alcoholism: The Genetic Factor

But there were troublesome questions: Can findings from research in mice or rats be generalized to humans? Because alcoholic animals can be bred, can we assume that genetics is an important factor in human alcoholism?

Affirmative answers began to emerge as early as 1972 when M. A. Schuckit, George Winokur, and D. W. Goodwin at the Washington University School of Medicine mounted a study of children in which it was found that genetic predisposition might be more important than childhood environment in the development of alcoholism (Schuckit et al., 1972).

In 1973, D. W. Goodwin and George Winokur and their colleagues at the Psykologisk Institut, Copenhagen, found further support for this thesis in a study based on a sample of 5,483 individuals in Denmark who had been adopted in early childhood. They found that the sons of alcoholics adopted by other families were more than three times more likely to become alcoholics than were the adopted sons of nonalcoholics, and at an earlier age (Goodwin, Schulsinger, Hermansen, Fluze, & Winokur, 1973).

Additional confirmation came in 1978 when Michael Bohman at Umea University in Sweden compared rates of alcohol abuse in 2,324 adoptees and their biological parents. The sample included 1,125 men and 1,199 women, adopted before the age of 3 years. The parents included 2,261 mothers and 1,902 fathers. Bohman found that adopted sons of alcoholic fathers were three times more likely to become alcoholic than adopted sons of nonalcoholic fathers. Adopted sons of alcoholic mothers were twice as likely to become alcoholic as those whose mothers were nonalcoholic (Bohman, Cloninger, Van Knorring, & Siguardsen, 1978).

These earlier studies came into focus in an important series of investigations of Swedish adoptees that were carried out by C. R. Cloninger and M. Bohman, and colleagues at the Washington University School of Medicine.

They sought to answer four questions:

- What characteristics of the *biological* parents influence the risk of alcohol abuse in the adoptees?
- What characteristics of the *adoptive* parents influence the risk of alcohol abuse in the adoptees?
- How do genetic and environmental factors interact in the development of alcohol abuse?
- Is the genetic predisposition to alcoholism expressed in other psychopathological ways, depending on the environment and sex of the individual?

The investigators studied 862 men and 913 women of known parentage who had been adopted before the age of 3 by nonrelatives. A total of 35.3% of the adopted children had at least one biological parent known to abuse alcohol. A careful study was made of the subjects, subdivided in terms of congenital background and post-natal home environment, and further divided into four subgroups according to their degree of alcoholism: none, mild, moderate, or severe. Characteristics of the biological parents were examined to identify those associated with a particular degree of alcoholism in the adoptees. To determine the effect of postnatal factors, the adoptive parents were also examined to identify influences that might be associated with particular degrees of alcoholism in the adoptees. Specific findings were:

- Of the sons of alcoholic biological fathers, 22.8% were alcoholic, compared with 14.7% of the sons who did not have an alcoholic biological parent.
- Of the sons of alcoholic biological mothers, 28.1% were alcohol abusers, compared with 14.7% of sons who did not have an alcoholic biological parent.
- Of the daughters of alcoholic biological mothers, 10.8% were alcohol abusers, compared with 2.8% of daughters who did not have an alcoholic biological parent.
- Alcoholism in the *adoptive* parents was not a factor in whether or not adoptees would become alcoholic, indicating that home environment and imitation of elders were not determining factors (Cloninger, 1983; Bohman et al., 1984).

Investigators identified two distinct types of genetic predisposition to alcoholism (Cloninger, Bohman, & Sigvardsson, 1981):

1. *Type I: milieu-limited alcoholism.* The investigators found this to be the most common type of alcoholism. Occurring in both males and females, this type of alcoholism requires both a genetic predisposition and triggering influences in the environment. Milieu-limited alcoholism is not likely to be severe and often goes untreated. It is usually associated with mild, untreated, adult-onset alcohol abuse in either biological parent. Typically, the alcoholic parent has not been a lawbreaker. Severity may be associated with low social status or unskilled occupation of the adoptive father. Milieu-limited alcohol abuse tends to have its onset after 25 years of age.

2. *Type 2: male-limited alcoholism.* The data suggested that this severe type of genetic predisposition occurs only in men. It is less prevalent than milieu-limited alcoholism and appears to be unaffected by environment. In families with male-limited susceptibility, alcohol abuse is found to be nine times greater in the adopted sons, regardless of the environment after their adoption. Male-limited susceptibility is related to severe alcoholism in the biological father, often severe enough to require treatment, and often involving law breaking, but is not associated with alcoholism in the biological mother. The onset of this particular type of alcoholism often comes early, before 25 years of age, and may be accompanied by serious encounters with the law. Postnatal influences in the adoptive family do not influence the development of alco-

holism in the son, but may affect its severity. An interesting sidelight is that adoptees with male-limited alcoholism generally are not as severely afflicted as their fathers.

These classifications represent an important contribution to our understanding of the interaction of genetics and environment, but some aspects relating to sex and age differences have proved controversial. When Marc Schuckit and his group, for example, attempted to correlate age of onset with the Type I and Type II classifications, they found that age of onset correlated not with types of alcoholism, but with antisocial personality disorder.

Schuckit's data emphasize the important association between early age at onset of alcoholism and more severe clinical characteristics, including the number of alcohol-related social complications, other drug use, and childhood criminality among primary alcoholics. The Type I-versus-Type II construct did not further contribute to the classification of alcoholic subtypes differing in clinical histories, suggesting that while this scheme is useful heuristically, further testing of its relevance is needed (Schuckit, 1990).

The National Institute on Alcohol Abuse and Alcoholism now believes that there are three types of alcoholism, with Type III characterizing individuals with antisocial personality disorders. The Type III classification is arbitrary and is based on Schuckit's findings that age of onset relates to antisocial personality rather than the Type I or Type II classification.

All of the human genetic studies discussed above help to establish a strong role for genetic predisposition and to clarify the role of environmental factors in activating that predisposition.

Electrophysiological Markers of Inherited Susceptibility in Humans

Toward the end of the 1970s, scientists were exploring a fascinating theory—that genetic susceptibility to alcoholism in humans may be accompanied by electrophysiological "markers" that can be detected and measured. Henri Begleiter and B. Porjesz at the State University of New York in Brooklyn pioneered this research beginning in the late 1970s and carried it forward in a series of highly innovative experiments that are continuing.

The researchers attached electrodes to the scalps of their subjects to detect, amplify, and characterize electrical events in the brain resulting from incoming stimuli or accompanying specific mental processes. They made recordings of electrical activity in response to stimuli, with particular attention to a waveform designated "P₃," or P300.

They compared 25 boys aged 7 to 13 years who were sons of alcoholic fathers with a control group of 25 boys who had no family history of alcoholism. None of the boys in either group used alcohol or drugs. The goal was to explore possible electrophysiological differences that might ultimately be used as a diagnostic tool, or "marker," to identify children at high risk. The investigators found that in response to visual stimuli, the P_3 wave had a markedly reduced amplitude in the sons of alcoholic fathers. They concluded, however, that the data were not sufficiently definitive for use as a clinical tool.

In 1984, Begleiter reported decreased amplitude in the P_3 wave in abstinent, formerly severe, chronic alcoholics. This study suggested that decreases in P_3 activity are not a consequence of years of heavy drinking, but are genetic antecedents of alcohol abuse. These neurophysiological observations of boys at risk for alcoholism are striking in that they were obtained without the use of alcohol in sons of alcoholics not previously exposed to alcohol as a drug of abuse. However, their data do not allow them to infer that the observed P_3 wave deficits in high-risk male children represent a predisposing factor for subsequent alcohol abuse.

Longitudinal studies to examine the relationship between the present neurological findings in male children and future patterns of alcohol intake are necessary. The results of the above experiments suggested that differences in the P_3 wave may be related more to genetics than to the pharmacological effects of alcohol. Begleiter and Porjesz (1990) most recently concluded that the P_3 wave provides a phenotype marker, distinguishing those at risk for alcoholism.

Genetic Factors in Sensitivity to Alcohol

By the mid-1980s, additional genetic questions were beginning to be asked. For example, assuming that children of alcoholics are at special risk for developing alcoholism, what are the specific genetic determinants of that risk? Are there other observable differences in bodily response to alcohol in animals and humans having a genetic predisposition?

Earlier, Elston, Blum, DeLallo, and Briggs (1982) found that alcohol-preferring mice required a higher dose of alcohol to disturb their ability to balance on a bar than did water-preferring mice. This suggested that alcohol-preferring mice are, to some degree, protected from the early adverse effects of intoxication.

Schuckit observed a similar reduction of sensitivity in humans. His group had studied 23 nonalcoholic males with close relatives who were alcoholics. He compared these people with a matched set of nonalcoholic males who had no family history of alcoholism. All the subjects received, in rapid succession, three drinks of a sweetened, noncarbonated beverage to which alcohol had been added. They were then asked to describe their feelings, either positive ("talkative, elated, high"), negative ("dizzy, tired, sad"), or both. The subjects who had close alcoholic relatives reported less intense *positive* and *negative* feelings following the beverage intake than those who had no alcoholic relatives (Schuckit, 1984).

In a subsequent experiment with two similar groups, Schuckit found an objective way to measure physiological responses to alcohol, without reliance on self-reporting. He developed a "body sway" test in which the subjects were asked to wear a harness connected by a rope to a pulley. Any change of body position caused a movement of the pulley, which was measured and recorded. It was found that, following the ingestion of alcohol, the degree of sway was significantly less in the nonalcoholic individuals who had close alcoholic relatives than in the nonalcoholic individuals who did not have close alcoholic relatives.

According to Schuckit (1985), even though a single genetic factor may not explain the predisposition in all individuals, it is possible that a simple behavioral measure of response to alcohol might be used as a marker to identify people at the highest risk. This could hold true even if alcoholism proves to be the result of multiple genetic factors interacting with multiple factors in the environment.

The fact that individuals from families with a history of alcoholism are less sensitive to the positive and negative effects of alcohol tends to encourage them to "take a chance" with drinking, opening the way to alcohol abuse since they perceive that they are more tolerant of alcohol than their peers. The experiments were reported accurately by the press, and helped to dispel the long-held myth that "he men" and strong-willed women can "hold their liquor." On the contrary, the findings suggested that people who do not "get drunk" easily in the beginning are the ones who are at the greatest risk of becoming alcoholics.

Electrophysiological Markers in Children at Risk: A Neurocognitive Profile

Noble and associates used electrophysiological techniques to investigate cognitive functions in alcoholic fathers and their sons. They selected 45 father–son pairs, a total of 90 subjects, and divided them into three groups:

1. Group A+, a high-risk group, had a strong family history of alcoholism. It consisted of 15 boys and their recovering alcoholic fathers. The fathers had at least one close alcoholic relative.
2. Group NA+, an intermediate-risk group, had a strong family history of alcoholism. It consisted of 15 boys whose fathers were not alcoholic. The fathers had at least one alcoholic relative.
3. Group NA–, a low-risk group, had no family history of alcoholism. It consisted of 15 boys and their nonalcoholic fathers. The fathers had no close alcoholic relatives.

In the experiment, electrodes were attached to the subjects' scalps through an electroencephalograph to monitor electrical activity in the brain following the presentation of visual stimuli on a video monitor. The stimuli consisted of different shapes and colors, with a number from 0 to 9 located in the center of each shape. The task was to count, silently, the number of times that two consecutive stimuli matched in all three dimensions—shape, color, and number. Four runs of 200 stimuli each were presented, separated by five-minute rest periods.

Noble's group found that (Whipple, Parker, & Noble, 1988):

1. In the electrical tests, the A+ boys (high risk) and their fathers showed the least ability to match sets of stimuli and the lowest magnitude of electrical response as measured by the P_3 waves. In the behavioral test, they showed the poorest visual perception and memory.
2. The NA+ boys (intermediate risk) and their fathers showed a somewhat better performance.
3. The NA− boys (low risk) and their fathers performed best of all.

The researchers concluded that the atypical neurocognitive profile found in this sample of high-risk boys may be a marker for alcoholism. Follow-up studies will be needed to determine whether individuals exhibiting this profile subsequently develop drinking problems. Ultimately, the results of such studies should facilitate the early identification and prevention of alcoholism. These findings confirmed and extended Begleiter's results, in which his group showed that boys at risk of developing alcoholism have a P_3 wave deficit.

Begleiter had raised the question of whether this P_3-wave deficit could be transferred from alcoholic father to son. Noble's answer was "yes," but he raised a further question: Is this deficit related to drug- and alcohol-seeking behavior in adult life? His further experiments verified the fact that NA+ boys used significantly more alcohol and smoked more cigarettes, as well as more marijuana, than NA− boys (Noble, 1990).

Some controversy still exists over the question of cognitive differences, however. Marc Schuckit, for example, was unable to confirm neurocognitive behavioral differences between sons of alcoholics and sons of nonalcoholics (Schuckit, Bulters, et al., 1987). But other research by Oscar Parsons and his group at the University of Oklahoma confirmed Noble's initial observations (Schaeffer, Parsons, Errico, 1988).

Hormonal Response to Alcohol in Sons of Alcoholics

Schuckit and his associates were also involved during this period in evaluating the effect of alcohol on levels of the hormone prolactin in the blood of sons of alcoholics. The researchers were aware of earlier findings that alcohol causes a profound increase in blood prolactin levels in humans; now they wanted to see whether alcohol causes a greater or lesser increase in sons of alcoholics in comparison with sons of nonalcoholics. They found little difference in prolactin levels between the two groups prior to alcohol administration, but after ethanol administration, the sons of alcoholics had significantly lower prolactin levels than did the sons of nonalcoholics.

Thus, in addition to seeing psychomotor and neuroelectrical differences in sons of alcoholics, there are hormonal differences as well. Such differences might well be a "window" into neurochemical anomalies in the brain (Schuckit, Gold, et al., 1987). Since prolactin release is regulated in part by the dopaminergic system and alcohol causes dopamine release, these differences in prolactin levels may indicate a genetic defect in the brain of sons of alcoholics that results in a predisposition to alcohol-seeking behavior.

ETHANOL AND NEUROMODULATOR INTERACTIONS: A CASCADE MODEL OF REWARD

A careful scrutiny of the literature reveals abundant studies suggesting that varied biogenic amines and peptides significantly affect human and animal alcohol intake (Topel, 1985). However, we do caution against overgeneralizing the key factors motivating alcohol drinking in humans since uncontrollable social elements such as stress, family pressure, interpersonal relationships, and economics also affect human neurochemistry. These social elements complicate comparisons between uncontrollable drinking in humans and drug-seeking behavior in animals. Although acute or chronic administration of ethanol alters various neurotransmitters and these neurotransmitters or neuropeptides affect alcohol intake in experimental animal studies, we cannot exclude the possibility that these effects may not be related to such intake. The possibility exists that such factors as tolerance of or dependence on alcohol may play important roles in ethanol-dependent events.

Neuromodulator Hypothesis

Ethanol administered in vitro after acute injection or following chronic administration has been shown selectively to alter certain neurochemical systems and to have profound effects on the function of brain neurotransmitters. We contend that chronic alcohol abuse produces long-term neurochemical deficits that influence future ethanol consumption.

Myers (1963) showed that preference for ethanol was decidedly enhanced in rats repeatedly infused with several different concentrations of ethanol solutions. The rats showed preferences for ordinarily noxious ethanol without prior oral exposure to this fluid. Myers proposed that chronic alcohol abuse can directly alter the brain's biochemical "environment" to produce significant changes in behavior. These findings may not parallel the effect of alcohol on human consumption. Nevertheless, the remarkably high relapse rate of the alcoholic following sound institutional support (Pettinati, Sugermann, DiPowato, & Maurer, 1982) would suggest a possible metabolic aberration of the central nervous system.

The following observations support our thesis that intricate relationships yield ethanol-induced rewards via a cascade of events involving certain monoamines and neuropeptides (Fig. 12-1). The schematic as presented represents a model of neuromodulator cascade of "reward."

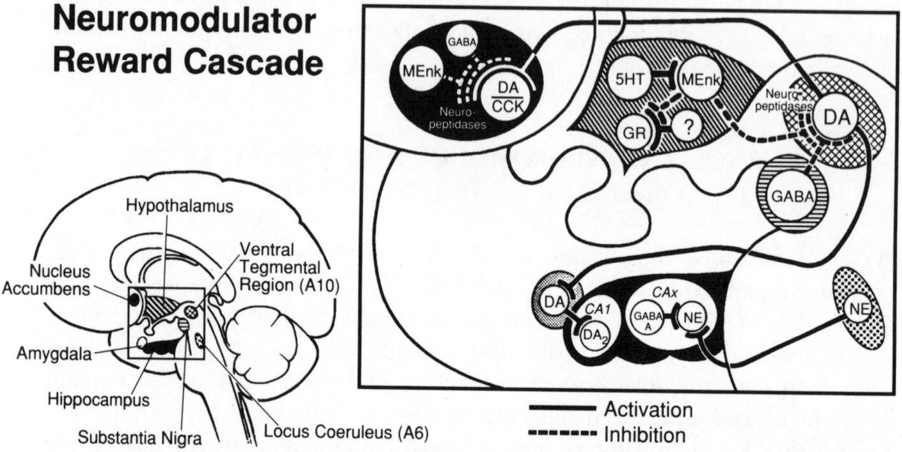

Neuromodulator Reward Cascade

Figure 12-1. *(A) A hemisection of the brain showing anatomical sites crucial to the "reward cascade" model. (B) The wiring diagram of these reward cascade sites, including neurotransmitters operating at each site. The 5-HT neurons in the hypothalamus project to met-enkephalin (MENK) neurons, which inhibit mesencephalic projections of GABA neurons that, in turn, inhibit DA neurons of the ventral tegmental region (A10). In the hypothalamus, the glucose receptor (GR), when activated, can also affect enkephalanergic neurons. The DA neurons project both rostrally to the nucleus accumbens and laterally to the DA neurons of the amygdala. In the nucleus accumbens, the interneuron GABA fine-tunes the DA and CCK. Neuropeptidase, substances involved with the destruction of opioid peptides, are involved in met-enkephalin activity in both the ventral tegmental region and the nucleus accumbens. The DA neurons of the amygdala project to the CA1 area of the hippocampus, and NE neurons of the locus coeruleus (A6) also project to areas of the hippocampus (CAx = several CA areas) that also contain NE. GABA neurons also projecting within the hippocampus go to a variety of NE-containing CA sites (CAx). The avenues of activation (continuous lines) and inhibition represent the predominant response resulting from a particular neurotransmitter. However, both activation and inhibition (interrupted lines) represent the predominant response resulting from a particular neurotransmitter. And both activation and inhibition result from the combined interactions between neurotransmitters and neuromodulators in a complex manner. When in balance, this circuit provides a homeostasis of activity and inactivity. But if a neurotransmitter or neuromodulator becomes deficient, or its receptor site is nonresponsive, then the homeostatic balance is upset, causing a change in behavior.*

Drug-Reward Mechanisms(s)

Never before has there been a unified consensus of how the earlier mentioned monoamines and opioid peptides function together to precipitate uncontrollable drinking. Now we believe that evidence supports the argument that changes in acetylcholine (ACH) and the monoamines dopamine (DA), norepinephrine (NE), and serotonin (5-HT) and γ-aminobutyric acid (GABA) under the influence of ethanol interrelate with the opioidergic system to promote a feeling of reward in the limbic area of the brain. Although it is unlikely that the cholinergic pathways directly affect this reward function (Zarevics, Weidley, & Setler, 1977), the dopaminergic system does appear to play an indirect, yet critical, role (Wise & Bozarth, 1985). Dopaminergic circuit elements mediate the rewarding effects of certain commonly abused drugs, such as opiates, cocaine, and alcohol. All of these drugs have been reported to facilitate brain stimulation reward (Crow, 1970; Koob, Spector, & Meyerhoff, 1975; Carlson & Lydic, 1976). Common mechanisms in the dopaminergic system probably mediate these drugs' rewarding effects, either within the DA cell bodies or at dopaminergic synaptic terminals (Wise & Bozarth, 1985).

Although the exact anatomical substrate of reward or positive reinforcement is unknown, various supraspinal sites have been suggested (Wise & Bozarth, 1985; German & Bowden, 1974; Olds & Olds, 1963). According to some investigators, reward circuits can be broken down into two categories: dopaminergic pathways and noradrenergic pathways (Lippa, Anlelman, Fisher, & Canfield, 1973; Poschel & Ninteman, 1963). Bozarth and Wise (1981) believe that DA is the reward substrate for both opiates and ethanol; others believe that NE is the final reward substrate for ethanol (Amit & Brown, 1982) (see Fig. 12-1). Some investigators consider it unlikely that noradrenergic pathways are directly involved in reward mechanisms (Yokel & Wise, 1975; Clavier, Fibiger, & Phillips 1976), but these conclusions are based on cocaine–DA-dependent reward systems.

Wise and Bozarth (1985) have postulated that dopaminergic systems are transsynaptically activated by rewarding brain stimulation. The descending fiber system that represents the major directly activated component of the mechanism of rewarding medial forebrain bundle (MFB) stimulation (Shizgal, Bielagan, & Kiss, 1980) terminates in the dopaminergic cells of the ventral tegmental area and substantia nigra (Corbett & Wise, 1980). Pharmacological blockade of DA receptors (Fouriezos, Hansson, & Wise, 1978), catecholamine-depletion studies with 6-hydroxydopamine (Spyraki, Fibiger, & Phillips, 1983), and anatomical mapping studies (Wise, 1980) have provided support to establish DA as the reward substrate.

The rewarding action of certain drugs such as amphetamine and cocaine involves a dopaminergic (DeWit & Wise, 1977), but not the noradrenergic, system (Spyraki, Fibiger, & Phillips, 1982). In fact, limbic dopaminergic projections appear to be most strongly involved in amphetamine reward. Intravenous amphetamine and cocaine self-administration have been greatly reduced when 6-hydroxydopamine

(Lyness, Friedle & Moore, 1979) or a DA receptor antagonist was used to destroy the catecholaminergic neurons in the nucleus accumbens, which lies in a terminal area of the mesolimbic dopaminergic pathways. Selective dopaminergic (but not noradrenergic) agonists have shown amphetamine-like rewarding properties (Baxter, Glackman, Stein, & Scerni, 1974; Davis & Smith, 1977). Similarly, evidence has implicated dopaminergic systems in the rewarding action of opiates.

Injections of opiates into various brain regions containing opioid receptors suggest that only the DA cell bodies of the ventral tegmental area are involved in the opiates' rewarding actions (Phillips & LePiane, 1980). Furthermore, opiate receptor antagonism restricted to the ventral tegmental area by local microinjection, an opiate antagonist, has reduced the rewarding impact of intravenous heroin (Britt & Wise, 1983). Other evidence involving the dopaminergic system includes DA-receptor blockade (Ettenberg, Pettit, Bloom, & Koob, 1982), whereby DA antagonists block place preferences established by rewarding opiate treatments (Spyraki et al., 1983). In brain-slice experiments, it has been reported that DA, cocaine, or the selective D_2 receptor agonist N0437 activates rewarding CA_1 target cells in the hippocampus (Stein & Belluzzi, 1986) (Fig. 12-1). Opioid peptides may be rewarding by themselves. Dynorphin-containing terminals have been demonstrated along with kappa opioid receptors in the CA_3 area of the rat hippocampus. Dynorphin is self-administered in the hippocampal Ca_3 area in experimental animals. Ionotophoresis into single neurons of dynorphin induces firing of CA_3 neurons, suggesting that dynorphin (or possibly other opioid peptides) may be a natural "reinforcement neurotransmitter" in the CA_3 area of the hippocampus (Stevens, Shiotsu, Belluzzi, & Stein, 1988). Direct or indirect stimulation of the hippocampus may occur at other distinct target cells and is, therefore, represented as CA_x target cells, as illustrated in Figure 12-1.

Opioids exert rewarding effects by activating dopaminergic cell bodies. Cocaine and amphetamines exert their rewarding effects at the dopaminergic synaptic terminals by augmenting DA release and inhibiting its reuptake (Dackis, Gold, Sweeney, Byram, & Climlco, 1987).

Wise (1980) has argued that DA is the catecholamine critically involved in the central mediation of reward. Amit and Brown (1982) argue, in contrast, that for ethanol the reward substrate is not DA, but NE.

Neurotransmitters—Common Mechanism(s) of Drug-Seeking Behavior

The consensus of the literature is that a possible common pathway of reward occurs with the abuse of alcohol, cocaine, and opiates. Neurochemical deficits have been demonstrated in both animals and humans with chronic use of these drugs.

Alcohol, cocaine, and heroin share the ability quickly to reinforce the behavior of using in experimental animals in self-administration paradigms. The rewarding properties of these seemingly diverse substances may activate a common system in the brain (Wise & Bozarth, 1987). Opiates are believed to interact with the brain reward circuits through opiate-receptor–mediated activation of the mesolimbic DA system, possibly at its origin in the ventral midbrain (Bozarth, 1983). Alcohol, through a cascade of events, including the interaction of 5-HT, endogenous opioids, and DA, activates the NE fibers of the mesolimbic circuitry (Blum & Kozlowski, 1990). In a more direct fashion, alcohol, through the subsequent formation of neuroamine condensation products, tetrahydroisoquinolines (TIQs), may interact with opioid receptors and stimulate mesolimbic catecholaminergic systems (Alraksinen et al., 1984). As an indirect agonist at catecholamine synapses (Wise, 1984), cocaine is believed to mediate reward at terminal regions of the mesolimbic DA system (Dackis & Gold, 1985), such as the nucleus accumbens (Zito, Vickers, & Roberts, 1985) and prefrontal cortex (Goeders & Smith, 1983), as well as CA1 hippocampal cells (Stein & Belluzzi, 1987).

Common pathway support for these drugs is provided by the finding that kainic-acid–induced lesions of the nucleus accumbens (Roberts & Koob, 1982) and 6-hydroxydopamine lesions of the mesolimbic DA receptors prevent the rewarding effects of opiates and cocaine (Spyraki et al., 1983), whereas blockade of NE sites similarly reduces alcohol intake (Amit & Brown, 1982). Narcotic antagonism similarly blocks the threshold-lowering action of cocaine (Bain & Kornetsky, 1987), reduces heroin reward (Bozarth & Wise, 1981), and attenuates the self-administration of ethanol in animals (Altshuler, Phillips, & Feinhandler, 1980). Additionally, opiate antagonists prevent the postshock increase of ethanol consumption in rodents (Volpicelli, Davis, & Olgin, 1986). In humans, naltrexone significantly reduces the relapse rate over a 95-day postdetoxification period in recovering alcoholics (Volpicelli et al., 1986).

Wise and Bozarth (1987), and others almost a decade earlier (Blum et al., 1976), proposed a theory suggesting that the common denominator of a wide range of addictive substances is their ability to cause psychomotor activation via activation of mesolimbic dopaminergic fibers. Recently, C57BL/6J mice have been observed to self-administer ethanol, opiates, and cocaine equally (Elmer, Meisch, & George, 1987). During acute intake, ethanol, heroin, and cocaine tend significantly to enhance the activity of neurotransmitters (i.e., 5-HT, DA, NE, GABA); however, during chronic abuse, amounts, receptor densities, and metabolic state of the neurotransmitters in tissue culture and humans are functionally at deficit (Charness, Gordon, & Amond, 1983; Javors, Blaisdell, Lee, & Bruden, 1987; Koob, Voccurino, & Amaric, 1987).

According to the available data, drug-seeking behavior results from a cascade of events in which drug-dependent processes stimulate the reward circuits of the brain via the dopaminergic/noradrenergic system(s). Figure 12-1 shows a model of the dopaminergic cascade of reward. This cascade is important since it attempts to relate both monoaminergic and peptidergic pathways as substrates of the reward process, as reviewed above.

Neurotransmitters and Food Cravings

The behavior that underlies uncontrollable ingestive activity for alcohol, drugs, and food (in particular, carbohydrates) is still unknown. However, these compulsive behaviors have been hypothesized to be caused by either predisposing environmental or congenital factors. Such factors may have as a prime feature certain alterations in brain neurochemical balance. These alterations seem to induce the phenomenon of compulsive alcohol-, drug-, and food-seeking behavior.

Previously, our laboratory proposed that a multineuronal cascade of reward may play a role in the neuropharmacology of compulsive-seeking behavior (Blum & Kozlowki, 1990). Others have hypothesized that multiple brain neurotransmitters play a significant role in the control of food intake, appetite for specific macronutrients, and patterns of meal-taking behavior. Based on extensive evidence, Leibowitz (1986) supports the idea that several brain monamines and neuropeptides control normal eating behavior. It is well established that ingestive behavior is regulated by a complex integrative network known as the mesolimbic reward circuitry (Wise, 1983). The medial and lateral portions of the hypothalamus, working in conjunction with forebrain and hindbrain sites and with peripheral autonomic endocrine pathways, together serve as important balancing signals for hunger and satiety. Additionally, similarities between animal and human neurotransmitter systems are further suggested by analyses of human cerebrospinal fluid, showing specific disturbances in brain or hypothalamic neurochemical function in association with abnormal eating patterns (Kaye et al., 1984, Kaye et al., 1985).

The primary neurotransmitters involved in eating behavior include the monoamines DA, NE, epinephrine (EPI), and 5-HT; the amino acid GABA; and a variety of neuropeptides, such as the pancreatic polypeptides, opioid peptides, hormone-releasing factors, and various gut–brain peptides.

Substantial evidence based on direct application of these neurotransmitters to neurons reveals four classes of eating-stimulatory neurotransmitters, whereas a considerably larger number of substances are shown to inhibit eating.

EATING-STIMULATORY NEUROTRANSMITTERS

The eating-stimulatory neurotransmitters include the catecholamine NE, acting through α_2-noradrenergic receptors, GABA, and three classes of neuropeptides, namely, the opioids β-endorphin, enkephalin, and dynorphin; the pancreatic polypeptide (neuropeptide Y and peptide YY); and galanin. These substances, when administered directly into the rat hypothalamus, encourage eating in satiated animals (Leibowitz, 1978).

Furthermore, chronic administration of certain monoamines (NE) and neuropeptides significantly alters daily food intake and weight gain (Stanley & Leibowitz, 1984; Lichtenstein, Marinescu, & Leibowitz, 1984).

EATING-INHIBITION NEUROTRANSMITTERS

The feeding-inhibitory neurotransmitters in the brain specifically include the monoamines DA, EPI, 5-HT, and the gut–brain peptides cholcystokinin (CCK), neurotensin, calcitonin, glucagon, and corticotropin-releasing factor (Inokuchi, Domura, Nishimura, 1984; Blundell, 1984; Bhakthavatsalam & Leibowitz, 1986; Leibowitz, Brown, & Treter, 1982).

The effects of these neurotransmitters on eating are characterized primarily by a specific change in macronutrient selection, rather than by an increase or decrease in total food intake. Many peptides, including CCK-8, bombesin, calcitonin, corticotropin-releasing factor, neurotensin, somatostatin, glucagon, and methionine-enkephalin have selective inhibitory actions on macronutrients (Dhatt, Rattan, & Mangat, 1988; Marks-Kauffman & Kanarch, 1980). Leibowitz and associates (Leibowitz et al., 1984; Leibowitz, 1985) reported that medial paraventricular nucleus (PVN) injections of NE in the rat induce a selective increase in carbohydrate ingestion with little or no change in fat and suppression of protein intake. Carbohydrate-craving behavior is consistently observed with chronic stimulation of NE and neuropeptide Y (Stanley, Daniel, et al., 1985; Stanley & Leibowitz, 1985). Certain brain monoamines also have selective actions on macronutrient intake. Dopamine-receptor blockade preferentially stimulates protein consumption, whereas catecholamine-releasing drugs such as amphetamine decrease protein ingestion (Blundell, 1983; Leibowitz et al., 1986). In contrast, 5-HT, in the medial hypothalamus, may selectively suppress carbohydrate intake, while sparing protein intake (Shor-Posner et al., 1986; Blundell, 1986).

Direct serotonergic agonists (e.g., quipazine), indirect serotonergic agonists (e.g., [+]–fenfluramine), or selective inhibitors of 5-HT uptake into serotonergic neurons (e.g., fluoxitine) decreased food ingestion in laboratory experiments (Samanin et al., 1977; Garattini et al., 1979; Goudie, Thornton & Wheeler, 1976). Borsini, Bendotti, and Samanin and colleagues (1985) reported that (+)–fenfluramine strongly reduced the consumption of a sucrose solution in nondeprived rats, while Leander (1987) demonstrated that fluoxitine suppresses the ingestion of saccharin solutions in normal rats. A similar finding was true for alcohol intake in alcohol rat lines bred to prefer alcohol (Murphy et al., 1988). Obviously, the motive to drink saccharin solutions depends only on the sweet taste, since they provide no calories. Both (+)–fenfluramine and quipazine, an indirect and a direct serotonergic agonist, respectively, produce similar dose-dependent suppression of cumulative consumption of a 5% sucrose solution by rats with gastric fistulas. This indicates that direct and indirect serotonergic agonists can strongly depress a feeding response activated by sweet taste.

OPIOID PEPTIDES AND MACRONUTRIENT SELECTION

Current evidence suggests that the effect of the pharmacology of the opioidergic system on eating behaviors is very complex and thus it would be difficult to ascribe a generalized role, particularly in view of the different effects observed with specific opioid peptides or macronutrient selection.

In support of this observation, both increases and decreases in food intake have been observed under a variety of experimental conditions (Bado, Roza, Lewin, & Dubrasguet, 1989; Gossnell, Levine, & Morley, 1986).

Different effects have also been observed with both opiate/opioid agonists and opiate antagonists, depending on duration or administration. In short-term experiments, administration of agonists, centrally or peripherally, results in feeding increases. In contrast, the peripheral administration of opiate antagonists diminishes the intake of sweet foods. The inference from these studies is that long-term use of opioid/opiate antagonists would result in a decrease in food intake (Morley & Levine, 1982; Morley, Parker, & Levine, 1985; Krahn, DeQuardo, & Gosnell, 1990).

The results have been far more complicated than expected. In general, chronic administration of antagonists has been disappointing (Atkinson, 1987). Naltrexone caused some reduction in binge eating in bulimics (Jonas & Gold, 1987). However, it also produced weight gain in anorectic patients (Moore, Mills, & Forster, 1985). Shimomura, Oku, Glick, & Bray, 1982) observed increased food intake with chronic naloxone treatment and decreased food intake with chronic morphine. Dhatt et al. (1988) had similar observations with chronic morphine administration.

These observations suggest that while in acute situations opioid agonists increase and antagonists decrease food intake, in chronic situations, opposite effects prevail.

One important problem in attempting to discuss and assign a specific pharmacological action of opiates/opioids appears to reside in obtaining exact information on the types of foods (macronutrient selection—lipids, proteins, and carbohydrates) consumed. In this regard, it is noteworthy that the opioid peptides, as well as opiates acting through μ, δ, and κ receptors, augment the ingestion of fat and protein, while actually suppressing the relative proportion of carbohydrates ingested (Shor-Posner et al., 1986; Tepperman & Hirst, 1982). The effects of opioid peptides on carbohydrate intake were investigated in animals made obese by neonatal monosodium glutamate (MSG) administration. This procedure results in reduced levels of brain endorphin (Krieger et al., 1979). These obese rats, compared with control animals, chose a greater percentage of their daily calories as carbohydrates and lower percentages as fat and protein (Shor-Posner, 1986).

Furthermore, research on the importance of endogenous opioid peptides in feeding behavior primarily focused on their stimulatory effects, especially their role in genetic predisposition to impulsive food intake. In comparison with lean littermates, increased levels of pituitary endorphin were observed in genetically obese mice (Ob/Ob) and rats (Fa/Fa) (Margules et al., 1978). However, it has been known for some time that diet choices made by genetically obese mice are similar to the changed choice behavior after morphine administration. Furthermore, obese mice are similar to the changed choice behavior after morphine administration. Furthermore, obese mice select lower proportions of their diets as protein and carbohydrate and higher proportions as fat (Mayer et al., 1951). Work by Gosnell and Majchrzak (1990) has concentrated primarily on the feeding effects of central injections of opioid agonists. This resulted in an increased consumption of both saccharin and salt solutions. Similarly, a low dose of the selective κ-agonist U-50,488H was found to facilitate the acquisition of a preference for a 20% sucrose solution (Lynch & Burns, 1987).

Based on these and other studies, it appears that opioid agonists and antagonists, respectively, increase and decrease preferences for palatable tastes. We argue that palatability is a different measure than macronutrient selection (e.g., carbohydrates), thus preventing any definitive conclusions with regard to feeding behavior.

The opioid peptides not only are involved in macronutrient intake, but have been implicated in compulsive alcohol and drug seeking (Blum et al., 1983), as well as brain self-stimulation behavior (Blum et al., 1983; Banks & Kastin, 1989). In fact, Blum et al. (1987) reversed alcohol-seeking behavior in genetically preferring C57/6J mice with the chronic administration of an enkephalinase inhibitor. Heibreder et al. (1988) showed that intracranial self-stimulation by rats was reduced by nucleus accumbens microinjections of kelatorphan, a potent enkephalinase inhibitor. In terms of food intake, Riviere and Bueno (1987) reported that central injections of the enkephalinase inhibitor thiorphan also reduced daily food intake in sheep. Since deficits have been found in neurotransmitter functions underlying craving behavior, and since these deficits may be alleviated by increased neurotransmitter release consequent to the use of drugs, alcohol, and food, the studies mentioned indicate that enkephalinase inhibition may similarly compensate for neurotransmitter imbalance (i.e., opioids, thereby attenuating craving behavior). These results suggest that human carbohydrate binging might be critically mediated by differences in patterns of endogenous peptides.

We believe that compulsive ingestive behavior is the response to one or more neurotransmitter deficits. Attempts to alleviate this neurotransmitter imbalance through drug-receptor activation (alcohol, heroin, cocaine, and glucose) will only substitute for the lack of reward and will yield a temporary sense of well-being (Chesselet et al., 1987).

REWARD-CASCADE MANIPULATIONS

There are numerous pharmacological agents that can alter the action of the reward cascade by pharmacological modification of neurotransmitter action: (1) dopaminergic agonists, such as bromocriptine (Tennant & Sagherian, 1987); (2) mixed opioid agonists-antagonists, such as buprenorphine (Mello, Mendelson, Brie, Lukas, 1989); (3) opioid antagonists, such as naltrexone (Volpicelli et al., 1986); (4) serotonergic reuptake inhibitors, such as citalopram (Gill & Amit, 1987; Naranjo, Sellers, & Lawrin, 1986); (5) catecholaminergic reuptake inhibitors, such as tricyclic antidepressants (Gawin & Kleber, 1984; Chiolo & Antelman, 1980); and (6) antianxiety agents with complex neurochemical action, such as buspirone (Collins & Myers, 1987). Each of these drugs enhances neurotransmitter availability by acting at pre- or postsynaptic receptor sites or via reuptake mechanisms.

An alternative method to enhance neurotransmitter availability uses the principle of amino-acid loading naturally to augment neurotransmitter synthesis and release (Hernandez & Hoevel, 1988; Wurtman, Hefti, & Melamed, 1981). As mentioned earlier, certain amino acids have been reported to reduce craving behavior in rodents by virtue of their ability to inhibit opioid peptide-degrading enzymes (Blum et al., 1987).

NEURONUTRIENTS AS ADJUNCTS TO THERAPY

Utilizing the reward-cascade mechanisms as a blueprint for the potential restoration of brain chemical imbalance, our laboratory began to test and develop certain amino-acid–mineral–vitamin enterals.

In searching for a nontoxic approach to the restoration of brain neurotransmitter supply in recovering chemically dependent patients, our laboratory decided to test the utility of select amino-acid precursors, as well as certain metals that act as cofactors in neurotransmitter synthesis. We have chosen the strategy of using naturally occurring food-based materials for several specific reasons: with food substances as precursors to alter brain neurotransmitters, responses to increased precursor availability are usually self-limited, and thus no known dependency occurs; excessive amino-acid substrate is metabolized along normal routes and is quickly eliminated; increases in neurotransmission brought about by precursors are particularly specific because they tend to work at only the synapses that use that transmitter; those neurons that are more active (e.g., as a consequence of exercise, stress, or mental disease) exhibit the greatest degree of precursor responsiveness; precursor amino-acid loading enhances transmitter synthesis and release; and precursors stimulate the function of these product amines in the brain (Yons, 1986).

Utilizing this approach, we have developed nutritional supplements of amino acids, vitamins, and minerals that assist in neurochemical restoration by virtue of precursor amino acids known to raise brain neurotransmitter levels and affect behavior (Sved, 1983), opioid peptide degradation inhibition known to reduce drug-seeking behavior (Blum et al., 1987), and transmitter synthesis and release enhancement by cofactors and minerals (Vereby & Gold, 1985).

Table 12-1 illustrates the contents and proposed actions of the individual ingredients of one of the nutritional formulas, SAAVE®, primarily intended for the alcohol and opiate abuser. Investigation of the potential benefit of this formula has resulted in one pilot double-blind study (Blum, Allison, Trachtenberg, Williams, & Loeblid, 1988a) and one double-blind, placebo-controlled study to date (Blum et al., 1988b). Table 12-1 also illustrates the contents and proposed actions of the individual ingredients of the nutritional formula, Tropamine®, primarily designed to act as an adjunct for the cocaine abuser. Experimentation with this supplement has resulted in an open-trial investigation (Blum et al., 1988b). Outpatient 12-month open-trial relapse studies have been completed on both SAAVE and Tropamine (Brown, Blum, & Tractenberg, 1990). Additionally, Table 12-1 also includes the contents of PhenaCal™, a supplement that showed benefits in an open trial for carbohydrate bingers (Blum, Trachtenberg, & Cook, 1990).

A summary of available data in patients with SAAVE, Tropamine, and PhenaCal is given in Table 12-2.

Early Testing of SAAVE

Our laboratory recently published the results of a double-blind type evaluation of the nutritional supplement SAAVE with regard to facilitating improvement in a 30-day inpatient alcohol and drug rehabilitation center (Blum, Trachtenberg, & Ramsey, 1988c).

SAAVE is formulated to elevate levels of enkephalin(s), 5-HT, catecholamines, and GABA, which are believed to be functionally deficient in alcoholics. Twenty-two patients were studied. The SAAVE patients, as compared with the control group, (1) had a lower BUD (building up to drink) score, one versus two; (2) required no p.r.n. benzodiazepines, 0 versus 94%; (3) ceased tremoring at 72 hours as compared with 96 hours in controls; and (4) had no severe depression on the Minnesota Multiphasic Inventory, in contrast to 24% of the control group.

Double-Blind Placebo-Controlled Study with SAAVE

The double-blind, placebo-controlled study (Blum et al., 1988b) suggests that SAAVE is efficacious as an adjunct in the detoxification, short-term, and continuing recovery of both alcohol and polydrug abusers. With the use of both nonrepeated- and repeated-measure statistical analyses, the following conclusions were reached regarding the potential clinical effects of SAAVE for inpatients:

1. A sixfold improvement is evident for the SAAVE groups in comparing frequency of AMA (withdrawal against medical advice) dropouts.
2. SAAVE improves the psychological status of the patient as measured by the BESS (behavioral, emotional, social, spiritual) score. The analysis-of-variance (ANOVA) scores of BESS scores were significant for the alcohol group, with the alcohol–SAAVE group demonstrating a greater improvement than the alcohol–placebo group. Higher BESS scores were consistently obtained with SAAVE for both groups relative to placebo. In fact, the BESS score was sig-

Table 12-1
SAAVE, Tropamine, and PhenaCal Composition and Rationale for Use

Ingredient	Amount[a]	Restorative action	Mechanism	Expected action	Product[b]
D-Phenylalanine	750 mg	Enkephalins	Enzyme inhibition	Anticraving, antidepression	T,S,P
L-Phenylalanine	750 mg	Dopamine norepinephrine	Precursor loading	Reward, antidepression	T,S,P
L-Tryosine	900 mg	Dopamine norepinephrine	Precursor loading	Reward, anticraving, antistress	T,P
L-Glutamine	300 mg	GABA	Precursor loading	Anticraving, antistress	T,S,P
Vitamin B complex		Neurotransmitter synthesis	Enzyme cofactors in transmitter synthesis, promotes GI absorption of amino acids	Facilitates action of neurotransmitters	T,S,P
Thiamine (HCl)—B$_1$	100 mg	Neurotransmitter synthesis	Enzyme cofactors in transmitter synthesis, promotes GI absorption of amino acids	Facilitates action of neurotransmitters	T,S,P
Riboflavin—B$_2$	15 mg	Neurotransmitter synthesis	Enzyme cofactors in transmitter synthesis, promotes GI absorption of amino acids	Facilitates action of neurotransmitters	T,S,P
Niacinamide—B$_3$	100 mg	Neurotransmitter synthesis	Enzyme cofactors in transmitter synthesis, promotes GI absorption of amino acids	Facilitates action of neurotransmitters	T,S,P
Pantothenic acid—B$_5$	90	Neurotransmitter synthesis	Enzyme cofactors in transmitter synthesis, promotes GI absorption of amino acids	Facilitates action of neurotransmitters	T,S,P
Pyridoxal-5'-phosphate—B$_6$	20 mg	Neurotransmitter synthesis	Enzyme cofactors in transmitter synthesis, promotes GI absorption of amino acids	Facilitates action of neurotransmitters	T,S,P
Folic acid—B$_9$	400 μg	Neurotransmitter synthesis	Enzyme cofactors in transmitter synthesis, promotes GI absorption of amino acids	Facilitates action of neurotransmitters	T,S,P

Cyanocobalamin—B$_{12}$	6µg	Neurotransmitter synthesis	Enzyme cofactors in transmitter synthesis, promotes GI absorption of amino acids	Facilitates action of neurotransmitters	T,S,P
Ascorbate (vitamin)—C	600 mg	Neurotransmitter synthesis	Enzyme cofactors in transmitter synthesis, promotes GI absorption of amino acids	Facilitates action of neurotransmitters and acids in withdrawal	T,S,P
Zinc (chelate)	30 mg	Neurotransmitter synthesis	Enzyme cofactor	Facilitates action of neurotransmitters	T,S,P
Calcium (chelate)	150 mg	Neurotransmitter promotor	Enzyme cofactor	Facilitates action of neurotransmitters	T,S,P
Magnesium (oxide)	150 mg	Neurotransmitter modulator	Regulates transmitter release	Calmative	T,S,P
Vitamin A (betacarotene)	2000 IU	Enhances immune response and reduces stress	Promotes proper structure and function of the adrenal gland	Assists in the fight–flight syndrome	S
Biotin (vitamin H)	0.3 mg	Promotes metabolism of carbohydrates	Enzyme cofactor	Enhances protein synthesis and reduces depression	S,P
Chromium (picolinate)	0.06 mg	Amino-acid-uptake promotor	Stimulates insulin and increases muscle utilization of valine and isolucine reducing carrier competition for L-phenylalanine and L-tryptophan	Increases blood–brain passage of neurotransmitter precursors	T,S,P
D-α Tocopherol succinate—vitamine E	30 IU	Protects cells against free radicals	Antioxidant	Retards aging process	S,P
Iodide (potassium Iodide)	0.15 mg	Enhances thyroid action	Restores thyroid hormone and increases neurotransmitter metabolism	Facilitates neurotransmitter metabolism	P

(Continued)

Table 12-1 (Continued)
SAAVE, Tropamine, and PhenaCal Composition and Rationale for Use

Ingredient	Amount[a]	Restorative action	Mechanism	Expected action	Product[b]
Copper (chelate)	2 mg	Neurotransmitter synthesis	Enzyme cofactor	Builds up dopamine	P
L-Carnitine	60 mg	Neuromodulator synthesis and mobilizes surface fat	Promotes production of endorphins	Reduces fat and acids in neuromodulator action	P
L-Arginine pyroglutamate	60 mg	Restores muscle transport and reduces fat and cholesterol	Vehicle for transport, storage and excretion of nitrogen	Increases muscle, not fat and enhances muscle energy sources like phosphoarginine	P
L-Ornithine (aspartate)	60 mg	Repairs tissue and muscle	May cause release of growth hormone and is converted to arginine	Muscle strength is enhanced	P
L-Selenomethionine	0.072 µg	Neurotransmitter modulator	Methyl donor, sulfur donor and precursor of sulfur amino acids	Facilitates action of neuromodulators	P
Iron (aspartate)	6 mg	Aids in oxygenation of tissues and in neurotransmitter storage	Constituent of hemoglobin and other proteins	Facilitates neurotransmitter function	S,P
	9 mg	Aids in oxygenation of tissues and in neurotransmitter storage	Constituent of hemoglobin and other proteins	Facilitates neurotransmitter function	T

[a]Amounts are for six capsules (daily dose) [b]These products are manufactured by Matrix Technologies, Inc., Houston, Texas: T=Tropamine; S-SAAVE; P=PhenaCal

Table 12-2

Summary of Clinical Experimentation with SAAVE, Tropamine, and PhenaCal

Drug Use	Treatment	Total No. of Patients	No. of Days Studied	Study Type	Significant Results	Reference
Alcohol	SAAVE	22	28	DB	100% decrease in BUD score; reduction in benzodiazepine requirement; reduction of withdrawal tremors after 72 hours; reduction in depression as measured by MMPI	Blum et al., 1988
Alcohol + polydrug	SAAVE	62	21	DBP	Reduced stress as measured by SCL, reduced BESS score; improved physical score; sixfold increased risk with placebo for leaving AMA post five days	Blum et al., 1989
cocaine	Tropamine	54	30	OT	Reduction of drug hunger compared with controls and SAAVE 4.17% AMA rate for Tropamine versus 28% for SAAVE and 37% for controls	Blum et al., 1988
Alcohol and cocaine	SAAVE and Tropamine	60	379	OT	The overall one-year recovery values were 73% for the alcoholics using SAAVE and 53% for the cocaine abusers using Tropamine	Brown et al., 1990
Carbohydrate + bingers	PhenaCal	27	90	OT	The PhenaCal group lost an average of 26.96 ± 2.7 pounds; the control group lost 10.0 ± 2.1 pounds. Only 18.2% of the PhenaCal group relapsed in contrast to 81.8% of the control group. Use of PhenaCal allowed overweight subjects to lose 2.7 times as much as patients without PhenaCal	Blum et al., 1990
Overweight	PhenaCal	247	730	OT	At two years, craving for food and binge eating were both reduced threefold in the group taking PCAL-103 compared with the control group. Subjects in the PCAL-103 group regained only 13.5% of the weight lost during fasting compared with 51% of the weight lost by the subjects in the control group	Blum et al., in preparation

Abbreviations: AMA = withdrawal against medical advice; BESS = behavioral, emotional, social, spiritual; BUD = building up to drink; DB = double blind; DBPC = double blind, placebo controlled; MMPI = Minnesota Multiphasic Personality Inventory; OT = open trial; SCL = skin conductance level.

nificantly improved for SAAVE patients seven days after cessation of its use. The data suggest that SAAVE is cumulative in its effect.

3. Patients on SAAVE showed significantly reduced stress manifestations, as measured by the autogen 3000 SCL (skin conductance level) in both the alcohol and polydrug groups. This indicates that SAAVE increases the rate of improvement. Effects for the alcoholics were more dramatic than for the polydrug abusers.

4. SAAVE improved physiological condition, as measured by the physical score (a measure of withdrawal signs) at the 10th day, for both the alcohol and polydrug groups. This finding is consistent with the clinical observations that patients have most detoxification somatic problems during the first 10 days, and then show improvement thereafter in a consistent fashion.

5. Patients using SAAVE in this inpatient setting improved about one week in advance of those not using SAAVE.

Open Clinical Trial with Tropamine

A clinical trial involving 54 patients was completed comparing the effects of Tropamine, SAAVE, and nothing (control group) (Blum et al., 1988c). In a 30-day inpatient treatment setting, Tropamine significantly reduced AMA and drug hunger. The AMA rate for controls was 37.5%, while for the Tropamine group, it was only 4.2%, and for the SAAVE group it was 28.6%. Within five days, Tropamine-treated patients showed a decided decrease in agitation, outside focus, and, most important, drug hunger. They were more compliant; there were much less acting out and drug craving. For both of these groups, the severity of the cocaine "crash" was reduced. Normally, discussing prior drug experience or viewing street corners associated with drug traffic and drug dealers' houses would trigger agitation and drug hunger in patients; with Tropamine, these were diminished. The patients were also more cooperative and more focused. The attending physicians reported that they had never seen more compliant cocaine patients. The difference in drug hunger was statistically significant for the entire treatment period with Tropamine, but significant only for the first 20 days for the SAAVE group. More rigorous studies are required to ascertain the extent of efficiency.

Open Trials in Outpatients

In a recent study by Brown et al. (1990), the neuronutrients SAAVE and Tropamine were studied in outpatient driving-under-the-influence (DUI) offenders with either alcohol- or cocaine-related problems. These neuronutrients were found significantly to reduce relapse rates and enhance recovery in these DUI outpatient offenders over a 10-week period. Follow-up on both the SAAVE and Tropamine groups after 10 months revealed a 73% and a 53% overall recovery rate respectively.

As patients proceed through recovery, they experience both negative and positive feelings. Negative feelings are often characterized as anxiety, depression, anger, irritability, and paranoia, all of which promote drug craving as a perceived solution. These feelings have been assayed and grouped under the heading BUR (building up to relapse). Gorski and Miller (1986) and Marlatt (1978) have commented on the progressive stages that lead to relapse. These negative emotions and the attendant reinforcing behaviors are central to their concept.

Both the alcoholics and cocaine addicts in the experimental groups exhibited a dramatic decrease in negative feelings, as compared with their control counterparts. The experimental groups attained minimal BUR score values after only four weeks in the program. In contrast, the control groups did not achieve comparably low values by 10 weeks. Thus individuals in the control groups remained significantly more at risk of relapse for a period more than 2.5 times longer than that of the experimental subjects.

The converse of the BUR is the RS, a measure of positive, self-enhancing feelings. As with the BUR, the RS leveled off asymptotically for the experimental patients at four weeks, while it improved far more slowly for the control patients. Even at 10 weeks, the RS had not attained the same level as the control subjects. The rate at which patients dropped out of the program mirrors the rate of improvement seen in the BUR and RS values for these two groups of patients.

The Brown study demonstrates that retention for the alcoholics at the end of 10 weeks was 87% for the experimental subjects, but only 47% for the control patients. For the cocaine addicts, these numbers are 80% and 13% respectively. These are dramatic differences. The recovery dropout pattern seen over the first 10 weeks continued in a like manner over the next 10 months. Thus, over the succeeding 10 months, the experimental group of alcoholics suffered only a further 7.7% patient loss. Similarly, after the first 10 weeks, the experimental group of cocaine patients lost an additional 14% over the next 10 months. Furthermore, the overall one-year recovery values of 73% for the alcoholics using SAAVE and 53% for the cocaine addicts using Tropamine in this outpatient setting compare favorably with the more intense intervention seen with inpatient treatment.

It should be noted that the subjects in the present study were resistant to 12-step programs, in spite of continual encouragement from the staff. On this basis, after correction of 87% reliability, the outcome data of recovery of 53% to 73% are quite favorable and suggest that neuronutrient supplementation assists in the recovery process.

Further support for these findings can be derived from numerous studies on outcome data on outpatients that have been conducted over the past three decades. An average 12-month relapse percentage of 67% for alcoholics was obtained by Hunt, Barnett, and Branch (1971). Additionally, Bill (1965) found that 34.6% of Alcoholic Anonymous (AA) members were abstinent at the end of the first year. Ditman (1967) supported Bill's finding when he reported that AA members have an abstinence rate of 30% to 35%. Baekeland, Lundwall, and Kissin (1975) reported that outpatient dropout rates for alcoholism treatment tend to be from 52% to 75%. Finally, Milkman and Sunderwirth (1987) stated that "aproximately 75% of all those who attempt abstinence from alcohol reverse their habits between three and six months after beginning a program for recovery." The present findings of facilitated recovery, both with SAAVE for the alcoholics and with Tropamine for the cocaine addicts, suggest that these neuronutrients—through possible chemical restoration— are important adjuncts to the treatment of drug dependency.

In observations in an outpatient setting, Horne (1988) also reported that the administration of these supplements improved client retention during the withdrawal and early recovery phases of treatment.

Open Clinical Trial of PhenaCal

Inasmuch as neurotransmitters and neuromodulators are known to stimulate or inhibit eating behavior, our laboratory (Blum et al., 1990) elected to examine the effects of precursor amino-acid loading and enkephalinase inhibition on compulsive eating and weight loss in a controlled-diet clinical setting. In a 90-day open trial, we investigated the effect of the experimental neuronutrient PhenaCal on weight loss, uncontrollable carbohydrate binging, and relapse rates in 27 outpatients attending a supervised diet-controlled treatment program. The patients were assigned, retrospectively, to two matched treatment groups: those receiving the neuronutrient (experimental group [E]; $n = 16$) and those not receiving the neuronutrient (control group [C]; $n = 11$). The E patients exhibited facilitated withdrawal from carbohydrates compared with the C patients. The E group lost an average of 26.96 ± 2.7 pounds; the C group lost only 10.0 ± 2.1 pounds. Only 18.2% of the E group relapsed in contrast to 81.8% of the C group. Use of the amino-acid supplement PhenaCal by chronic carbohydrate bingers allowed overweight individuals to lose 2.7 times as much weight as patients without the benefit of this product.

Numerous studies have implicated the interaction of opiates, opioid peptides, CCK-8, glutcagon, DA, and insulin in glucose utilization and the selective intake of carbohydrates (Ottavlani & Riley, 1984; Wurtman & Wurtman, 1986).

Although we cannot, at this time, provide an exact mechanism of action for this neuronutrient mixture, nor can we pinpoint which ingredient or combination of ingredients best suppresses carbohydrate binging in the study, an underlying presumption in the field is that a derangement or imbalance of the actions of some or all of this neurochemistry is responsible for eating disorders. Further, the principal candidate region for such imbalance is in the mesolimbic area. Similar data and logic underly thinking about drug-dependent disorders. Thus alcohol, opiates, cocaine, and glucose induce reward by activating the mesolimbic reward multineuronal circuitry. The importance of both the nucleus accumbens and enkephalins in this complex circuit is attested to by the report of Heidbreder et al. (1988).

Additionally, using a push–pull cannula technique, Chesselet et al. (1981) were able to induce DA release in the striatum after local application of enkephalin, which suggests regulation by δ-receptor stimulation. Indeed, kelatorphan may also protect against possible CCK-8 degradation by brain peptidases. This important satiety neuropeptide is colocalized with DA in the nucleus accumbens and there is a close interaction between CCK-8, DA, and endogenous opioid peptides (Matsumura et al., 1984; Heremansen, 1983; Frohman, 1943; Fullerton et al., 1985; Gilman & Lichtigfeid, 1986).

Pharmacological Adjuncts

In addition to nutritional adjuncts, certain pharmacological adjuncts are beginning to appear.

ALCOHOL-DRINKING DETERRENTS

The prototype of this class is disulfiram (Antabuse), which is given daily to deter drinking in individuals who need motivation to stay sober. Antabuse is nonaddictive, and alone it has no pharmacological effect. In the presence of alcohol, however, high levels of acetaldehyde build up in the blood because the disulfiram blocks the enzyme aldehyde dehydrogenase and the person becomes sick. Currently, there is disagreement concerning the effectiveness of Antabuse in alcoholism treatment (Banys, 1990). A more promising area of research utilizing the concepts of immunology involving antibodies directed toward acetaldehyde may provide a means to develop natural antibuselike substances (Israel, Hurwitz, Niemela, & Arnon, 1986).

EUPHORIANT-BLOCKING DRUGS

Opiate antagonists such as naloxone (Trexan®) have been used to facilitate opiate detoxification and also as blocking drugs for relapse prevention based on drug-extinction principles (Herridge & Gold, 1988; Volpicelli, Alterman, Hayashido, Muenz, & O'Brien, 1988).

In the treatment of alcoholism, for example, the narcotic antagonist Trexan has been found, in a double-blind, placebo-controlled study of detoxified alcoholics, to reduce relapse. In this regard, many biomedical (basic science) researchers believe that the pathology of brain reward pathways leads to the loss of control over drinking. This pathology may be related to genetically induced neurochemical abnormalities that theoretically could be reversed with chemical "antagonists" to the specific neurochemical defect.

Our earlier theory, known as the "genotype theory of drug-seeking behavior" (Blum et al., 1983), states that one type of alcoholism may be caused by brain endorphin deficiency. Replacing the lost endorphins with synthetic endorphins could overcome the addiction. Raising opioid levels with inhibitors of their degrading enzymes (i.e., enkephalinase inhibitors) has been shown to reduce craving behavior in both animals (Blum et al., 1987) and humans (Blum, Trachtenberg, Eliot, & Samuels, 1989; Brown et al., 1990).

Since all available endorphins are known to be addicting, chemists are being challenged to design new, nonaddicting endorphin molecules, or endorphin substitutes. These compounds could reverse basic neurochemical pathology, thereby overcoming the cause of one type of alcoholism and potentially compulsive disease.

ANTICRAVING DRUGS

Bromocriptine is a DA-receptor stimulator. In a six-month, placebo-controlled trial involving chronic alcoholics, bromocriptine improved treatment outcome, measured by the amount of alcohol consumed and psychological functioning. Its use in the treatment of cocaine addiction is well known (Tennant & Sagherian, 1987). Recent clinical research has found, almost by accident, that a patient's desire to drink is significantly reduced by antidepressant drugs given to treat alcoholic depression. Based on earlier animal studies showing lower levels of the brain chemical 5-HT in alcohol-preferring rats and mice (compared with nonpreferring animals) and reversal of alcohol preference by drugs that raise brain 5-HT levels, the clinical findings have been interpreted to mean that the "craving" for alcohol is caused by 5-HT dysfunction in critical brain areas. Thus antidepressants that block 5-HT inactivation are seen as overcoming the basic, pathological, compulsive urge to drink. Future studies will likely develop more specific and less toxic drugs to take advantage of this approach. (Antidepressant drugs are generally believed to be nonaddicting.)

One new example being actively explored is citalopram. This drug, which enhances the supply of 5-HT at the synapse, has been found in a double-blind, placebo-controlled study to increase significantly the days of abstinence in outpatients under treatment for alcoholism. Further, tricyclic antidepressants have been observed to reduce cocaine usage over an eight-week clinical trial (Naranjo et al., 1986).

EATING-DISORDER DRUGS

Studies are under way to evaluate the effects of Trexan on the prevention of relapse in carbohydrate binging and bulimia (Jonas & Gold, 1987). Various other drugs, such as fluoxetine, which also enhances the supply of 5-HT at the synapse, are being investigated as treatment adjuncts for patients with eating disorders (Leander, 1987; Borsini et al., 1985).

CLINICAL SUMMARY OF ELECTROPHYSIOLOGICAL ABNORMALITIES

Taken as a whole, in looking at all the research associated with the electrophysiology of alcoholism and substance abuse, it becomes apparent that there are electrophysiological abnormalities in both alcoholics and drug addicts and that substance abuse is an organic brain disease. In their 1990 paper, Begleiter and Porjesz (1990) demonstrated conclusively that the P300 is the most reliable indicator of risk for development of alcoholism in children of alcoholics, as well as for regression to alcoholism in alcoholics. These data are further supported by the neuropsychiatric data of Whipple, Parker, and Noble (1988), indicating that neuropsychological testing can also be an indicator and predictor. Begleiter and others (Begleiter & Porjesz, 1990; Naitoh, 1973; O'Connor & Tasman, 1990) also suggest that reductions in α waves from the lobe, as well as right temporal and parietal lobe electrophysiological abnormalities, may be biological indicators of a high risk of alcohol abuse. In combining these findings with the works of Blum (Blum et al., 1989) and Thatcher (Thatcher et al., 1982, 1984, 1985; Fishbein, Thatcher, et al., 1990), it becomes clear that genetic tendencies combine with environmental factors to produce neurophysiological and biochemical alterations.

Thatcher has shown that decreased amplitudes of evoked potentials are related to exposure to environmental toxins such as lead cadmium and possibly intake of refined carbohydrates. This has led many to believe that one would be able to do quantified electroencephalograms and biochemical tests and identify with relative certainty who is at risk and who would become more at risk. Braverman, Blum, and Smayda (1990) have shown that once substance abuse begins, electrophysiological abnormalities probably become much more heterogeneous and occur in virtually all cases of significant substance abuse (Table 12-3). It is common to find electrophysiological abnormalities on BEAM (brain electrical activity mapping) that are extremely diverse and not significantly different from other organic brain disease groups and to conclude that although certain electrophysiological predictors probably exist, specifically the P300 wave, most substance abusers begin with a small amount of brain disease (as a result of genetic tendency and environmental action) and progress to a more global brain disease. From the biochemical point of view, many of these individuals can be analyzed for nutritional deficiencies with tests for plasma, amino acids, vitamin profiles, minerals, essential fatty acids, and trace metals. Substance abusers are frequently low in amino-acid precursors such as tryptophan, tyrosine, phenylalanine, and methionine, and low in trace elements such

Table 12-3
**BEAM Abnormalities, by Components, in 60 Mixed-Substance Abusers
and Cocaine Addicts**

Components	Normal	Abnormal
BEAM test total	3	57
Electroencephalogram	43	17
Spectral analysis	30	30
Auditory evoked response	11	49
Visual evoked response	17	43

as zinc and selenium, and even elevated in copper (Braverman & Pfeiffer, 1987). Nutritional precursor therapy alone is successful (Blum et al., 1989), but needs to be augmented by the use of multivitamins, B complex, trace elements, and so on to help the substance abuser reach full recovery (Blum et al., 1989; Brown et al., 1990).

The need for medications such as antidepressants, most notably Prozac, and anticonvulsants (Tegretol and benzodiazepines, i.e., Clonazepam) to deal with the electrophysiological imbalances is also critical in achieving healing rates. Drug therapies have mixed results, and the concern about using drugs to stop the abuse of drugs has increasingly made nutritional alternatives more attractive. It appears that the combination of nutritional with electrophysiological treatment may be the best first approach, followed by drug therapies as a last resort (Braverman et al., 1990). A recent study by Braverman, Smith, Smayda, and Blum showed that the P300 amplitude can be increased significantly (alcohol lowers the P300 amplitude) by cranial electrotherapy stimulation (CES). This is the Food and Drug Administration's (FDA) term for an electric device that can be worn on the mastoids, emitting a frequency of 100 pulses per second, 1.5 milliamperes, 20% duty cycle, and a sinusoidal or square waveform. The FDA has permitted this device to be marketed for anxiety, insomnia, and depression, which frequently occur in substance-abuse patients. Smith of our group (Schmitt, Capo, Fraizier, & Bore, 1984; Smith, 1982, 1985) has studied over 400 alcoholics and polysubstance abusers and has shown the usefulness of this therapy alone in improving mood states (i.e., anxiety, depression, insomnia) as well as cognition. The effect of reducing alcoholic recidivism can last up to a year after only three weeks of treatment. Recent studies done in our laboratory with children of alcoholics, as well as with alcoholics and patients with organic brain disease, show a significant increase in the P300 amplitude (about 3 dV) when the CES device is worn in the left wrist/central forehead position (Table 12-4). The increase in P300 may peak 30 minutes after use, but may continue to increase with daily use for three weeks or more. Furthermore, significant electrophysiological normalizations of spectral analysis do occur (Braverman et al., 1990). The CES device can normalize many types of abnormal electrophysiology on spectral power analysis, including both excess and decreases of delta, theta, alpha, or beta, because the CES apparently corrects brain irregularities somewhat as a

Table 12-4
Patients with Modification of P300 Amplitude in Organic Brain Diseases wearing
CES in left wrist/central forehead position for 40 minutes; $N = 14$

	After	Before
Time	317.1 ± 26	308 ± 24
Voltage (amplitude)	9.9 ± 6.1*	7.0 ± 4.1

*$p < 0.03$ by paired-t test

defibrillator defibrillates a heart arrythmia. It probably accomplishes this action by altering brain neurotransmitters (Grinenko et al., 1988).

In conclusion, substance abusers have probably taught us a tremendous amount, which we can be thankful for, about the biochemical origin and treatment of anxiety and depression and other psychiatric diseases. When behavior is severely disturbed, it almost always has an organic basis, and substance abuse is probably one of the end points, when people are so desperately ill that they self-medicate with substances that cause further brain disease or damage. We now have a healing approach that includes a combination of amino-acid and nutrient formulas with cranial electrical stimulation. It should not surprise us that the nutritional and electrophysiological approaches combined produce the most outstanding results because the human brain is truly both nutritional and electrical. This does not mean that the drug model is completely done away with. In fact, within the judgment of each physician, there are still many marvelous things that can be accomplished through the use of antidepressants and anticonvulsants, and probably less through the use of benzodiazepines and antipsychotics. Nonetheless, certain basic studies can become important parts of the complete evaluation of substance abusers. This includes routine medical and nutritional (amino acids, trace elements, etc.) and toxicology profiles (lead cadmium, etc.), as well as neuropsychological and BEAM techniques. It is not difficult to imagine that if these approaches were used and combined properly, the national appetite for substance abuse would be reduced. We can predict this if we correctly believe in the data about the P300 amplitude as predictive and that CES can indeed change the P300 amplitude consistently as our data suggest for a prolonged period of CES use. Daily CES is like a daily ritual that may also contribute in its further effectiveness of antidoting compulsive behavior. Electrical therapies change brain electricity and thereby change brain chemistry. Additionally, there is growing evidence that neuroelectro training based on the work of Peniston (Peniston and Kulkosky, 1989) utilizing biofeedback techniques significantly reduce recidivism rates in male alcoholics. In an attempt to incorporate brain-wave mapping, P300 wave analysis, amino acid precursor loading techniques, and neuroelectro training (biofeedback), specialized clinics have been developed to facilitate patient recovery processes (Blum, 1991). We believe that the data require further evaluation, but that, because of the drug-abuse crisis, cojoint therapies based on our model should be included in our armamentarium to treat the drug and alcohol abuser.

Finding a Suspect Alcogene

As cited earlier in conjunction with E. P. Noble and our associates, Kenneth Blum reported on an allelic association of the human dopamine D_2 (DR D_2) receptor gene in alcoholism.

The work of Pickens and associates (Pickens et al., 1991) suggests that the genetic inheritable coefficient significantly increases with the more serious of several forms of either alcoholism or drug dependence. In this regard, following the initial discovery of an allelic association of the A1 allele of the DRD$_2$ receptor gene in severe alcoholics, other work clearly supports this specific gene association with not only severe alcoholism but drug dependence as well. (Blum et al., 1990, Blum et al., 1991, Noble et al., 1991, Parsian et al., 1991, Comings et. al., 1991, Uhl et al., 1991, Blum et al., 1992, Noble et al., 1992). In terms of support for a significant gene-behavior association, Cloninger (1991) reviewed all studies up to October 1991. This showed the D$_2$ A1 allele was present in 45% of 330 alcoholics versus 21.5% of 158 controls known not to be alcoholic; only 20% of 330 caucasian "control" individuals with varying degrees of clinical classification were A1 positive. This data from six published articles provide substantial evidence for a significant gene-behavior association at a p<10-7.

As shown in Figure 12-2, chromosome 11, the site of the DR D$_2$ receptor gene, has been implicated not only in alcoholism, but also in other aberrant behaviors. For example, the gene that controls the enzyme tyrosine hydroxylases, which is involved in the synthesis of DA and NE, has been implicated in manic-depressive illness. In numerous

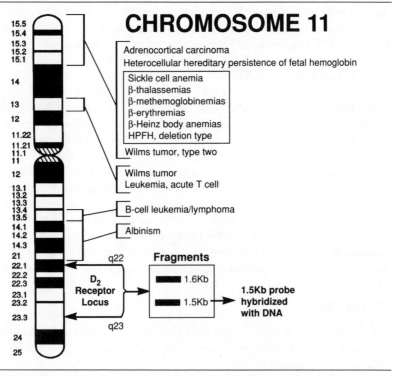

Figure 12-2. *Dopamine D$_2$ receptor gene locus. Additional polymorphisms at the 3 and 5 sites on the DNA.*

studies, the DR D$_2$ receptor has been implicated in various compulsive pleasure-seeking behaviors, including drug abuse, excessive sex, and eating disorders. This suggests the possibility that, as well as finding an alcogene, we have found a gene associated with early deviant behaviors and reward-seeking behavior.

A Word of Caution

In the paper published in the *Journal of the American Medical Association* of April 18, 1990, Blum, Noble, and colleagues pointed out that this initial finding was based on a limited sample, that other genes and other factors such as environment must be considered, and that future work must include DNA obtained from large groups of living alcoholics and their relatives.

We now realize that there is another problem that will be faced by other researchers seeking to replicate or extend our findings: The alcoholics in our sample were all representatives of a particularly virulent form of the disease, characterized by repeated relapses and eventual death due to alcohol-related problems. In addition, they were all 50 years of age or older, which meant they had years of opportunity to break the habit. These two factors make phenotype determination more difficult, particularly when living alcoholics are involved. It may prove that, insofar as alcoholism is concerned, the A$_1$ allele is specific for this virulent form.

Another interesting question was: Is it possible that these genetic anomalies were consequences of alcohol abuse, rather than causes of alcoholism?

Fortunately, that question had already been answered by Olivier Civelli and his group. They found the presence of the A$_1$ allele of the DR D$_2$ receptor gene in 39 children who had not been exposed to alcohol. This indicates that this polymorphism is genetically transmitted, not the result of alcohol intake.

IMPLICATIONS FOR NOW AND THE FUTURE

If our findings are correct, they constitute a powerful argument in favor of the disease concept of alcoholism and the importance of the genetic factor. This controversy is still raging, and in many quarters alcoholism is still considered a product of weak moral character and lack of willpower. Even the U.S. Supreme Court seemed to side with this viewpoint in a much-publicized 1988 decision. We hope that our findings will remove much of the stigma, enable more individuals to accept their craving as a symptom of an illness, and make it easier for them to seek treatment and affiliation with self-help 12-step programs.

For the future, the first step we can envision is the development of a diagnostic tool—a blood test, for example—that will identify children at risk in alcoholic families.

As more is learned about genetic anomalies and their effect on the brain's neurochemistry, we may be able to design more effective adjuncts to treatment; in other words, we will be able to fine-tune our pharmacological intervention in terms of genotype as well as phenotype.

Several questions growing out of the experiments also need to be answered. Is the D_2 receptor gene itself the direct cause of the alcohol syndrome? Or is it another gene nearby on the chromosome? Or is it two or more genes working together? Does the fact that one third of the alcoholics in the sample did not show the A_1 allele indicate that other, as yet undetected, genes may be involved? Or do some forms of alcoholism develop from environmental rather than genetic causes?

Furthermore, the question of privacy and labeling of individuals who test positive for this or other putative alcogenes is a cause for concern. With blood tests plausible within the next five years, will children who test positive be branded "alcoholic"? Will they be discriminated against because of this label? What if an employer or insurance company finds out that a person has alcogenes? What about entrance to health professions as well as other critical societal professions for individuals testing positive for these genes? These are disturbing questions with no simple answers, but progress in the genetics of alcoholism and other compulsive diseases must be pursued with great vigor if we want truly to understand their root causes.

These questions would have been pointless only a few years ago. We did not have the insights, the knowledge base, the technology, or the techniques to seek the answers. We had not yet made the leap to the concept of somatopsychic disease in which neurochemical imbalances or deficiencies—often resulting from genetic anomalies—lead not only to physical disabilities, but to behavioral aberrations as well. But now we have the concepts and, increasingly, the tools to research and understand many diseases that once were cloaked in mystery. It is our hope that out of this research will come knowledge that will enable us to prevent, treat, and cure a wide variety of diseases, including such compulsive diseases as alcoholism and drug addiction.

REFERENCES

Alraksinen, M.M., Saano, V., Stidel, E., Juronen, H., Huhtikansas, A. & Gynther, J. (1984). Binding of beta-carbolines and tetrahydroisoquisolines by opiate receptors of the delta-type. *Pharmacologica et Toxicologica, 55,* 380–385.

Altshuler, H.L., Phillips, P.E., & Feinhandler, D.A. (1980). Alteration of ethanol self-administration by naltrexone. *Life Sciences, 26,* 679–688.

Amit, Z., & Brown, Z.W. (1982). Actions of drugs of abuse on brain reward systems: A reconsideration with specific attention to alcohol. *Pharmacology, Biochemistry and Behavior, 17,* 233–238.

Atkinson, R.L. (1987). Opioid regulation in food intake and body weight in humans. *Federation Proceedings, 46,* 178–182.

Bado, A., Roze, C., Lewin, M.J.M., & Dubrasquet, M. (1989). Endogenous opioid peptides in the control of food intake in cats. *Peptides, 10,* 967–971.

Baekeland, F., Lundwall, L., & Kissin, B. (1975). Methods for the treatment of chronic alcoholism: A critical appraisal. In R. Gibbons, Y. Israel, H. Kalant, R. Popham, W. Schmidt, & R.G. Smart (Eds.), *Research advances in alcohol and drug problems,* Vol. 2. New York: Wiley.

Bain, G.T., & Kornetsky, C. (1987). Naloxone attenuation of the effect of cocaine on rewarding brain stimulation. *Life Sciences, 40,* 1119–1125.

Banks, W.A., & Kastin, A.J. (1989). Inhibition of the brain to blood transport system for enkephalins and Tyr-Mif-1 in mice addicted or genetically predisposed to drinking ethanol. *Alcohol, 6,* 53–57.

Banys, P. (1986). Clinical use of disulfiram (Antabuse): A review. *Journal of Psychoactive Drugs, 20,* 243–262.

Baxter, B.L., Gluckman, M.I., Stein, L., & Scerni, R.A. (1974). Self-injection of apomorphine in the rat: Positive reinforcement by a dopamine receptor stimulant. *Pharmacology, Biochemistry and Behavior, 2,* 387–391.

Begleiter, H., & Porjesz, B. (1990). Neuroelectric processes and individuals at risk for alcoholism. *Alcohol and Alcoholism, 25,* 251–256.

Begleiter, H., Porjesz, B., Biharis, B., & Kissin, B. (1984). Event-related brain potentials in boys at risk for alcoholism. *Science, 225,* 1493–1495.

Bhakthavatsalam, P., & Leibowitz, S.F. (1986). Morphine-elicited feeding: Diurnal rhythm circulating corticosterone and macronutrient selections. *Pharmacology, Biochemistry and Behavior, 24,* 911–917.

Bill, C. (1965). The growth and effectiveness of Alcoholics Anonymous in a southwestern city. *Quarterly Journal of Studies on Alcohol, 26,* 279–284.

Blum, K. (with J. E. Payne) (1991). *Alcohol and the Addictive Brain.* New York: The Free Press.

Blum, K., Hamilton, M.L., & Wallace, J.E. (1976). Alcohol and opiates: A review of common neurochemical and behavioral mechanisms. In K. Blum (Ed.), *Alcohol and opiates: Neurochemical and behavioral mechanisms,* (pp. 203–206). New York: Academic Press.

Blum, K., Elston, S.F., DeLallo, A., et al. (1983). Ethanol acceptance as a function of genotype amounts of brain [met]-enkephalin. *Proceedings of the National Academy of Sciences (U.S.A.), 80,* 6510–6512.

Blum, K., Briggs, A.H., Trachtenberg, M.C., et al. (1987). Enkephalinase inhibition: Regulation of ethanol intake in genetically predisposed mice. *Alcohol 4,* 449–456.

Blum, K., Allison, D., Trachtenberg, M.C., Williams, R.W., & Loeblich, L.A. (1988). Reduction of both drug hunger and withdrawal against advice rate of cocaine abusers in a 30-day inpatient treatment program by the neuronutrient Tropamine[TM]. *Current Therapeutic Research, 43,* 1204–1214.

Blum, K., Trachtenberg, M.C., Elliot, C.E., Dingler, M.L., Sexton, R.L., Samuels, A.L., & Cataldie, L. (1988b). Enkephalinase inhibition and precursor loading improves treatment of alcohol and polydrug abusers: Double-blind placebo controlled study of the nutritional adjunct SAAVE[TM]. *Alcohol, 5,* 481–493.

treatment of alcohol and polydrug abusers: Double-blind placebo controlled study of the nutritional adjunct SAAVE™. *Alcohol, 5*, 481–493.

Blum, K., Trachtenberg, M.C., & Ramsey, J.C. (1988c). Improvement of inpatient treatment of neurotransmitter restoration: A pilot study. *International Journal of the Addictions, 23*, 991–998.

Blum, K., Trachtenberg, M.C., Eliot, C., & Samuels, A. (1989). Enkephalinase inhibition and precursor amino acid loading improves inpatient treatment of alcohol and polydrug abusers: Double-blind placebo-controlled study of the nutritional adjunct SAAVE. *Alcohol, 5*, 481–493.

Blum, K., Noble, E.P., Sheridan, P.J., Montgomery, A., Ritchie, T., Jagadeeswaran, P., Nogami, H., Briggs, A.H., & Cohn, J.B. (1990a). Allelic association of human dopamine D_2 receptor gene in alcoholism. *Journal of the American Medical Association, 263*, 2055–2060.

Blum, K., Noble, E.P., Sheridan, P.J., Finley O., Montgomery, A., Ritchie, T., Ozkaragoz, T., Fitch, R.J., Sadlack F., Sheffield, D., Dahlmann, T., Halbardier, S., and Nogami, H. (1991). Association of the A1 allele of the D_2 dopamine receptor gene with severe alcoholism. *Alcohol, 8*, 406–416.

Blum, K., & Kozlowski, G.P. (1990b). Ethanol and neuromodulator interactions: A cascade model of reward. In H. Oliat, S. Parvez, & H. Parvez, (Eds.), *Progress in alcohol research* (pp. 131–147). Utrecht: VSP.

Blum, K., Trachtenberg, M.C., & Cook, D.W. (1990c). Neuronutrient effects of weight loss in carbohydrate bingers: An open clinical trial. *Current Therapeutic Research, 48*, 217–233.

Blum, K., Noble, E.P., Sheridan, P.J., (1992). *Genetic Predisposition to alcoholism: Association of the dopamine D_2 receptor Taq1 B1 RFLP with severe alcoholics*. C.I.N.P. XVIII Congress, Nice France.

Blundell, J.E. (1983). Problems and processes underlying the control of food selection and nutrient intake. In R.J. Wurtman & J.J. Wurtman (Eds.), *Nutrition and the brain* (pp. 163–222). New York: Raven Press.

Blundell, J.E. (1984). Serotonin and appetite. *Neuropharmacology, 23*, 1537–1551.

Blundell, J.E. (1986). Serotonin manipulations and the structure of feeding behavior. *Appetite, 7*, 39–56.

Bohman, M. (1978). Some genetic aspects of alcoholism and criminality: A population of adoptees. *Archives of General Psychiatry, 35*, 269–276.

Bohman, M., Cloninger, C.R., Van Knorring, A.L., & Sigvardson, S. (1984). An adoption study of somatosome disorders. *Archives of General Psychiatry, 41*, 872–878.

Borsini, F., Bendotti, C., & Samanin, R. (1985). Salbutanol, d-amphetamine and d-fenfluramine reduce sucrose intake in freely fed rats by acting on different neurochemical mechanisms. *International Journal of Obesity, 9*, 277–283.

Bozarth, M.A. (1983). In J.E. Smith & J.D. Lane, (Eds.), *The neurobiology of opiate reward processes* (pp. 331–359). New York: Elsevier.

Bozarth, M.A., & Wise, R.A. (1981). Heroin reward is dependent on a dopaminergic substrate. *Life Sciences, 29*, 1881–1886.

Braverman, E.R., Blum, K., & Smayda, R.J. (1990). A commentary on brain mapping in

60 substance abusers: Can the potential for drug abuse be predicted and prevented by treatment? *Current Therapeutic Research, 48,* 1990.

Braverman, E.R., & Pfeiffer, C.C. (1987). *The healing nutrients within.* New Canaan, CT: Keats.

Braverman, E.R., Smith, R.B., Smayda, R.J., & Blum, K. (1990). Modification of P300 amplitude and other electrophysiological parameters of drug abuse by cranial electrical stimulation. *Current Therapeutic Research, 48.*

Britt, M.D., & Wise, R.A. (1982). Ventral tegmental site of opiate reward: Antagonism by a hydrophilic opiate receptor blocker. *Brain Research, 258,* 105–108.

Brown, R.J., Blum, K., & Trachtenberg, M.C. (1990). Neurodynamics of relapse prevention: A neuronutrient approach to outpatient DUI offenders. *Journal of Psychoactive Drugs, 22,* 173–187.

Carlson, R.H., & Lydic, R. (1976). The effects of ethanol upon threshold and response rate for self-stimulation. *Psychopharmacology (Berlin), 50,* 61–64.

Charness, M.E., Gordon, A.S., & Amond, I.D. (1983). Ethanol modulation of opiate receptors in cultured neural cells. *Science, 222,* 1246–1248.

Chesselet, M.F., Chermany, A., Reisine, T.D., et al. (1981). Morphine and delta-opiate agonists locally stimulate in vivo dopamine release in cat caudate nuclei. *Nature, 322,* 291–320.

Chiolo, L., & Antelman, S. (1980). Repeated treatment with tricyclic antidepressant induces a progressive dopamine autoreceptor subsensitivity independent of daily drug treatment. *Nature, 287,* 451–453.

Clavier, R.M., Fibiger, H.C., & Phillips, A.G. (1976). Evidence that self-stimulation of the region of the locus coerulens in rats does not depend upon noradrenergic projections to telencephalon. *Brain Research, 113,* 71–81.

Cloninger, C.R. (1983). Genetic and environmental factors in the development of alcoholism. *Journal of Psychiatric Treatment and Evaluation, 5,* 487–496.

Cloninger, C.R. (1991). D2 dopamine receptor gene is associated but not linked with alcoholism. *JAMA, 266,* 1833–1834.

Cloninger, C.R., Bohman, M., & Sigvardsson, S., Inheritance of alcohol abuse. *Archives of General Psychiatry.* 38:861–868.

Collins, D.M., & Myers, R.D. (1987). Buspirone attenuates volitional alcohol intake in the chronically drinking monkey. *Alcohol, 4,* 49–56.

Comings, D.E., B.G., Comings, D., Muhlemann, G., Dietz, B., Shahbahrami, D., Tast,. (1991). The dopamine D2 receptor as a modifying gene in neuropsychiatric disorders. *JAMA, 266,* 1793.

Corbett, D., & Wise, R.A. (1980). Intracranial self-stimulation in relation to the ascending dopaminergic systems of the midbrain: A moveable electrode mapping study. *Brain Research, 185,* 1–15.

Crow, T.J. (1970). Enhancement by cocaine of intra-cranial self-stimulation in the rat. *Life Sciences, 9,* 375–381.

Dackis, C.A., & Gold, M:S. (1985). New concepts in cocaine addiction: The dopamine depletion hypothesis. *Neuroscience and Biobehavioral Research, 9,* 469–477.

mine receptor blocker pimozide, but not with the noradrenergic blockers phentolamine or phenoxybenzamide. *Canadian Journal of Physiology, 31*, 195–203.

Dhatt, R.K., Rattan, A.K., Mangat, H.K. (1988). Effect of chronic intracerebroventricular morphine to feeding responses in male rats. *Physiology and Behavior, 43*, 553–557.

Ditman, K.S. (1967). A controlled experiment on the use of court probation for drunk arrests. *American Journal of Psychiatry, 124*, 160–163.

Elmer, G.I., Meisch, R.A., & George, F.R. (1987). Mouse strain differences in operant self-administration of ethanol. *Behavior Genetics, 17*, 439–451.

Elston, S.F.A., Blum, K., DeLallo, L., & Briggs, A.H. (1982). Ethanol intoxication as a function of genotype dependent responses in three inbred mice strains. *Pharmacology, Biochemistry and Behavior, 16*, 13–15.

Ettenberg, A., Pettit, H.O., Bloom, F.E., & Koob, G.F. (1982). Heroin and cocaine intravenous self-administration in rats: Mediation by separate neural systems. *Psychopharmacology (Berlin), 78*, 204–209.

Fishbein, D.H., Thatcher, D.W., & Cantor, D.S. (1990). Ingestion of carbohydrates varying in complexity produce differential brain responses. *Clinical Electroencephalography, 21*(1), 5–11.

Fouriezos, G., Hansson, P., & Wise, R.A. (1978). Neuroleptic-induced attenuation of brain stimulation reward in rats. *Journal of Comparative Psychology, 92*, 661–671.

Frohman, L.A. (1983). CNS peptides and glucoregulation. *Annual Review of Physiology, 45*, 95–107.

Fullerton, D.T., Getto, C.J., Swift, W.J., et al. (1985). Sugar, opioids, and binge eating. *Brain Research Bulletin, 14*, 673–680.

Garattini, S., Caccia, S., Mennini, T., et al. (1979). Biochemical pharmacology of the anorectic drug fenfluramine: A review. *Current Medical Research and Opinion, 6*, 15–27.

Gawin, F.H., & Kleber, H.D. (1984). Cocaine abuse treatment: Open pilot trial with desipramine and lithium carbonate. *Archives of General Psychiatry, 41*, 903–909.

German, D.C., & Bowden, D.M. (1974). Catecholamine systems as the neural substrate for intracranial self-stimulation: A hypothesis. *Brain Research, 73*, 381–419.

Gill, K., & Amit, Z. (1987). Effects of serotonin uptake blockade on food, water and ethanol consumption in rats. *Alcoholism: Clinical and Experimental Research, 11*, 444–449.

Gilman, M.A., Lichtigfeld, F.J. (1986). The opioids, dopamine, cholecystokinin and eating disorders. *Clinical Neuropharmacology, 9*, 91–97.

Goeders, N.E., & Smith, J.E. (1983). Cortical dopaminergic involvement in cocaine reinforcement. *Science, 221*, 773–775.

Gomez, E., & Mikhail, A.R. (1979). Treatment of methadone withdrawal with cerebral electrotherapy (electrosleep). *British Journal of Psychiatry, 134*, 111.

Goodwin, D.W., Schulsinger, F., Hermansen, L., Fuze, S.B., & Winoken, G. (1973). Alcohol problems in adoptees raised apart from alcoholic biologic parents. *Archives of General Psychiatry, 28*, 238–243.

Gorski, T.T., & Miller, M. (1986). *Staying sober: A guide for relapse prevention.* Independence, MO: Independence Press.

Gosnell, B.A., Levine, A.S., & Morley, J.E. (1986). The stimulation of food intake by selective agonists of mu, kappa and delta opioid receptors. *Life Sciences*, 38, 1081–1088.

Gosnell, B.A., & Majchrzak, M.J. (1990). Effects of a selective mu opioid receptor agonist and naloxone on the intake of sodium chloride solutions. *Psychopharmacology*, 100, 66–71.

Goudie, A.J., Thornton, D.W., & Wheeler, T.J. (1976). Effects of Lilly 110140, a specific inhibitor of 5-hydroxytryptamine uptake, on food intake and on 5-hydroxytryptophan-induced anorexia. Evidence for serotoninergic inhibiton of feeding. *Pharmaceutical Pharmacology*, 28, 318–320.

Grinenko, A., et al. (1988). Metabolism of biogenic amines during the treatment of alcohol withdrawal syndrome by transcranial electrical treatment. *Biogenic Amines*, 5, 427–436.

Heidbreder, C., Roques, B., Vanderhaeghen, J.J., et al. (1988). Kelatorphan, a potent enkephalinases inhibitor, presents opposite properties when injected intracerebroventricularly or into the nucleus accumbens on intracranial self-stimulation. *Neurochemistry International*, 3, 347–350.

Hermansen, K. (1983). Enkephalins and the secretion of pancreatic somatostatin and insulin in the dog: Studies in vitro. *Endocrinology*, 113, 1149–1154.

Hernandez, L., & Hoevel, B.G. (1988). Food reward and cocaine increase extracellular dopamine in the nucleus accumbens as measured by microdialysis. *Life Sciences*, 42, 1705–1712.

Herridge, M.D., & Gold, M.S. (1988). Pharmacological adjuncts in the treatment of opioid and cocaine addicts. *Journal of Psychoactive Drugs*, 20, 233–242.

Horne, D.E. (1988). Clinical impressions of SAAVE[TM] and Tropamine[TM]. *Journal of Psychoactive Drugs*, 20, 333–336.

Hunt, W.A., Barnett, L.W., & Branch, L.G. (1971). Relapse rates in addiction programs. *Journal of Clinical Psychology*, 27, 355.

Inokuchi, A., Domura, Y., & Nishimura, H. (1984). Effect of intracerebroventricularly infused glucagon on feeding behavior. *Physiology and Behavior*, 33, 397–400.

Irwin, M., Schuckit, M. & Smith, T.L. (1990). Clinical importance of age at onset in type 1 and 2 primary alcoholics. *Archives of General Psychiatry*, 47, 320–323.

Israel, Y., Hurwitz, E., Niemela, O., & Arnon, R. (1986). Monoclonal and polyclonal antibodies against acetaldehyde-containing epitopes in acetaldehyde-protein adducts. *Proceedings of the National Academy of Sciences*, (U.S.A.), 83, 7923–7927.

Javors, M., Blaisdell, G., Lee, J., & Bowden, C. (1987). Binding of imipramine to platelet membranes is lower in alcoholics than in controls. *Alcohol and Drug Research*, 7, 453–459.

Jonas, J.M., & Gold, M.G. (1987). The use of opiate antagonists in treating bulimia: A study of low-dose versus high-dose naltrexone. *Psychiatry Research*, 24, 195–199.

Kaye, W.H., Elbert, M.H., Gwirtsman, H.E., et al. (1984). Differences in brain serotonergic metabolism between non-bulimic and bulimic patients with anorexia nervosa. *American Journal of Psychiatry*, 141, 1558–1601.

Kaye, W.H., Gwirtsman, H.E., Lake, C.R., Slever, L.J., Jimerson, D.C., Elbert, M.H.,

& Murphy, D.L. (1985). Disturbances of ne metabolism and alpha-2 adrenergic receptor activity in anorexia nervosa: Relationship to nutritional state. *Psychopharmacology Bulletin, 21*(3), 419–423.

Koob, G.F., Spector, N.H., & Meyerhoff, J.L. (1975). Effects of heroin on lever pressing for intracranial self-stimulation. Food and water in the rat. *Psychopharmacologia, 42*, 231–234.

Koob, G.F., Voccurino, F.J., & Amaric, M. (1987). Neurochemical substrates for opiate reinforcement. In S. Fisher, A. Raskin, & E.H. Uhlenhuth (Eds.), *Aspects* (pp. 80–108). New York: Oxford University Press.

Krahn, D.D., DeQuardo, J., & Gosnell, B.A. (in press). Opiate addiction and anorexia nervosa: A case report. *International Journal of Eating Disorders.*

Krieger, D.T., Liotta, A.S., Nicholsen, G.,et al. (1979). Brain ACTH and endorphin reduced in rats with monosodium glutamate-induced arcuate nuclear lesions. *Nature, 278*, 562–563.

Leander, J.D. (1987). Fluoxetine suppresses palatability-induced ingestion. *Psychopharmacologia (Berlin), 91*, 285–287.

Leibowitz, S.F. (1978). Paraventricular nucleus: A primary site mediating adrenergic stimulation of feeding and drinking. *Pharmacology, Biochemistry and Behavior, 8*, 163–175.

Leibowitz, S.F. (1985). Brain neurotransmitters and appetite regulation. *Psychopharmacology Bulletin, 21*, 412–418.

Leibowitz, S.F. (1986). Brain monamines and peptides: Role in the control of eating behavior. *Federation Proceedings, 45*, 1396–1403.

Leibowitz, S.F., Brown, D., & Treter, J.R. (1982). Peripheral and hypothalamic injections of α-adrenergic and dopaminergic receptor drugs have specific effects on nutrient selection in rats. *Proceedings of the Eastern Psychological Association, 53*, 136.

Leibowitz, S.F., Roland, C.R., Hor, L., et al. (1984). Noradrenergic feeding elicited via the paraventricular nucleus is dependent upon circulating corticosterone. *Physiology and Behavior, 32*, 857–864.

Leibowitz, S.F., Shor-Posner, G., Maclow, C., et al. (1986). Amphetamine: Effects on meal patterns and macronutrient selection. *Brain Research Bulletin, 17*, 681–689.

Leibowitz, S.F., Weiss, G., Yee, F., et al. (1985). Noradrenergic innervation of the paraventricular nucleus specific role in control of carbohydrate ingestion. *Brain Research Bulletin, 14*, 561–567.

Lichtenstein, S.S., Marinescu, C., & Leibowitz, S.F., (1984). Chronic infusion of norepinephrine and clonidine into the hypothalamic paraventricular neucleus. *Brain Research Bulletin, 13*, 591–595.

Lippa, A.S., Antelman, S.M., Fisher, A.E., & Canfield, D.R. (1973). Neurochemical mediation of reward: A significant role for dopamine? *Pharmacology, Biochemistry and Behavior, 1*, 23–28.

Lumeng, L., Hawkins, T.D., & Li, T.-K. (1977). In R.G. Thurman, J.R. Williamson, H. Drott, & B. Chance (Eds.), *Alcohol and aldehyde metabolising systems*. (Vol. 3, p. 567). New York: Academic Press.

Lynch, W.C., & Burns, G. (1987). Enhancement of sucrose intake by the kappa opioid agonist U-50, 488H persists beyond the period of drug exposure. *Society on Neuroscience Abstracts, 13,* 878.

Lyness, W.H., Friedle, N.M., & Moore, K.E. (1979). Destruction of dopaminergic nerve terminals in nucleus accumbens: Effect on d-amphetamine self-administration. *Pharmacology, Biochemistry and Behavior, 11,* 553–556.

Margules, D.L., Moisset, B., Lewis, M.J., et al. (1978). B-endorphin is associated with overeating in genetically obese mice (Ob/ob) and rats (fa/fa). *Science, 202,* 988–991.

Marks-Kaufman, R., & Kanarch, T.B. (1980). Morphine selectively influences macronutrient intake in the rat. *Pharmacology, Biochemistry and Behavior, 12,* 427–430.

Marlatt, G.A. (1978). Craving for alcohol, loss of control, and relapse: A cognitive-behavioral analysis. In P.E. Nathan, G.A. Marlatt, & T. Lobers (Eds.), *Alcoholism: New direction in behavioral research and treatment.* New York: Plenum.

Matsumura, M., Fukushima, T., Saito, H., et al. (1984). In vivo and in vitro effects of beta-endorphin on glucose metabolism in the rat. *Hormone and Metabolic Research, 16,* 27–31.

Mayer, J.M., Dickie, M., Bates, M.W., et al. (1951). Free selection of nutrients by hereditarily obsese mice. *Science, 113,* 745–746.

McClearn, G.E., & Rodgers, D.A., (1959). Differences in alcohol preferences among inbred strains of mice. *Quarterly Journal of Studies on Alcohol, 20,* 691–695.

Mello, N.K., Mendelson, J.H., Bree, M.P., & Lukas, S.E. (1989). Bupremorphine suppresses cocaine self-administration by rhesus monkeys. *Science, 245,* 859–862.

Milkman, H., & Sunderwirth, S. (1987). *Craving for ecstasy: The consciousness and chemistry of escape.* Lexington, MA: Lexington Books.

Mirone, L. (1957). Dietary deficiency in mice in relation to voluntary alcohol consumption. *Quarterly Journal of Studies on Alcohol, 18,* 552–560.

Moore, R., Mills, I.H., & Forster, A. (1982). Naloxone in the treatment of anorexia nervosa: Effect on weight gain and lipolysis. *Journal of the Royal Society of Medicine, 74,* 129–131.

Morley, J.E., & Levine, A.S. (1982). Corticotropine releasing factor, grooming and ingestive behavior. *Life Sciences, 31,* 1459–1464.

Morley, J.E., Parker, S., & Levine, A.S. (1985). Effect of butyrphanol tantrate on food and water consumption in humans. *American Journal of Clinical Nutrition, 42,* 1175–1178.

Murphy, J.M., Waller, N.D., Galto, W., et al. (1988). Effects of fluoxetine on the intragastric self-administration of ethanol in the alcohol-preferring p lines of rats. *Alcohol, 5,* 283–286.

Myers, R.D. (1963). Alcohol consumption in rats: Effects of intracranial injections of ethanol. *Science, 142,* 240–241.

Naitoh, P. (1973). The value of electroencephalography in alcoholism. *Annals of the New York Academy of Sciences, 215,* 303–320.

Naranjo, C.A., Sellers, E.M., & Lawrin, M.O. (1986). Modulation of ethanol intake by serotonin uptake inhibitors. *Journal of Clinical Psychiatry, 47,* 16–22.

Noble, E.P. (1990). Alcoholic fathers and their sons: Neuropsychological, electro-

Naitoh, P. (1973). The value of electroencephalography in alcoholism. *Annals of the New York Academy of Sciences, 215,* 303–320.

Naranjo, C.A., Sellers, E.M., & Lawrin, M.O. (1986). Modulation of ethanol intake by serotonin uptake inhibitors. *Journal of Clinical Psychiatry, 47,* 16–22.

Noble, E.P. (1990). Alcoholic fathers and their sons: Neuropsychological, electropsychological, personality and family correlates. In *Banbury Report 33: Molecular genetics and biology of alcoholism.* Cold Spring Harbor, NY: Cold Spring Harbor Laboratory Press.

Noble, E.P., Blum, K., and Khalsa, H. (1992). Allelic association of the D_2 dopamine receptor gene in cocaine dependence. C.I.N.P. XVIII Congress, Nice, France.

Noble, E.P., Blum, K., Ritchie, T., Montgomery, A., Sheridan, P.J. (1991). Allelic association of the D_2 dopamine receptor gene with receptor binding characteristics in alcoholism. *Archives of General Psychiatry, 48,* 648–656.

O'Connor, S., & Tasman, A. (1990). The application of electrophysiology to research in alcoholism. *Journal of Neuropsychiatry, 2,* 149–158.

Olds, M.E., & Olds, J. (1963). Approach-avoidance analysis of rat diencephalon. *Journal of Comparative Neurology, 120,* 259–295.

Ottaviani, R., & Riley, A.L. (1984). Effect of chronic morphine on the self-selection of macronutrients in the rat. *Nutrition and Behavior, 2,* 27–36.

Parsian, A., Todd, R.D., Devor, E.J., O'Malley, K.L, Suarez, B.K., Reich, T., Cloninger, C.R. (1991). Alcoholism and alleles of the human dopamine D_2 receptor locus: Studies of association and lineage. *Archives of General Psychiatry, 48,* 655–663.

Peniston, E.G., & Kulkosky, P.J. (1989). Alcoholism: Clinical and experimental research. Brainwave Training and B-Endorphin levels in alcoholics. *13,*(2) 271–279.

Pettinati, H.M., Sugermann, A.A., DiPowato, N., & Maurer, H.S. (1982). The natural history of alcoholism over four years after treatment. *Quarterly Journal of Studies in Alcohol, 43,* 201–215.

Phillips, A.G., & LePiane, F.G. (1980). Reinforcing effects of morphine microinjection into the ventral tegmental area. *Pharmacology, Biochemistry and Behavior, 12,* 965–968.

Pickens, R.W., Svikes, D.S., McGue, M, Lykken, K.T., Heston, L.L., Clayton, P.J. (1991). Heterogeneity in the inheritance of alcoholism: A study of male and female twins. *Archives of General Psychiatry, 48,* 19–28.

Poschel, B.P., & Ninteman, F.W. (1963). Norepinephrine: A possible excitatory neurophormone of the reward system. *Life Sciences, 10,* 782–788.

Riviere, P.J.M., & Bueno, L. (1987). Origin of the stimulation of food intake by oral administration of enkephalinase inhibitors in sheep. *Life Sciences, 41,* 333–339.

Roberts, D.C.S., & Koob, G.F. (1982). Disruption of cocaine self-administration following 6-hydroxydopamine lesions of the ventral tegmental area in rats. *Pharmacology, Biochemistry and Behavior, 17,* 901–904.

Samanin, R., Bendotti, C., Candelaresi, G., et al. (1977). Specificity of serotoninergic involvement in the decrease of food intake induced by quipazine in the rat. *Life Sciences, 21,* 1259–1266.

Schaeffer, K.W., Parsons, O.A., & Errico, A. (1988). Abstracting deficits in childhood con-

Schuckit, M.A. (1984). Subjective responses to alcohol in sons of alcoholics and control subjects. *Archives of General Psychiatry, 41,* 879–884.

Schuckit, M.A. (1985). Ethanol-induced changes in body sway in men at high alcoholism risk. *Archives of General Psychiatry, 42,* 375–379.

Schuckit, M.A. (1990). Progress in the search for genetic markers of an alcoholism risk. In H. Ollat, S. Parvez, & H. Parvez (Eds.), *Progress in alcoholism research,* (Vol. 2, pp. 1–14). Utrecht: VSP.

Schuckit, M.A., Bulters, N., Lyn, L., & Irwin, M. (1987). Neuropsychologic deficits and the risk for alcoholism. *Neuropsychopharmacology, 1,* 45–53.

Schuckit, M.A., Godwin, D.A., & Winokur, G. (1972). A study of alcoholism in half-siblings. *American Journal of Psychology, 128,* 1132–1136.

Schuckit, M.A., Gold, E., & Risch, C. (1987). Serum prolactin levels in sons of alcoholics and control subjects. *American Journal of Psychiatry, 149,* 854–859.

Shimomura, Y., Oku, J., Glick, Z., & Bray, G.A. (1982). Opiate receptors, food intake and obesity. *Physiology and Behavior, 28,* 441–445.

Shizgal, P., Bielajen, C., & Kiss, I. (1980). Anodal hyperpolarization block technique provides evidence for rostro-caudal conduction of reward related signals in the medial forebrain bundle. *Society for Neuroscience Abstracts,* p. 422.

Shor-Posner, G., Azar, P.A., Filart, R., et al. (1986). Morphine-stimulated feeding analysis of macronutrient selection and paraventricular nucleus lesions. *Pharmacology, Biochemistry and Behavior, 24,* 931–939.

Shor-Posner, G., Grinker, J.A., Marinescu, C., et al. (1986). Hypothalamic serotonin in the control of meal patterns and macronutrient selection. *Brain Research Bulletin, 17,* 663–671.

Smith, R.B. (1982). Confirming evidence of an effective treatment for brain dysfunction in alcoholic patients. *Journal of Nervous and Mental Disease, 170,* 275–278.

Smith, R.B. (1985). Cranial electrotherapy stimulation. In J.B. Myklebust, J.F. Cusick, A. Sanies, & S.J. Larson (Eds.), *Neural stimulation* (Vol. II, pp. 129–150). Boca Raton, FL: CRC Press.

Spyraki, C., Fibiger, H.C., & Phillips, A.G. (1982). Dopaminergic substrates of amphetamine-induced place preference conditioning. *Brain Research, 253,* 185–193.

Spyraki, C., Fibiger, H.C., & Phillips, A.G. (1983). Attenuation of heroin reward in rats by disruption of the mesolimbic dopamine system. *Psychopharmacology (Berlin), 79,* 278–283.

Stanley, B.G., Daniel, D.R., Chin, A.S., et al. (1985a). Paraventricular nucleus injections of peptide YY and neuropeptide Y preferentially enhance carbohydrate ingestion. *Peptides, 6,* 1205–1211.

Stanley, B.G., & Leibowitz, S.F. (1985). Neuropeptide Y injected in the paraventricular hypothalamus: A powerful stimulant of feeding behavior. *Proceedings of the National Academy of Sciences, (U.S.A.), 82,* 3940–3943.

Stanley, B.G., & Leibowitz, S.F. (1986). Neuropeptide Y: Stimulation of feeding and drinking by injection into the paraventricular nucleus. *Life Sciences, 35,* 2635–2642.

Stein, L., & Belluzzi, J. (1986). Second messengers, natural rewards, and drugs of abuse. *Clinical Neuropharmacology, 9,* 205–207.

hypothalamus: A powerful stimulant of feeding behavior. *Proceedings of the National Academy of Sciences, (U.S.A.), 82,* 3940–3943.

Stanley, B.G., & Leibowitz, S.F. (1986). Neuropeptide Y: Stimulation of feeding and drinking by injection into the paraventricular nucleus. *Life Sciences, 35,* 2635–2642.

Stein, L., & Belluzzi, J. (1986). Second messengers, natural rewards, and drugs of abuse. *Clinical Neuropharmacology, 9,* 205–207.

Stein, L., & Belluzzi, J.D. (1987). Reward transmitters and drugs of abuse. In J. Engel & L. Oreland (Eds.), *Brain reward systems and abuse* (pp. 19–33). New York: Raven Press.

Stevens, K.E., Shiotsu, G., Belluzzi, J.D., & Stein, L. (1988). Dymorphin A: Self-administration in CA_3 hippocampal field in the rat. *Society for Neuroscience Abstracts.*

Sved, A. (1983). Precursor control of the function of monoaminergic neurons. In R.J. Wurtman and J.J. Wurtman (Eds.), *Nutrition and the brain* (pp. 223–275). New York: Raven Press.

Tennant, F.S., Jr., & Sagherian, A.A. (1987). Double-blind comparison of amantadine and bromocriptine for ambulatory withdrawal from cocaine dependence. *Archives of Internal Medicine, 147,* 109–112.

Tepperman, F.S., & Hirst, M. (1982). Concerning the specificity of the hypothalamic opiate receptor for food intake in the rat. *Pharmacology, Biochemistry and Behavior, 17,* 1141–1144.

Thatcher, R.W., Lester, M.L., McAlaster, R., & Horst, R. (1982). Effects of low levels of cadmium and lead on cognitive functioning in children. *Archives of Environmental Health, 37,* 159–166.

Thatcher, R.W., Lester, M.L., McAlaster, R., & Cantor, D.S. (1985). Comparisons among nutrition, EEG and trace elements in predicting reading ability in children. *Annals of the New York Academy of Sciences, 433,* 87–96.

Thatcher, R.W., McAlaster, R., & Lester, M.L. (1984). Evoked potentials related to hair cadmium and lead. *Annals of the New York Academy of Sciences, 425,* 23–31.

Topel, H. (1985). Biochemical basis of alcoholism: Statements and hypotheses of present research. *Alcohol, 2,* 711–788.

Traynor v. Turnage, Administrator, Veterans Administration et al., and McKelvey v. Turnage, Administrator, Veterans Administration et al. 108 SCT 1372, 99, 1988.

Verebey, K., & Gold, M.S. (1985). Psychopharmacology of cocaine. Behavior, neurophysiology, neurochemistry and proposed treatment. In D.W. Morgan (Ed.), *Psychopharmacology: Impact on clinical psychiatry* (pp. 219–241). St. Louis: Ishiyaku.

Volpicelli, J.R., Davis, M.A., & Olgin, J.E. (1986). Naltrexone blocks the post-shock increase of ethanol consumption. *Life Sciences, 38,* 841–847.

Volpicelli, J.R., O'Brien, C.P., Alterman, A.I., and Hayashida, M. (1986). Naltrexone and the treatment of alcohol dependence: Initial observations. In L.D. Reid (Ed.) *Opioids, bulimia and alcohol abuse and alcoholism.* (pp. 195–214). New York: Springer Verlag.

Waller, M.B., McBride, W.J., Gaho, G.J., Lumeng, L. & Li, T.-K. (1984). Intragastric self-

Genotropic factors in the etiology of alcoholism. *Archives of Biochemistry*, 23, 235–290.

Wise, R.A. (1980). Action of drugs of abuse on brain reward systems. *Pharmacology, Biochemistry and Behavior*, 13, 213–223.

Wise, R.A. (1983). Brain neuronal systems mediating reward processes. In J.D. Smith & J.D. Cane (Eds.), *The neurobiology of opiate reward processes* (pp. 361–402). Amsterdam: Elsevier Biomedical.

Wise, R.A. (1984). Neural mechanisms of the reinforcing action of cocaine. In J. Grabowski (Ed.), *Cocaine: Pharmacology, effects and treatment of abuse*. Rockville, MD: NIDA Research Monograph 50, pp. 15–33.

Wise, R.A., & Bozarth, M.A. (1985). Actions of abused drugs on reward systems in the brain. In K. Blum & L. Manzo (Eds.), *Neurotoxicology, Drug and chemical toxicology*. Vol. 3. F.J. DiCarlo, and F.W. Oehme, (Eds.). New York: Marcel Dekker. 111–133.

Wise, R.A., & Bozarth, M.A. (1987). A psychomotor stimulant theory of addiction. *Psychological Review*, 94, 469–492.

Wurtman, H., Hefti, F. & Melamed, E. (1981). Precursor control of neurotransmitter synthesis. *Pharmacological Reviews*, 32, 315–335.

Wurtman, J.J., & Wurtman, R.J. (1979). Drugs that enhance serotonergic transmission diminish elective carbohydrate consumption by rats. *Life Sciences*, 24, 895–904.

Yokel, R.A., & Wise, R.A. (1975). Increased lever pressing for amphetamine after pimozide in rats: Implications for a dopamine theory of reward. *Science*, 187, 547–549.

Young, S.N. (1986). The clinical psychopharmacology of tryptophan. In R.J. Wurtman & J.J. Wurtman (Eds.), *Nutrition and the brain* (pp. 49–88). New York: Raven Press.

Zarevics, P., Weidley, E. & Setler, P. (1977). Blockade of intracranial self-stimulation by antipsychotic drugs: Failure to correlate with central alpha-noradrenergic blockade. *Psychopharmacology (Berlin)*, 53, 283–288.

Zito, K.A., Vickers, G. & Roberts, D.C.S. (1985). Disruption of cocaine and heroin self-administration following kainic acid lesions of nucleus accumbens. *Pharmacology, Biochemistry and Behavior*, 23, 1029–1036.

13

Under the Influence: Early Object Representation and Recovery in Alcoholic Women

Therese M. Unumb, Ph.D.

The intent of this chapter is to highlight one of the major findings of a recent exploratory study conducted by the author that addresses recovering alcoholic women's perceptions of the early experience with parental figures and their relationship to personality functioning, and to discuss some possible implications of these findings for both future research on women and alcoholism and the psychotherapeutic process. Specifically, it will be argued that the attainment of "object permanence" represents a useful way of conceptualizing the psychological development of some female alcoholics, and that differing patterns of identifications with each parent have importance for understanding processes of internalization and identity formation.

The rationale for the particular research thrust that guides this discussion is perhaps best explained by the observation that while more recent formulations on the etiology of female alcoholism have been illuminating, relatively little is known about the nature of earliest familial relationships or about differences in the alcoholic women's early relationships with each parent. Moreover, because themes set forth in the psychological literature on women and alcoholism have affirmed the critical role of the family of origin in personality development, consideration of these issues is clearly pertinent.

Theoretical contributions on object relations, for example, represent one area of discourse that has received much attention in the psychoanalytic literature in recent years (Greenberg & Mitchell, 1983) and one that also has begun to attract the interest of alcoholism researchers (cf. Scott, 1983). Thus this concern with the actual and perceived familial influences on character formation provides one rich conceptual framework in which to investigate relationships with early caretakers and has served as the one around which the study was organized. More specifically, the investigation began with an assumption that perceptions of early experiences with primary caretakers were important for understanding personality functioning in adulthood.

After briefly summarizing the research methodology employed, an integration of qualitative and quantitative methods of analysis was selected to examine the experiences of 30 middle-class white women, with a design based on a "data triangulation" strategy. The women completed a 90-minute interview and two adapted versions of the Family Environment Scale (Moos, 1973). Three earliest memories were also elicited from each subject and evaluated for level and quality of self-object differentiation using the Assessment of the Quality and Structural Dimensions of Object Representations (AQSDOR) scale (Blatt, Chevron, Quinlan, & Wein, 1981). Interjudge ratings on the scale were acceptable. In commenting on this use of multiple methods of data collection as an operational strategy for validating observations and hypotheses, Filstead (1979) has observed that the ability to arrive at similar conclusions about certain phenomena using different data sources enhances the validity of the observations made about those events (p. 44).

LEVEL AND QUALITY OF OBJECT REPRESENTATIONS

In an effort to describe some of the identifiable patterns of perceptions and events that characterized the study women's recollections of their early relations with their parents, it is necessary first to consider the major study finding, which demonstrated that, psychologically, the subjects had attained a level of object representation indicating the capacity for "object constancy." Importantly, this ability to substitute a mental representation of the primary caretaker in the caretaker's absence is considered the hallmark of this phase of emotional development. Practically speaking, it may be interpreted as evidence that the study women have a representation of the mother as available to them in much the same manner as the primary caretaker was previously available to them for sustenance, comfort, and love (Mahler, Pine, & Bergman, 1975), and it is this parental imago that facilitates the ability to self-soothe when threatened by anxiety.

Critical to this theoretical formulation is that the women, having internalized the mother in this way, experienced her apart from her need-satisfying functions and her presence is no longer essential for the maintenance of well-being. Translated, the internalization of the mother in this manner attests to a higher level of functioning than would be seen in more severely emotionally disturbed individuals. The achievement of the level of emotional object constancy also implies the capacity to recognize and tolerate loving and hostile feelings for the same object, thereby indicating that the mental splitting of objects (i.e., as either "all good" or "all bad") has been replaced by an ability to synthesize and tolerate ambivalence (Burgner & Edgecombe, 1972).

Given these criteria, and on the basis of the research data, an argument against the attainment of a level of object constancy also might be made, however, supported by qualitatively derived evidence that the study women were not well able to articulate ways in which these significant others had been "internalized." A common response to questions about ways in which they were like or unlike their parents, for example, was one of an expressed desire to disavow any identifications with parental behaviors and attitudes. Citing the importance of "doing things differently" and of "not making the same mistakes my parents made" were familiar themes expressed. These reactions were often accompanied by an emphatic statement of the subjects' belief that despite their rejection of "parental ways," they believed their parents had "done the best they could with what they had." For some, this statement appeared to serve as an acknowledgment that familial bonds were stronger than even massive disappointment, while for others, it conveyed a sense of resignation tinged with resentment.

Furthermore, the generally disparate precepts of mothers and fathers that emerged when perceptions were articulated might be construed as representing "object splitting," thereby also suggesting that the capacity to synthesize and tolerate ambivalence had not been achieved. Following are two illustrations of how expressions of unambiguous high regard for the fathers were juxtaposed with tensions either with or involving the mother:

> He was the one who always said, "You can do whatever you want. You're as smart as any man . . ." When I started fighting with my mother to the point that it was just unbearable, he got frustrated . . . he'd say "You know, I'm stuck in between you two." It was his calm way of looking at life. I always wanted to be like him . . . he was my idol.

And as another subject stated:

> Oh, I was crazy about him, he was my idol, and he played me against her . . . I was the in-between. He was very, uh, I guess very unhappy with her because she wasn't what he wanted her to be.
>
> (Unumb, 1988, p. 88)

Still, rather than demonstrating the implausibility of the interpretation that a stable concept of the self and the other (i.e., object constancy) had been attained, these discrepancies might be understood in another way. That is, given that the concept of object constancy, as measured by the AQSDOR scale represents a blend of the definitions formulated by Piaget (1954) and Mahler (Mahler et al., 1975), it is possible that this blending may not adequately reconcile the different meaning each theorist attributed to the object-constancy phenomenon. Greenberg and Mitchell

(1983), for example, note that Piaget's work focuses on the child's relations with inanimate things, with the notion of object permanence referring to the cognitive capacity for things to continue to exist in the child's mind even when they are not present. Such capacity is thought to appear at about 18 months of age, well before the development of constancy in the libidinal sense described by Mahler: "The reason for this lag is that, in speaking of the constancy of the human, libidinal cathected object, we are referring to a situation far more affectively charged than is Piaget" (p. 279).

In this way, Mahler's notion of object constancy presupposes, but is not identical to, the capacity for object permanence as defined by Piaget. Consequently, the apparent discrepancies in the interpretation of the study findings pertaining to object representation may be attributable, at least to some extent, to a mixing of the definitional terms and to the authors' greater adherence to the Piagetian concept of object constancy on the AQSDOR scale than was initially appreciated.

Of course, our understanding of the findings is also well served by the reminder that levels of psychological development are not static entities, but carry with them the remnants of earlier modes of experiencing others, as well as strivings toward a more sophisticated conceptualization of objects. The recognition, then, that the achievement of object constancy represents a gradual process of psychological development accompanied by both regressions and forward thrusts offers an even more convincing way of reconciling seeming contradictions in the data.

PATTERNS OF PERCEPTION OF EARLY PARENTAL FIGURES

Since a major question that guided this investigation was whether there was any relationship between the nature and quality of study women's earliest perceptions of either their mothers or fathers and the assessment of character structure, with support for such a relationship having been demonstrated, a central task was further to tease out the meanings associated with the internalization of parental images. In this way, it was believed that the characteristics of the internalizations that defined the stage of object constancy and described the study women might be better delineated.

Schafer's (1968) definition of internalization, which was formulated as part of a larger-scale effort to bring preciseness and clarity to psychoanalytic thinking, is used here and refers to "all those processes by which the subject transforms real or imagined regulatory interactions with this environment into inner regulations and characteristics" (p. 9). Within this context, Schafer further defines identifications as one important kind of internalization; as such, a focus on identification phenomena as they pertained to the study women becomes meaningful to the present discussion.

Based on the research findings, it is proposed here that an understanding of how the study women internalized the experience of the relationship with their parents, as well as the implications of these internalization processes, is best clarified around two central ideas. First, it is proposed that the study women's denial of identifications with parenting figures, when it occurred, represented a psychological press for autonomy and a denial of dependency longings. Second, it is proposed that the disparate perceptions of and identifications with parental figures that also were demonstrated represented problems in the integration and internalization of the conflicting attributes, values, principles, and feelings of these significant others.

REJECTION OF IDENTIFICATIONS AND THE THRUST TOWARD AUTONOMY

Jacobson (1964) has written on the process of identity formation and has described the identification process as representing the "rebellious struggle for the development and maintenance of one's own independent identity, bringing the individual closer and closer to the time when parents become dispensable" (p. 66). She further describes the increasing selectivity of identifications that occurs over the course of early development as meaning: "In this respect I like you and want to be like you, but in other respects, I don't like you and don't want to be like you; I want to be different" (p. 9).

From this perspective, the rejection of identifications with her parents may well represent a statement about the importance of the recovering alcoholic female's need to individuate and clearly distinguish herself as independent. In this manner, the strength of the denial of similarity to the parents may serve as one important indicator for assessing the power of the need to deny dependence.

Blos (1967) has described the wholesale rejection of the family of origin as "a frantic circumvention of the painful disengagement process." While his work focused particularly on developmental processes associated with adolescence, his description of the individuation process has relevance for understanding, in a more general way, failures that preclude maturation (cf. Colarusso & Nemiroff, 1981). Here, for example, he describes the incapacity to separate from internal objects except by detachment and rejection as the subjective experience of a sense of alienation that represents a failure adequately to resolve the process of individuation (in Miller, 1987).

If the denial of identifications is indeed associated with problems in individuation, the question of why this occurs arises. Mahler (Mahler et al., 1975) has opined that in order for an inner sense of autonomy to develop, the individuation process must be gradual and progressive and include the mother's sustained emotional availability and consistency. If we consider, then, what needs to happen in order for object constancy to take place, our attention is drawn more specifically to Mahler's notion of developmental events preceding this phenomenon, with particular attention accorded the "rapprochement phase." During this period, it is believed that the mother must be able to tolerate her own wishes for dependency and autonomy in order to respond in an empathic way to the corresponding wishes in the child and in this manner avoid retaliation against or withdrawal from the child.

From a theoretical perspective on psychological development, it might be speculated that the residual difficulties in individuation, as manifested by failures in identification with parenting figures, may be attributable to either too sudden or inconsistent relations with the early caretakers at a time when vacillation between leaving the mother and returning to her predominated. One potentially productive area of research, then, would be to ascertain whether the denial of identifications with parental figures is indeed characteristic among alcoholic women, and if so, whether this phenomenon is correlated with the need for autonomy and denial of dependency longings.

In light of the body of research on alcoholism, there is certainly nothing novel regarding the notion that dependency issues are intimately linked with addictive behavior, but it is nonetheless important to understand better, among other things, the implications of dependency tendencies for women who no longer drink. How, for example, are dependency longings managed when the alcohol is no longer considered a viable means for self-soothing? And to what degree, if any, do other activities—such as participation in Alcoholics Anonymous—or interpersonal relations with significant others serve as "symptom substitutions" for the alcohol use, and for which individuals? We might also wonder if these activities shift and/or change over time and under what circumstances such changes might occur.

Yet another issue important to the understanding of differences in the nature of dependency longings and how they might be manifested in sobriety involves an examination of the effects of early experiences with an alcoholic mother. While this thrust was not the central focus of the research described here, perceptions of the early relationship with an alcoholic mother, when they were described, were remarkable for the harsh criticism that distinguished them from all other depictions of mothers and fathers.

Describing the unpredictability of life with an alcoholic mother, for example, one woman recalled how she coped with the attendant stress:

> Uh, just recently, I've been able to say my mother's an alcoholic . . . but when I was growing up—I'd say from about the fourth grade on, she was on my back. I, uh, these mood swings, these mood shifts, were just unbearable, I mean, they were just incredible. I didn't know when she was going to explode, or when she was going to be O.K. And I, for one, walked around on eggshells my entire life at home. (Unumb, 1988, p. 99)

Interestingly, the depictions of these early experiences with an alcoholic mother tended to be global rather than to involve any distinction between periods when the mother was drinking and when she was sober, implying that there may have been a central need to "predict" the parent, possibly as a means for facilitating the development of object constancy and a sense of autonomy. These negative depictions also imply that the experience of failures in need gratification was a pervasive one. The following portrayal of the relationship with her alcoholic mother highlights one woman's sense of deprivation, despite her assertion of a positive bond:

> . . . The sad, the really sad part of it was the fact that so often, that the only time she was the least bit nice to me was when she was drinking. You know? Because a drunk will talk to anybody. They get somebody on the phone, who-ever's there will do, you know? [laughs] And there were times when she was drinking that she would become affectionate, not affectionate . . . but, you know, she would tell me she loved me.

This same subject, now in her mid-30s and sober for approximately four years, also described having been twice divorced, her "workaholic" life style, and her unwillingness to "rely on anybody to meet my needs," while acknowledging an emerging awareness of how strong feelings of "abandonment" by her mother had influenced these adaptations to adulthood and the difficulties met along the way. In this manner, it might be speculated that perceived failures in nurturance by an alcoholic mother resonate both long and in some fairly predictable ways.

To date, however, the paucity of research on recovery in alcoholic women over the life course precludes any hard and fast conclusions about how dependency issues are managed in adulthood or, more particularly, at different periods in adulthood. Certainly, the high recidivism rate among alcoholics helps to explain why research efforts thus far have focused on the manifest chemical dependency itself, rather than on psychological and relational factors associated with long-term sobriety. Still, the formulation and testing of hypotheses about the correlation between management/resolution of dependency longings and the maintenance of sobriety represent an important arena of study and one where clinical findings would seem to play an important role.

IMPLICATIONS OF DISPARATE PERCEPTIONS AND IDENTIFICATIONS FOR PERSONALITY FUNCTIONING

Since not all of the study women rejected identifications with their parents, it is also important to consider the nature of identifications with parental figures when they did occur. It was found, for example, that when similarities to their parents were reported, they tended to be organized around identifications with either the alcoholic father's values and abilities or the mother's alcoholism. From an object-relations perspective, this pattern is consistent with the positive/negative split that characterized perceptions of the fathers versus perceptions of the mothers more generally.

Because it was the study women who recalled having had alcoholic fathers who were most apt to describe identifications with them, but in terms of the father's values and skills rather than his alcoholism, we might wonder whether recovering alcoholic women need to deny identifications with paternal alcoholism in order to sustain a positive image of the father and internalize a "good" representation of him. Conceptually, this pattern of positive identifications with their fathers and the father's "goodness" may serve as a way of splitting off or denying the "bad" perceptions of the experiences with the paternal figure and of themselves. Conversely, the identification with the mothers around the experience of alcoholism might be viewed as a way of "containing" the bad self and object experiences within this relationship in an effort to control destructive wishes and fears associated with their own and their parents' drinking behaviors, while protecting the internalized experience of the "good self" and the "good object" (cf. Klein, 1975).

Alternatively, this lower level of object relations could, as proposed earlier, serve as a means for asserting control and autonomy in an unpredictable environment. Yet another hypothesis might be proffered here, as well. That is, rather than the "object splitting" representing a way of defending against primitive anxiety, the identification with a "negative" mother might be thought of as a means for promoting, albeit rather unsuccessfully, the resolution of the oedipal conflict and the attainment of gender identity and autonomy.

Again, while some of these speculations about object "splitting" might seem to contradict the object-constancy phenomenon, it bears remembering that what is being described is a developmental process rather than an "event." Moreover, it makes intuitive sense to presume that not all of the subjects were alike in all ways, so that while they generally fit the criteria for a certain diagnostic "picture," the different patterns of identification may be reflective of some relative variations within a diagnostic schema.

At issue at this juncture is the question of the implications of these disparate perceptions of parental figures for personality functioning in adulthood. Colarusso and Nemiroff (1979, 1981) suggest that the fundamental issues of childhood continue as central aspects of adult life, but in altered form, and have emphasized the importance of adult experiences for understanding processes of individuation subsequent to childhood. Given this premise, that there is some link between developmental processes in childhood and in adulthood, it is worthwhile to consider not only how the study women's early perceptions of their parents correlate with expressed patterns of identification with them, but also the implications of these patterns, so as to understand how alcoholic women negotiate the individuation process in adulthood.

In essence, then, the aforementioned data demonstrated that identifications, when reported at all, involved either a "positive" identification with the father or an essentially "negative" identification with the mother, with little intermingling of positive and negative percepts when describing parental figures. Thus it is reasonable to hypothesize that, from a psychological perspective, the dichotomized perceptions and identifications of the parental figures represent not only difficulties in the study women's capacities for integrating and internalizing conflicting attributes, values, principles, and feelings of the parental figures, but also, unless reconciled, failures in integration that may serve further to hinder the process of individuation and the development of a more stable feminine identity.

In this regard, it becomes especially important to consider how recovering alcoholic women negotiate the mother–daughter relationship in adulthood when negative perceptions of their mothers predominate, particularly since there is good empirical support to demonstrate that the nature of the mother–daughter identification is a crucial correlate of the individuation process for women (Lebe, 1982; Wilk, 1981; Miller, 1987; Cohler, Weiss, & Grunebaum, 1981). Specifically, it seems likely that the female alcoholic's success or failure in reconciling the difficulties in her relationship with her mother has important implications for the way in which issues of autonomy, dependence, and gender identity are managed, and it becomes important to understand what kind of experiences in adulthood foster, as well as impede, this reconciliation process. Undoubtedly, knowledge about how these relationships are negotiated will also have bearing in the therapeutic setting. Consequently, some thoughts about psychotherapy for this population of women are in order.

FURTHER DIRECTIONS FOR FUTURE RESEARCH

The efficacy of the hypothesis regarding failures in the integration and internalization of object representations among recovering alcoholic women raises a number of questions that await further investigation. To illustrate, we might wonder about particular "arenas of vulnerability" that emerge over the life course, evoking unresolved psychological issues and resulting in an increased proneness to the development of, or relapse into, alcoholism. In this regard, one potentially productive focus of research would be to investigate predispositional factors associated with female alcoholism and their possible links with certain life-stage phenomena. Looking at the issue of arenas of vulnerability from a social-psychological perspective would, of course, also be useful. Neugarten (1968), for example, has proposed that it is the *unexpected* event in adulthood, rather than the anticipated change, that signals crisis in individuals' lives, often leading to maladaptive methods of coping. If accurate, it might be anticipated that the rapid cultural shifts and social role changes currently affecting women's lives would result in additional psychological stress and crises. Alcohol abuse and alcoholism thus might represent one means for managing these problems, thereby warranting inquiry into the role of unanticipated events in the onset of female alcoholism in adulthood.

In the past several years, some investigators interested in object-relations theories have focused their attention on a proposed link between female alcoholism and a borderline level of personality organization (Hartocollis & Hartocollis 1980; Gleissner, 1986). Often, substantiation of this association has been based on findings that confirm evidence of mental "splitting" of objects into good/bad dichotomies. While evidence of splitting was demonstrated in this study, this characteristic is frequently and erroneously described as the distinguishing feature of the borderline diagnostic category. Future research efforts, therefore, should be directed toward providing a more sophisticated understanding of personality functioning in alcoholic women, relying on a range of diagnostic indicators and methods of evaluation for making their assessments.

Finally, and in a related vein, since it was demonstrated that the study women's level of representations was somewhat higher, and, by inference, more closely associated with the phase of phallic narcissism, it is necessary to ascertain whether these findings can be replicated. If replicable, there would be stronger evidence to support the hypothesis that recovering alcoholic women experience problems in integrating and internalizing higher-level attributes of early caretakers (i.e., the capacity for appreciating the complex and often contradictory nature of others' values, feelings, and actions). In order to test whether these difficulties actually interfere with the process of individuation and identity formation, a study of current relationships with significant other persons might be undertaken. This study could include relationships with spouses, important female friends, and daughters as a way of determining whether the patterns of individuation in these relationships are consistent with or differentiated from the perceptions of the relationship with the early caretakers.

SOME THOUGHTS ON THERAPEUTIC INTERVENTION

All but two of the study women reported a current or past involvement in some form of psychotherapy, including long-term outpatient treatment, thereby testifying to the need for consideration of appropriate therapeutic interventions for female alcoholics.

The assertion that AA played, and continues to play, a vital role in the sustained recovery from alcohol addiction was unanimously supported by the study women. Consequently, an appreciation, especially among mental health professionals, for the critical function AA serves in both normalizing the experience of alcoholism and providing a solid support network for recovery undoubtedly would facilitate the building of a stronger alliance between professional and self-help forms of intervention.

Because the study women differed in their view of how central AA was in their lives, however (Unumb, 1988, Appendix A), it seems possible that the level and intensity of involvement in AA might be one indicator of the degree of dependency on external supports present at any given period in recovery, thus signaling what the therapeutic issues and tasks will be. Some of the women reported, for example, that they felt less of a need to organize their lives around meetings than a need to utilize their AA involvements as simply one important way of fostering personal growth. Others described involvements in a variety of self-help groups, which served as the fabric of their social relationships and represented their hold on sobriety. While it is not certain which factors contribute most to these differing perspectives, knowledge about patterns of involvement in self-help organizations like AA and the other "anonymous" groups might more richly illuminate how strivings toward autonomy and dependency longings are manifested in help-seeking behaviors. Going a step further, and musing about the *interface* between self-help groups and individual psychotherapy, an issue that arises is the manner in which involvement in self-help activities may serve, if unexamined, to mask or diffuse dependency longings by externalizing them to a group rather than facing them in a one-to-one relationship.

Additionally, the tendency to possess negative perceptions of and specific identifications with their mothers suggests that alcoholic women may have internalized a skewed, and perhaps primitive, percept of female role models that have correspondingly negative implications for their perceptions of themselves. Therapeutic interventions aimed toward the internalization of a more balanced representation of the mothering figure, then, would be expected to facilitate the psychological growth of the formerly addicted female, while also evoking speculation about whether a same-sex therapist would be more effective in this enterprise.

Speaking to the issue of how the therapist can intervene as the mediator in the patient's achievement of higher developmental levels of object representation, Blatt, Wild, and Ritzler (1975) note:

If the internalization of object relations results in the formation of psychic structures during normal development, then the internalization of significant interactions between the patient and the analyst must play an important role in the therapeutic process. According to Loewald (1960, p. 18), the analyst becomes available as a new object by eliminating, step by step, the transference distortions which interfere with the establishment of new object relationships. And it is the internalization of new and relatively undistorted relations with the analyst which leads to therapeutic change. The consideration of psychopathological conditions as disturbances in object relations and representations offers the potential for integrating the study of impairments in cognitive processes, interpersonal relationships, and the representation of the self and the object world within a theoretical model which has etiological, as well as therapeutic implications. (pp. 280–281)

Although not detailed in this chapter, data that also bear on the question of the therapeutic intervention and provide a counterpoint to the above are those that described many of the study women's object representations as consistent with a "concrete-perceptual" level of development. The concrete-perceptual level is described by Blatt et al. (1981) as including those memories in which the person is defined as a separate entity, but the definition is primarily in concrete literal terms, often characterized in terms of physical attributes. As Blatt points out, "there is a literalness, a globality, and a concreteness to the description. There is little emphasis on part properties, attributes, or features, but rather the person is experienced as a literal, concrete totality. Emphasis is often on what the person looks like in its external characteristics or physical properties, in a literal concrete sense."

Given the propensity to conceptualize the object (parent) as a concrete, fixed construct that is not understood in terms of the parts that make up the whole, and where, as a consequence, extremely contradictory experiences with the object are met with confusion (cf. Blatt et al., 1981), it should not be surprising that for many of the study women, there was a lack of enthusiasm for the deeper exploration of psychological issues. For example, as a group, the study subjects demonstrated little interest in describing or exploring the issue of motivations for drinking. Some subjects described the need to know "why" as likely to open a floodgate to rationalizations and justifications for drinking abusively. The response perhaps most eloquent in its simplicity, as well as for its depiction of environmental influences, however, was that provided by a 35-year-old subject whose mother had been actively alcoholic since the subject's early childhood. Explaining why the question of impetus for drinking did not engender curiosity, she said, "I lived with it for so long, I guess the 'why' isn't important" (Unumb, 1988, p. 83). Consideration of all these factors, as well as the possible wish to mask dependency longings via participation in less "scrutinizing" endeavors, becomes important, then, particularly when designing treatment goals for individual psychotherapy and making a decision to adopt a support-oriented versus an insight-oriented or uncovering therapy approach.

Finally, given some other findings of this study, which were consistent with published research on the intergenerational link to alcoholism (Roe, 1944; Cotton, 1979; Fox, 1972; Clemmons, 1979), the importance of aggressive interventions at a family-systems level certainly cannot be discounted. Perhaps what is specifically needed, however, is a greater appreciation among therapists of the particular impact that maternal alcoholism can have on the family system than has been acknowledged (let alone understood!). Moreover, as was seen in this particular study, where the reported presence of maternal alcoholism during the subject's formative years almost always coexisted with paternal alcoholism, it becomes critical to consider the implications of working with recovering alcoholic women who both may have been reared by two alcoholic parents and now, as mothers themselves, find themselves rearing their own children in an environment in which both parents are chemically dependent.

It is not difficult to accept that this schema would have particular implications for the way in which family tensions and deficits in caretaking are manifested, but it is perhaps less obvious, and therefore important, to appreciate how, on a very primitive level, family members' capacities for "reality testing" are at an even higher risk of becoming severely compromised in an environment where there is no parental anchor of stability and predictability. By reality testing, reference here is made not only to what the study women described as utter confusion regarding "socially appropriate" ways of communicating anger and love, but especially to the difficulties in accurately assessing interpersonal cues, problems that occurred when family members colluded to deny another's alcoholism. Consequently, as a desperate means of protecting the self against object splitting, fears of attack, emotional withdrawal, and even psychic fragmentation, defenses that impede "seeing things as they really are" need to be respected and very carefully explored by the clinician treating these families and the individuals they comprise.

SUMMARY

As with most attempts to describe and understand the meaning of interpersonal relationships, perceptions of one's parents are fraught with complexities and contradictions, factors that are not easily captured, let alone readily explained. Thus an attempt has been made here to impart some of the broad-brush findings that described and distinguished subjects' early perceptions of their mothers and fathers and also to report some of the different colorations that emerged when findings from the various data sources were compared, contrasted, and, when appropriate, integrated.

The investigation reported on in this chapter demonstrated that there are identifiable patterns of perceptions and events that characterize recovering alcoholic women's recollections of their early relationships with parents, and that these perceptions are influenced, at least to some degree, by the presence of parental alcoholism in childhood, and particularly by the issue of predictability. The study also provided support for the hypothesis that there is an association between how alcoholic females perceive characteristics of the early relationship with parental caretakers and the level and quality of object representations, as measured by their earliest memories of these figures. Specifically, it was found that the study women were more homogeneous than dissimilar when one aspect of personality was measured. As a group, it was found that the subjects had attained a level of development in which object constancy, or a clear differentiation of self from others, had been achieved.

With regard to methodological issues, the integration of qualitative and quantitative research methods provided a useful way of approaching the investigation of factors associated with psychological development. The heavier emphasis on the qualitative analysis of the data offered a richness that fosters a deeper appreciation of the complexities inherent in the way in which individuals' perceptions, motives, and assessments of important relationships are formulated. Because the assessment of the conceptual level of object representation was limited to one measure of quantitative evaluation, however (i.e., the AQSDOR scale), with some question about the definition employed to describe the level of object constancy, the investigation would have been strengthened by the use of an additional measure; unfortunately, few instruments are available to assess this construct.

Finally, a limitation, as well as a strength, of the study findings described here was demonstrated by the composition of the sample. The focus on White, middle-class females precludes generalizability of the findings to other populations of alcoholic women who have achieved sobriety, while the number of professional women who were represented signified a needed departure from previous studies in which samples more typically have been solely constituted of middle-class homemakers.

Regarding treatment issues, it has been argued here that there is a need for a greater appreciation among mental health professionals for the role of self-help groups in the long-term recovery and psychological growth of the alcoholic female. In this vein, closer attention to the ways in which such involvements can serve to undermine, as well as augment, the therapeutic process is necessary.

Data that demonstrated that the study women harbored more negative perceptions of and identifications with their mothers certainly have import for the treatment process and raise the question of whether the internalization of a more balanced representation of the mothering figure might prove more viable via work with a female therapist. An appreciation for the quality of alcoholic women's object relatedness also has meaning in the selection of a particular individual therapy approach, whereby the alcoholic's interest in and capacity for exploring motivations for drinking may function as a useful diagnostic indicator when considering a supportive versus a depth-oriented treatment approach.

No intent has been made in this discussion to compare or contrast various treatment modalities. It bears mentioning, however, that consideration of treatment issues associated with intervention at a family-systems level may prove particularly illuminating when closer scrutiny is accorded the effect of maternal alcoholism on family members. Here, with a focus on the "impaired caretaker," the issue of predictability again becomes a salient one and has important ramifications for understanding family members' vulnerabilities as they pertain to reality testing.

In closing, it is reasonable to assume that until women are more adequately represented in research studies on alcoholism, clear conceptualizations of the antecedents associated with this disorder specific to females will remain elusive. From a psychological perspective, it has been proposed here that the formulation of meaningful hypotheses about why women become addicted to alcohol is dependent, at least in part, on the consideration of internal processes that intercede in their experiences, influence their interpersonal relations, and shape the way in which they function over the life course. Clearly, knowledge about these phenomena will be important not only from a treatment perspective, but also for identifying women at high risk.

REFERENCES

Blatt, S., Chevron, E., Quinlan, D., & Wein, S. (1981). Manual for the assessment of qualitative and structural dimensions of object representations. Unpublished manuscript, Yale University.

Blatt, S., Wild, C.M., & Ritzler, B. (1975). Disturbances of object representations in schizophrenia. *Psychoanalysis and Contemporary Science, 4,* 235–288.

Blos, P. (1967). The second individuation process in adolescence. *Psychoanalytic Study of the Child, 27,* 168–182.

Burgner, M., & Edgecombe, R. (1972). Some problems in the conceptualization of early object relationships: 2. The concept of object constancy. *Psychoanalytic Study of the Child, 27,* 315–333.

Clemmons, P. (1979). Issues in marriage, family and child counseling in alcoholism. In V. Burtle (Ed.), *Women who drink* (pp. 127–144). Springfield, IL: Charles C. Thomas.

Cohler, B., Weiss, J., & Grunebaum, H. (1981). *Mothers, grandmothers and daughters: Personality and childcare in three-generation families.* New York: Wiley.

Colarusso, C., & Nemiroff, R. (1979). Adult development. *International Journal of Psychoanalysis, 60,* 59–71.

Colarusso, C., & Nemiroff, R. (1981). *Adult development.* New York: Plenum Press.

Cotton, N. (1979). The familial incidence of alcoholism. *Journal of Studies on Alcohol, 40,* 89–116.

Filstead, W. (1979). Qualitative methods: A needed perspective in evaluation research. In T. Cook & C. Reichardt (Eds.), *Qualitative and quantitative methods in evaluation research* (pp. 33–47). Beverly Hills, CA: Sage.

Fox, R. (1972). Children in the alcoholic family. In W.C. Bier (Ed.), *Problems in addiction: Alcoholism and narcotics.* New York: Fordham University Press.

Gleissner, M. (1986). Alcoholism and impaired object relations in females. *Dissertation Abstracts International, 46.* 8-A, 2441. University Microfilms.

Greenberg, J., & Mitchell, S. (1983). *Object relations in psychoanalytic theory.* Cambridge, MA: Harvard University Press.

Hartocollis, P., & Hartocollis, P. (1980). Alcoholism, borderline and narcissistic disorders: A psychoanalytic overview. In W. Fann (Ed.), *Phenomenology and treatment of alcoholism* (pp. 93–110). New York: SP Medical and Scientific Books.

Jacobson, E. (1964). *The self and the object world.* New York: International Universities Press.

Klein, M. (1975). *Envy and gratitude and other works, 1946–1963.* New York: Delacorte Press.

Lebe, D. (1982). Individuation of women. *Psychoanalytic Review, 69,* 63–73.

Mahler, M., Pine, F., & Bergman, A. (1975). *The psychological birth of the human infant.* New York: Basic Books.

Miller, A. (1987). Attachment and autonomy: Individuation themes in the relationships of 20–40 year old women and their mothers. *Dissertation Abstracts International.* University Microfilms.

Moos, R. (1973). *The family environment scale.* Palo Alto, CA: Consulting Psychologists Press.

Neugarten, B. (Ed.). (1968). Adult personality: Toward a psychology of the life cycle. In *Middle age and aging* (pp. 137–147). Chicago: University of Chicago Press.

Piaget, J. (1954). *The construction of reality in the child.* New York: Basic Books.

Roe, A. (1944). The adult adjustment of children of alcoholic parents raised in foster homes. *Quarterly Journal of Studies on Alcohol, 5,* 378–393.

Schafer, R. (1968). *Aspects of internalization.* New York: International Universities Press.

Scott, E. (1983). Object relations theory: Expanded and applied to the treatment of certain alcoholics. *International Journal of Offender Therapy and Comparative Criminology, 27,* 99–109.

Unumb, T. (1988). Early object relations and recovery in alcoholic women. *Dissertation Abstracts International.* University Microfilms.

Wilk, C. (1981). The dual-career dilemma: A psychosocial study of the decision to have children. *Dissertation Abstracts International.* University Microfilms.

14

Recovery from Cocaine/Crack Abuse: A Follow-up of Applicants for Treatment

Paula H. Kleinman, Ph.D.

Sung-Yeon Kang, Ph.D.

George E. Woody, M.D.

Robert B. Millman, M.D.

Thomas C. Todd, Ph.D.

Douglas S. Lipton, Ph.D.

Cocaine/crack is the source of more professional and public concern than any other illicit drug. It is the sole illicit substance whose use was on the increase through the mid-1980s (Schuster, 1988). Treatment for cocaine/crack abuse is still in its infancy (Kleber & Gawin, 1984; Millman, 1988; Rosecan, Spitz, & Gross, 1987; Washton & Gold, 1987), and research about abuse of the drug is also relatively sparse. There are few follow-up studies of cocaine abusers (Waldorf, Murphy, & Reinarman, 1988; Wallace, 1989) and little information about use patterns over time. As with other addictive drugs, there is uncertainty about recovery and the extent to which treatment affects the recovery process (Schachter, 1982). The sample discussed here consists of persons who applied for outpatient treatment of cocaine/crack abuse in New York City during 1988–1989, with special emphasis on those who were reinterviewed six to 12 months after initial contact with the program.

In this chapter, we first present the drug-use history of this sample and findings on psychopathology at the time of application for treatment. Second, we review findings on the rate of retention in treatment. Next, data on drug use and other problem behavior in the follow-up period are discussed. Finally, attention is focused on recovery from cocaine abuse and on the factors that are related to it.

METHODS

Subjects

The analyses reported here are based on three different samples drawn from the same larger group: (1) 168 adults with cocaine-use disorders who attended at least one assessment session with an outpatient drug-free treatment program in New York City between February 1988 and July 1989 (baseline data, shown in Table 14–1, are based on this sample); (2) A subsample of the first 76 persons to be seen for at least one assessment session (data on psychopathology are drawn on this sample); and (3) A subsample of 122 persons who were reinterviewed six to 12 months later (all follow-up data are based on this sample). The initial intention was to conduct follow-up interviews six months after initial contact, but difficulties in locating certain members of the sample produced a time lag that was longer than expected for those who were hardest to reach. The 122 persons in the follow-up sample represent 73% of those who were seen at the program at least once.

All persons admitted to the study were classified at intake as having both lifetime and current cocaine-use disorders according to criteria set forth in the revised third

Table 14-1
Demographic Characteristics of Baseline and Follow-up Samples

Variables		Baseline (N = 168), %	Follow-up (N = 122), %
Sex	1. Male	86	85
	2. Female	14	15
Education	1. <12 years	26	25
	2. 12 years	41	40
	3. >12 years	33	35
Age	1. 20–29	52	46
	2. 30–39	40	46
	3. 40–49	8	8
Ethnicity	1. White	16	16
	2. Black	62	64
	3. Hispanic	21	19
	4. Other	1	1
Occupation	1. White collar	32	34
	2. Blue collar (or unemployed)	68	66

edition of the *Diagnostic and Statistical Manual of Mental Disorders* (DSM-III-R). At the time of entry, their history of cocaine use ranged from one to 31 years, with an average of eight years. Clients who were reinterviewed closely resembled the entire population of persons admitted to the study in terms of demographic characteristics (see Table 14-1). The majority in both samples were non-White and male, with 12 or fewer years of education. Most had held a full-time job in the three years prior to entry into treatment, and of these, most had blue-collar jobs. More than half had been arrested at least once, about two thirds of these on non–drug related charges.

Measurement of Variables

All subjects received an extensive intake battery, which included the Addiction Severity Index (McLellan, Luborsky, Woody & O'Brien, 1980), the Beck Depression Inventory (Beck & Steer, 1981), the Structured Clinical Interview for DSM-III-R (Spitzer et al., 1986), and a Drug History instrument designed by the authors.

ADDICTION SEVERITY INDEX

The Addiction Severity Index (ASI) is a structured clinical research interview designed to provide information about various areas of a patient's life in which there is often dysfunction associated with drug abuse. These potential problem areas are as follows: (1) medical, (2) legal, (3) drug abuse, (4) alcohol abuse, (5) employment, (6) family, and (7) psychiatric. Reliability and validity data for the ASI have been extensively reported (McLellan et al., 1980, 1982, 1985; Rounsaville, Kosten, & Weissman, 1986), and it has become one of the most commonly used evaluation instruments in clinical studies of substance abuse. A composite score, based on the sum of several individual questions within each problem area, has been developed for each area by McLellan and his associates (McGahan, Griffith, Parente & McLellan, *Composite Scores from the Addiction Severity Index* [unpublished manual], pp. 1–14) and is used in this chapter.

BECK DEPRESSION INVENTORY

The Beck Depression Inventory (Beck & Steer, 1981) is a self-administered 21-item self-rating scale of depression. It rates cognitive, affective, somatic, and behavioral/vegetative symptoms of depression on a scale from 0 to 3. The scale has been validated with other measures of depression, including the SCL-90.

STRUCTURED CLINICAL INTERVIEW FOR DSM-III-R (SCID)

The Structured Clinical Interview for DSM-III-R (SCID) is a relatively new, interviewer-administered schedule designed to diagnose DSM-III-R Axis I and Axis II disorders. Developed by Spitzer et al. (1987), it was designed to improve upon the Schedule for Affective Disorders (SADS), an instrument previously designed for the same purpose. The SCID-OP and SCID II are relatively new measures and only preliminary reliability studies have been reported to date. Reliability of the diagnosis of cocaine dependence was reported to be κ = 1.0 and for major depression, preliminary results were reported to be κ = .60 (Gibbon, M., personal communication).

DRUG HISTORY

The Drug History is a structured interview designed for this study to describe past and current cocaine use in some detail. It also includes questions about age at first cigarette use, level of current cigarette smoking, first illicit drug used, age at which that drug was used, and other drugs used, both at the beginning of cocaine use and during the period of heaviest cocaine use.

Methods of Analysis

Data are analyzed by simple correlation coefficients, paired t-tests measuring the significance of the difference in means at two different points in time for the same group, analysis of covariance, and discriminant function analysis.

RESULTS

Drug-Use History

The mean age at first cocaine use was 21.5 years, with a range of 12 to 45 years; the mean age at first use of any illicit drug was 16.5 years, with a range of 11 to 39 years. Almost all (91%) had used cocaine three or more times a week for at least a month, with a third (34%) having used three or more times a week for four years or more. Although 96% began using cocaine by the intranasal route ("snorting"), crack or free-base inhalation was the current ingestion route for about three quarters of the sample (72%) in the 30 days prior to first program contact. About half (46%) had spent over $450 on cocaine/crack in the 30 days prior to entering into treatment.

As expected, most clients were users of cigarettes, alcohol, and marijuana, as well as cocaine. Eighty-six percent were current smokers, 71% had used marijuana at least three times a week for a month or more at some time in their lives, and 26% had drunk alcohol to intoxication at least that often. Regular use of other drugs was lower—14% had used hallucinogens, 12% had used amphetamines, and 7% or fewer had used any of a number of other illicit drugs (heroin, methadone, other opiates, sedatives, barbiturates, PCP, inhalants, quaaludes) three or more times a week for at least a month. Almost four fifths (79%) had had no previous treatment for drug use.

Psychopathology of Sample

AXIS I DISORDERS

Over one quarter (28%) of the clients were diagnosed as having a current (within the last 30 days) major depressive syndrome. An additional 12% were diagnosed as having had a major depressive episode at some time in their life. Six percent were dysthymic at the time of the interview and 1% were suffering from a depressive illness not otherwise specified (NOS). In total, the percentage of clients suffering from some type of lifetime depressive illness was 47%. (This high level of depression is consistent with findings of previous studies of heroin addicts [Rounsaville et al., 1982; Woody et al., 1983], and of those with cocaine-use disorders [Weiss et al., 1986]). In addition to depression, the only other Axis I diagnoses were phobic disorders (social phobia, 5%; agoraphobia, one person; simple phobia, one person), and panic disorder, one person). All who were found to have phobic disorders also were diagnosed as having one of the forms of depressive disorder discussed above. (Kleinman, et al., [1990b] present additional details on these findings.)

AXIS II DISORDERS

Among many persons in this sample, several personality disorders were diagnosed in the same individual, as is consistent with the SCID-II format and the cluster concept of DSM-III-R (American Psychiatric Association, 1987). (Forty percent were found to have two or more Axis II disorders.) Similarly, many of the subjects who were diagnosed as having Axis I disorders also were diagnosed as having Axis II disorders. At the same time, the sample included 32 persons (42%) who were diagnosed as having no Axis II personality disorders.

Previous studies of cocaine-use disorders in middle-class populations have reported that borderline and narcissistic personalities were predominant and anti-social personalities were not represented (Resnick & Resnick, 1986; Weiss et al., 1986). In their most recent work, however, Weiss et al. (1988) report a substantial representation (19.3%) of anti-social personality disorders among treated cocaine abusers. Findings in this population are somewhat different: Four disorders, including both borderline and antisocial personalities, were found to be most common. These four most common diagnoses were antisocial (21%), passive-aggressive (21%), borderline (18%), and self-defeating (18%) personality disorders.

Retention in Treatment

The follow-up sample resembled the admission sample closely in terms of number of therapy sessions received. In both groups, over one third received no therapy sessions (i.e., they dropped out of the study after one or two pretreatment assessment interviews). Thirty-five percent of the follow-up sample and

32% of the admission sample dropped out between the first and fifth therapy sessions, and 28% of the follow-up group and 24% of the intake sample attended six or more sessions. The most common reasons given by clients in the follow-up interview to explain why they had dropped out of treatment were conflicts with work, family, school, or finances (23%); conflicts within themselves about stopping their use of cocaine (23%); and wanting to stop use in their own way or with the help of family (20%).

Trends in data previously analyzed indicated that both individual and family therapy were somewhat (but not significantly) more powerful than paraprofessionally led group therapy in effecting retention in treatment (Kleinman et al., 1990a). The same study showed that the rate of retention in treatment for four sessions or more varied widely by therapist, from 14% of the clients of one to 81% of the clients of another.

Of the 122 persons who were interviewed at follow-up, fully half (51%) sought other treatment after their contact with our center. The most frequently sought types of further treatment were residential treatment (43%) and Narcotics or Cocaine Anonymous (38%). Among the 61 persons who sought treatment elsewhere, only 30 actually received such treatment. We are uncertain exactly how much treatment they obtained, but no relationship between abstention from cocaine and receiving additional treatment was found.

Behavior in the Follow-up Period as Compared with the Initial Contact Period

COMPARISON OF DRUG USE AND OTHER PROBLEMS

Initial and follow-up ASI scores are seen in Table 14-2. Drug use was significantly lower in the follow-up period than it was at the time of initial contact. The composite drug score is significantly lower in the 30 days preceding the follow-up interview, as are the number of days of cocaine use, the number of days of marijuana use, the amount spent on drugs, and the number of days of drug problems. Psychiatric/psychological problems as measured by the psychiatric severity score are also significantly less serious at follow-up, and there is a significant decline in family/social problems.

Although the alcohol composite score, the amount spent on alcohol, and the number of days of alcohol problems were almost unchanged, the number of days of alcohol use in the past 30 days increased significantly between intake and follow-up. Though superficially this might suggest that drug substitution is taking place, a more refined examination of the relationship between alcohol problems and length of abstinence from cocaine/crack showed that those who had an alcohol problem at follow-up were also more likely to be using cocaine/crack at follow-up ($r = -0.22$ $p < 0.01$). This suggests that alcohol and cocaine are used together or that there is a pattern of cocaine use followed by alcohol intake aimed to reduce the dysphoria associated with the stimulating effects of cocaine, and is consistent with clinical reports. There were no changes between intake and follow-up in medical, employment, or legal problems.

COMPARISON OF IMPACT OF TREATMENT ON COCAINE USE AND OTHER PROBLEM AREAS

We find a suggestion, but no convincing evidence, that the treatment, as delivered under the conditions of this study, was responsible for the improvements seen. This conclusion is reached primarily because the number of sessions received was not significantly related to number of days of cocaine use or to improvement in other scores. When the sample was divided into two extreme groups i.e., those who had no therapy sessions and those who had 13 or more sessions, the same absence of a relationship between cocaine use and number of therapy sessions was found. However, there were nonsignificant trends in the data suggesting that the number

Table 14-2
Differences in Mean Scores Between Intake and Follow-up for Each Problem Area

	Intake	Follow-up	P*
Medical composite/cal	0.15	0.12	n.s.
Days medical problem†	2.70	2.06	n.s.
Employment composite	0.58	0.59	n.s.
Days worked‡	13.94	13.00	n.s.
Money earned‡	11.63	10.51	n.s.
Alcohol composite	0.09	0.08	n.s.
Days alcohol	1.06	1.90	≤ 0.05
Amount spent	1.22	0.84	n.s.
Days alcohol problem	0.50	0.64	n.s.
Drug composite	0.20	0.11	< 0.0001
Days cocaine	11.54	5.48	< 0.0001
Days marijuana	4.83	2.13	< 0.0001
Amount spent	8.43	2.86	< 0.0001
Days drug problem	14.42	7.19	< 0.0001
Legal composite	0.07	0.05	n.s.
Crime days	0.65	0.20	n.s.
Family/social composite	0.42	0.25	< 0.0001
Days problem with family	7.35	3.42	< 0.0001
Days problem with other people	2.222	1.31	n.s.
Psychiatric composite	0.26	0.20	< 0.01

*Probability based on paired t-tests.
†Days in this table refers to the number of days in the 30 days prior to interviews.
‡For these two items only, higher scores indicate less severity.

of days of alcohol problems, the number of days worked, and the number of days of problems with others improved more among persons who had six or more sessions than among those who had less treatment.

Impact of Cocaine Use on Other Drug Use and on Other Problem Areas

Persons who did not use cocaine in the past 30 days had (expectably) lower scores on both the drug composite index and selected individual drug items than did continuing users. This group also had significantly greater improvement in the alcohol, employment, family/social, and psychiatric areas than did those who continued to use cocaine (Table 14-3). (However, no differences were seen between abstainers and continuing users in the areas of medical and legal problems.) In short, there was a clear relationship between continuation of the cocaine-use disorder and dysfunction in several important areas of daily life.

Table 14-3
Differences in Mean Scores for ASI Problem Areas Between Nonusers of Cocaine and Users at Initial Contact and at Follow-Up

| | Nonusers (N = 53) | | Users (N = 66) | | |
	Initial Contact	Follow-Up	Initial Contact	Follow-Up	p^*
Drug composite	0.19	0.03	0.21	0.17	<0.0001
Days of cocaine use	10.24	0.00	12.58	9.84	<0.0001
Days of marijuana use	3.51	0.82	5.89 ·	3.17	<0.05
Amount spent on drugs	7.62	0.14	9.06	4.98	<0.0001
Days of drug problem	13.37	0.27	15.25	12.70	<0.0001
Alcohol composite	0.06	0.05	0.10	0.10	≤0.01
Days of alcohol use	1.18	1.37	0.97	2.33	n.s.
Amount spent on alcohol	0.73	0.63	1.61	1.02	n.s.
Days alcohol problem	.37	0.18	0.61	1.02	n.s.
Medical composite	0.15	0.10	0.15	0.13	n.s.
Days of medical problem	2.08	1.94	3.19	2.16	n.s.
Employment composite	0.57	0.52	0.59	0.64	<0.05
Days worked	14.37	15.12	13.59	11.30	n.s.
Money earned	11.78	12.59	11.52	8.92	<0.05
Legal composite	0.06	0.04	0.08	0.06	n.s.
Days criminal activity	0.40	0.04	0.85	0.33	n.s.
Family/social composite	0.40	0.11	0.43	0.37	<0.0001
Days problem with family	7.28	0.54	7.40	5.71	<0.0001
Days problem with other people	1.42	1.02	2.86	1.54	n.s.
Psychiatric composite	0.25	0.09	0.27	0.28	<0.0001

*Analysis of covariance conducted on follow-up scores using pretreatment scores as covariates.

Recovery from Cocaine Abuse

A DEMANDING TEST OF ABSTENTION FROM COCAINE USE IN THE FOLLOW-UP PERIOD

A more conservative measure of abstention from cocaine use than the one used above was developed by combining self-report for an extended period with results of urine testing at the time of follow-up. In order to qualify as "clean," the client had to have a negative urine result *and* to report no use of cocaine in the prior three months (and, as a reliability test, no use of cocaine in the past 30 days). For those clients who were not able to report to our site for a urine test, the criterion was self-report of no cocaine in the prior *six* months, with additional confirmation of non-use by special follow-up phone call to a member of the client's family. Using this conservative definition, 19% of all followed-up clients were found to be clean, 74% were determined to be abusing, and determination could not be made about 7%.

It should be noted that this definition of abstention does not fully reflect cocaine-use patterns. Whereas the use patterns of other drugs include "periods of abstention followed by relapse," cocaine abuse is unique in that typically the drug is used intermittently by some people; there are periods of no drug use of days, weeks, or even months, punctuated by binges.*

PREDICTORS OF RECOVERY

In previous studies of heroin, alcohol, and psychotherapy treatment, four variables have been reported fairly consistently as influencing success: employment history, criminal history, length of time in treatment, and psychological health. Pretreatment employment has repeatedly predicted success in drug and alcohol-abuse treatments (Cooper, 1983; DeFleur, Ball, & Stuart, 1969; Roizen, Cahalan, & Shanks, 1976; Vaillant, 1966). Involvement with the criminal justice system has predicted failure in drug-abuse treatment programs (Cooper, 1983; McGlothlin, Anglin, & Wilson, 1977; Simpson, Savage, Lloyd, & Sells, 1978). Length of time in treatment generally has been associated with success of drug treatment (McLellan, 1983). Psychological health at initial contact was positively related to success in psychotherapy according to a number of studies (Luborsky, Crits-Christoph, Mintz, & Auerbach, 1988). Persons with high scores on a psychiatric severity index were unlikely to benefit from standard methadone treatment, but improved following methadone treatment combined with psychotherapy (Woody et al., 1984). Relationships between sociodemographic factors and outcome have been more variable. Conflicting findings have been reported regarding age, eth-

---

*Thus many persons classified as "abusers" according to this classification scheme have in fact experienced periods of nonuse of cocaine during the past six months. Likewise, a few of those classified as "clean" even by this conservative definition may be expected to engage in cocaine binges at some later time.

nicity, and sex, suggesting that the relationships found in particular studies may be chance associations, or that they may be products of specific staff–client or program–client interactions (Kleinman et al., 1990a).

In our sample, the bivariate relationship of seven variables to recovery was examined (Table 14-4). Clients who had never been arrested were most likely to stop using cocaine ($r = 0.26$). Age, form of cocaine used at entry (powder versus crack or free-base), and length of lifetime use of cocaine were modestly, although not significantly, related to recovery. Level of education, level of depression at time of application for treatment, and number of therapy sessions received were unrelated to recovery.

The relationship of the same seven variables to recovery was analyzed by means of a discriminant function analysis (Table 14-5). One function was revealed by this analysis, and it was found to account for a meaningful portion of the variance in the data (Wilk's lambda = 0.86; chi-square value = 12.86, $p < 0.10$). Seventy percent of the cases were correctly classified by this function—62% of those who were cocaine users and 73% of those who were cocaine-free. Consistent with the bivariate relationships shown above, only the coefficient for arrest history had a significant F ratio. When all discriminating variables were considered simultaneously, having no arrests had the strongest power in predicting recovery (standardized coefficient = 0.91) and none of the other variables included had significant standardized coefficients.

Table 14-4
Intercorrelation Matrix of Dependent and Independent Variables

	1	2	3	4	5	6	7	8
1. Cocaine use (nonuser vs. user)	—							
2. Criminal history (no arrest vs. any arrest)	0.26*	—						
3. Number of therapy sessions	−0.00	−0.06	—					
4. Age	0.10	−0.22	−0.09	—				
5. Lifetime use of cocaine	0.09	−0.04	0.06	0.13	—			
6. Form of cocaine (powder vs. crack)	0.10	−0.10	−0.07	0.06	0.01	—		
7. Depression score	0.04	0.14	−0.11	−0.01	0.04	0.11	—	
8. Education	−0.07	−0.25*	−.08	0.01	0.23*	0.04	−0.20†	—

†$p < 0.05$
*$p \leqslant 0.01$

DISCUSSION

Persons with cocaine-use disorders, like heroin addicts, have been shown here to have unusually high rates of depressive disorders. In disagreement with some early reports on Axis II disorders of persons with cocaine-use disorders, antisocial, passive-aggressive, and self-defeating personality disorders were found as frequently as borderline disorders.

A significant improvement in both psychological functioning as measured by the ASI psychiatric severity score and family–social functioning was noted for the sample as a whole. However, those who were not using cocaine at follow-up accounted for virtually all of this improvement. This suggests that improvement in a range of areas that are impaired during the course of a cocaine-use disorder is tied very directly to abstinence. The close association between cocaine/crack use in the 30 days before follow-up and the psychiatric composite score of the ASI is noteworthy. It strongly suggests, as previous investigators (Gawin & Kleber, 1986) have proposed, that use of the drug produces or exacerbates symptoms of psychiatric disturbance. The current data add strength to that hypothesis. Users and nonusers at follow-up had closely similar scores at initial treatment contact and the dramatic decline in scores was noted only among persons not currently using cocaine; the scores of those who continued to use remained unchanged or increased between entry and follow-up.

The powerful relationship found here between recovery and arrest history is important. It confirms a number of studies based on a variety of treatment settings. Persons who have been arrested probably have a weaker prosocial support system than others. They may have more personality impairment as well. Whatever the

Table 14-5
Univariate F Ratio and Discriminant Function Coefficient

Variable	F	Unstandardized Coefficient	Standardized Coefficient
Criminal history	7.47*	1.90	0.91
Age	0.83	0.08	0.48
Form of cocaine	0.75	0.39	0.34
Lifetime use of cocaine	0.96	0.00	0.30
Number of therapy sessions	0.28	0.10	0.29
Education	0.43	−0.00	−0.21
Beck depression score	0.09	−0.00	−0.02
(Constant)		−5.75	

*$p<0.01$.
Note: Wilk's Lambda = 0.86, χ^2 = 12.86 (df = 7), $p <0.10$

reasons, validation underscores the finding that when persons with criminal justice records are seen in treatment, extraordinary measures are needed to promote problem remission.

Recovery from use of cocaine for a period of at least three months characterized 19% of persons followed up in this study. This abstinence rate probably represents spontaneous remission in a group of patients with enough motivation to seek treatment, as number of therapy sessions attended was not related to improvement. Studies of alcoholics (Knupfer, 1972), tobacco smokers (Schachter, 1982), heroin addicts (Biernacki, 1986), and cocaine abusers (Waldorf et al., 1989) show that spontaneous remission of problem use of addictive substances is possible.

The finding of no association between number of treatment sessions and improved performance is at variance with other studies that have shown a relationship between amount of treatment received and outcome following treatment (Smith & Glass, 1977). Studies of psychotherapy (Woody et al., 1983) and family therapy (Stanton et al., 1982) performed with heroin addicts maintained on methadone have shown treatment effects, but both studies offered therapy in addition to methadone, drug counseling, supervised urine testing, rules, and other structures offered by the treatment program.

CONCLUSIONS

It is our impression that a more intensive outpatient treatment model would have been more effective with variable-length inpatient stays available for those who require them. A number of clinicians working with cocaine addicts have reported success by using a more intensive approach, in which drug-free group therapy, education, and individual or family therapy are delivered in three to five two-to-six hour sessions a week for the first four to eight weeks of outpatient contact (Pettinati, 1990; Rawson, Obert, McCann, & Mann, 1985; Washton, 1989). Less intensive treatment, as was offered here, is reserved for follow-up treatment for those who respond to the initial, more intense phase. The need for a more intensive initial phase of treatment is suggested by the fact that many of the patients who entered this study sought residential treatment in another setting at a later time.

When ideas about cocaine treatment were in the initial stages of development in the early 1980s, a commonly held view in the field was that cocaine was not an addictive drug. As such, in offering once-a-week outpatient treatment, providers may have been guided by a "mild problem" model, one that increasingly has been seen to be inadequate for the real severity of cocaine addiction. Based on the success of methadone in the treatment of heroin addiction, the search for pharmacotherapeutic aids in the treatment of cocaine disorders is well advised (Gawin & Kleber, 1984; Rosecan & Nunes, 1987; Kosten, 1990). Future studies could explore the interactions among pharmacotherapies, patient characteristics, and treatment structure and intensity in developing effective treatments for persons with cocaine-use disorders.

REFERENCES

American Psychiatric Association (1987). *Diagnostic and statistical manual of mental disorders* (rev. 2nd ed.). Washington, DC: Author.

Beck, A. & Steer, R. (1981). *Beck depression inventory manual.* New York: Harcourt Brace Jovanovich.

Biernacki, P. (1986). *Pathways from heroin addiction: Recovery without treatment.* Philadelphia: Temple University Press.

Carroll, K. (1989). Psychotherapy and counseling in the treatment of cocaine abuse. Presented at NIDA Technical Review Meeting on Psychotherapy and Counseling in the Treatment of Drug Abuse, Rockville, Md.

Cooper, J.R. (Ed.) (1983). *Research on the treatment of narcotic addiction.* Rockville, MD: National Institute on Drug Abuse.

DeFleur, F., Ball, J. & Snarr, R. (1969). The long term correlates of opiate addiction. *Social Problems, 17,* 223–233.

Gawin, F.H., & Kleber, H.D. (1986). Abstinence symptomatology and psychiatric diagnosis in cocaine abusers. *Archives of General Psychiatry, 43,* 107–113.

Kang. S.Y., Kleinman, P.H., Woody, G.E., et al.: (1991). Outcomes for cocaine abusers after once-a-week psychosocial therapy. *American Journal of Psychiatry,* 148, 630–635.

Kleber, H.D., & Gawin, F.H. (1984). The spectrum of cocaine abuse and its treatment. *Journal of Clinical Psychiatry, 45,* 18–23.

Kleinman, P.H., Kang, S.Y., Lipton, D.S., et al. (1990a). Retention of cocaine abusers in outpatient psychotherapy. *American Journal of Drug and Alcohol Abuse.* In Press.

Kleinman, P.H., Miller, A.B., Millman, R.B., et al. (1990b). Psychopathology among cocaine abusers entering treatment. *Journal of Nervous and Mental Disease, 178,* 442–447.

Knupfer, G. (1972). Ex-problem drinkers. In M. Roff, L. Robins, & M. Pollack (Eds.), *Life history research in psychopathology* (Vol. 2, pp. 256–280). Minneapolis: University of Minnesota Press.

Kosten, T.R. (1989). Pharmacotherapeutic interventions for cocaine abuse: Matching patients to treatments. *Journal of Nervous and Mental Disease, 177,* 379–389.

Luborsky, L., Crits-Christoph, P., Mintz, M., & Auerbach, A. (1988). *Who will benefit from psychotherapy.* New York: Basic Books.

McGlothlin, W.H., Anglin, M.D., & Wilson, B.D. (1977). An evaluation of the California Civil Addict Program. Washington, D.C.: U.S. Government Printing Office.

McLellan, A.T. (1983). Patient characteristics associated with outcome. In J.R. Cooper, (Ed.), *Research on the treatment of narcotic addiction.* Rockville, MD: National Institute on Drug Abuse.

McLellan, A.T., Luborsky, L., Cacciola, J., et al. (1985). New data from the Addiction Severity Index: Reliability and validity in three centers. *Journal of Nervous and Mental Disease, 173,* 412–428.

McLellan, A.T., Luborsky, L., O'Brien, C., et al. (1982). Is treatment for substance abuse effective? *Journal of the American Medical Association, 247,* 1423–1428.

McLellan, A.T., Luborsky, L., Woody, G.E., & O'Brien, C.P. (1980). An improved diagnostic evaluation instrument for substance abuse patients. *Journal of Nervous and Mental Disease, 168,* 26–33.

Millman, R.B. (1988). Evaluation and clinical management of cocaine abusers. *Journal of Clinical Psychiatry, 49,* 27–33.

Nunes, E. (1989). Personal communication.

Pettinati, H. (1990). Personal communication.

Rawson, R.A., Obert, J.L., McCann, M.J., & Mann, A.J. (1986). Cocaine treatment outcome: Cocaine use following inpatient, outpatient and no treatment. In *Problems of drug dependence, 1985,* NIDA Research Monograph 67, Washington, D.C.

Roizen, R., Cahalan, D., & Shanks, P. (1976). Spontaneous remission among untreated problem drinkers. Presented at Conference on Strategies of Longitudinal Research on Drug Use. San Juan, Puerto Rico.

Rosecan, J.S., & Nunes, E.V. (1987). Pharmacological management of cocaine abuse. In H.I. Spitz & J.S. Rosecan (Eds.), *Cocaine abuse: New directions in treatment and research.* New York: Brunner/Mazel.

Rosecan, J.S., Spitz, H.I., & Gross, B.G. (1987). Contemporary issues in the treatment of cocaine abuse. In H.I. Spitz & J.S. Rosecan (Eds.), *Cocaine abuse: New directions in treatment and research* (pp. 299–324). New York: Brunner/Mazel.

Rounsaville, B.J., Kosten, T., Weissman, M.M., et al. (1986). Prognostic significance of psychopathology in treated opiate addicts. *Archives of General Psychiatry, 43,* 739–745.

Rounsaville, B.J., Weissman, M.M., Crits-Christoph, K., Wilber, C., & Kleber, H. (1982). Diagnosis and symptoms of depression in opiate addicts. *Archives of General Psychiatry, 39,* 151–156.

Schachter, S. (1982). Recidivism and self-cure of smoking and obesity. *American Psychologist, 37,* 436–444.

Schuster, G. (1988). Initiatives at the National Institute on Drug Abuse. In *Problems of drug dependence 1987: Proceedings of the 49th Annual Scientific Meeting.* NIDA Research Monograph 81, Rockville, MD.

Simpson, D.D., Savage, J.L., Lloyd, M.R., & Sells, S.B. (1978). *Evaluation of drug abuse treatments based on the first year after DARP.* Services Research Monograph Series, DHEW Pub. No. ADM 78-701. Washington, DC: NIDA.

Spitzer, R., Williams, J., & Gibbons, M. (1987). *Instruction Manual for the Structured Clinical Interview for DSM-III-R* (SCID, 4/1/87 Revision). New York: Biometrics Research Dept., N.Y.S. Psychiatric Institute.

Smith, M.L., & Glass, G.V. (1977). Meta-analysis of psychotherapy outcome studies. *American Psychologist, 32,* 752–760.

Stanton, M.D., Todd, T.C., et al. (1982). *The family therapy of drug abuse and addiction.* New York: Guilford Press.

Vaillant, G.E. (1966). Twelve year follow-up of New York narcotic addicts: I—The relation of treatment to outcome. *American Journal of Psychiatry, 122,* 727–737.

Waldorf, D., Murphy, S., & Reinarman, C. (1988). Social-psychological strategies of cessation from cocaine abuse. Presented at the 38th Annual Meeting of the Society for the Study of Social Problems, Atlanta.

Wallace, B.C. (1989). Psychological and environmental determinants of relapse in crack cocaine smokers. *Journal of Substance Abuse Treatment, 6,* 95–106.

Washton, A.M. (1989). *Cocaine addiction: Treatment, recovery and relapse prevention.* New York: W.W. Norton & Co.

Washton, A.M., & Gold, M.S. (1987). *Cocaine: A clinician's handbook.* New York: Guilford.

Weiss, R.D., Mirin, S.M., Griffin, M.L., Michaels, J.K. (1988). Psychopathology in cocaine abusers: Changing trends. *Journal of Nervous and Mental Disease, 176,* 719–725.

Woody, G.E., Luborsky, L., McLellan, A.T., et al.: (1983). Psychotherapy for opiate addicts: Does it help? *Archives of General Psychiatry, 40,* 639–645.

15

Family Therapy and the Therapeutic Community: The Chemically Dependent Adolescent

Arthur A. Weidman, Ph.D., ACSW, M.B.A.

This chapter will describe the results of two research projects and their implications for the treatment of chemically dependent adolescents. One project
explored the relationship between family therapy and reductions in treatment
dropout among chemically dependent adolescents in a therapeutic community
(TC), and the other explored the relationships among adolescent chemical
dependency, psychological differentiation, locus of control, and family process.
The first study found that involvement in family therapy made a significant difference in reducing the number of youths who dropped out of a TC. The second study found that chemically dependent adolescents are psychologically
undifferentiated. These teens are involved in a pseudoindividuated relationship
with one parent who is psychologically and emotionally unavailable, while the
other parent is peripheral. It was found that these teens become more undifferentiated with increasing time in the residential program. The residents internalized the TC belief system of personal responsibility while substituting
dependency on one parent and drugs for dependency on the TC.

The chemically dependent adolescent is a difficult and challenging client with
whom to work. Coupled with the normally stormy nature of adolescence is the
very destructive problem of substance abuse. Frequently, such youths come from
quite dysfunctional families. The therapist is faced with a very complex task.
The therapist who has a viable framework for understanding substance abuse
and specific interventions to use will be more effective in these circumstances.

One may view the family as the context within which identity emerges. The family is a developing system that may facilitate or hinder an individual member's devel-

opment. When a family is having difficulty negotiating a particular phase of its development, an individual member may express the difficulty in the form of a symptom or problem behavior. Problems may be viewed as being maintained by the family and as maintaining family stability. Individual and family problems may be seen as attempts to cope with a developmental issue; however, the attempt is not adequate given the family's limited view of the problem, previous deficits, or scarce resources. The family's attempt to cope is often well intentioned, and the resulting dysfunction is often quite unintended. A question that is sometimes useful to pose is: How does this problem help the family, dyad, or individual maintain stability? Or, to what developmental issue is this problem a response? Substance abuse may be seen as developing in response to a particular set of family problems and dynamics. One consequence of this view of substance abuse is that in order to understand and treat the etiology and maintaining dynamics of a problem, one will need to work with the family.

Another reason for working with families is that families are powerful groups of people who exert significant influence on their members. In treatment, families can be either a tremendous support or an impediment that can undermine and sabotage treatment.

One may view compulsive substance abuse as a symptom that serves defensive functions the purpose of which is to maintain family stability. Compulsive substance abuse may be related to a symbiotic relationship between an adolescent and a parent (Alexander & Dibb, 1977; Attardo, 1965; Ziegler-Driscoll, 1978). Viewed in this manner, compulsive substance abuse may be seen as an attempt to cope with the developmental issues of separation and individuation that precede the youth's leaving home. The drug abuser has never fully achieved separation from the parent and is still in a dependent and symbiotic relationship (Weidman, 1983a). The parents of the drug abuser do not encourage the abuser to individuate and separate from the family. Compulsive substance abuse may be seen as a pseudoseparation, in which the apparently independent and defiant use of drugs maintains the drug abuser in a dependent position vis-à-vis the family of origin. This substance dependency, which is an exchange of dependency on parents for dependency on drugs, serves to maintain a drug abuser's dependency on his or her parent(s).

An example of pseudoseparation is that of an adolescent who is using drugs and is engaged in other self-destructive, antisocial behavior and whose parents still support the youth by allowing use of the family car or providing pocket (read "drug") money and money for legal fees and bail. Frequently, the teenager disobeys the parents, steals from the family, may be violent with family members, and is arrested. The dependent and fused nature of the parent–adolescent relationship is shown by the fact that, even with all of the adolescent's self-destructive acting out, the parents still try to help by giving the teenager "one more chance." Were the parents to try to stop the acting out by not rescuing the youth, removal from the home and placement in a treatment program or detention center would be the most likely outcome. The parents and the adolescent often experience a profound and unconscious fear of object loss. Since the adolescent and parents are involved in a fused relationship, one often observes a significant depression develop in both the parents and the adolescent when they are separated. When, with support, parents are able to take a firm and consistent position and get the adolescent into treatment, the adolescent typically becomes enraged and depressed.

The importance of family processes in the development of compulsive substance abuse is further outlined in the work of Chien, Gerald, Lee, and Rosenfeld (1964), who stated, "The overall results of the analysis of our indexes gives strong support to the view that family experiences play an important role in the etiology of addiction" (p. 271). If family processes play a significant role in the development and maintenance of substance abuse, then family therapy should have a significant effect on this problem.

The impact of family therapy on the drug abuser's family may be seen in a number of areas, including disengaging the fused family system and moving the drug abuser from a state of pseudoseparation to one of relative differentiation and fostering a sense of autonomy and of separate identity.

An important dynamic operating in the families of chemically dependent teenagers is defensive delineation. Delineations are the view one person has of another as revealed implicitly or explicitly in the behavior of that person with the other. When the delineation contains evidence of distortion of the other person related to the individual's defense structure, then it can be termed a defensive delineation. For example, the parents of one teenager saw him as still being a failure despite his one and a half years in a TC, his obtaining of a high-school diploma, and the evaluations of the staff that he was ready to move out on his own. The teenager's father had never achieved any of his own dreams. The son's achievements confronted the father with his own failure.

Typically, what is found in such cases is a pattern of anxiety in the parents over the adolescent's potential for individuation and separation. This parental anxiety over the adolescent's developmental growth is a major cause of parental defensive delineations; the adolescent's maturation stirs up conflicts and anxieties in the parent, who projects onto the adolescent one part of a previously internalized conflict. Externalizing the conflict onto an interpersonal relationship diminishes parental anxiety. A significant component of this process is the willingness, conscious and unconscious, of the recipient of the projection to accept the projection. The teenager colludes with the parent in providing vicarious gratification of the unacceptable and unconscious desires. The motivation for the adolescent's collusion in this process is the gratification received by reducing parental anxiety. Since a relatively fused state exists between the adolescent and parent, what is anxiety reducing for the parent is gratifying for the adolescent.

STUDY 1

There is a large body of literature on the efficacy of family therapy in the treatment of a variety of problems (Gurman & Kniskern, 1978). In addition, family therapy has proved to be an effective tool in the treatment of drug abuse (Kaufman & Kaufmann, 1979; Stanton et al., 1982). Weidman (1983b) discussed a family therapy approach to adolescent substance abuse that relies on the theoretical formulation previously discussed. Stanton (1979) found that structural family therapy, when compared with no treatment and methadone-maintenance treatment, substantially increased the percentage of drug-free days. He stated, "The practice of treating the drug abuser and his family members separately or concurrently does not appear to be as promising or efficacious as treating them together. . . . The point is, if treatment is not construed to directly intervene in and change the family process surrounding detoxification, such treatment is much less likely to success" (p. 13). Stanton and associates (1982) found that after one year, drug abusers who had received 10 sessions of structural family therapy had a mortality rate of 2% while those who received no treatment or methadone maintenance treatment had a mortality rate of 10%. These findings are particularly significant since the drug abusers were randomly assigned to treatment groups. The researchers write, "It seems safe to conclude that the effectiveness of a short-term structural-strategic family therapy approach to this acknowledgedly difficult population is significant" (p. 421).

There is a large body of literature on factors affecting dropping out of treatment (Baekeland & Lundwall, 1975), however, not much of this literature focuses on the role of family factors in this regard. Zax, Marsey, and Biggs (1961) found that social isolation was predictive of dropping out of outpatient alcoholism treatment. Dropouts were more likely to be single or not living with their spouses. Baekeland, Lundwall, and Shanahan (1973) found that clients at an alcohol clinic who failed to return after the first visit were more likely to be living alone, while clinic attenders were described as socially intact individuals. One interpretation of these findings is that dropouts have a less cohesive support network to encourage them to remain in treatment. Baekeland and Lundwall (1975), in their review of the literature, found that family pathology, attitudes, and behavior were important in predicting dropping out of treatment in eight out of 10 studies. They stated, "One gathers from the clinical literature that family pathology, attitudes, and behavior help to determine whether patients stay in psychotherapy, get treatment for alcoholism and drug addiction and then stay in it. . . . Unfortunately, systemic studies are lacking in these areas" (p. 169).

There are contradictory findings for the effects of family support of or pressure on drug abusers remaining in residential treatment. Ward and Hemsley (1982) found that social pressure on the drug abuser by family members to seek treatment was significantly and inversely related to length of stay ($r = -0.307$). On the other hand,

Gossop (1978) found a positive relationship between family pressure and length of stay in residential treatment. LeFave (1980) found a number of factors, including attendance of the father at intake and subsequent treatment sessions, predictive of a family's continuing on conjoint family therapy.

In the present study, family support is viewed as involvement in and cooperation with the residential treatment program, which is operationally defined as attending conjoint family therapy. The significance of the research reported here lies in its attempt to fill a void in the research on family factors that may affect dropping out of residential treatment for drug abuse. Length of involvement in residential treatment for drug abuse has been found to be significantly associated with number of treatment outcomes, including abstinence, increased number of months employed, decreased criminal activity (DeLeon & Andrews, 1978), decreased objective indicators of psychopathology (Sacks & Levy, 1979), and increased psychological and interpersonal levels of differentiation (Weidman, 1983a). Therefore, factors that may facilitate drug abusers' remaining in residential treatment will have a direct bearing on successful treatment outcome along a number of dimensions.

The aim of this study was to take advantage of a naturally occurring experiment in which one of the facilities of a TC in suburban Washington, D.C. (facility A) changed its treatment philosophy to include structural family therapy (Minuchin & Fishman, 1981; Stanton et al., 1982) in its orientation and approach to treatment, while another facility (facility B) did not make such a change. This change provided the opportunity to explore the effects of structural family therapy and staff training on an important dimension in the residential treatment of drug abusers, that of dropping out. The only difference between facility A and facility B was the introduction of structural family therapy into the treatment approach at facility A. The research found that on the main variables used in this study, facility A and facility B were not significantly different before the introduction of structural family therapy into facility A. It was also found that after the training, the facilities did significantly different.

Four periods were compared: the nine months preceding and the nine months following the introduction of structural family therapy into facility A's treatment approach and the concurring two nine-month periods for facility B. It was found that the introduction of structural family therapy into treatment and the staff training necessary to accomplish this introduction had an effect on practice in a number of areas.

Three hypotheses were generated. First, it was hypothesized that there would be a decrease in the number of TC residents dropping out of treatment as a result of the introduction of a family systems orientation to treatment. It was expected that the addition of structural family therapy to the traditional TC treatment approach would result in increased family involvement in treatment, which, in turn, might result in increased support for treatment and, therefore, increased support for the residents remaining in treatment. The result thus would be a decrease in the number of dropouts from facility A, but not from facility B. The second hypothesis was that the changed treatment approach would result in an increase in the number of families being seen in family therapy during the first month the adolescent was in treatment. It was believed that this early involvement may have contributed to reducing dropping out. Previous research (Stanton et al., 1982) had indicated that involving the family early in treatment was important to the drug abusers' remaining in treatment. It was expected that if the number of dropouts were reduced, one would also find an increase in the number of families being seen during the first month of residential treatment. Third, it was hypothesized that families that had a dropout attended family therapy at a lower rate and had a greater number of months with no family therapy sessions than families who continued in treatment. It was assumed that the changed treatment approach in facility A would result in greater program support for family therapy and the expectation that families would be involved in treatment.

STUDY 2

The second study took place at the same residential treatment facility using the same adolescent and family members. There is substantial literature on substance abuse and locus of control. Generally, powerless groups and maladjusted groups tend to perceive locus of control as being external (Lefcourt, 1966, 1976). This finding is related to the finding of Rotter, which indicated that situational variables may affect a person's perception of locus of control. Powerless groups' external scores on locus of control may reflect an accurate perception of their situation. One would expect chemically dependent adolescents to have an external locus of control, but most studies find that these youths are significantly more internal than normal populations (Berzins & Ross, 1973; Calicchia, 1974; Smithyman, Plant, & Southern, 1974). This internality has been interpreted as a drug-engendered pseudointernality (Berzins & Ross, 1973). The addict's extensive experience with self-control by self-administering opiates to control mood states leads to a generalized belief by the addict that he or she controls the reinforcements important to him or her.

Tobacyk, Broughton, and Vaught (1975) found that congruent groups (field-independent internals and field-dependent externals) were better adjusted psychologically than incongruent groups (field-independent externals and field-dependent internals). The relationship that seems to exist is that poor adjustment and locus-of-control differentiation incongruence are associated. Compulsive adolescent substance abuse may be viewed as a separation–individuation problem involving a low level of psychological differentiation as evidenced by involvement in symbiotic family relationships. It follows that given the low level of psychological differentiation between the adolescent substance abuser and parent, the adolescent will show an incongruence between locus of control and psychological differentiation. It can be expected that the adolescent will be field dependent internally. This hypothesized finding could be interpreted as representing diffuse psychological boundaries. It would suggest that the substance-abusing adolescent, because of diffuse psychological differentiation, will have difficulty in accurately distinguishing external from internal locus of causality and so inaccurately hold a belief in internal locus of control. This inaccurate perception, based on a relatively diffuse level of psychological differentiation, is analogous to Mahler, Pine, and Berman's (1975) description of the infant before the rapprochement subphase of the separation-individuation process.

This study explored the relationships among adolescent and parental levels of differentiation, adolescent beliefs about locus of control, and adolescent substance abuse. The specific hypotheses were that:

1. Among compulsive adolescent substance abusers, locus of control and differentiation are significantly related. Adolescents who have a lower level of differentiation have more internal locus of control beliefs than do adolescents who have higher levels of differentiation.
2. Maternal and adolescent levels of differentiation are related. Mothers who score high on the fusion scale of the Boundary/Fusion Questionnaire have adolescents who also score high on the fusion scale. Mothers who score high on the boundary scale have adolescents who score low on the boundary scale. Paternal and adolescent levels of differentiation are not related.
3. Adolescents in more advanced phases of treatment are more differentiated than adolescents in earlier stages of treatment.

METHODOLOGY

The study design involved a review of the agency's statistical forms for an 18-month period. The forms were completed monthly by the family therapy staff. The data from the forms were collected by the author, who was one of the two family therapists at facility A. These forms record the number of conjoint family therapy sessions and whether or not the resident left the facility against advice (dropped out). The settings for this study were two facilities of a residential TC for substance abusers located in the Washington, D.C., metropolitan area. Facility A and facility B both had identical treatment approaches and philosophies. During the nine months prior to the program change, both programs provided family therapy, but it was begun in the third to sixth month after admission. Admission criteria required: (1) a voluntary request by the client, although frequently the choice was between jail and treatment; and (2) drug abuse of such magnitude that it markedly interfered with the adolescent's family, school, or social functioning. Facilities A and B, being two facilities of a four-facility residential TC for substance abusers, had a common director, deputy director, and administration. Intake workers for the TC admitted people into all facilities. Each facility had separate house directors, house staff, education staff, and family therapy staff. Both A and B are in suburban locations. Each facility had been operating for over five years with the same house director. Long-term retention rates and recidivism were not significantly different between the two facilities. When applying the chi-square test to the figures on dropouts for A and B in the nine months before the program change, the following results were seen: $\chi^2 = 0.67$, $p =$ n.s.

The TC is a drug-free residential facility for the rehabilitation of drug abusers. Such facilities are highly structured and directive. The house staff members, who are largely ex-addicts themselves, provide the day-to-day treatment. The family therapists have M.S.W. degrees and the intake and vocational rehabilitation staff members have various master's-level degrees. The education staff members are all state-certified teachers, some of whom are provided by the county board of education. Treatment usually involves a number of modalities, the most ubiquitous being the confrontation–encounter group. The TC employee community imposes sanctions, as well as advancement of status and privileges, as part of the recovery and growth process. Personal responsibility for one's own life and for self-improvement is emphasized. The program consists of an induction phase followed by three other phases of treatment. Adolescents typically are residents of the program for one year.

As a result of the requirements of one of the funding sources of facility A, that facility had to change its treatment approach by adding structural family therapy as an orientation to the methodology for treatment. Facility B, which had a different funding source, was not required to make this change. The change in treatment approach involved the introduction and integration of a family systems approach into the traditional TC approach (Hinshelwood & Manning, 1979). Attempts were made to introduce this new approach into all aspects of facility A's program, including viewing the facility as a large family, using structural concepts in group work, and having the family therapists use the structural approach in their work with families. All staff members at facility A were involved in a weekly training program over a period of nine months, for a total of 107 hours. The training involved didactic presentations of structural family concepts and techniques, as well as the use of videotapes and live supervision using a one-way mirror and telephone system. The consultants who directed the training were on the staff of a local family-therapy institute.

The subjects were the 43 adolescents of facility A and the 49 adolescents of facility B during the 18 months covered by this study. The data were gathered from both facilities for the period including nine months before and nine months after the change in treatment approach at facility A. See Table 15-1.

There were no statistically significant differences between the samples from facility A and facility B along such dimensions as age, race, sex, socioeconomic level of the parents, or length of stay in treatment as measured by the t-test. There were also no statistically significant differences among the above demographic items of information between facility A and B during the first or second nine-month period. The main variables for this study include:

1. Dropout. A dropout is a resident of one of the facilities who left against staff advice and who did not graduate or complete the program.
2. Attender. An attender is a resident of one of the facilities who did not leave against staff advice during the period of this study.
3. No-show month. A no-show month is a month during which the family was not involved in family therapy.

The subjects of the second study were residents of the TC's facility A age 20 and younger and their parents. There were 14 residents and 27 parents. All eligible residents and parents agreed to participate in the study. All residents were male; 12 were White and two were Black. All the residents had had at least one felony drug charge and a history of drug use of at least four years. These adolescents were compulsive drug users in that they exhibited a high frequency and intense level of drug usage of relatively long duration involving either physiological or psychological dependence such that they had been unable to discontinue use at will. Eight of the families were headed by a mother and father, three by a mother and a stepfather, one by a father and stepmother, one by a single mother, and one by a grandmother and mother.

Instruments

The measure of interpersonal differentiation was the Boundary/Fusion Questionnaire, a 41-item instrument in which each item is scaled on a seven-point

Table 15-1
Demographic Data

	Facility A	Facility B	Total
N	43	49	92
Average age	17 yrs	16.6 yrs	16.8 yrs
Age range	14–20 yrs	14–20 yrs	14–20 yrs
Male	79%	80%	79%
Female	21%	20%	19%
White	81%	80%	80%
Black	19%	20%	20%
Average length of drug use	5.9 yrs	5.8 yrs	5.9 yrs
Average educational level of parents	12.4 yrs	12.3 yrs	12.4 yrs

scale from "strongly agree" to "strongly disagree" (Miller, 1980). It yields two scores, a boundary and a fusion score. The questionnaire was used to measure the relationship between parental and adolescent levels of differentiation. The boundary score measures the individual's effort to demarcate the self psychologically from the environment. The fusion score measures the individual's tendency to incorporate external experiences of others and their feelings into the individual's self-image; that is, the extent to which a person relies on others to provide a clear definition of self. The scales are orthogonal to each other. Split-half reliability coefficients for the boundary and fusion scales are 0.76 and 0.75 respectively.

The measure of intrapsychic differentiation was the Embedded Figures Test (Witkin, Oltman, Raskin, and Karp, 1971). The score is the accurate time required to extract simple figures from each of 12 complex figures. Reliability coefficients range from 0.61 to .91.

The measure of locus of control was the Nowicki-Strickland Locus of Control Scale for Adolescents. This scale is a paper-and-pencil measure of 40 items to be answered "yes" or "no" (Nowicki & Strickland, 1973).

Adolescents were administered the Embedded Figures Test, Boundary/Fusion Questionnaire, and Locus of Control Scale, in that order, at the TC. Four sets of parents who lived further than a drive of an hour and a half from the facility were administered the Boundary/Fusion Questionnaire over the telephone. A t-test comparing the scores on telephone administrations of the scale with a random sample of parents in the larger sample showed no significant difference between groups ($p < 0.50$, two-tailed).

FINDINGS

Study 1

The findings for study 1 were analyzed using the chi-square statistic and, if this was to be found significant, Cramer's Measure of Association ($\emptyset$) was used to measure the strength of the association between the variables. The t-test was also used. The first hypothesis tested was whether there was a decrease in the number of dropouts associated with the introduction of structural family therapy into residential treatment. To test this hypothesis, the numbers of dropouts and of attenders were compared before and after the program change. An inspection of Tables 15-2 and 15-3 reveals that, as expected, there was a significant decrease in the number of residents of the TC dropping out of treatment for the nine-month period following the program change for facility A, but not for facility B.

The second hypothesis tested was whether the change in treatment approach was associated with an increase in the number of families being seen in family therapy during the first month of treatment. To test this hypothesis, the numbers of families seen and not seen in family therapy during the first month of treatment were compared before and after the program change.

Prior to the program change at facility A, most residents of both facilities began family therapy after they had been in treatment for a period of between three to six months. After the program change at facility A, residents were involved in conjoint family therapy on a regular basis beginning with the first month of treatment, while no such change occurred in facility B. Tables 15-4 and 15-5 reflect these findings.

The third hypothesis tested was whether families who had a dropout attended family therapy at a lower rate and had a greater number of months with no family therapy sessions than families who remained in treatment. To test this hypothesis, the strength of the association between dropping out and having a month with no family therapy was calculated (Table 15-6) and the rates of attendance in family

Table 15-2
Comparison of Dropouts and Attenders
by Time Period at Facility A

	Dropout	Attender	
Nine months preceding program change	19 (37%)	9 (18%)	28 (55%)
Nine months following program change	7 (14%)	16 (31%)	23 (45%)
Total	26 (51%)	25 (49%)	52

$\chi^2 = 4.0822$, $p<0.05$, $\emptyset = 0.28$

Table 15-3
Comparison of Dropouts and Attenders
by Time Period at Facility B

	Dropout	Attender	
Nine months preceding program change	6 (12%)	5 (10%)	11 (22%)
Nine months following program change	15 (31%)	23 (47%)	38 (78%)
Total	21 (43%)	28 (57%)	49

$\chi^2 = 0.3066$, $p=$ n.s.

Table 15-4
Comparison of Attendance in Family Therapy at Facility A During the First Month
of Treatment, by Time Period

	No Family Therapy	Family Therapy	
Nine months preceding program change	22 (54%)	6 (15%)	28 (69%)
Nine months following program change	3 (7%)	10 (29%)	13 (31%)
Total	25 (61%)	16 (39%)	41

$\chi^2 = 9.6129$, $p<0.01$, $\emptyset = 0.48$

therapy for dropouts and attenders were calculated (Table 15-7). As previously suggested, families who had a dropout attended family therapy at a lower rate and had a greater number of months without family therapy sessions than did families who continued in treatment. Tables 15-6 and 15-7 support these findings. Their significance lies in the hypothesized connection between greater involvement in family therapy as measured by rate and regularity of attendance and support for the resident to remain in treatment. The family involved in treatment may feel identified with the treatment success or failure of its drug-abusing member and, therefore, support the adolescent's staying in treatment.

Since 85% of the no-show months for dropouts occurred in their first month of treatment, the chi-square statistic was calculated for a two-by-two contingency table of dropouts and attenders differentiated by those who had no family therapy during their first month of treatment and those who had family therapy during their first

Table 15-5

Comparison of Attendance in Family Therapy at Facility B During the First Month of Treatment, by Time Period

	No Family Therapy	Family Therapy	
Nine months preceding program change	13 (38%)	6 (18%)	19 (56%)
Nine months following program change	11 (32%)	4 (12%)	15 (46%)
Total	24 (70%)	10 (30%)	34

$\chi^2 = 0.01$, $p = $ n.s.

Table 15-6

Dropouts and Attenders Differentiated by Those Who Had and Those Who Never Had a No-Show Month (Facility A)

	Dropout	Attender	
One or more no-show months	25	7	32
No no-show months	3	8	11
Total	28	15	43

$\chi^2 = 6.5094$, $p<0.02$ $\emptyset = 0.39$

Table 15-7

Comparison of Dropout and Attender Monthly Rate of Attendance in Family Therapy (Facility A)

	Dropout	Attender
χ^2	0.75	2.12
SD	0.97	1.23
N	26	17

$t = 4.01$, $df = 41$, $p<0.001$

month of treatment. The following information was generated: $\chi^2 = 6.6609$, $p<0.01$, $N = 43$, $\emptyset = 30$. These findings indicate that dropouts were more likely to have not had family therapy during their first month of treatment and complement those presented in Tables 15-4 and 15-5, which show a significant increase in the number of families being seen in family therapy in facility A after the program change there.

Study 2

A Pearson correlation analysis was used to test the hypothesis that adolescents who have a lower level of differentiation have more internal locus-of-control beliefs that do adolescents who have higher levels of differentiation. It was found that the correlation between a score on the Embedded Figures Test and a score on the Nowicki-Strickland Locus of Control Scale was not significant, thereby refuting the first hypothesis that level of differentiation and locus of control among compulsive adolescent substance abusers are related.

A series of Pearson correlation analyses were used to test the second hypothesis that maternal and adolescent levels of differentiation are related while paternal and adolescent levels of differentiation are not related. To test this hypothesis, the correlation coefficient between the adolescent's score on the Boundary/Fusion Questionnaire and the maternal and paternal scores on this questionnaire were computed. Table 15-8 presents these findings, which, while not statistically significant, are in the expected direction.

A Pearson correlation analysis showed that the relationship between the adolescent's level of differentiation as measured by the Embedded Figures Test and the adolescent's length of stay in weeks in the TC are related in the opposite

Table 15-8
Correlation Between Adolescent, Maternal, and Paternal Scores on the
Boundary Fusion Questionnaire

| | Adolescent | |
	Boundary	Fusion
Mother[a]		
Boundary	−0.24*	0.01
Fusion	−0.04	0.38†
Father		
Boundary[b]	0.19	−0.42†
Fusion	0.36*	0.08

[a]$N = 14$
[b]$N = 11$
*$p<0.12$
†$p<0.08$

from the expected direction, $r = 0.42$ ($p = 0.06$), thus refuting the third hypothesis.

Table 15-9 presents a comparison of the norms for the Embedded Figures Test and Locus of Control Scale with the mean scores and the standard deviations. As expected, the residents were significantly less differentiated than the normative group. An unexpected finding was that the residents were not significantly different from the normative group on locus-of-control scores. However, when the sample was divided by the median length of stay, residents who had been in the facility longer had significantly more internal locus-of-control beliefs than the normative group ($t = 1.63$, $p<0.05$). Residents who had been in the facility fewer than the median number of weeks were no different in their locus-of-control scores than the normative group. The possibility remains that the findings for the effect of time in treatment on locus of control may be due to chance.

Table 15-10 presents a comparison of the norms for the Boundary/Fusion Questionnaire with the mean scores for subjects. The original normative data for

Table 15-9
Comparison of Resident's Embedded Figure Test Scores and Locus of Control Scores with Norms for Those Tests

	Resident's Mean Score[a]	Normative Group's Mean Score	t Score
Locus of Control	10.29	11.38	1.09
Embedded Figures Test	60.00	32.00	3.01*

Note: Normative data on the Locus of Control Scale are from Nowicki and Strickland (1973): N = 39 males, age 18. Normative data on the Embedded Figures Test are from Witkin et al. (1971). N = 23 males, age 17
[a]N = 14
*$p<0.005$ (two-tailed)

Table 15-10
Comparison of Subject Scores on the Boundary/Fusion Questionnaire with Normative Scores

Resident[a]	Mother[b]		Father[c]			
	Mean	t Score	Mean	t Score	Mean	t Score
Boundary	65.1	1.80*	81.3	2.49†	76.6	0.97
Fusion	69.1	1.07	64.4	2.51‡	65.0	2.39‡

Note: Normative data on the Boundary/Fusion Questionnaire are from Miller (1981): N = 602, mean boundary score = 71.9, mean fusion score = 72.8
[a]N = 14
[b]N = 14
[c]N = 12
*$p<0.05$ (two-tailed)
‡$p<0.02$ (two-tailed)
†$p<0.01$ (two-tailed)

the Boundary/Fusion Questionnaire are based on a sample of 602 college students (Miller, 1981). Miller also collected data on a sample of blue-collar adult men and women in New Haven, Conn. He found that the means on the Boundary/Fusion Questionnaire for this sample were not significantly different from the means calculated on the original sample of 602.

DISCUSSION OF RESULTS

Study 1

This study produced two major findings. First, there was a significant decrease in dropping out for facility A, but not facility B, between the nine months preceding and the nine months following the program change at facility A. Second, dropouts were characterized by having attended family therapy at a significantly lower rate than those who continued and as having missed one or more months, particularly the first month, of family therapy significantly more often than those who continued.

A third finding was that there was an increase in attendance in family therapy during the first month of treatment at facility A but not at facility B for the same period. However, this finding is not surprising since facility A required such attendance, while facility B's clients were not asked to engage in family therapy until the third or sixth month after admittance. The finding does suggest that increased involvement in family therapy may be secured by simply requiring it. Staff training may also help to facilitate the process of involvement in family therapy.

The findings for the third hypothesis could be attributed to the fact that only motivated families remain in treatment. However, this explanation is obviated by findings for the first two hypotheses. If it were motivation and not family treatment and staff training that caused the differences in the rates and frequency of attendance in family therapy between attenders and dropouts, there should be no differences at facility A before and after the program change. In addition, there should be no differences between facility A and facility B in the frequency of family therapy attendance and dropping out. The first two sets of findings contradict their expectations. One could conclude from this that it is important to involve the family in structured family therapy early and on a regular basis in the residential treatment of the adolescent drug abuser since this may preclude dropping out. Attendance in family therapy by the adolescents early in treatment is also associated with a decrease in the number of dropouts. In addition, one could also conclude that staff training in structural family therapy may result in fewer dropouts and greater attendance in family therapy as a result of increased confidence and competence. Attendance in family therapy early in treatment is also associated with a decrease in the number of dropouts.

An early staff–family connection may be a predictor of outcome and attendance in family therapy because of the effect of training on staff morale. Staff members who receive training may feel more competent and confident than they did prior to training. These factors may lead to higher staff morale and a greater sense of an ability to help clients. When this feeling is communicated to clients, the clients may respond by being more amenable to involvement in treatment. These effects may be the result of staff enthusiasm caused by being involved in a training program. These effects of staff training could have been controlled at facility B had the staff there been involved in another training program, such as group psychotherapy. However, increase in staff morale is not the only outcome of training. Other outcomes included a program commitment to using structural family therapy and to involving families in treatment at the beginning of the adolescent's treatment.

One major policy change at facility A as the result of training was that all residents, adults and adolescents, were to be in conjoint family therapy. Tables 15-4 and 15-5 show that there was an increase in the number of families seen during the first month that the adolescent was in treatment at facility A, but not facility B, after the program change and training. Another policy change was that adolescents were only accepted into treatment if their parents agreed to participate. It should be noted that no family refused to be involved. The staff began using structural family therapy as a way of conceptualizing dynamics in the facility and developed a common language across disciplines.

Earlier and increased involvement in family therapy may have led to reduced dropping out as a result of a number of factors. One such factor may be that involving families early in treatment reduces the effectiveness of splitting by the adolescent. The use of denial, splitting, and projection as defenses by drug abusers is well documented (Krystal, 1977; Masterson, 1972; Weidman, 1983b; Wurmser, 1978). It may be that when families are involved in treatment there is less of a chance for the adolescent to create a situation in which the treatment facility is viewed as "bad" while the family is viewed as "good." When the parents are involved in treatment, they have a chance to compare the adolescent's perceptions with their own perceptions. Early involvement of the family may result in the family's feeling identified with the treatment facility rather than antagonistic. Ideally, the family therapist joins with the family, and all work together to contain the adolescent's acting out. When the treatment facility and family do not cooperate early in treatment, the dynamics of the situation are similar to those seen in a custody battle. The family and treatment facility fight each other over who is to control the situation and direct the adolescent's treatment. This divisiveness results in the adolescent's being able to manipulate both parties in the "custody battle" so that the drug abuser is pulled out of treatment by the family or pushed out by the treatment facility. The therapeutic task for the family therapist is to get the parents to cooperate so that the family power balance and hierarchy are re-sorted with the parents in charge working as a team. When the family is involved with the TC from the beginning, the family and staff are better able to cooperate and the hierarchy is restored, with the adults in charge of the adolescent.

Another factor that may explain how the increased and early use of family therapy leads to less dropping out is the increased stake the family has in keeping the adolescent in treatment. The family that had repeatedly failed in conscious attempts to help its child may unconsciously resist and sabotage treatment, perhaps because of a fear of appearing incompetent if treatment succeeds. The family has a large stake in the outcome of treatment because the members are involved in the treatment, having put in time and effort. When the family is involved in treatment, the successful outcome for the adolescent directly reflects on the family's efforts and competencies.

Study 2

The findings of this study parallel the findings of others in the field (Eldred & Washington, 1976; Gossop, 1978), who found a significant positive relationship between family pressure to remain in treatment and length of stay. The family exerts a powerful influence on its members to remain in or to drop out of treatment. If the family needs a deviant member to maintain homeostasis and deflect tension, and if this need is not handled appropriately, the family will sabotage treatment and act to regain its regulator of homeostasis. Family factors play a crucial role in the etiology and maintenance of substance abuse (Stanton et al., 1982). A family approach that focuses on those areas of the family process that continue to maintain substance-abusing behavior will be effective as a treatment approach. If some of the same family processes that maintain substance-abusing behavior also lead to dropping out, one may expect that a family approach will reduce dropping out of treatment, as the present study indicates.

The finding of no relationship between locus of control and level of differentiation among compulsive adolescent substance abusers is consistent with previous research (Lefcourt & Telegdi, 1971; Tobacyk, et al., 1975). The hypothesized relationship between locus of control and level of differentiation was built on the formulation that compulsive adolescent substance abusers are poorly differentiated and have internal-locus-of-control beliefs. The youths in this study, while being poorly differentiated as measured by the Embedded Figures Test, surprisingly were not different in their locus-of-control scores from the normative groups. It may be that the violation of this assumption led to the finding of no relationship between locus of control and level of differentiation.

The relationship between locus of control and level of differentiation for residents who had been in the facility fewer than the median number of weeks, while not significant, was in the expected direction ($r = 0.37$). The lack of significance may be attributable to the small sample size ($n = 7$). It may be that the relationship between locus of control and level of differentiation only holds for residents in an early phase of treatment when they are not yet well adjusted. Researchers have found that residents of TCs exhibit increased psychological and social adjustment with increasing lengths of stay (DeLeon, Skodol, & Rosenthal, 1973).

In addition, it may also be that these youths are able accurately to determine the locus of causality because their levels of differentiation are not low enough to affect their reality-testing abilities. It may be that locus of control and psychological differentiation will only show the expected relationship among more disturbed youths—those with borderline and psychotic disorders.

As predicted, there are relationships that approach statistical significance between adolescent and parental level of differentiation as measured by the Boundary/Fusion Questionnaire. These correlations may not have reached statistical significance because of the small sample size.

The correlation between adolescent and maternal fusion scores suggests that the adolescent and mother are involved in a symbiotic relationship in which they rely on each other to provide a clear definition of self (Alexander & Dibb, 1977). It may be inferred, following the findings of Witkin, Dyk, Faterson, Goodenough, and Karp (1962), that the more differentiated mothers have more differentiated adolescents.

The inverse relationship between maternal and adolescent boundary scores suggests that as mothers are increasingly distant and bounded in their relationships, their adolescents tend to become less bounded. As the maternal figure becomes less emotionally available to the adolescent, the adolescent becomes more needy of a relationship with her. This inverse relationship may be taken as supporting the conceptualization that compulsive adolescent substance abuse had its roots in the rapprochement subphase of the separation–individuation process (Mahler et al., 1975). As Mahler et al. stated, "The less emotionally available the mother is at the time of rapprochement, the more insistently and even desperately does the toddler attempt to woo her" (p. 80). It is out of this early experience that the pseudoindividuation behavior of compulsive substance abuse emerges. In both the rapprochement subphase and the substance abuse, the child is attempting to coerce the parent into functioning as a quasi-external ego (McDevitt & Mahler, 1980). It is the maternal figure's unavailability that is crucial in the development of rapprochement difficulties and later substance abuse.

When one looks at the pattern of maternal scores compared with the normative group on the Boundary/Fusion Scale, one finds that these mothers have significantly higher boundary and lower fusion scores. This pattern of scores indicates that these mothers are less psychologically available to their children. They may be described as more highly demarcated from the environment and distant and less able to incorporate the experiences of others, particularly their children. The drug abuser's pseudoindividuation may be viewed as an attempt to cope with this maternal unavailability. Drug abuse may be viewed as a search for an alternative source of psychological and emotional support when the youth enters the second individuation process of adolescence. However, because the youth has not experienced sufficient emotional involvement by the maternal figure, the youth is unable to separate and individuate. The drug-abusing adolescent experiences the normal developmental pull toward autonomy and independence, while not having internalized sufficient psychological involvement and emotional supplies to be able to separate and individuate.

The relationships among paternal and adolescent levels of differentiation are difficult to interpret as the correlations that approach statistical significance are between different scales of the Boundary/Fusion Questionnaire. The correlation between the father's fusion and adolescent's boundary scores suggests that as these fathers' use of others to define self increases, their adolescents' boundedness also increases. In other words, the father's decreasing level of differentiation is associated with the adolescent's increasing need for structure in the environment, as indicated by higher boundary scores. The negative correlation between the father's boundary and the adolescent's fusion scores indicates that the father's need for structure increases in association with the adolescent's decreasing tendency to rely on others for self-definition. It may be that the father's rigidity precludes a relationship developing between himself and the adolescent, and hence we have the negative correlation between paternal boundary and adolescent fusion scores. This interpretation is further strengthened by the very low and nonsignificant correlation between adolescent and paternal fusion scores, indicating the father's peripheral position in the family with respect to the adolescent.

The significance of the above relationships between the adolescent and paternal levels of differentiation may be found in the discussions by object-relations theorists (Mahler et al., 1975; Horner, 1979) on the significance of the father during early development. These theorists have described the role of the father during separation—individuation as the bridge between the symbiotic maternal relationship and the environment. It may be interpreted that the father's decreased ability to function as the bridge to reality is associated with the adolescent's decreased level of differentiation and increased use of others to develop a definition of self.

Although the above findings may be due to chance, these findings and their interpretation are consistent with previous research on family relationships among compulsive adolescent substance abusers (Chien et al., 1964; Stanton et al., 1978; Vaillant, 1966; Ziegler-Driscoll, 1978, 1979). This literature describes the father as being peripheral and distant while the mother is described as overinvolved and symbiotic with the drug abuser.

The relationship between the adolescent's level of differentiation and length of stay in the TC was opposite from the expected direction, becoming less differentiated over time. These results may be a function of the adolescent's increasing acceptance of and dependence on the TC. One of the effects of treatment is that the resident's dependence shifts to the program; the resident becomes involved in a symbiotic relationship with the program. These youths come to treatment in a pseudoindividuated state with strong unmet dependency needs. Their parents have been unable to assist them in the separation–individuation process of developing autonomy and independence. The TC offers a consistent, expectable, and reliable environment in which emotional support enables the drug-abusing adolescent to reexperience the pervasive ambivalence and demandingness of the rapprochement subphase. The TC by its structure allows the youth to become dependent on it. In this sense, it acts as an external ego, regulating time and activities and defining reality by explaining the reasons for behavior. The TC acts as an external superego and ego ideal by defining right and wrong, by critically evaluating behavior, and by levying consequences for behavior. It may be that the internalization process only begins as the youths start to separate from the program by living and working outside the facility and returning once a week for groups.

It might be argued that the more psychologically differentiated residents are the ones who leave treatment against program advice, so that those who continue in treatment are only the least psychologically differentiated. If this were true, one would expect that phase 1 residents would exhibit greater variance in their level of differentiation than phase 2 and phase 3 residents, who have been in treatment longer. Most persons leave treatment against program advice during phase 1. A test for the equality of variance between phase 1 residents and those in phase 2 and 3 revealed no significant difference between the groups.

Another element of this pattern of decreasing differentiation over time is the operation of denial. The compulsive adolescent substance abuser is often forced into treatment. All the youths in this study were given a choice by the Juvenile Court of either going to the TC or to a state training school. The lack of voluntary involvement in treatment coupled with pseudoindividuation suggests that these youths strongly deny their dependency. As they progress through treatment, their denial decreases and their dependency emerges. They then become increasingly dependent on the program and less differentiated.

CONCLUSION

Involving the families of adolescent substance abusers in family therapy appears to reduce dropping out of treatment; for one thing, it may result in the family's having a greater investment in keeping the adolescent in treatment, thereby reducing attempts to sabotage treatment. The clear implication is that work with chemically dependent adolescents should include family treatment as a major component of treatment.

The second study provided support for the theoretical constructs that intrapsychic and interpersonal levels of differentiation play a key role in the adolescent's substance abuse. Family therapy is a treatment modality that enables the clinician to focus on the reciprocal nature of the relationships among family members. The chemically dependent adolescent's pseudoindividuation may be treated as an attempt to cope with an overinvolved and emotionally unavailable mother and a peripheral father. In addition, the adolescent's behavior may be seen as a means of deflecting parent attention away from marital conflicts and thus reducing parental anxiety. It then follows that family therapy, which focuses on the interactional aspects of the separation–individuation process, will positively affect the level of differentiation of family members.

Increasing the adolescent's intrapsychic and interpersonal levels of differentiation from the maternal figure is a desired outcome of treatment in family therapy facilities.

REFERENCES

Alexander, B. K., & Dibb, G. A. (1977). Interpersonal perception in addict families. *Family Process, 16,* 17–28.

Attardo, N. (1965). Psycho-dynamic factors in the mother-child relationship in adolescent drug addiction. *Psychotherapy Psychosomatic, 13,* 249–255.

Baekeland, F., Lundwall, L., & Shanahan, T. M. (1973a). Dropping-out of treatment: A critical review. *Psychological Bulletin, 82,* 738–783.

Baekeland, F., Lundwall, L., & Shanahan, T. J. (1973b). Correlates of patient attrition in the outpatient treatment of alcoholism. *Journal of Nervous and Mental Disease, 157,* 99–107.

Baekeland, F., & Lundwall, L. (1975). Dropping-out of treatment: A critical review. *Psychological Bulletin, 82,* 738–783.

Berzins, J. J., & Ross, W. F. (1973). Locus of control among opiate addicts. *Journal of Consulting and Clinical Psychology, 40,* 84–91.

Calicchia, J. P. (1974) Narcotic addiction and perceived locus of control. *Journal of Clinical Psychology, 30,* 499–504.

Chien, I., Gerald, D. L., Lee, R. S., & Rosenfeld, E. (1964) *The road to H.* New York: Basic Books.

DeLeon, G., & Andrews, M. (1978). Therapeutic community drop-outs five years later: Preliminary findings on self-reported status. In O. E. Smith, S. M. Anderson, M. Buston, N. Gottlieb, W. Harvey, & T. Chungs (Eds.), *A multi-cultural view of drug abuse: Proceedings of the National Drug Abuse Conference, 1977.* Cambridge, MA: Schenken.

DeLeon, G., Skodol, A., & Rosenthal, M. (1973). Changes in psychopathological signs of resident drug addicts. *Archives of General Psychiatry, 28,* 131–135.

Eldred, C. A., & Washington, M. N. (1976). Interpersonal relationships in heroin use by men and women and their role in treatment outcome. *International Journal of Addictions, 11,* 117–130.

Goldstein, M. (1976). Maternal perception and locus of control in male opiate addicts of different ages and races. *Dissertation Abstracts International*, 37, 2740A.

Gossop, M. (1978). Drug independence: A study of the relationship between motivational, cognitive, social and historical factors, and treatment variables. *Journal of Nervous and Mental Disease*, 166, 44–50.

Gurman, A. S., & Kniskern, D. P. (1978). Research on marital and family therapy: Progress perspective. In S. L. Garfield & A. E. Bergin (Eds.), *Handbook of psychotherapy and behavior change: An empirical analysis* (2nd ed.). New York: Wiley.

Hinshelwood, R. D., & Manning, N. (1979). *Therapeutic communities: Reflections and progress*. London: Routledge & Kegan Paul.

Horner, A. (1979). *Object relations and the developing ego in therapy*. New York: Jason Aronson.

Kaufman, E., & Kaufmann, P. (1979). *Family therapy of drug and alcohol abuse*. New York: Gardner Press.

Krystal, H. (1977). Self and object-representation in alcoholism and other drug dependence. In J. D. Blaine & D. A. Julius (Eds.), *Psychodynamics of drug abuse*. (NIDA Research Monograph No. 2, Department of Health, Education, and Welfare Publication no. 77–470.) Washington, DC: U.S. Government Printing Office.

LeFave, M. K. (1980). Correlates of engagement in family therapy. *Journal of Marriage and Family Therapy*, 10, 75–81.

Lefcourt, H. M. (1976). *Locus of control*. Hillsdale, NJ: Lawrence Erlbaum Associates.

Lefcourt, H. M. (1966). Belief in personal control of reinforcement: A review. *Psychological Bulletin*, 65, 206–220.

Lefcourt, H. M., & Telegdi, M. S. (1971). Perceived locus of control and field dependence as prediction of cognitive activity. *Journal of Consulting and Clinical Psychology*, 37, 53–56.

Mahler, M. S., Pine, F., & Berman, A. (1975). *The psychological birth of the human infant*. New York: Basic Books.

Masterson, J. F. (1972). *Treatment of the borderline adolescent*. New York: Wiley.

McDevitt, J. B., & Mahler, M. S. (1980). Object constancy, individuality and internalization. In S. I. Greenspan & G. H. Pollock (Eds.), *The course of life, Volume I*. (Mental Health Study Center, U.S. Department of Health and Human Service Publication No. 80–786.) Washington, DC: U.S. Government Printing Office.

Miller, J. (1981). Personal communication.

Miller, K. (1980). Psychological differentiation, social factors and meeting sequence in large group process. Doctoral dissertation, George Washington University.

Minuchin, S., & Fishman, H. C. (1981) *Family therapy techniques*. Cambridge, MA: Harvard University Press.

Nowicki, S., & Strickland, B. R. (1973). A locus of control scale for children. *Journal of Consulting and Clinical Psychology*, 40, 148–154.

Rotter, J. B. (1975). Some problems and misconceptions related to the construct of internal vs. external control of reinforcement. *Journal of Consulting and Clinical Psychology*, 48, 56–67.

Rotter, J. B. (1976). *Locus of control*. Hillsdale, NJ: Lawrence Erlbaum.

Sachs, J. G., & Levy, N. M. (1979). Objective personality changes in residents of a therapeutic community. *American Journal of Psychiatry*, 136, 796–799.

Smithyman, S. D., Plant, W. T., & Southern, M. L. (1974). Locus of control in two samples of chronic drug abusers. *Psychological Reports*, 34, 1293.

Stanton, M. D. (1979). Family treatment of drug problems: A review. In R. L. Depont, A. Goldstein, & J. O'Connell (Eds.), *Handbook of drug abuse*. (National Institute on Drug Abuse and Office of Drug Abuse Policy, Executive Office of the President.) Washington, DC: U.S. Government Printing Office.

Stanton, M. D., Todd, T. C., et al. (1982). *The family therapy of drug abuse and addiction*. New York: Guilford.

Stanton, M. D., Todd, T. C., Heard, D. B., Kirschner, S., Kleiman, J. I., Mowatt, D. T., Riley, P., Scott, S. M., & Van Deusen, M. M. (1978). Heroin addiction as a family phenomenon: A new conceptual model. *American Journal of Drug Abuse*, 5, 125–150.

Strassberg, S., & Robinson, J. (1974). The relationship between locus and control and other personality measures in drug abusers. *Journal of Consulting and Clinical Psychology*, 42, 744–745.

Tobacyk, J. J., Broughton, A., & Vaught, G. M. (1975). Effects of congruence between locus of control and field dependence on personality functioning. *Journal of Consulting and Clinical Psychology*, 43, 81–85.

Vaillant, G. E. (1966). A 12-year follow-up of New York narcotic addicts. III, Some social and psychiatric characteristics. *Archives of General Psychiatry*, 15, 559–609.

Ward, E. S., & Hemsley, D. R. (1982). Social and psychological factors associated with length of stay on an inpatient drug dependency treatment unit. *International Journal of Addictions*, 16, 1281–1288.

Weidman, A. (1983a). The compulsive adolescent substance abusers: Psychological differentiation and family process. *Journal of Drug Education*, 13, 161–172.

Weidman, A. (1983b). Adolescent substance abuse: Family dynamics. *Family Therapy*, 10, 47–55.

Weidman, A. (1983c). Psychological differentiation and locus of control among compulsive adolescent substance abusers and their parents. *Dissertation Abstracts International*, 44, 3948-B. (University Microfilms DA8405718.)

Witkin, H. A., Dyk, R. B., Faterson, H. F., Goodenough, D. R., & Karp, S. A. (1962). *Psychological differentiation*. New York: Wiley.

Witkin, H. A., Oltman, P. K., Raskin, E., & Karp, S. A. (1971). *Manual for the Embedded Figures Test*. Palo Alto, CA: Consulting Psychologists Press.

Wurmser, L. (1978). *The hidden dimension*. New York: Jason Aronson.

Zax, M., Marsey, R., & Biggs, C. F. (1961). Demographic characteristics of alcoholic outpatients and tendency to remain in treatment. *Quarterly Journal of Studies on Alcohol*, 22, 98–105.

Ziegler-Driscoll, G. (1978). Family treatment with parent addict families. In D. E. Smith, S. M. Anderson, M. Buston, N. Gottlieb, W. Harvey, & T. Chung (Eds.), *A multi-*

cultural view of drug abuse: Proceedings of the National Drug Abuse Conference 1977. Cambridge, MA: Schenken.

Ziegler-Driscoll, G. (1979). The similarities in families of drug dependents and alcoholics. In E. Kaufman & P. Kaufmann (Eds.), *Family therapy of drug and alcohol abuse.* New York: Gardner Press.

PART V

POPULATION CHARACTERISTICS: IMPLICATIONS FOR TREATMENT AND RECOVERY

16

Cultural Factors in the Assessment and Treatment of African-American Addicts: Africentric Considerations

Rosalyn Harris-Offutt, B.S., CRNA, NCC, CPC

"We Wear The Mask"

We wear the mask that grins and lies,
It hides our cheeks and shades our eyes,
This debt we pay to human guile,
With torn and bleeding hearts we smile,
And mouth with myriad subtleties.

Why should the world be overwise
In counting all our tears and sighs?
Nay, let them see us, while
We wear the mask.

. . .

Paul Lawrence Dunbar (1913)

"How It Feels To Be Colored Me"

But I am not tragically colored. There is no great sorrow damned up in my soul, nor lurking behind my eyes. I do not mind at all. I do not belong to the sobbing school of negrohood who hold that nature somehow has given them a lowdown dirty deal and whose feelings are hurt about it. . . . No, I do not weep at the world. I am too busy sharpening my oyster knife.

Zora Neale Hurston (1928)

Recovery from drug addiction is a two-stage process. The first stage, called detoxification, focuses on allowing the body an environment in which it can begin to return to a greater level of physiological homeostasis. This stage begins with the patient entering drug abstinence and withdrawal. Withdrawal can be defined as a reactive process of the cells of the body attempting to readjust to functioning without the presence of drugs or chemicals or any of the by-products of their chemical breakdown. This stage can express itself on a polaric continuum of benign to deadly malignant to terminal. Many variances, including type of drug, progressed stage of disease, sex, state of physical health, and age, play a significant role in the degree of vehemence with which it occurs. This stage often requires medical intervention and management to protect and sustain life. Its acute duration is generally accepted medically as extending from five to seven days, unless physiological crises occur.

CONTINUING RECOVERY
AND AFRICENTRIC CONSIDERATIONS

The second stage begins only after abstinence has been attained. This stage, for purposes of both identification and simplicity, will be referred to throughout this chapter as "continuing recovery."

Continuing recovery from drug addiction is an ongoing process that requires the patient to confront his or her distorted beliefs and self-defeating behavioral patterns. Effective treatment of addictive disease is based on awareness with understanding of any factors that affect the patient's personal and cultural belief systems. Nearly everything that is known and practiced in the psychotherapeutic realm is based on Eurocentric models of personality development. They define psychopathology as well as accepted and approved therapeutic modalities. Usually these models are inadequate in providing the therapist with a working knowledge of Africentric cultural values and concomitant beliefs and behaviors. The Eurocentric model does not acknowledge the cultural forces that shape this population's ethnic belief system. The Eurocentric treatment model, including psychological testing instruments, does not distinguish between beliefs and behaviors that are the outcome of racial enculturalization, ethnic self-concept/worth, or reactive defendedness used to protect the self from perceived or authentic racial assault. Lack of attention to the presence of these variances can yield therapeutic bias and create a negative impact on the recovery process.

Therapists need more than a working knowledge of the Africentric cultural value system and emotional survival skills. Many African-Americans suffer the pain of a low ethnic sense of self, and their attempt to avoid acknowledging, feeling, or reducing the pain may cause them to be more driven to self-medication and addictive drug use. Thus these patients are likely to be more vulnerable to a higher incidence of relapse. When White therapists are not aware of these factors, therapeutic effectiveness is limited. Unless recognized, the outcome undermines the therapeutic process, ultimately affecting therapeutic effectiveness and hindering continuing recovery of the African-American patient.

African-Americans, from their arrival on America's shores, have been required to live in two worlds. The dictates of slavery permitted no choice in learning or not learning European cultural rituals and beliefs. The entire African definition of family spirituality, personhood was devalued and dehumanized. The results of having to survive and live the dichotomy created by this cultural assault continues to create internal conflict in African-Americans today. This conflict expresses itself as distress, emotional pain, and negative self-concept.

Clark and Clark (1939), in studies of doll-color preference, identified and reported how self-rejection begins early in childhood. This preference for things white indicated how early in development African-Americans begin to react to what they perceive and experience as society's edict of what is acceptable and approved. This early emergence of racial awareness and the perception of how the larger culture perceives things that are black is supported historically by the overt existence of slavery and racism. Racism became an institution—an institution to defend one's self from, to be coped with, to be overtly opposed at risk, to covertly oppose at all times.

Even for contemporary African-Americans, nothing has changed. Thus African-American society continues to live in varying degrees of reactive formation. The explicitly taught and implicitly modeled belief passed from generation to generation is: It is not safe to talk, honestly, to Whites, to trust Whites, or to allow them to know how you feel. Permission is given to keep secrets. Grier and Cobbs (1986) refer to this as "cultural paranoia." They proceed to define this paranoia as the "reluctance to trust people of different color, lifestyle, class, etc.; regarded as a healthy response to racism, discrimination, and oppression."

African-Americans frequently approach therapy with a lack of trust that is well grounded in their experiences of racial prejudice as expressed in various forms of discrimination. This "cultural paranoia" has a great impact on their perception of safety in the therapeutic setting. It will influence the engagement and rapport establishment phase of the therapeutic process, and it will have a direct effect on the disclosure and uncovering phases. Boyd-Franklin (1989) suggests that (1) sensitivity to judgments made by Whites may cause Black patients to withhold information; (2) therapeutic approaches that focus on initial extensive history intake may increase hesitancy and suspicion, rather than facilitate the process of joining; and (3) the use of one-way mirrors and taping equipment can heighten a patient's suspiciousness about therapy.

Boykins (1983) describes nine dimensions of beliefs, whose roots are African-American based, that continue to have an impact on African-Americans today. These beliefs play a significant role in how they experience their world, and they affect all facets of the African-American psychosocial life experience. They are:

1. *Spirituality*—a belief that powers greater than humans exist and are at work.
2. *Harmony*—a belief that human beings and their environment are interdependently connected. This applies to living in harmony with nature rather than trying to control it and integrating the parts of one's life into a harmonious whole.
3. *Movement*—a rhythmic orientation to life that may be manifested in music and dance, as well as in behavior and approach.
4. *Verve*—the psychological aspect of the movement dimension. This involves a preference to be simultaneously attuned to several stimuli rather than a singular, routinized, or bland orientation; energetic, intense.
5. *Affect*—emotional expressiveness and sensitivity to emotional cues; integration of feeling with cognitive elements.
6. *Communalism*—interdependence of people; social orientation.
7. *Expressive individualism*—focus on a person's unique style or flavor in an activity; spontaneity; manifested as a unique tilt of one's hat, a walk, a jazz musician's rendition.
8. *Orality*—importance of information learned and transmitted orally; call and response pattern.
9. *Social time perspective*—viewing time in terms of the event rather than the clock, for example, the event begins when everyone arrives.

Baldwin (1989) suggests that the "European worldview upon which Western Psychology itself is based is diametrically opposed to the psychological development, survival, and liberation of Black people." Eurocentric psychology devalues or denies any worldviews other than its own. Lack of awareness or acceptance of other existing worldviews creates an unspoken, predisposed bias in any therapist whose clients are of African descent.

In the course of assessment, disclosure, and uncovering during the therapeutic process, the therapist is likely to observe or learn belief and/or behavioral patterns related to issues of communication, family structure, parenting, and spirituality. Many of these may appear to be dysfunctional relative to Eurocentric standards. The possibility/probability that these beliefs and behaviors are based on Africentric cultural values must always be considered. When psychological tests are used to assist in assessment and diagnosis, it becomes crucial that their results be interpreted in light of African-Americans' unique world view and the set of life's experiences that distinguishes them from the Eurocentric experience on which these instruments were based. These considerations allow the therapist to assess with healthy discernment, thus supporting a more authentic process of assessment, diagnosis, choice of therapeutic modalities, focus, and goals of therapy.

CULTURAL THERAPIST BIAS AND EFFECTS ON THERAPEUTIC MANAGEMENT

The exploration by therapists of their own race and class biases is absolutely required. How therapists experience their world will affect the patient–therapist relationship, the process, and consequently determine outcome.

Myers (1988) suggests that a lack of understanding and acceptance of the Afrocentric worldview creates a sub-optimal environment where oppression reigns. Therapeutic oppression whether overt or covert is racism. Therapeutic racism is assaultive and dehumanizing.

Therapists who are stuck in an interpersonal style of overt or covert bias support the re-creation of the slave–master relationship. This countertherapeutic relationship is based on self-righteousness and/or pretense, thus representing defendedness. It encourages suppression and oppression rather than patient expression or openness.

When race is not an issue and therapists identify these styles of relating by a patient to his or her family or significant other, assessment indicates the presence of a dysfunctional process. The family system is identified and diagnosed as a dysfunctional system. In the subspecialty of addiction, it is frequently referred to as codependent, coaddictive, or addictive dependency. We use language to explain what supports the patient's continuing to function with the dysfunction. Some examples of that language are: (1) denial, (2) intellectualization, (3) rationalization, (4) external locus of control, and, (5) object orientation. The underlying issue is seen as one of control and power. The system is viewed as reactive. Labels have been created to identify examples of reactive relationships, such as, battered spouse syndrome, abusive, pimp/prostitute, parasitic, dictatorial. In some instances, pathological personality processes are named and diagnosed. Treatment models are formed and goals of therapy are created that are focused on confronting and reframing in the hope of guiding the patient/system into healthier ways of functioning and relating.

Unless White therapists are aware of their own beliefs and own issues and recognize the necessity to confront and process these issues, the entire therapeutic process with African-American patients is suspect. The process will support continued disorder and the patient will continue to be reactive and to express behaviors rooted in ethnic emotional survival skills.

ORDER VERSUS DISORDER

All theories of personality development affirm the impact that childhood learning has on the development of the mature, healthier, psychological/emotional self. For the African-American woman or man, healthy development of the ethnic personality is always affected by the presence of societal/institutional racism. As previously stated, the experience of racism and the reaction to it begins as early as childhood. While this experience is shared by both sexes, Grier and Cobbs (1968) suggest that the time frame in which it occurs and its intensity differ among African-American children. They suggest an earlier and greater intensity for African-American females in early childhood because of what happens in order for them to be seen as "acceptably groomed," for example, the texture of their hair, or the size of their feet. Girls are personally exposed earlier, both implicitly and explicitly, to racial and societal definitions of good versus bad and beauty versus ugliness. The experience for African-American males focuses less on physical attributes and more on issues of self-assertion versus suppression of self-assertion. During slavery, this was a major survival skill to be learned. The fear of pain, punishment, or death for honest self-assertion was real. Learning to live this emotional dichotomy, regardless of how conflicted it felt, was a life-saving skill.

There is a cross-integration of learning that takes place between the sexes. Bowles (1983, 1988) suggests that a fourth task or added dimension in development exists for African-American children. She identifies that task as the establishment of ethnic-defined self-representation and states that an appreciation of how a positive ethnic sense of self unfolds will aid practitioners, educators, and mental health professionals to better assess the internal resources available to African-Americans. This active awareness allows the therapist to relate to the patient from a position of empowerment rather than inadequacy. An understanding of what healthy functioning is within this added dimension compared with what is less than healthy is of utmost importance. This allows the therapist to remain cognizant of the "added dimension" where order/disorder may exist for African-Americans, its origin, its impact, and its direct effect on therapeutic management.

EFFECTS OF CULTURAL CONSIDERATIONS ON THERAPY

The goal of treatment, both medical and psychotherapeutic, is freedom from drug use and repetitive relapse. Psychotherapeutic treatment addresses the added dimension of facilitating—healing of personality splits, improving coping skills, and development of a healthier sense of self-worth. The goal of psychotherapy is self-empowerment.

When treating African-American addicts it is necessary for the therapist to be cognizant, accept, and respect the Africentric value system. This belief system has an effect on how the patient ethnically perceives him/her self. The patient's ethnic perception of self influences his/her concept of self-worth and self-power, thereby affecting how he/she relates to the society in which one lives. Accepting and understanding the African value system allows therapists to guide patients towards a healthier sense of ethnic self-worth and empowerment.

When treating African-American addicts, therapeutic assessment or definition of therapeutic objectives needs to consider Africentric values. Boyd Franklin (1989) describes this sensitivity as especially important in light of slavery and a history of racism.

Among examples of this consideration are:

1. The inclusion of the extended-family system in identifying the family support system.
2. The use of music as a safe way to express feeling.
3. An increase in the amount of shared conversation during sessions.
4. The avoidance of suggesting or implying a complete trust in the social environment.
5. The avoidance of the use of first names or pet names until given permission.
6. The offer of a choice of seating arrangements for both therapist and patient (sensitivity toward patient's need for freedom of movement, as well as decreasing the perception of the therapist as the ultimate authority).
7. The use of a less sterile therapeutic setting incorporating color, live vegetation, scents (in our office, oil essence simmers, and patients often state that they feel much less anxious and safer as soon as they enter and smell the essence).
8. The use of spontaneous laughter.
9. The avoidance of extensive history taking initially (Boyd-Franklin, 1989).
10. A sensitivity to Black religious beliefs and their importance to the patient.
11. The inclusion of art as a form of therapy. Even in individual therapy, the use of collage as a form of art is workable.

CONCLUSION

Admittedly, there are many factors that act to determine effective therapeutic management of the drug or chemically dependent patient. This chapter focuses on differences to be considered in the therapeutic management of African-American patients and on identifying added dimensions or systems to be aware of during such therapeutic management—and how the added systems are understood and can be utilized by therapists to aid the African-American addict who is struggling to maintain continuing recovery. Therapists practicing in the area of addiction have to guide recovering patients (1) in learning new, different, and healthier ways of structuring their lives; (2) in applying decision-making strategies; (3) in becoming cognizant of the definition and purpose of limits/boundaries; (4) in becoming aware of the need for limits; (5) in learning healthier ways of managing stressful or oppressive environments; (6) in defining healthier ways of coping with feelings; and (7) in defining or redefining their beliefs regarding their relationships with themselves and with others. Therapists who treat African-American addicts also have the added dimension of being challenged to aid the patient in understanding how his or her differences can be experienced as an enhancement of continuing recovery.

REFERENCES

Baldwin, J. A. (1989). The role of black psychologist in black liberation. *The Journal of Black Psychology, 16*(1), 67–76.

Barksdale, R. K., & Kinnamon, K. (Eds.). (1972). *Black writers in America: A comprehensive anthology, 1920–1970.* New York: Macmillan.

Bontemps, A. (Ed.). (1974). *American Negro poetry: An anthology.* (rev. ed., p. 14). New York: Hill & Wang.

Bourne, B. G., & Fox, R. (1973). *Alcoholism: Progress in research and treatment.* New York: Academic Press.

Bowles, D. D. (1983). *Collected works.* Northhampton, MA: Smith College.

Bowles, D. D. (1988). *Culture and ethnicity.* Silver Springs, MD: NASW.

Boyd-Franklin, N. (1987). The contribution of family therapy models to the treatment of Black families. *Psychotherapy, 24,* 621–629.

Boyd-Franklin, N. (1989). *Black families in therapy: A multisystems approach.* New York: Guilford.

Boykins, A. W. (1983). *Achievement and achievement motives* (pp. 324–337). Boston: W. H. Freeman.

Boykins, A. W., & Toms, F. D. (1985). Black child socialization: A conceptual framework. In H. P. McAdoo & J. L. McAdoo (Eds.), *Social educational and parental environments* (pp. 32–52). Beverly Hills, CA: Sage.

Cannon, K. G. (1988). *Black womanist ethics.* Atlanta: Scholar Press.

Catanzaro, R. J. (1968). *Alcoholism.* Springfield, IL: Charles C. Thomas.

Cermak, T. L. (1986). *Diagnosing and treating co-dependence.* MN: Johnson Institute Books.

Clark, K. B., & Clark, M. P. (1939). The development of consciousness of self and the emergence of racial identification in negro pre-school children. *Journal of Social Psychology, 10,* 591–599.

Clark, K. B., & Clark, M. P. (1940). Skin color as a factor in racial identification of negro pre-school children. *Journal of Social Psychology, S.P.S.S.I. Bulletin, II,* 159–169.

Dunbar, P. L. (1913). *Complete poems of Paul Lawrence Dunbar.* New York: Dodd, Mead.

Grier, W. H., & Cobbs, P. M. (1986). *Black rage.* New York: Basic Books.

Griffith, E. H., English, T., & Mayfield, V. (1980). Possession, prayer, and testimony: Therapeutic aspects of the Wednesday night meeting in a Black church. *Psychiatry, 43,* 120–128.

Harrison, D. K. (1975). Race as a counselor-client variable. *Counseling Psychologist, 5,* 124–133.

Hunt, P. (1987). Black clients: Implications for supervision of trainees. *Psychiatry, 24,* 114–119.

Hurston, Z. N. (1928). How It Feels to Be Colored Me! *The World Tomorrow*, 11(5), 215–216.

Jenkins, A. (1982). *The psychology of the Afro-American; Afro-American self-concept: Sustaining self-esteem* (pp. 22–51). New York: Pergamon.

Lindbald-Goldberg, M., Dukes, J., & Lasley, J. (1988). Stress in Black, low-income, single-parent families: Normative and dysfunctional patterns. *American Journal of Orthopsychiatry*, 58, 104–120.

Looney, J. (1988). Ego development and Black identity. *Journal of Black Psychology*, 15, 44–56.

Mayfield, W. (1972). Mental health in the Black community. *Social Work*, 17, 106–110.

McCarthy, J., & Yancey, W. (1971). Uncle Tom & Mr. Charlie: Metaphysical pathos in the study of racism and personal disorganization. *American Journal of Sociology*, 76, 648–672.

McGoldrick, M., Rearce, J., & Giordano, J. (1982). *Ethnicity and family therapy*. New York: Guilford.

Mitchell, H., & Lewter, N. (1986). *Soul theology: The heart of American Black culture*. San Francisco: Harper & Row.

Myers, L. J. (1988). *Understanding an Afrocentric world view: Introduction to an optimal psychology*. Dubuque, Iowa: Kendall/Hunt.

Nobles, W. W. (1974). Africanity: Its role in Black families. *Black Scholar*, 5, 10–17.

Peters, M., & Massey, G. (1983). Mundane extreme environmental stress in family stress theories: The case of Black families in White America. *Marriage and Family Review*, 6, 193–218.

Royse, D., & Turner, G. (1980). Strengths of Black families: A Black community's perspective. *Social Work*, 25, 407–409.

Scanzoni, J. (1971). *The Black family in modern society*. Boston: Allyn & Bacon.

Siegel, J. M. (1974). A brief review of the effects of race in clinical service interactions. *American Journal of Orthopsychiatry*, 44, 555–562.

Smerdlow, A., & Lessinger, H. (1983). *Class, race and sex: The dynamics of control*. Boston: G. K. Hall.

Terry, R. W. (1970). *For Whites only*. Grand Rapids, MI: William B. Eerdmans.

Torrey, E. F. (1982). *Witchdoctors and psychiatrists: The common roads of psychotherapy and its future* (Rev.). New York: Harper & Row.

Weaner, D. (1982). Empowering treatment skills for helping Black families. *Social Casework*, 6, 100–105.

White, J. S. (1969). *African religions and philosophies*. Garden City, NY: Anchor Books.

Willis, M. G. (1989). A review of African-American children: A review of the literature and interventions. *Journal of Black Psychology*, 16, 47–65.

17

Issues in the Treatment of the Dual-Diagnosis Patient

Joan Ellen Zweben, Ph.D.

In recent years, increasing attention has become focused on the dual-diagnosis patient, as greater understanding in the separate fields of psychopathology and substance abuse permit a more effective integration of approaches to take place. The term "dual diagnosis" is used in this chapter to refer to the coexistence of substance abuse and other psychological disorders. It is not restricted to the psychotic and major mood disorders alone, as it is sometimes used, but includes anxiety disorders, eating disorders, moderate depression, and other disorders that interfere with full well-being and functioning. These conditions influence the timetable of recovery and play an underestimated role in relapse.

The early optimism on the part of many substance-abuse practitioners that most problems would be ameliorated by abstinence and meaningful involvement in a 12-step recovery program has shifted to renewed appreciation for the fact that many patients have other problems that need to be addressed. As substance-abuse treatment systems have matured, increased efforts are being made to meet the needs of these patients.

Multiple obstacles combine to impair our ability to address these needs. This chapter describes their sources, current status, and some approaches that hold promise. The long-standing gulf between the mental health system and the chemical-dependency treatment system has resulted in serious problems in assessment and treatment. Despite the fact that drugs and alcohol are frequently

ACKNOWLEDGMENT. Thanks are due Marta Obuchowsky, M.A., MFCC, for editorial assistance.

influential in determining presenting symptomatology, one cannot take it for granted that a competent and systematic assessment has been done on patients within the mental health system. Diagnostic problems are compounded by the fact that substance-abuse problems readily imitate every other entity found in clinical practice. In the absence of adequate assessment, it is not surprising that these problems are not effectively addressed in the treatment plan. Historical mistrust of professionals has created a complementary problem in the chemical-dependency treatment system: psychopathology is often underdiagnosed, leading to unrealistic expectations and poor treatment planning for the subgroup of patients with coexisting disorders. At present, the patient is often in the confusing position of drawing what he or she needs from each of the separate systems, meeting demands that may even conflict.

This chapter discusses treatment issues from the standpoint of recovery-oriented psychotherapy. In this model, the clinician adapts the therapeutic strategy to meet the changing needs of the patient in recovery. Abstinence is viewed as the foundation of therapeutic progress and is a clearly stated goal of early treatment. The task of the clinician is to address the psychiatric disorder in a manner consistent with the patient's stage in recovery. Special considerations in using psychotropic medications with dual-diagnosis patients in recovery are presented.

Finally, the chapter raises training considerations for all practitioners, from the position that the needs of dual-diagnosis patients cannot be effectively met by maintaining two separate treatment systems.

IMPEDIMENTS IN THE MENTAL HEALTH AND CHEMICAL-DEPENDENCY TREATMENT SYSTEMS

Historically, the mental health and substance-abuse treatment systems have had separate evolutions and diverse factors have perpetuated the gulf (Zweben, 1989; Clark & Zweben, 1989). Psychotherapists often assumed that drug and alcohol problems were symptoms of underlying conflicts and would resolve once these were addressed. Since they seldom did systematic assessment, they could continue to underestimate the role of substance abuse in their patients' symptomatology. Although the negative impact on treatment has been discussed and documented for over a decade (Galanter, 1989; Peyser, 1989; Vaillant, 1981; Hall, Popkin, DeVaul, & Stickney, 1977, 1978), substance abuse continues to be considered as an elective rather than a core element in a clinician's training (Selin & Svanum, 1981; Schlesinger, 1984). Separate funding empires exacerbate the problem by promoting treatment responses that are tailored to patients with either mental health or substance-abuse problems. Those with both may find themselves ineligible for treatment in either setting.

Assessment of substance abuse is still frequently omitted from admission screening, despite studies documenting its frequency in medical and psychiatric settings (Abanth et al., 1989; Moore et al., 1989; Menicucci, Wermuth, & Sorensen, 1988; Crowley et al., 1974). Wolfe and Sorensen (1989) note that it is so prevalent among the psychiatric population that it is desirable to approach the intake from the perspective of ruling it out. Psychiatric facilities often make substance abuse an exclusion criterion, encouraging the patient seeking admission to minimize or deny the substance-abuse problem. Psychiatrists may prescribe medication without taking adequate drug and alcohol histories (Brown & Schuckit, 1988) or without doing toxicology screens, thus maintaining the impression that physicians overprescribe, misprescribe, or cloud the diagnostic picture by using medication in situations that would clear adequately without them within a few days or at most several weeks (Kosten & Kleber, 1988). Psychologists may administer expensive test batteries without allowing adequate time for the cognitive impairments associated with withdrawal and early abstinence to clear. Halfway-house placements may be unsafe because drug and alcohol use by inhabitants is usually unchallenged or handled ineffectively.

Patients who had spent many years in therapy struggling to achieve slow progress sometimes discovered on their own the important role of drug or alcohol use in their distress and became embittered when mental health practitioners failed to give factor this adequate attention. Anyone attending 12-step program meetings has heard troubling stories of therapists who ignored the problem, even when the patient tried repeatedly to bring it to their attention; who told the patient it would go away once the "underlying" problems were addressed; who continued for many years to assist alcoholics in attempts at controlled drinking while their physical and mental condition deteriorated. Other therapists underestimate the prolonged vulnerability of early recovery and contribute to relapse by attempting anxiety-provoking exploration prematurely. These practices have created a backlash in which many recovering persons with coexisting disorders are reluctant or unwilling to seek the therapeutic help that could make it possible for them to live more comfortably without drugs and alcohol.

Within the addiction treatment system, other factors operate to prevent effective treatment. Chemical-dependency programs relying exclusively or heavily on recovering staff members, many of whom may have had little training in treating psychopathology, may fail to recognize or adequately address a disorder that is minimally disguised. Although the number of highly trained professionals who are also in recovery is growing rapidly, it is still quite common to find chemical-dependency programs without a sophisticated diagnostician as part of their regular staff. Often, the program physician is an internist without systematic training in assessing psychopathology. Many staff members, especially recovering ones, share negative experiences about professionals and are understandably mistrustful. Many treatment programs have a uniform approach that undermines individualized treatment planning. What Washton (1989) describes as an "enabling phobia" may lead the staff to equate responding to the unique needs of the dual-diagnosis patient as "letting him (her) get away with being treated as special." Other programs assure patients that consistent 12-step program participation will remedy all problems encountered in recovery. Lack of understanding and negative attitudes perpetuate resistance to the appropriate use of psychotropic medication. In an earlier work, (Zweben, 1989), the vulnerabilities of the conventionally trained mental health therapist are contrasted with the difficulties often seen among those whose primary experience base is substance-abuse treatment. These factors limit the practitioner's ability to meet the needs of the dual-diagnosis patient.

Wallen and Weiner (1989) discuss larger impediments affecting both systems that further compound the problem. Reimbursement policies can present major obstacles. Often, chemical dependency is not covered, or the patient cannot get reimbursed for psychiatric and chemical-dependency treatment at the same time, as it is rare for one setting to be able to do both. They point to the need for the networking of agencies to develop integrated treatment programs. Many clinicians are deeply frustrated by the absence of longer-term residential programs for dual-diagnosis patients, particularly for the severely disturbed.

GUIDELINES FOR DIAGNOSIS

Sorting out the effects of substance abuse from the influence of underlying psychopathology can be a major challenge in differential diagnosis. Several authors speak to this issue (Kosten & Kleber, 1988; Schuckit, 1988). A longitudinal approach is necessary, with repeated observations to distinguish between drug-related symptoms and psychopathology. When two or more disorders are present, it is important to try to establish whether the psychiatric syndrome was ever observed before the onset of substance abuse or during a period of extended abstinence. History from the patient, the patient's family and significant others, and cousers can be vital in making a determination. Physical examinations and toxicology screens are crucial, as presenting symptoms may result from acute intoxication, overdose, withdrawal, rebound, or protracted abstinence effects. Many symptoms clear within days or weeks, so it is important initially to make provisional diagnoses and to observe carefully; many substance abusers appear far more disturbed on admission than they do once abstinent for a while. If the intent is to assess stable characteristics, psychological testing should be deferred for several weeks and possibly until 60 to 90 days of abstinence have been achieved. However, some testing may be useful to assess impairments that affect the ability to utilize treatment (Meek, Clark, & Solana, 1989). In terms of prognosis, Stoffelmayr and his colleagues (Stoffelmayr, Benishek, Humphreys, Lee, & Mavis, 1989) have suggested that the global severity of the psychopathology, coexisting with social instability (e.g., unemployment, absence of intact family, legal problems), is more important than a specific diagnosis in determining treatment outcome.

INTEGRATING PSYCHIATRIC AND SUBSTANCE-ABUSE TREATMENT

Optimally, the elements of substance-abuse treatment would be integrated into the treatment of the psychological disorder by clinicians whose skill repertoire enabled them to handle both. The recovery-oriented therapy model (Zweben, 1986, 1987, 1989; Krystal & Zweben, 1988, 1989) provides a description of the stages and tasks of recovery and how the clinician can adapt therapeutic strategies to meet the changing needs of the patient. These tasks are (1) obtaining an abstinence commitment, (2) breaking the addiction cycle, (3) establishing and consolidating abstinence and creating new life-styles, (4) renegotiating relationships, and (5) exploring long-term psychological issues, such as management of affect and impulse, development of self-care mechanisms, and improvement of self-esteem.

Obtaining an Abstinence Commitment

General approaches for breaking through denial and obtaining an abstinence commitment have been described in the recovery-oriented therapy series (especially Zweben, 1986, 1987, 1989). Certain elements are worthy of additional emphasis when working with someone with a coexisting psychological disorder. The educational component of treatment creates the foundation on which to interpret resistance. Patients typically lack a clear understanding of alcohol and drug effects and attempts at self-medication play a significant role in their behavior. They deeply fear that giving up their drugs will make them feel worse or leave them indefinitely at the mercy of painful states. This process may not be conscious, but may need to be elucidated by careful exploration of the times the patient used and the events and feelings surrounding the occurrences. A link is thus established between uncomfortable feeling states and drug and alcohol use. Many patients are misled by the initial drug effects, which may be pleasurable or only a welcome shift from one painful state to another that is merely different. Sometimes control issues are central. Treece and Khantzian (1986) note, "The need for a sense of control and mastery over affects has led to a preference for the drug-induced dysphoria that the user can control over the sense of helplessness and unpredictability experienced without drugs" (p. 401).

Patients need to be educated about the realities of self-medication—that though it initially may seem to improve things, it is likely to worsen the preexisting disorder in a number of ways. Many do not appreciate the biphasic properties of certain drugs. For example, alcohol initially produces euphoria, but is, in fact, a central nervous system depressant and has that effect each time it is used. Alcohol and drugs, used regularly, tend to lower stress tolerance and to exacerbate negative mood states, in addition to the undermining effect of drug-seeking preoccupation and behaviors. Alcohol and drug use also tend to interfere with the action of the most appropriate medications given for psychiatric disorders (Schuckit, 1988). At this stage, the therapist should emphasize that while abstinence will not fix everything, drinking and using undermine one's resources to deal with problems in a way that can only become clear once the patient has been alcohol- and drug-free for a time. Drake and Wallach (1989) studied chronically mentally ill patients and reported that the one third who abused alcohol and drugs were less able to maintain good community adjustment (regular meals, adequate finances, stable housing, regular activities); showed greater hostility, suicidality, and speech disorganization; and had poorer medication compliance. These patients were almost twice as likely to be rehospitalized during the follow-up period.

Marijuana use illustrates many of these issues. Negrete and Knapp (1986) studied the effects of cannabis use on the clinical condition of schizophrenics over a six-month period. Patients were assigned to use categories based on the medical record, interview data and toxicology screens. Clinical condition was assessed by the following criteria: (1) frequency of service contacts (scheduled versus emergency visits), (2) degree of delusional activity (absent, transient, continuous), and (3) degree of hallucinatory activity. They found that the clinical condition varied according to the patient's use status. The group of active users had the highest incidence of continuous delusional or hallucinatory activity and also required the most intense therapeutic intervention. The authors proposed several possible explanations. The first explanation is the possibility that cannabis has a disorganizing effect on psychic function, which causes an actual worsening of symptoms; the second is that it causes a toxic psychosis that blends with the schizophrenic symptoms and makes them appear more pronounced. The third, most interesting explanation, and one to explore further, is the possibility that cannabis neutralizes the effects of the antipsychotic medication by actually blocking the neuroleptics (Knudsen & Vilmar, 1984). Thus marijuana has effects that are not recognized as drug effects by the user because they may occur from 12 hours to several days after the actual use (Zweben & O'Connell, 1987). It is this phenomenon of delayed effects to which patients must be alerted; the therapist must challenge the patient's conviction (tacit or stated) that the drug use is helping. At that point, a therapeutic alliance can be formed on the basis of an "experiment," in which the patient explores the question of whether abstinence makes things better or makes difficulties more manageable.

The educational tasks in treatment can be accomplished partly through group presentations, but it is important that the program provide an arena in which to monitor how the information is assimilated. Even patients who are not seriously disturbed need some help in applying the concepts to their situation. In the psychoeducational model, the information is interwoven into a variety of treatment activities. It is crucial that the therapist be able to discern when the patient needs information and when the therapeutic issues need further clarification in order to make the information relevant. Sometimes practitioners lecture when skilled inquiry is in order. In the case of the patient with a thought disorder, it is particularly important to be attentive to the patient's degree of lucidity and to be flexible in timing.

When the patient indicates a readiness actually to give up drugs and alcohol, a detoxification plan that includes medical and psychological interventions should be formulated (Zweben, 1986; Zweben & O'Connell, 1988). For the dual-diagnosis patient, this formulation ideally occurs in the context of an established relationship that offers considerable support, as painful feeling states will inevitably surface. It is especially helpful to offer more intense outpatient treatment while the patient is giving up alcohol and drugs, replacing drinking and using by increased structure and more frequent contact with the therapist and support groups.

Issues in Ongoing Treatment

Dual-diagnosis patients need treatment that focuses on reality-oriented issues in a supportive manner. Inasmuch as anxiety exacerbates both the psychiatric symptoms and the substance abuse (Wallen & Weiner, 1989), it is desirable to avoid intensive uncovering therapy in order to minimize the emergence of anxiety. However, many patients are troubled by traumatic experiences such as incest or family violence and raise these issues early in the treatment. For some, painful memories haunt them once they are abstinent for a brief while. Certainly the clinician should not foster denial by sending the message that these topics are inappropriate to discuss, but it is important that the goals remain clear. Early in treatment, the clinician's goal is to help the patient contain or express feelings and anxiety without returning to drug use. Later, once abstinence has been consolidated, it may be more appropriate for the therapist to attempt therapeutic work aimed at the resolution of some of these issues. For some patients, a marginal stability is all that is possible. It is very important that the clinician have realistic expectations, but also that he or she does not avoid hard challenges because of deficits in his or her own skills repertoire.

Confrontation is an issue on which the chemical-dependency and mental health systems are often at odds. Breaking through denial, penetrating the character armor, is seen by many in addiction treatment as a central task, and many programs rely heavily on direct, intense confrontation to achieve this. Patients with dual disorders, particularly those who are severely disturbed, can be extremely vulnerable to aggressive exchanges. Firm feedback can improve reality testing and address denial, but must be given in a supportive atmosphere. Peer pressure is helpful if applied in a nurturant way. For these reasons, it is desirable to offer separate recovery groups for dual-diagnosis patients and separate program components within therapeutic community settings. It is essential that staff members have skills that extend well beyond aggressive confrontation.

Individualizing treatment while maintaining consistency of approach is another challenging task. Many chemical-dependency programs have a fixed set of activities in which everyone participates and are very negative toward the patient who is labeled as manipulative. Patient attempts to be treated as special often elicit highly punitive staff attitudes and behaviors. Unfortunately, it can be difficult to distinguish intact patients from the disturbed ones who protect themselves and others from recognizing deficits by manipulative behaviors. For example, many cognitively impaired patients are accused of resistance or lack of motivation because their deficits are unrecognized (Zweben, 1989; Meek et al., 1989). Dual-diagnosis patients need individualized treatment planning, and this must be balanced with the need for program consistency. Disturbed patients fluctuate in their levels of functioning which is very difficult for staff members who like consistent, uniform rules. It is important that the program leadership set a tone that allows for individualized response to patient needs without sacrificing basic structure.

Relapse is an area in which the needs of the dual-diagnosis patient often go unmet. The chemical-dependency treatment system can be very unforgiving of patients who relapse multiple times. Until recently, program emphasis has been on inpatient treatment. With changing insurance reimbursement policies, programs are now developing outpatient services, but many do not have the long-term experience that allows them to put relapse in an appropriate context. Inpatient referral is often seen as the solution to relapse, instead of relapse being viewed as part of the recovery process. Many programs insist on terminating patients who relapse several times, lest staff members be found guilty of "enabling" by their colleagues. The concept of enabling, which refers to protecting someone from the consequences of drug and alcohol use, has become a justification for terminating the patient who manifests the problem for which he or she is in treatment. On closer examination, however, a chronic pattern of relapse is often associated with a coexisting psychiatric disorder, possibly undiagnosed in the chemical-dependency treatment setting. A stance in which the practitioner tries to maximize the gains of a period of intact functioning and to cushion the negative impact of regressive periods is more appropriate to this patient population.

Medication Issues

Medication compliance is a key issue for dual-diagnosis patients (Drake & Wallach, 1989; Minkoff, 1989), with special complications because of the emphasis in addiction treatment on avoiding drug-taking behavior (Zweben & Smith, 1989). Control issues are central in that the patient must transfer control of the drug supply and regimen to the physician. This alliance is often a turbulent one. The patient must also be educated about the interaction between medication and alcohol and other drugs; drugs of abuse usually interfere with the action of the most appropriate medications given for the primary disorder (Schuckit, 1988).

Other problems in using medication with patients with dual disorders are discussed by Zweben and Smith (1989). One major caution pertains to the use of haloperidol (Haldol) by the patient who appears in the psychiatric emergency room in a psychotic state. A stimulant psychosis may be indistinguishable from mania or agitated paranoid schizophrenia; the use of haloperidol may precipitate a medical emergency if the psychosis is due to stimulant use (Kosten & Kleber, 1988).

Benzodiazepines (Valium, Librium, Xanax, Ativan, Clonopin, Halcion, Serax, Dalmane, etc.) are usually contraindicated for persons with a personal or family history of chemical dependency, except as an anticonvulsant precaution during detoxification from alcohol (Smith & Wesson, 1985). These drugs often become a substitute addiction or set the stage for relapse to the primary drug of abuse. Recovering patients with anxiety disorders have been successfully treated with tricyclic antidepressants, which hold fewer hazards for this group.

Twelve-Step Program Participation

The recovery resources and support network offered by 12-step programs is invaluable, especially for the dual-diagnosis patient, who usually has limited financial resources. However, it is important that the therapist make an effort to offset potential problems by carefully preparing patients for meetings. Many programs develop a network of other patients who can take a newcomer to an appropriate meeting, a practice that works especially well once the patient's fears and concerns have been discussed.

One serious problem that arises in meetings is the tendency of some members to pressure others into discontinuing prescribed medication on the mistaken presumption that recovery does not count unless it is entirely drug-free. To clarify this issue, Alcoholics Anonymous (AA) has published an excellent pamphlet, *The AA Member—Medications and Other Drugs. Report from a Group of Physicians in AA* (Alcoholics Anonymous, 1984). The patient can be assured that AA clearly states that no member is to play doctor in the case of appropriately prescribed medication. Preparing the patient by providing a historical background on why medications are viewed with suspicion, and some reassurance that in this self-help group members say what they wish, but that a criticism of psychotropic medication does not reflect the organization's stance, often gives the patient the support necessary to weather the peer pressure.

"Double trouble" meetings are proliferating in many cities and offer dual-diagnosis patients an alternative. These meetings may be less discouraging to patients who compare their own recovery process unfavorably with that of others who are more intact. Issues about medication or seeing a psychotherapist are similarly neutralized.

One problem that arises with dual-diagnosis patients is the tendency of some to incorporate 12-step concepts into their delusional system. The paranoid patient may complain about the coerciveness of the group or the rigidity of the rules. The Higher Power concept may be incorporated into the delusional system in negative ways. When this occurs, the patient must be allowed some distance and offered some reality testing. Spiritual concepts incorporated into a delusional system in frightening ways may be approached in some patients through visualization, in a manner described by Krystal and Zweben (1988, 1989). Using this approach, positive allies are introduced who tame or disempower the menacing elements in the delusional system.

Training Considerations

The problem of addiction ultimately is best addressed by cross-training, in which we develop a cadre of practitioners who can respond to both psychiatric and recovery issues. Many times, the patient would not require a specialized addiction treatment program if elements of substance-abuse treatment were incorporated into the psychiatric setting. Even moderate substance use can worsen the psychiatric picture, but such problems may yield easily to some basic information and attention on the part of the therapist. Therapists within one system need to be familiar with the basic assumptions and language of professionals in the other system in order to collaborate effectively. All therapists working with the dual-diagnosis population need to be capable of good clinical observation, flexibility, and ambiguity tolerance, a task that can be difficult for the recovering therapist who has not adequately addressed those issues in his or her own recovery (Zweben, 1989). In addition to enriching therapists' skills, the gaps in the treatment system must be remedied. One important endeavor is to develop drug-free residential settings ranging from minimally to highly structured. These are essential to meet the needs of the patient who requires long-term care, but whose functioning can be optimized by appropriate treatment. Chronic problems cannot be remedied by the quick-fix approach, and it is necessary for practitioners who understand the needs to be advocates to obtain the resources required to address these complex problems.

REFERENCES

Abanth, J., Vandewater, S., Kamal, M., Brodsky, A., Gamal, R., & Miller, M. (1989). Missed diagnosis of substance abuse in psychiatric patients. *Hospital and Community Psychiatry, 40*, 297–299.

Alcoholics Anonymous (1984). *The AA member—medications and other drugs. Report from a group of physicians in AA.* New York: Alcoholics Anonymous World Services.

Brown, S., & Schuckit, M. (1988). Changes in depression among abstinent alcoholics. *Journal of Studies on Alcohol, 49,* 412–417.

Clark, H. W., & Zweben, J. E. (1989). Legal vulnerabilities in the treatment of chemically dependent dual diagnosis patients. *Journal of Psychoactive Drugs, 21,* 251–257.

Crowley, T. J., Bhesluk, D., Dilts, S., & Hart, R. (1974). Drug and alcohol abuse among psychiatric admissions: A multidrug clinical-toxicological study. *Archives of General Psychiatry, 30,* 13–20.

Drake, R. E., & Wallach, M. A. (1989). Substance abuse among the chronic mentally ill. *Hospital and Community Psychiatry, 40,* 1041–1045.

Galanter, M. (1989). The current status of psychiatric education in alcoholism and drug abuse. *American Journal of Psychiatry, 146,* 35–39.

Gawin, F. H., & Ellinwood, E. H. (1988). Cocaine and other stimulants: Actions, abuse, and treatment. *New England Journal of Medicine, 318,* 1173–1182.

Hall, R. C., Popkin, M. K., DeVaul, R., & Stickney, S. K. (1977). The effect of unrecognized drug abuse on diagnosis and therapeutic outcome. *American Journal of Drug and Alcohol Abuse, 4,* 455–465.

Hall, R. C., Popkin, M. K., DeVaul, R., & Stickney, S. K. (1978). Covert outpatient drug abuse: Incidence and therapist recognition. *Journal of Nervous and Mental Disease, 166,* 343–348.

Knudsen, P., & Vilmar, T. (1984). Cannabis and neuroleptic agents in schizophrenia. *Acta Psychiatrica Scandinavica, 69,* 162–174.

Kosten, T. R., & Kleber, H. D. (1988). Differential diagnosis of psychiatric comorbidity in substance abusers. *Journal of Substance Abuse Treatment, 5,* 201–206.

Krystal, S., & Zweben, J. (1988). The use of visualization as a means of integrating the spiritual dimension into treatment. *Journal of Substance Abuse Treatment, 5,* 201–206.

Krystal, S., & Zweben, J. (1989). The use of visualization as a means of integrating the spiritual dimension into treatment: Part II, Working with emotions. *Journal of Substance Abuse Treatment, 6,* 223–228.

Meek, P. S., Clark, H. W., & Solana, V. L. (1989). Neurocognitive impairment: The unrecognized component of dual diagnosis in substance abuse treatment. *Journal of Psychoactive Drugs, 21,* 153–160.

Menicucci, L. D., Wermuth, L., & Sorensen, J. L. (1988). Treatment providers' assessment of dual-prognosis patients: Diagnosis, treatment, referral, and family involvement. *International Journal of the Addictions, 23,* 617–622.

Minkoff, K. (1989). An integrated treatment model for dual diagnosis of psychosis and addiction. *Hospital and Community Psychiatry, 40,* 1031–1036.

Moore, R. D., Bone, L. R., Geller, G., Mamon, J. A., Stokes, E. J., & Levine, D. M. (1989). Prevalence, detection and treatment of alcoholism in hospitalized patients. *Journal of the American Medical Association, 261,* 403–407.

Negrete, J. C., & Knapp, W. P. (1986). The effects of cannabis use on the clinical condition of schizophrenics. In L. S. Harris (Ed.), *Problems of Drug Dependence, 1985. Proceedings of the 47th Annual Scientific Meeting, Committee on Problems of Drug*

Dependence, NIDA Research Monograph 67. Rockville, MD: Department of Health and Human Services.

Peyser, H. (1989). Alcohol and drug abuse: Underrecognized and untreated. *Hospital and Community Psychiatry, 40,* 221.

Schlesinger, S. E. (1984). Substance misuse training in graduate psychology programs. *Journal of Studies on Alcohol, 45,* 131–137.

Schuckit, M. (1988). Evaluating the dual diagnosis patient. *Drug Abuse and Alcoholism Newsletter, 17,* 1–4.

Selin, J., & Svanum, S. (1981). Alcoholism and substance abuse training: A survey of graduate programs in clinical psychology. *Professional Psychology, 12,* 717–721.

Smith, D. E., & Wesson, D. R. (1985). Benzodiazepine dependency syndromes. In D. E. Smith, & D. R. Wesson (Eds.), *The benzodiazepines: Current standards for medical practice.* Boston: MTP Press.

Stoffelmayr, B. E., Benishek, L. A., Humphreys, K., Lee, J. A., & Mavis, B. E. (1989). Substance abuse prognosis with an additional psychiatric diagnosis: Understanding the relationship. *Journal of Psychoactive Drugs, 21,* 145–152.

Treece, C. T., & Khantzian, E. J. (1986). Psychodynamic factors in the development of drug dependence. *Psychiatric Clinics of North America, 9,* 399–412.

Vaillant, G. (1981). Dangers of psychotherapy in the treatment of alcoholism. In M. Bean & N. Zinberg (Eds.), *Dynamic approaches to the understanding and treatment of alcoholism.* New York: Free Press.

Wallen, M. C., & Weiner, H. D. (1989). Impediments to effective treatment of the dually diagnosed patient. *Journal of Psychoactive Drugs, 21,* 161–168.

Washton, A. (1989). Motivational factors in cocaine relapse and recovery. Presented at Alcohol and Cocaine Relapse Prevention Conference; San Francisco.

Wolfe, H. L., & Sorensen, J. L. (1989). Dual diagnosis patients in the urban psychiatric emergency room. *Journal of Psychoactive Drugs, 21,* 169–175.

Zweben, J. E. (1986). Recovery oriented psychotherapy. *Journal of Substance Abuse Treatment, 3,* 255–262.

Zweben, J. E. (1987). Recovery oriented psychotherapy: Facilitating the use of 12 step programs. *Journal of Psychoactive Drugs, 19,* 243–251.

Zweben, J. E. (1989). Recovery oriented psychotherapy: Patient resistances and therapist dilemmas. *Journal of Substance Abuse Treatment, 6,* 123–132.

Zweben, J., & O'Connell, K. (1988). Strategies for breaking marijuana dependence. *Journal of Psychoactive Drugs, 20*(1), 121–128.

Zweben, J. E., & Smith, D. E. (1989). Considerations in using psychotropic medication with dual diagnosis patients in recovery. *Journal of Psychoactive Drugs, 21,* 221–229.

Zweben, J. E., & Wallace, J. W. (Eds.) (1989). Dual diagnosis: Clinical and research perspectives (issue theme) *Journal of Psychoactive Drugs, 21.*

18

Toward Effective Treatment Models for Special Populations: Criminal, Pregnant, Adolescent, Uninsured, HIV-Positive, Methadone-Maintained, and Homeless Populations

Barbara C. Wallace, Ph.D.

In the preceding two chapters, we have seen how important it is to consider the distinct characteristics of individual chemically dependent patients. Specifically, we saw how the distinct characteristics of the population of the dually diagnosed or of those with an African-American racial identity suggest specific clinical concerns and sensitivities we must possess when designing and delivering treatment interventions. In this chapter, we extend the philosophy that the characteristics of special-treatment populations must be considered as we examine seven contemporary populations of chemically dependent patients: (1) criminal or prison-based populations, (2) pregnant women, (3) adolescents, (4) persons without medical insurance, (5) persons who have tested positive for the human immunodeficiency virus (HIV) or present with the acquired immune deficiency syndrome (AIDS), (6) methadone-maintained clients, and (7) homeless chemically dependent persons. The way in which population characteristics influence treatment program design is explored.

PRISON-BASED POPULATIONS

A major population yet to be adequately treated is that of the criminal chemically dependent. The extent to which chemically dependent persons have been involved

310

in criminal behaviors and enterprising but illegal endeavors to support costly drug habits has been well documented (Johnson et al., 1985). However, without access to treatment, many of these individuals who are motivated to seek such treatment are locked into a cycle of continued criminal involvement, and compulsive drug use in response to brain-driven cravings (Rosecan & Spitz, 1987) and face the risk of incarceration (Glaberson, 1990).

Drug-related criminality typically involves the sale and distribution of drugs either to insure the user's access to the drug or to produce income to support expensive drug habits. Violence and criminal prosecution also follow territorial drug disputes. Other users engage in the informal exchange of sex for crack or in prostitution. Merely by virtue of possessing cocaine, crack, or other illegal drugs, charges of possession or of intent to distribute (depending on the amount in one's possession) can result in one's achieving the status of criminal. In this way, the crack and cocaine epidemic of the 1980s has played a major role in contributing to the growth of chemically dependent prison-based populations.

New York State

TRENDS IN CRACK-RELATED CRIMINALITY

New York State statistics document a cocaine and crack epidemic–related trend of rising arrest rates and a growth in the incarcerated population. Glaberson (1990) cites statistics from a New York study showing that 23% of Black men between the ages of 20 and 29 are in state prisons, local jails, on probation, or on parole—a number double that of Black men enrolled in colleges in the state.

This report further questions whether New York law enforcement is skewed against minorities since 95% of the inmates in New York City jails are Black or Hispanic (Glaberson, 1990, p. B6). Such questioning seems reasonable in light of National Institute for Drug Abuse survey findings that Blacks made up 11% of those people who had used illegal drugs, Hispanic groups made up 7%, and Whites accounted for 80% (Glaberson, 1990, p. B6).

NATIONAL TRENDS

With regard to national trends, the number of inmates in state and federal prisons reached a record high (755,425) in the first half of 1990, with 42,862 additional inmates during this period. For the one-year period of June 1989 to June 1990, a record annual increase of 80,000 prisoners represents the largest growth in 65 years of prison-population statistics. This rise is attributed to the enactment of mandatory minimum sentences for drug crimes and repeat offenders. Of note is the finding that the increase in the number of female prisoners continued to exceed the increase for male prisoners; the number of female prisoners rose 7.1% in the first half of 1990, while the number of male inmates rose by 5.9%. Also, the highest rate of incarceration was in the South, followed by the West, Midwest, and Northeast respectively (*New York Times*, 1990a).

The 13% growth in the nation's prison population in 1989 is related to another national trend involving a 12.1% increase in 1989 in the number of convicts paroled from prison (*New York Times*, 1990b), with parole used to reduce prison crowding and defendants given probation as an alternative to prison. Thus, as a consequence of caps on facilities' populations and street-level dealers and users being incarcerated, a system in chaos resorts to increases in those paroled. More alternatives to incarceration are needed, but until they are implemented, states such as Texas, California, Pennsylvania, New York, Rhode Island, Oregon, and Florida (*New York Times*, 1990b) will probably continue to show increases in those paroled.

These data support the assertion that the cocaine and crack epidemic of the 1980s created a diverse cohort of cocaine and crack cocaine users nationwide who are at risk of arrest and incarceration as a consequence of being charged with the possession, sale, or distribution of drugs; with crimes designed to secure funds for the purchase of drugs; or with violence associated with drug dealing or territorial drug disputes. Females are also at risk of being criminally charged with exposing a fetus to cocaine when they become pregnant or with child abuse and neglect (Chavkin, 1990). High arrest rates and stiff penalties may reflect societal intolerance of drug-related crimes, which affect everyone regardless of sex, race, or ethnicity. For example, Michigan has the stiffest penalties of any state for possession of more than 650 grams of cocaine, or about 1.5 pounds. In Michigan, the penalty for possession of such quantities is life in prison without parole even for first-time offenders (Greenhouse, 1990, p. A16). Thus a diverse national criminal cohort includes people of both sexes and all races and classes.

Implications for Program Design

The implications of prison-population characteristics for the design of prison-based chemical-dependency treatment are several. Programs need to recognize the diverse characteristics of the prison population. Culturally sensitive interventions may be necessary for minorities. Similarly, empathic and sensitive interventions are necessary that recognize the needs of women who are concerned about child care and may wish to be reunited with their children. The likelihood that prison populations will include women and other minorities who may be angry about the criminal proceedings against them, as well as others who are bitter about lengthy sentences that may constitute cruel and unusual punishment (Greenhouse, 1990, p. A16), is great. This suggests the need for preventative rehabilitation services to reduce the risk of angry acting out and recidivism upon release from prison.

In contrast to the recommendations that criminals be treated with respect and receive rehabilitation services, incarceration in today's jails and prisons is primarily characterized by conditions that are inhumane and indecent by virtue of overcrowding (Malcolm, 1990). Warehousing of people must be replaced with a nationwide system of intermediate sanctions for nonviolent felonies that can spare someone guilty of possession of an illicit drug from exposure to such commonplace prison atrocities as gang rape (Lay, 1990).

Whether designing prison-based treatment programs, designing programs for individuals on probation and parole, or establishing programs for mandatory participation as an alternative to incarceration, these population characteristics should affect the program designs.

Model Programs Worthy of Replication

Several treatment approaches address the special needs of criminal chemically dependent populations. These model programs are discussed in this section.

PRISON AND COMMUNITY-BASED THERAPEUTIC COMMUNITIES

Among the approaches to rehabilitation of the prison-based chemically dependent, the "Stay 'N Out" prison-based therapeutic community (TC) represents a model approach (Wexler & Williams, 1986; Wexler, 1987; Wexler, Lipton, & Johnson, 1988). For individuals who are mandated to treatment, the community-based residential TC has been a valuable rehabilitative tool as an alternative to incarceration for many found guilty of drug-related crimes (Sandberg, 1986). Residential TCs are capable of producing positive attitudinal and behavioral change in angry and bitter prisoners. Moreover, TCs assist clients in systematically learning how better to regulate feelings, impulses, and behavior in interpersonal relationships (see Chapter 4). Also, TCs have long worked with the consequences of childhood development in dysfunctional families and spend substantial time in group-therapy contexts helping members to integrate traumatic and painful experiences and to function more effectively despite childhood trauma.

Wexler and Williams (1986) discuss the kind of modifications necessary in a prison setting in order to implement a prison-based TC program successfully. These include less use of humiliation and punishment and somewhat less use of confrontation, which might provoke a violent reaction. By utilizing the knowledge gained from model prison-based drug-treatment programs, other prison facilities might realize less recidivism, less reinvolvement in drug use after prison release time, and higher rates of employment and constructive life involvement.

ACUPUNCTURE IN PRISONS AND OUTPATIENT SETTINGS

Another promising approach utilized with those on probation and implemented in jail and prison settings involves the use of acupuncture (Smith, 1989). Acupuncture decreases craving and induces relaxation. At the Lincoln Hospital Acupuncture Clinic in New York, it has shown some success in helping those on probation to maintain abstinence. However, acupuncture is only part of a comprehensive treatment approach that includes daily urine testing, individual counseling to address psychosocial problems, and on-site Narcotics Anonymous meetings. Acupuncture in jail and prison settings is popular because it is so inexpensive. However, Smith (1989) cautions against utilizing this procedure alone without addressing the psychosocial problems and needs of clients. When outpatient program referrals are arranged for probationers, acupuncture represents a promising treatment adjunct. However, as Smith (1989) cautions, it is just one part of a total treatment approach.

TWELVE-STEP PROGRAMS

For many of the incarcerated, access to 12-step programs in prison and jail settings constitutes the only intervention they receive to address their drug and alcohol problems and more such programs are needed. We must neither overlook nor underestimate their value as a vehicle for rehabilitation. On the other hand, the needs of clients for a more comprehensive and intensive set of interventions—beyond what 12-step program involvement provides—also must not be underestimated in view of the many histories of severe chemical dependence necessitating criminal behavior to support it. Inmates should not have to rely on "self-help" alone, when state and federal institutions are obligated to provide for their needs. And the need for rehabilitation and treatment of severe chemical dependency cannot be denied for a significant portion of today's burgeoning prison population.

THE NEED FOR TREATMENT MODELS

Wallace (1991a) has reviewed treatments that seem to work and that are promising with the cocaine and crack dependent in general. Outpatient program models that might be adapted for use with probationers or those mandated to treatment can follow models proved to be effective with the cocaine and crack dependent and those abusing multiple substances. Programs are generally intensive (four to five days a week during the first six months of abstinence) and comprehensive (providing urine tests, family education, couples counseling, family therapy, relapse prevention, recovery groups—see Chapter 3). The availability of such intensive outpatient rehabilitation for mandated referrals might substantially reduce relapse to chronic drug use and recidivism to crime.

Value of Professional Therapy in Programs

University-based training programs for counselors, psychologists, social workers, and psychiatrists must also consider the provision of individual psychotherapy and the running of group therapy sessions in prison settings. The use of those in training and the establishment of stipend-funded externships and internships could be cost-effective. Such programs could be based in TCs in prison settings, or could be non-TC drug rehabilitation programs or community-based TC programs. While such programs could provide professional therapy and enhance rehabilitation efforts at the same time, the problem of too few mental health professionals with training in chemical-dependency treatment also could be remedied. The cocaine and crack epidemic of the 1980s has created a cohort of relapse-prone chemically dependent clients who will require continuing or intermittent treatment into the coming decades, even if they do not receive treatment until they have completed lengthy mandatory sentences. Such a program of internships and externships anticipates a critical treatment need.

Carroll and Sobel (1986) have argued for the need successfully to integrate more mental health professionals into TC settings. Schiffer's (1988) work substantiates the value of delivering long-term professional psychotherapy to facilitate the successful recovery of cocaine patients because so many have experienced childhood trauma that needs resolution in this kind of treatment. The work of several authors suggests that the chemically dependent who end up in the criminal justice system may have histories of childhood molestation or sexual, physical, or emotional abuse (Sandberg, 1986; Rohsenow, Corbett, & Devine, 1988; Wallace, 1990, Young, 1990; Bollerud, 1990). Such histories argue for the implementation of professional therapy services as one component of a rehabilitation or residential TC program. Also, the increasing and significantly high levels of psychopathology found both in jail populations (Teplin, 1990; Shenson, Dubler, & Michaels, 1990) and among residential TC populations underscore the importance of providing professional mental health treatment to these populations (DeLeon, 1989; Blume, 1989; Stoffelmayr, Benishek, Humphreys, Lee, & Mavis, 1989). In fact, the current lack of provision of mental health services to a population with higher rates of severe mental disorder than the general population may constitute violation of Eighth Amendment guarantees against cruel and unusual punishment (Teplin, 1990).

In sum, the cocaine and crack epidemics of the 1980s challenge the criminal justice system to incorporate true rehabilitation goals by establishing prison-based drug treatment and community-based treatment alternatives to incarceration. The prison-based TC, the residential community-based TC, the use of promising treatments such as acupuncture as just one part of a comprehensive treatment approach, and long-term outpatient treatment models are all viable options. But, most important, this prison-based population must be recognized as having critical treatment needs. The cost of recidivism, relapse to compulsive drug use, and continued criminality by even more angry, bitter, and resentful parolees argues for the establishment of rehabilitation goals that include drug rehabilitation.

CHEMICALLY DEPENDENT PREGNANT WOMEN

As pointed out earlier, the female chemical user is at risk of being charged with delivering illicit drugs to a minor, with homicide against a fetus, or with child abuse or neglect (Chavkin, 1990). Even though cocaine deaths are decreasing, other cocaine-use indicators continue to rise—such as the birth of babies exposed to cocaine in the womb (*Outlook*, 1990). Thus chemically dependent pregnant women represent another population with critical treatment needs.

Readers are referred elsewhere for evidence that cocaine and other drug use is placing infants at risk (Chasnoff, Landress, & Barrett, 1990; Petiti & Coleman, 1990; Chavkin, 1990; Joyce, 1990) and for a detailed discussion of the treatment needs of pregnant chemically dependent women currently being threatened with criminal sanctions (Wallace, 1991b). However, several points can be advanced here.

Inpatient detoxification units can effectively treat pregnant women (Wallace, 1991a) and more residential TC programs must admit such women. Actually, pregnant women require specially designed programs that combine outpatient and some option for inpatient or residential treatment. These programs need to have several special features based on this population's characteristics.

Model treatment programs must offer prenatal medical care, pediatric follow-up, social-service case management, chemical-dependency treatment on site, interdisciplinary staff, parent education, home visits, child care, 24-hour hotline, a drop-in center, and support groups. They also must provide community outreach services to women who may fear criminal sanctions and punishment and so are avoiding prenatal care; a drug-free residential option is frequently necessary as well (Kronstadt, 1989; McRobbie, Mata, & Kronstadt, 1990).

Residential treatment may be essential for a compulsive chemical user at risk of relapsing and exposing her developing fetus to these chemicals. Many women who have escalated to compulsive self-administration of chemicals have experienced psychosocial deterioration and have lost their homes. Others are partners of men who openly use drugs in front of them, if they do not entice or force them to do the same. The availability of drug-free housing, therefore, is often a critical need for these women. Thus halfway houses or modified residential TCs need to be part of comprehensive and intensive treatment services.

The kind of treatment that the chemically dependent pregnant woman requires must include genuine empathy and respect. Women must be assisted in understanding that neurochemically based cravings (Rosecan & Spitz, 1987) contributed to compulsive drug-use patterns that may have been damaging to the self and the fetus. This kind of education can begin to reduce levels of shame and guilt by explaining how compulsive drug use continued in response to intense neurochemically based cravings. Education can also focus on the responsibility clients have to protect themselves and their fetuses from conditioned environmental stimuli that may trigger relapse, and from high-risk situations in general, and how crucial involvement in long-term treatment is to the recovery process. Empathy and psychodynamic interventions also help clients to regulate and manage painful feelings over the loss of child custody, feelings of guilt and shame over informal prostitution, or feelings of ambivalence regarding a pregnancy. Again, for a more detailed discussion of these issues, readers should consult other sources (Wallace, 1991a,b).

ADOLESCENT POPULATIONS

Growth in the number of drug-abusing and drug-dependent adolescents has been facilitated by the widespread availability of such a cheap and potent high as that provided by crack vials often sold as "two for the price of one" $5 crack specials. The good news is that the use of crack cocaine is no longer chic among adolescents who have been bombarded, in cities like New York, by the daily presence on the streets of thin, dirty, and often homeless crack addicts. However, the sadder news is that, also in New York City, crack-busting gangs include such adolescents, who harass and violently attack suspected crack users (Kolata, 1990).

Our concern here, however, is those adolescents who continue to use cocaine, crack, alcohol, heroin, "ice" methamphetamine, marijuana, and any other new and fashionable chemical that becomes available. The use, and abuse, of anabolic steroids by adolescents is also of concern (Gough, 1989; Daigle, 1990). Other authors have provided detailed discussions of adolescent chemical-dependency issues and the kind of counseling and program modifications adolescents require (George, 1990; Van Meter & Rioux, 1990; also see Chapter 15). Nonetheless, from this author's perspective, several themes can be briefly addressed here to convey the special characteristics of this population and the kinds of interventions needed.

Impact of Dysfunctional Family Dynamics

Factors to consider in assessment and treatment planning include the consequences of adolescents currently living in, having negotiated critical childhood periods in, or having run away from a dysfunctional family system (Wood, 1990; Flewelling & Bauman, 1990; Kandel, 1990; Powers, Eckenrode, & Jaklitsch, 1990; Wallace, 1990).

The Need for Psychoeducation

Adolescent clients may need psychoeducation (Wallace, 1991a, 1990b) on what constitutes a dysfunctional family dynamic or trauma and the impact of these events, and may require treatment for attendant emotional and psychological scars. Psychoeducation may assist adolescents in discontinuing a pattern of running away from home, prostituting themselves, and placing themselves at risk for AIDS (Kearon, 1990). Other adolescents may be in a state of denial regarding the effect and meaning of incest, and may unwittingly continue to place themselves at risk for continued sexual abuse, even though they resort to the use of chemicals to cope.

Continuing contact with abusive pimps or imposing stepfathers and a willingness to sell their bodies informally when they have run away from home all illustrate how chemically dependent adolescents may be caught in destructive and damaging cycles of behavior. Psychoeducation can outline the possible developmental effect of trauma, spell out the link between childhood/adolescent trauma and substance abuse, explain self-medication and defenses such as denial, and serve as an introduction to the process of therapy (Wallace, 1991a, 1990b).

The Need for Professional Therapy

Adolescents require therapeutic assistance in learning better to process painful feelings without developing rigid character armor, or splitting off, or repressing trauma. Some may actually present with posttraumatic stress disorder or be prone to dissociative states (Wallace, 1991a) as a consequence of severe sexual or physical abuse. Therapeutic interventions may begin to compensate for an inherent ego weakness, difficulties in managing impulses, and poor reality testing. Also, a number of adolescents continue to cope on a daily basis with dysfunctional family dynamics, such as an alcoholic parent or bickering and violent parents. Where separation from the family is not indicated or feasible, and running away from home is not an issue, adolescent clients need tremendous therapeutic support in coping with prolonged periods of high stress, anxiety, and fear. How can clinicians assist adolescents in not becoming the target of physical abuse by a potentially violent parent? How can adolescents avoid acting out their legitimate anger in a destructive and dangerous way? It is more adaptive for clients to express and work out feelings of ambivalence in therapy than it is for them to learn to disconnect from the feeling world, become desensitized to chaotic and harmful dysfunctional family dynamics, routinely and unconsciously act out feelings and impulses, and mask psychiatric symptoms with chemical use. A therapeutic dialogue and processing of feelings must replace silence, repression, splitting, destructive acting-out behavior, and self-medication patterns.

Thus professional individual and group therapies can be important adjuncts to adolescent chemical-dependency services and to programs for runaways. Adolescent clients also need to have more specialized adolescent residential TCs that include services such as the routine provision of family therapy (see Chapter 15). The inclusion of family therapy recognizes the role of dysfunctional family dynamics as a possible etiological factor in adolescent substance abuse and prevents families from continuing negative enabling behavior and from possibly sabotaging the treatment process.

Primary and Secondary Prevention

Models of primary, secondary, and tertiary prevention, such as the DARE model of chemical dependency (see Wallace, 1991a), may be more effective in deterring chemical use than public-service announcements that submit that doing drugs is analogous to frying an egg. Within the DARE model of chemical dependency, prevention education explains that Dependency follows abuse, Abuse follows recreational use, and Recreational use follows Experimental use; thus, the mnemonic or acronym "DARE." This model of prevention warns that chemical use may not be fun, but instead may be quite risky for individuals who possess certain high-risk characteristics. Would one DARE smoke crack, for example, knowing that one is an adult child of an alcoholic, harbors intense anger at an alcoholic and abusive father, possesses low self-esteem, disconnects from one's feelings, and tends to please one's peers because one fears rejection? Within the DARE model of chemical dependency, such an adolescent is at a much greater risk of advancing from experimental to recreational use of chemicals, and ultimately at greater risk of advancing to the abuse and dependence syndromes.

Therapists are urged to engage in a thorough assessment and to gather the kind of detailed psychosocial data that can assist in spelling out the particular way in which the individual adolescent may be uniquely at risk for advancing through the stages of the DARE model (Wallace, 1991a). It can be quite a powerful prevention intervention to spell out in detail to an adolescent how he or she may be different from those peers who are beginning to smoke crack or drink vodka in the school lavatory. You can explain the unique risk the adolescent faces for advancing to abuse and dependence syndromes in light of a characteristic pattern of defenses, ego weakness, and deficits in self-regulatory capacities.

Education on the Biological Risk

As Blum and coauthors begin to suggest in Chapter 12, prevention efforts with adolescents one day may involve the discussion of possible possession of the alcogene, brain-wave patterns, or neurochemical responses to chemicals that may signal a biological risk for developing chemical dependency. A future test may even determine the presence of this biological risk. Meanwhile, our interventions with adolescents can also include discussion of the possible risk of developing alcohol abuse and dependence if their father is an alcoholic. Data that 51% of the crack cocaine dependent had either a biological parent or stepparent who was alcoholic (Wallace, 1991a, 1990) also suggest the kind of education we can offer as part of primary and secondary prevention efforts with adolescents.

Prevention of Steroid Use

Adolescents increasingly are engaging in weight-lifting training and are subjected to role models who attribute their success in athletics partly to the use of anabolic steroids; many adolescents face the risk of utilizing anabolic steroids as early as junior high school (Daigle, 1990; Gough, 1989). Through education, adolescents must be informed of the physiological and psychological side effects of steroid use (Daigle, 1990; Gough, 1989).

Prevention education needs to convey the notion that experimental use can lead to occasional use and occasional use (rather than the term "recreational use") may gradually lock one into a cycle of avoiding withdrawal or abstinence side effects by using more steroids. The acceptance of negative physical and psychological side effects and continued use despite knowledge of these side effects can justify education on how steroid abuse can follow occasional use. We may even wonder whether or not some older or professional athletes meet the criteria for dependence on steroids, by virtue of loss of control, repeated attempts to stop or cut back without success, and continued use despite knowledge of negative consequences. Such case scenarios can be shared with adolescents as a part of prevention education, thus revealing how serious physical damage and illness are experienced by many long-term steroid users.

Prevention education must expose society's misplaced emphasis on winning, competition, and physical attractiveness at the cost of risking one's health. Adolescents must be assisted in critically evaluating these kinds of misplaced values and the media that convey such messages. Excessive concentration on improving one's physical appearance or reliance on the mood-enhancing effects of steroids must also be revealed as a poor and superficial alternative to working more directly at improving a low self-esteem, learning to achieve self-love, and gaining greater self-acceptance.

MEDICALLY UNINSURED POPULATIONS

As a consequence of living in a society in which large numbers of individuals lack health insurance, the plight of the medically uninsured chemically dependent deserves recognition. I have dealt with many clients who may have qualified for Medicaid payment of inpatient detoxification, but would not qualify for outpatient Medicaid. These clients had worked recently in the past, and some were confident of reemployment in the near future. Others disliked the idea of going on welfare in order to receive medical benefits.

Overreliance on 12-Step Programs as Aftercare

In making postdetoxification treatment arrangements for these clients, one faces a disturbing dilemma. In such cases, the recommendation to attend 12-step program meetings in a pattern of "90 meetings in 90 days" and the securing of a sponsor as soon as possible have constituted the best aftercare treatment recommendation.

Fortunately, the wide availability of 12-step programs in the New York metropolitan area has made such a treatment option a somewhat viable route for recovery here. However, when severe chemical dependency and other aspects of psychosocial functioning suggest the need for participation in the kind of intensive outpatient rehabilitation model described in Chapter 3, I sometimes felt as though I were throwing clients to the wolves. Yet I did all I could to break through denial and narcissistic inflation that fueled beliefs that intense, daily meetings were not necessary. Moreover, I conveyed the expectation that clients could "make it" and that they were fortunate to have access to such meetings in the New York area, and I explained the TC treatment alternative if relapse became a problem.

In this way, for many individuals who lack medical insurance, Alcoholics Anonymous, Narcotics Anonymous, and Cocaine Anonymous groups represents the main avenue by which they seek recovery. They cannot take advantage of progressive outpatient programs offering neuronutrients and pharmacological adjuncts. They cannot benefit from sophisticated relapse-prevention strategies arising out of the social learning and cognitive-behavioral field. And such clients may never begin to work in individual and group psychotherapy on childhood trauma, poor self-regulatory capacities, and psychopathology that may continue to place them at risk of relapse.

Reliance on Other Self-Help Groups

To compensate for the limited "free" services to which clients had access, I also recommended other kinds of 12-step groups. For those attending the recommended 12-step-based Adult Children of Alcoholics and Incest Survivors groups, the relative benefits of professional analysis of transference states and unconscious behavioral dramas may not be received; tension-producing, problematic patterns of behavior may continue even if abstinence is maintained. Feelings and memories may be powerfully accessed in anonymous self-help groups. However, sufficient time and individual attention or therapeutic interpretation of material may not be available. On the other hand, the invaluable role of group members in providing critical interpretations of other members' dynamics cannot be overlooked. So overall, the diverse and individual character, maturity, and success of self-help groups should not be underestimated.

In fact, I suggest that, in this time of crisis, creative people start more self-help groups. Without access to adequate treatment, such groups are needed for grandmothers raising their chemically addicted children's children, for the adolescent children of crack addicts, and for adult children of dysfunctional families.

Beyond Self-Help: Comprehensive Treatment for the Uninsured

Nevertheless, the point to be made is that people with problems such as these need access to more than self-help modalities. This is particularly true when dealing with severe chemical dependency, especially dependence on crack cocaine.

Intensive and comprehensive inpatient and outpatient programs of the kind discussed in Chapters 2 and 3 are needed for medically uninsured persons who currently can have access only to 12-step programs.

CHEMICALLY DEPENDENT AIDS PATIENTS

The AIDS epidemic has created a population of chemically dependent patients who have special needs as a result of HIV infection in addition to continuing drug dependence. These clients need programs that provide several kinds of interventions, including access to quality medical treatment; receipt of appropriate medications, such as AZT; nutritional counseling to avoid illness; education on safe-sex, AIDS-risk-reduction behaviors, such as condom use, avoidance of needle sharing, and proper cleaning of needles with bleach; inpatient hospitalization for medical crises and relapses to compulsive drug use; access to halfway houses and long-term, residential-based medical and drug treatment; participation in 12-step Positive Anonymous (PA) groups, professionally led support groups; and individual counseling; and family services that include education, family support groups, and family therapy.

A number of authors have described contemporary patterns of AIDS infection that should inform the design of prevention programs, addressed AIDS education and prevention issues, discussed AIDS and the needs of special minority populations, and described some promising programs of potential value with AIDS-positive and AIDS-at-risk chemically dependent populations (Holmes, Karon, & Kreiss, 1990; Chitwood, et al., 1990; Fullilove, Fullilove, Haynes, & Gross, 1990; Nyamathi & Vasquez, 1990; Morales, 1990; Sufian, Friedman, Stepherson, Rivera-Beckman, & Des Jarlais, 1990; Des Jarlais & Friedman, 1990; Schilling et al., 1989; Levy, Tendler, VanDevanter, & Cleary, 1990; Liebman, McIlvaine, Kotranski, & Lewis, 1990; Bracho de Carpio, Carpio-Cedraro, & Anderson, 1990; Schilling, El-Bassel, Schinke, Gordon, & Nichols, 1991). Readers are referred to these sources to get a sense of contemporary issues, the latest research trends, and state-of-the-art program models. The remaining parts of this section will raise issues that are derived from the author's clinical experiences with HIV-positive and AIDS-at-risk chemically dependent populations.

Difficult Questions To Be Answered

For many chemically dependent clients, a positive test result, enjoyment of a general state of health, preventative administration of AZT, and participation in PA groups may merely augment their regular TC program or outpatient clinic program involvement.

Many clients who pursue inpatient detoxification are or may be positive for the AIDS virus. Inpatient detoxification programs have to struggle with the decision of whether to routinely test their intravenous-drug-using and their crack-smoking clients; each group is at risk for AIDS as a result of their needle sharing and promiscuous sexual activities respectively. For this reason, AIDS education needs to be a routine service on inpatient detoxification and outpatient rehabilitation units. Should HIV testing be reserved for those with symptoms suggestive of AIDS or the AIDS-related complex? Or should all clients who report needle sharing and unprotected sex within the crack culture be tested?

Some programs elect as part of their AIDS education, to warn all clients who engage in high-risk behaviors that they have roughly a 50% chance of being HIV positive and so should act as though they might be infected and use condoms routinely. Others argue that an inpatient stay and the first access to quality medical care after perhaps a year of compulsive drug use and related behaviors necessitate giving patients an opportunity to discover their HIV status. Another view is that clients who are psychologically vulnerable when newly abstinent and already face a great risk of relapse when they encounter classically conditioned stimuli upon their release from the hospital are also too vulnerable in the first three to six months of recovery to handle a positive result. A newly abstinent patient, upon receiving a positive diagnosis, might react catastrophically, immediately relapse, and resume the very behaviors (needle sharing and unprotected promiscuous sex) that will place others at risk and further compromise the patient's own immune system.

It might be better not to recommend an HIV test until at least 90 days of abstinence have been achieved. However, here all bets are on an effective AIDS education program that convinces patients that they should act on the assumption they are positive and should use condoms, and thereby also encourages a delay in having children. The ethics of inadvertently encouraging abortions further complicates the issue.

Will a client who has achieved three to six months of recovery handle a positive test result better than someone who has been drug-free for 21 days? How does the risk of infecting others when abstinent and ignorant of one's HIV status weigh against the risk of a newly abstinent person's immediately relapsing upon news of a positive test result? Will this distressed, HIV-positive client who returns to drug use out of despair use a condom, clean needles with bleach, and avoid sharing needles? Would it be ethical and safe to test clients during inpatient detoxification if we knew we could place them directly in a residential TC where a safe supportive environment could prevent the worst-case scenario of immediate relapse and reckless infection of others? These are the kinds of questions and issues that need to be considered and ultimately resolved.

Combating Denial in Those Who Feel and Look "Healthy"

In the case of clients who feel and appear generally healthy, the treatment staff must pay particular attention to tendencies to deny the positive test result and to engage in acting-out behavior such as sex without a condom. The chemically dependent, who are already prone to profound levels of denial, present a considerable challenge when they exhibit persistent denial regarding their HIV-positive status. Many continue to harbor beliefs that they can have sex without a condom. Such entrenched levels of denial can even permit an HIV-positive client to do so even after a potential partner specifically asks about HIV status and suggests the use of a readily available condom! For such clients, confrontation by PA group members and in individual psychotherapy are necessary to prevent what constitutes reckless acting-out behavior even though they have achieved substantial periods of abstinence.

Special Needs of the Ill

On the other hand, clients who become quite ill pose other problems for the more traditional chemical-dependency treatment programs. Treatment may be interrupted by brief or extended hospitalizations. A risk of relapse may be great at times of high anxiety, fear, and pain related to illness. Programs have to handle such relapse episodes sensitively, departing from some standard punitive measures employed with "well" clients. Clients who are quite symptomatic may require medically oriented halfway-house and residential treatment services. Programs must provide the kind of comprehensive services listed in the beginning of this section, focusing on services for family members and therapeutic death and dying interventions.

Special AIDS inpatient treatment units geared toward the resolution of medical crises cannot overlook patients' chemical dependency. The staff must be prepared for patients' efforts to secure drugs, the sneaking of drugs into units, the outright delivery of drugs to patients on such units, and the need to initiate discussion of how continued chemical use may further compromise vulnerable immune systems. Chemical-dependency counselors may need to be added to what was originally conceived of as a medical unit for AIDS-related medical problems.

METHADONE-MAINTAINED CLIENTS

Kolar, Brown, Weddington, and Ball (1990) assert that the cocaine epidemic has created a crisis in methadone-maintenance treatment programs (MMTPs). This is consistent with assertions that cocaine and crack were used in the 1980s by diverse groups of individuals, including those within MMTPs. Also, the AIDS epidemic is forcing MMTP programs to give priority treatment to intravenous drug users testing positive for HIV or suffering from AIDS, and for such clients, methadone for life may be a valid goal, as some clinicians suggest (Sorenson, Batki, Good, & Wilkinson, 1990).

Many MMTPs, however, have long had problems with illicit drug use, as well as other problems. Rawson (1991) describes some of the newer problems with MMTPs. He points out that, during an era characterized by providing even more intensive and comprehensive services in the private sector to cocaine patients (in response to the same cocaine and crack epidemic affecting MMTPs), there has been a trend in some parts of the country toward reducing services in MMTPs. According to Rawson these efforts result in eliminating the perceived MMTP "frills" of counseling and urine testing as programs attempt to move toward just the delivery of methadone. Rawson appropriately asks what evidence exists that methadone alone constitutes a viable path to recovery.

As a clinician, I have made observations and gained impressions regarding deficits in contemporary MMTPs and developed a vision of what these programs should become, as described in the following.

Critical Observations

Recently, some have cited evidence that high doses of methadone, constituting what has been called a blockade dosage (typically 70 mg or more), can reduce the risk of HIV infection by reducing intravenous drug use (Joseph, 1990). This has created a climate in which more federal authorities and treatment professionals are advocating the routine use of high or blockade doses of methadone as a response to the AIDS epidemic. I question this recommendation as the primary thrust for improving today's MMTPs. Instead, should not the primary thrust for improving MMTPs follow the private trend of providing more intensive and comprehensive services that might permit a goal of gradually giving lower doses of methadone and helping clients to become more functional, if not ultimately employed? Among the services added, should we not include empirically tested models of AIDS prevention education (Schilling et al., 1990) within MMTPs?

In 1986, prior to Interfaith Medical Center's becoming a specialized crack cocaine unit, and for a two-year period (1986–1988) during which we detoxified the cocaine-dependent patients referred from MMTPs, I made several observations. Also, I had prior experiences working as a psychology intern in a Veterans Administration (VA) outpatient MMTP, corunning a weekly group therapy session. Many of the clients in the VA MMTP seemed to benefit from group therapy and were on doses of methadone that permitted them to work at full-time jobs. These earlier VA MMTP experiences colored my observations of cocaine- and crack-dependent clients who were referred for detoxification by MMTPs and influenced my responses to clients' descriptions of programs. In general, what the MMTP clients described did not compare favorably with my knowledge of the VA MMTP.

Clinically, I have noted with interest the seeming relationship between high "blockade dosages of methadone" (70 mg and higher) and the intravenous cocaine use and crack smoking of clients who enter inpatient detoxification. When I encountered clients sent to detoxify from cocaine and crack whom we were to maintain on, a high dose of methadone and refer back to the MMTP, I was struck by their behavior. Frequently, these clients were totally incapable of not engaging in a nearly continuous "nod" or stuporous state for substantial periods. My most frequent observation involved the following hypothesis: These clients need the stimulant effects of cocaine or crack administered chronically in order just to function or to maintain a functional state of awareness.

In support of this hypothesis and the earlier position of Rawson (1991), consider the remarks of Szalavita (1990), a recovering heroin addict detoxed from methadone:

> Methadone's main effect on me was to increase my intravenous cocaine use— the most dangerous kind of intravenous use for acquired immune deficiency syndrome transmission because, due to the nature of the high, one injects coke far more frequently than heroin . . . The second reason methadone fails is pharmacological. On a neurological basis, substituting methadone for heroin is similar to substituting vodka for gin: this is how it "blocks" opiates. It gets one too high (blocks all endorphin receptors by activating them) to feel the heroin . . .
> Methadone is no solution to the drugs and AIDS crisis, especially without counseling. Counseling—which leads addicts toward drug-free and AIDS-safe ways of dealing with problems—is the only thing methadone programs have going for them. The belief that taking a drug will solve an addict's problems is at the root of those problems, and the idea that methadone alone is an effective treatment merely illustrates that addicts reflect what society teaches them. Without counseling, methadone clinics are legal drug dispensaries and a good source of income for junkies. (p. A30)

This last remark by Szalavita takes us to a second hypothesis I advanced when a MMTP client detoxifying from cocaine or crack appeared to be "too high" on the unit. This hypothesis was that clients habitually sold, or "spit back," their methadone so frequently that they could not tolerate the high dose of methadone we were told by the MMTP staff to administer. We hypothesized, or were told, that the reason that clients sold part of their methadone was to finance the purchase of other drugs for their personal use. Other heroin addicts described buying street methadone regularly to detoxify themselves after an escalating heroin habit began to produce problems. These assertions supported the hypothesis that MMTP clients regularly sold their methadone on the streets.

If the second hypothesis is true, then it points toward another problem with MMTPs—the extent to which clients are regularly able to sell methadone even though a pattern of dirty urines and illicit drug use might suggest noncompliance and the necessity for some program action. Programs did indeed respond at times by referring clients to us for detoxification. But such referrals are only possible when urines are tested regularly, and in many programs this is not done often enough. Some outpatient clinics, however, in responding to the cocaine and crack epidemic, initiated the leasing of urine-testing machines so that clients could have their urine screened on a daily basis (Smith, 1989)—a change consistent with the trend Rawson (1991) recommends toward the provision of more intensive services. MMTPs might need to follow this lead, with the support of federal funding agencies.

To be fair, we must recognize the diversity of practices among different MMTPs and the fact that many people, such as Szalavita (1990), did benefit from counseling and did achieve stable long-term abstinence from all chemical use. Also, all treatment programs have been challenged by the cocaine and crack epidemic and any program weaknesses became much more glaring in this decade of the dual AIDS and crack epidemics.

Program Embodiment of Low Client Expectations

One weakness worthy of discussion is that some MMTPs may embody for and subtly project upon clients negative and low expectations.

In this regard, we could posit that those clients selling methadone for money, such as to purchase other drugs, are still manifesting their sociopathy or antisocial personality disorders. An alternative thesis is that clients respond to programs that embody negative and low expectations and behave accordingly. Possible negative and low expectations may be expressed via the concept that MMTP involvement is for life and that the highest methadone doses possible are "best" for clients. But how can the highest doses be best if clients are "too high" to be able to do anything other than sit, nod, and barely function beyond a sedentary level of behavior? Is anything other than a negative and low expectation for a client's entire life prospects conveyed by the notion of methadone maintenance at a high dose for life? Do programs in any way set clients up for outside illicit stimulant chemical use and perhaps for the occasional use of heroin? Could such illicit chemical use represent a form of healthy client rebellion, an indication that clients need to have greater control over their lives and need relief from the effects of high methadone doses? What about the concept that clients should be gradually achieving more control over their own behavior, such as is implicit in no longer having to "hustle" criminally to support a costly heroin habit? Were MMTPs supposed to be about gaining gradual control over criminal behavior, problematic feelings, impulses, interpersonal behaviors, and one's ability to maintain employment?

A Vision of More Intensive and Comprehensive MMTPs

Regarding this last question, I do believe that MMTPs were and are supposed to assist clients in gaining gradual control over various aspects of their adult functioning and in gradually achieving autonomy in that they no longer need to rely on the self-administration of illicit chemicals or on high doses of methadone. My experiences in working in a VA MMTP and professional contacts with such MMTP success stories support this belief.

My vision of MMTPs involves clients initially needing to be maintained on a high dose of methadone or a dose that is commensurate with their heroin habit. But, over the course of two to three years, clients should be afforded the following as part of an MMTP's intensive and comprehensive services:

1. Daily urine tests (via leased equipment) with the daily computerized test results monitored and reviewed by the staff.
2. Weekly or biweekly counseling to assist clients with program compliance, management of relapses to illicit chemical use, and support in coping with general life problems.
3. Professional psychotherapy, for those with significantly severe psychiatric symptoms (McLellan, 1986), which addresses underlying problems with anxiety, depression, low self-esteem, trauma from childhood or Vietnam, and poor self-regulatory capacities.
4. Group counseling to provide psychoeducation and therapeutic interaction that resolve attitudinal and behavioral problems.
5. A formal relapse-prevention program that teaches clients how to respond to triggers and high-risk situations to avoid a slip or relapse.
6. Programs that offer vocational testing and training or education to prepare clients for jobs.
7. Vocational counseling to assist clients with the stress of job interviews and job searches.
8. Programs that provide on-site couples counseling, child therapy, and family therapy or refer clients to appropriate mental health centers to receive such services.

As a part of this vision, at the end of two to three years of receiving these kinds of intensive and comprehensive services in MMTPs, clients can then enter into and maintain employment on perhaps 20 mg of methadone. Others may gradually decrease to 10 or 5 mg, but may decide to maintain these low levels for several more years, if not for life. However, at this point, these employed individuals who have learned a great deal about managing life's problems, preventing relapse, and improving self-regulatory capacities are now receiving only take-home methadone in weekly or biweekly batches.

Programs would also recognize that their populations are heterogeneous and would match clients to treatment goals and strategies based upon thorough assessments, such as that obtained with the Addiction Severity Index (McLellan, 1986) or a clinical interview (Wallace, 1991a). Some may require, and need to be matched to, professional individual psychotherapy (Woody, Luborsky, McLellan, & O'Brien, 1986). Other clients could be referred to residential TCs that permit them to be maintained on methadone while they gradually, over a two-year stay, achieve a goal of either low-dose methadone or the discontinuation of methadone. Meanwhile, such TCs would assist clients through the traditional TC strategies of providing counseling, opportunities for achieving positive attitude and behavioral changes, educational and vocational training, employment, and reentry into society as independent, employed citizens.

Such a vision is in line with the trend in private outpatient clinic treatment that Rawson (1991) observes: services have become increasingly intensive and comprehensive. The work of McLellan (1986) and his associates (Woody et al., 1986) indicates that VA MMTPs continue to model progressive developments in the delivery of services to addicts, beyond my first-hand positive experiences as a psychology intern at a VA MMTP. Also, I am sure that there are many other MMTPs that approximate this ideal level of service delivery to their clients, but are forced to recognize the reality of client diversity and the matching of different clients to different treatment goals and strategies. However, I am also appalled by the trend toward the elimination of services Rawson (1991) describes as occurring in MMTPs in some parts of the country and feel compelled to support him in articulating an alternative vision for the future of MMTPs.

In concluding, the question I am forced to pose is "Why do we not follow research and suggestive clinical findings regarding what can effectively rehabilitate severely dependent clients (McLellan, 1986; Woody et al., 1986; Wallace, 1991a; Rawson, Obert, McCann, Smith, & Ling, 1990; Washton & Stone-Washton, 1990) and begin to modify our MMTPs so that they can better meet the challenges of the cocaine, crack, and AIDS epidemics?

HOMELESS CHEMICALLY DEPENDENT CLIENTS

A homeless chemically dependent client requires a long-term stay in a residential TC. However, in New York State, two groups of homeless clients are barred from immediate referral to a TC—those who are dually diagnosed and those who have been incarcerated.

Needs of the Homeless Dually Diagnosed

Persons with a history of psychiatric hospitalizations and who are being maintained on either antipsychotic medication, antidepressant medication, or lithium are inappropriate candidates for the traditional TC for the chemically dependent. The lack of adequate medical and psychiatric staff prevents TCs from admitting these clients. Also, TCs use good judgment in anticipating that even today's relatively benign use of verbal haircuts or reprimands and harsh work assignments or loss of status as punishment and the forms of confrontation utilized in groups are techniques that the fragile egos and poor reality testing of the psychiatrically impaired cannot tolerate without the risk of regression and fragmentation. Frequently, suicidal ideation and high levels of anxiety and depression temporarily result even for the healthier individuals in TCs who are merely suffering from the post traumatic stress disorder or other personality disorders.

Thus modified TCs are required for homeless dually diagnosed patients that furnish medical and psychiatric services and an appropriately modified environment. A number of halfway house or residential programs are in existence in New York State that meet this special population's critical treatment needs. However, more such programs are needed, including more residentially based 12-step programs. Program developers need to follow the recommendations of Evans and Sullivan (1990) regarding how to structure programs for the dually diagnosed once they are in treatment and off the streets. Among key recommendations are to integrate the mental health and recovery models, modify work on the 12-steps in specific ways based on a client's specific psychiatric diagnosis, and educate clients on both the psychiatric and the addictive disease.

Needs of the Formerly Incarcerated, Homeless Client

A number of homeless clients have no psychiatric illness, but may have histories of serious and violent assaults. Some will be denied access to residential TCs because, in the screening process, that history will come to light. At that point, a clinical decision is made regarding the chances of the person's responding with explosive violence to limits, punishments, confrontation, and verbal haircuts or reprimands. Since the potential for violence is so hard to predict, a history of past violence is the best reason to deny this client entrance into a TC. These homeless clients require comprehensive and intensive day treatment services while they live in shelters and gradually are placed in independent housing.

Other people who were incarcerated experience the kind of inhumane treatment, atrocities, and warehousing behind bars discussed earlier in this chapter. The main consequence of such incarceration is feelings of abhorrence at the idea of not being able to leave a facility or at having restrictions placed on their liberty. Since former inmates have such strong feelings against and resist any kind of confinement, and since TCs restrict clients' freedom to leave the facilities for up to the first three months in residence, a large cohort of former inmates outrightly refuse the TC option. Also, persisting myths that all TCs still engage in what is perceived as brutal treatment—shaving heads or forcing residents to walk around with humiliating signs around their necks or to clean floors with a toothbrush—make the TC referral quite unattractive. Other clients have not been incarcerated, but fear TCs for some of these same reasons. Thus a relatively large group of clients must attempt to access day treatment program services while they use the shelter as their "home" base, holding the hope of assistance in gaining housing.

Since some of this resistance to TCs is based on misconceptions, myths, and exaggerated fears, day treatment programs need to add yet one more set of regular group meetings. Programs should schedule at least biweekly one-hour meetings at which current TC members furnish information about the TC to which they belong. Typically, two or three TC members discuss in these groups how their TC is run, the program components, and their personal experiences in adjusting to the TC environment. I have found that TCs welcome the opportunity to schedule such groups regularly and feel that it is a good experience for their residents who have accumulated eight or more months in residence. Program staff members can even request that a formerly incarcerated TC resident be included in the discussions.

In this way, both a recruiting mechanism for TC induction is established and important myths about TCs can be debunked. A large number of the clients languishing on long waiting lists for independent housing arrangements and chronically relapsing in depressing, drug-saturated shelters—even though day treatment programs for the homeless may provide fairly intensive and comprehensive services— may thereby pursue entrance into TCs. The bottom line is that the ideal treatment for the homeless chemically dependent client who can meet entrance criteria is an 18- to 24-month stay in a TC. The promise of receiving a high school equivalency diploma (GED), job training, and job placement, and having $3,000 in the bank and their own apartment within roughly two years is quite compelling for most homeless, addicted "down and outers."

For clients who rightfully exercise their free will, or perhaps use good judgment in estimating their intolerance for a TC environment, and reject it as an option, and for those who cannot meet TC entrance criteria, outpatient/day treatment programs need to include certain critical components, such as on-site counseling in shelters and halfway houses; random or routine urine testing on a frequent basis, and ideally on a daily basis; regular 12-step-program group meetings on the program site, as well as active encouragement to utilize outside meetings and to secure a sponsor; a solid five or six days' worth of intensive and comprehensive services such as GED preparation, individual counseling, group therapy, relapse-prevention groups, exercise groups, AIDS-prevention groups, parenting skills groups, and TC representatives' groups. The kind of services these clients require again should approximate a model of intensive and comprehensive services. The expectation of attaining independent housing or group housing and eventual employment (at least part-time activities for psychiatric clients) needs to be embodied in programs for homeless chemically dependent clients. And again, clients can be matched to different and appropriate treatment goals and interventions, based on the assessment findings.

CONCLUSION

This chapter has examined the way in which the distinctive characteristics of seven special populations of chemically dependent clients informs the recommended design of treatment programs. Specifically, it examined the characteristics of criminal, pregnant, adolescent, medically uninsured, AIDS, methadone-maintained, and homeless clients and briefly outlined pertinent issues that should influence program design. Repeated emphasis was placed both on the way in which both special program features in view of population characteristics must be set in place and on the need to move service-delivery systems toward more intensive and comprehensive designs. We also saw that the cocaine and crack epidemic, as well as the AIDS epidemic, has presented quite a challenge to programs, creating some new treatment dilemmas and bringing to light program weaknesses. Throughout the chapter, mention was made of the need both to engage in a thorough, individualized assessment of clients and to match clients to appropriate treatment goals and strategies. This underlying theme is consistent with a biopsychosocial approach to addiction and indicates that, regardless of the special population we may treat, certain elements of a practical treatment approach (Wallace, 1991a) prevail.

Although the chapter covered numerous special populations possessing distinct treatment needs, the needs of the chemically dependent elderly were not discussed; readers should see George (1990) for a discussion of these issues. Children remain neglected in the literature and must receive greater attention in the future.

REFERENCES

Bollerud, K. (1990). A model for the treatment of trauma-related syndromes among chemically dependent inpatient women. *Journal of Substance Abuse Treatment, 7*, 83–87.

Blume, S. B. (1989). Dual diagnosis: Psychoactive substance dependence and the personality disorders. *Journal of Psychoactive Drugs, 21*, 139–144.

Bracho de Carpio, A., Carpio-Cedraro, F. F., & Anderson, L. (1990). Hispanic families learning and teaching about AIDS: A participatory approach at the community level. *Hispanic Journal of Behavioral Sciences, 12*, 165–176.

Carroll, J. F., & Sobel, B. S. (1986). Integrating mental health personnel and practices into a therapeutic community. In G. DeLeon & J. T. Ziegenfuss, (Eds.), *Therapeutic communities for addictions.* Springfield, IL: Charles C. Thomas.

Chasnoff, I. J., Landress, H. J., & Barrett, M. E. (1990). The prevalence of illicit-drug or alcohol use during pregnancy and discrepancies in mandatory reporting in Pinellas County, Florida. *New England Journal of Medicine, 322*, 1202–1206.

Chavkin, W. (1990). Drug addiction and pregnancy: Policy crossroads. *American Journal of Public Health, 80*, 483–487.

Chitwood, D., McCoy, C., Inciardi, J., McBride, D., Comerford, M., Trapido, E., McCoy, V., Page, J., Griffin, J., Fletcher, M., & Ashman, M. (1990). HIV seropositivity of needles from shooting galleries in South Florida. *American Journal of Public Health*, 80, 150–152.

Daigle, R. D. (1990). Anabolic steroids. *Journal of Psychoactive Drugs*, 22, 77–80.

DeLeon, G. (1989). Psychopathology and substance abuse: What is being learned from research in therapeutic communities. *Journal of Psychoactive Drugs*, 21, 177–188.

Des Jarlais, D., & Friedman, S. (1990). Shooting galleries and AIDS: Infection probabilities and "tough" policies. *American Journal of Public Health*, 80, 142–144.

Evans, K. & Sullivan, J. M. (1990). *Dual diagnosis: Counseling the mentally ill substance abuser*. New York: Guilford.

Fram, D. H., Marmo, J., & Holden, R. (1989). Naltrexone treatment—the problem of patient acceptance. *Journal of Substance Abuse Treatment*, 6, 119–122.

Flewelling, R. L., & Bauman, K. E. (1990). Family structure as a predictor of initial substance use and sexual intercourse in early adolescence, *Journal of Marriage and the Family*, 52, 171–181.

Fullilove, M., Fullilove, R., Haynes, K., & Gross, S. (1990). Black women and AIDS prevention: A view towards understanding gender rules. *Journal of Sex Research*, 27, 47–64.

George, R. (1990). *Counseling the chemically dependent: Theory and practice*. Engelwood Cliffs, NJ: Prentice-Hall.

Glaberson, W. (1990, October 4). One in 4 young Black men are in custody, study says. *New York Times*, p. B6.

Greenhouse, L. (1990, November 6). Gay soldier wins battle to re-enlist. *New York Times*, p. A16.

Gough, D. (1989). Steroids in athletics: Is the edge worth the risk? A review and commentary. *Journal of Alcohol and Drug Education*, 35, 28–34.

Herridge, P., & Gold, M. S., (1988). Pharmacological adjuncts in the treatment of opioid and cocaine addicts. *Journal of Psychoactive Drugs*, 20, 233–242.

Holmes, K. H., Karon, J. M., & Kreiss, J. (1990). The increasing frequency of heterosexually acquired AIDS in the United States, 1983–1988. *American Journal of Public Health*, 80, 858–863.

Johnson, B. D., Goldstein, P. J., Preble, E., Schmeidler, J., Lipton, D. S., Spunt, B., & Miller, T. (1985). *Taking care of business: The economics of crime by heroin abusers*. Lexington, MA: Lexington Books, D.C. Heath and Company.

Joseph, H. (1990). A report on the activities of the Cocaine/Crack working group. New York State Division of Substance Abuse Services.

Joyce, T. (1990). The dramatic increase in the rate of low birthweight in New York City: An aggregate time-series analysis. *American Journal of Public Health*, 80, 682–684.

Kandel, D. B. (1990). Parenting styles, drug use, and children's adjustment in families of young adults. *Journal of Marriage and the Family*, 52, 183–196.

Kearon, W. G. (1990). Deinstitutionalization, street children, and the coming AIDS epidemic in the adolescent population. *Juvenile and Family Court Journal*, pp. 9–18.

Kolar, A. F., Brown, B., Weddington, W., & Ball, J. C. (1990). A Treatment crisis: Cocaine use by clients in methadone maintenance programs. *Journal of Substance Abuse Treatment, 7,* 101–107.

Kolata, G. (1990, July 23). Old, weak, and a loser: Crack user's image falls. *New York Times,* pp. A1, B4.

Kronstadt, D. (1989). *Pregnancy and cocaine addiction: An overview of impact and treatment.* San Francisco: Far West Laboratory for Educational Research and Development.

Lay, D. P. (1990, October 22). Our justice system, so-called. *New York Times,* p. A13.

Levy, R., Tendler, C., VanDevanter, N., & Cleary, P. D. (1990). A group intervention model for individuals testing positive for HIV antibody. *American Journal of Orthopsychiatry, 60,* 452–459.

Liebman, J., McIlvaine, D. S., Kotranski, L., & Lewis, R. (1990). AIDS prevention for IV drug users and their sexual partners in Philadelphia. *American Journal of Public Health, 80,* 615–616.

Malcolm, A. H. (1990, October 10). New strategies to fight crime go far beyond stiffer terms and more cells. *New York Times,* p. A16.

McLellan, A. T. (1986). "Psychiatric severity" as a predictor of outcome from substance abuse treatments. In R. E. Meyers (Ed.), *Psychopathology and addictive disorders,* New York: Guilford.

McRobbie, J., Mata, S., & Kronstadt, D. (1990). *Proceedings Papers December 1989: A Conference on Drug Free Pregnancy.* San Francisco: Far West Laboratory for Educational Research and Development.

Morales, E. S. (1990). HIV infection and Hispanic gay and bisexual men. *Hispanic Journal of Behavioral Sciences, 11,* 212–222.

New York Times (1990a, October 8). Number of inmates in U.S. reaches record. *New York Times,* p. A8.

New York Times (1990b, November 5). Number of parolees rose by 12% in 1989, Justice Department says. *New York Times,* p. A15.

Nyamathi, A., & Vasquez, R. (1990). Impact of poverty, homelessness, and drugs on Hispanic women at risk for HIV infection. *Hispanic Journal of Behavioral Sciences, 11,* 299–314.

Outlook (1990). Cocaine: 80s growth tend weakens? *Outlook on substance abuse in New York State.* New York State Division of Substance Abuse Services.

Petiti, D. B., & Colemen, C. (1990). Cocaine and the risk of low birth weight. *American Journal of Public Health, 80,* 25–28.

Powers, J. L., Eckenrode, J., & Jaklitsch, B. (1990). Maltreatment among runaway and homeless youth. *Child Abuse and Neglect, 14,* 87–98.

Rawson, R. A. (1991, in press). Chemical dependence treatment: The integration of the alcoholism and drug addiction systems. *International Journal of the Addictions.*

Rawson, R. A., Obert, J. L., McCann, M. J., Smith, D. P., & Ling, W. (1990). Neurobehavioral treatment for cocaine dependency. *Journal of Psychoactive Drugs, 22,* 283–297.

Rohsenow, D. J., Corbett, R., & Devine, D. (1988). Molested as children: A hidden contribution to substance abuse? *Journal of Substance Abuse Treatment, 5,* 13–18.

Rosecan, J. J., Spitz, H. I. (Eds.). (1987). *Cocaine abuse: New directions in treatment and research.* New York: Bruner/Mazel, Inc.

Sandberg, D. N. (1986). The child abuse—delinquency connection: Evolution of a therapeutic community. *Journal of Psychoactive Drugs, 18,* 215–220.

Schiffer, F. (1988). Psychotherapy of nine successfully treated cocaine abusers: Techniques and dynamics. *Journal of Substance Abuse Treatment, 5,* 131–137.

Schilling, R. F., El-Bassel, N., Schinke, S. P., Gordon, K., & Nichols, S. (1991). Building skills of recovering drug users to reduce heterosexual AIDS transmission. *Public Health Reports, 106,* 297–304.

Schilling, R. F., Schinke, S. P., Nichols, S. E., Zayas, L. H., Miller, S. O., Orlandi, M. A., & Botvin, G. (1989). Developing strategies for AIDS prevention research with Black and Hispanic drug users. *Public Health Reports, 104,* 2–12.

Shenson, D., Dubler, N., & Michaels, D. (1990). Jails and prisons: The new asylums? *American Journal of Public Health, 80,* 655–656.

Smith, M. (1989). Interview by author August 1989 at Lincoln Hospital Acupuncture Clinic, South Bronx, New York.

Spitz, H. I., & Rosecan, J. J. (Eds.). (1987). *Cocaine abuse: New directions in treatment and research.* New York: Bruner/Mazel.

Sorenson, J. L., Batki, S. L., Good, P., & Wilkinson, K. (1989). Methadone maintenance program for AIDS-affected opiate addicts. *Journal of Substance Abuse Treatment, 6,* 87–94.

Stoffelmayr, J., Benishek, L. A., Humphreys, K., Lee, J. A., & Mavis, B. E. (1989). Substance abuse prognosis with an additional psychiatric diagnosis: Understanding the relationship. *Journal of Psychoactive Drugs, 21,* 145–152.

Sufian, M., Friedman, S. R., Stepherson, B., Rivera-Beckman, J., & Des Jarlais, D. (1990). Impact of AIDS on Puerto Rican intravenous drug users. *Hispanic Journal of Behavioral Sciences, 11,* 122–134.

Szalavita, M. (1990, April 28). Methadone addicts are as far from recovery as heroin addicts. *New York Times,* p. A30.

Teplin, L. A. (1990). The prevalence of severe mental disorder among male urban jail detainees: Comparison with epidemiologic catchment area program. *American Journal of Public Health, 80,* 663–669.

Van Meter, W., & Rioux, D. (1990). The case for shorter residential alcohol and other drug abuse treatment of adolescents. *Journal of Psychoactive Drugs, 22,* 87–88.

Wallace, B. C. (1990). Crack cocaine smokers as adult children of alcoholics: The dysfunctional family link. *Journal of Substance Abuse Treatment, 7,* 89–100.

Wallace, B. C. (1991a). *Crack cocaine: A practical treatment approach for the chemically dependent.* New York: Bruner/Mazel.

Wallace, B. C. (1991b). Chemical dependency treatment for pregnant addicts: Beyond the criminal sanctions perspective. *Psychology of Addictive Behaviors, 5,* 23–35.

Washton, A. M., & Stone-Washton, N. (1990). Abstinence and relapse in outpatient cocaine addicts. *Journal of Psychoactive Drugs, 22,* 135–147.

Wexler, H. K. (1987). Therapeutic communities within prisons. In G. DeLeon & J. T.

Ziegenfuss (Eds.), *Therapeutic communities for addictions*. Springfield, IL: Charles C. Thomas.

Wexler, H. K., Lipton, D. S., & Johnson, B. D. (1988). A criminal justice strategy for treating cocaine-heroin abusing offenders in custody. *National Institute of Justice Issues and Practices*: U.S. Department of Justice, National Institute of Justice, Office of Communications Research.

Wexler, H. K., & Williams, R. (1986). The stay 'n out therapeutic community: Prison treatment for substance abusers. *Journal of Psychoactive Drugs, 18*, 221–230.

Wood, K. M. (1990). The family of the juvenile delinquent. *Juvenile and Family Court Journal*, 19–37.

Woody, G. E., Luborsky, L., McLellan, A. T., & O'Brien, C. P. (1986). Psychotherapy as an adjunct to methadone treatment. In R. E. Meyers (Ed.), *Psychopathology and addictive disorders*. New York: Guilford.

Young, E. B. (1990). The role of incest issues in relapse. *Journal of Psychoactive Drugs, 22*, 249–258.

19

Conclusion: Future Directions in Chemical-Dependency Treatment and the Need to Break the Silence on Child Abuse

Barbara C. Wallace, Ph.D.

The chapters in this book summarize contemporary clinical and research efforts currently going on in the field of chemical-dependency treatment. Clinicians across the United States are refining clinical techniques in their own work with addicted patients. Many have felt isolated because the field of mental health has yet to produce a cadre of professionals possessing the skills necessary to deal effectively with the chemically dependent. The contributors to this volume are integrating "this and that" from psychodynamic, cognitive-behavioral, and psychoeducational approaches. These professionals are moving disease-model Alcoholics Anonymous (AA) and individual psychotherapy advocates toward a conciliatory stance permitting the utilization of both modalities (Yalisove, Rothschild, Derby). Zweben similarly urges the integration of psychiatric and substance-abuse treatment to meet the needs of the dual-diagnosis client.

These pioneers in the addictions field are also doing long-term dynamic individual and group psychotherapy (Yalisove, Rothschild, Derby, Wallace), even as dissenters and objectors say it cannot and should not be done with this population. Nonetheless, answers to questions about appropriate technique are discovered through diligent work with clients. The analysis and working through of transference even occur with clients relatively early in treatment, bespeaking the advantages of group therapy (Wallace; Chapter 4). The contributors to this volume have sought to describe and theoretically justify their actions in their various chapters.

Other researchers, such as Blum and his colleagues, work hard to embrace a broad understanding of addictions and compulsions. His group has discovered the alcogene, unraveled mysteries of the neurogenetics of compulsive disease, and challenges the field to develop ethical primary and secondary prevention strategies for the biologically predisposed. At the same time, their appreciation of the role of stress, social environment, and psychological factors in the etiology of compulsive disease plays a vital part in forging integrated and comprehensive treatment approaches. Their support of psychologically based, and even spiritual, AA treatment approaches exemplifies the kind of integrative approach and broad thinking beyond rigid dogmatic attitudes necessary to advance the field of chemical-dependency treatment. Also, even as Blum and his associates pioneer "hard" scientific contributions, they, too, must cope with the dissenters and objectors who chant that it cannot and should not be done or that a disease-model view is absurd. The work of Hawkins suggests that those who yell loudest are often heard, while it reveals that many social-learning proponents can pioneer a refreshing, reconciliatory integration of theory and technique that substantively moves the field forward as well.

The research of other contributors to the volume also exemplifies an integration of quantitative and qualitative research methods (Unumb) and the bringing together of the psychodynamic concepts of differentiation and the cognitive-behavioral concepts of locus of control in examining treatment process and outcome (Weidman). Kleinman and colleagues' research reflects the importance of outcome-evaluation research, the follow-up of clients, and their thorough assessment; accumulated data permit us to understand the range of psychiatric disturbance that clients possess and to utilize research findings to create treatment models that are appropriately intensive to facilitate the achievement and maintenance of abstinence. This research justifies the assertions by me (Wallace) that inpatient treatment during a withdrawal phase may be important for some of our most severely addicted clients who are in need of this kind of intensive intervention. Similarly, Kleinman's findings validate Tatarsky and Washton's implementation of a long-term intensive outpatient treatment model that offers comprehensive services.

Long-term residential therapeutic community (TC) stays—spanning early, middle, and later phases of recovery—also receive validation from Kleinman's conclusion that many of her clients who sought outpatient treatments actually needed more intensive variable length inpatient treatment, which a TC provides. I describe developments in a progressive TC, Damon House New York Inc., but the recommendation that TCs offer a variable length of stay (three, six, nine months) has yet to be followed, although the successful integration of professional consultants into TC structure is transpiring.

Both my inpatient treatment model and TC consultation work, as well as Tatarsky and Washton's outpatient treatment approach, reflect modifications of clinical technique in work with the chemically dependent (as discussed in Part II). From the different vantage points of inpatient, outpatient, and residential TC settings, we discover, nonetheless, that the integration of psychoeducational, cognitive-behavioral, and psychodynamic (insight-oriented) interventions is essential.

The work of various contributors also serves as validation for their efforts undertaken in relative isolation across the country as evidenced in their attempts to make treatment more intensive, the use of the concept of phases of recovery, and the adoption of a biopsychosocial approach. Perhaps most striking is the articulation by numerous authors that treatment must address, as Wurmser states, both the surface phenomena (primary view) and the unconscious depths (secondary view). With regard to the secondary view, we have seen repeated emphasis on addressing addicts' poor self-care and deficient self-regulation of affects, low self-esteem, tendencies to act on impulse, and interpersonal behavior; Harris-Offutt would add, from their work with African-Americans, a low ethnic sense of self. And from her work with numerous special populations, this author cites treatment issues of which practitioners and researchers should be aware, while comments of authors earlier in the volume provide support for many of the views expressed in that chapter.

As this edited volume illustrates, only through the integration of approaches and the welding of techniques and interventions arising out of diverse theoretical approaches, if not opposing "camps," can we cope with this chemical-dependency "elephant." If I am an expert on the elephant's trunk and you are an expert on his tail, another is an expert on his torso, and yet another has done extensive research on his massive legs, is it not obvious that our arrogance and contempt for each other only blocks resolution of the mystery of how we are to deal with the total elephant?

Another point is that not all elephants are the same, although there may be certain commonalities. The field of chemical-dependency treatment must evolve toward the routine provision of thorough individualized assessments and the matching of clients to specific techniques. Our treating of all addicts as being the same, as a monolithic group, will be looked back on as a low point in our history—but only if the field sufficiently evolves.

The concept of phases of recovery and treatment takes us a step further, even beyond forging an integrated theory and advancing a biopsychosocial approach. This concept tells us when to weld and administer what part of our multifaceted techniques or multimodal treatment. The treatment may reflect the integrated use of diverse—if not once opposing—treatment interventions, but each treatment has its time for delivery. The idea of phases of treatment and recovery yields the concept of the correct "timing" of the delivery of a specific treatment intervention, depending on the phase of recovery the patient is currently negotiating.

In sum, this edited volume has presented the work of clinicians and their important research findings and has described the needs of special populations in an effort fundamentally to advance the state of chemical-dependency treatment. The principles illustrated in this volume and which are necessary to guide the continuing evolution of the field include that practice must be grounded in a theoretical rationale, that treatment models must be repeatedly refined in light of research findings, and that the special characteristics of patient populations must be considered in treatment design.

Before we conclude, there is yet another issue that deserves attention. It is one which we are reluctant to consider and it involves yet another special population—if not a large subset of the entire population of those who are chemically dependent and behaviorally compulsive. Although Zweben has discussed the dual-diagnosis patient, whose treatment needs have been thoroughly outlined in her chapter, some additional discussion about the plight of the victim of child abuse seems essential.

CAN WE BREAK THE CODE OF SILENCE ON CHILD ABUSE?

Recently, I had several experiences that bear directly on the future of the field of chemical dependency. Upon my arrival for consultation work at Damon House (described in Chapter 14), I was told about the recent dismissal from treatment of several of their therapeutic community (TC) residents. Individuals had "dropped guilt" they were holding for themselves as well as others. Two of the women with whom I had worked (and some male clients as well) either were discharged or "served" punishments for newly discovered sexual acting-out behavior. Both of the women were incest survivors. (However, the childhood and adolescent experiences of one of the women were so horrendous that the term sexual abuse fails to capture the magnitude of her experience.)

When clients admitted major sexual acting out that was revealed by those "dropping guilt," dismissals from the TC followed. Where it was minor kissing behavior, punishments were served. In estimating the chances that the "dismissed" could avoid a relapse (70 to 30 in favor of relapse, a counselor estimated) and pursue recovery beyond Damon House, one counselor shared a problematic observation that suggested to him a poor prognosis. These individuals displayed no regrets over their sexual acting-out behavior and had been capable of looking one straight in the eyes and lying. It was frightening and seemed to be a poor prognostic indicator for maintenance of a clean and sober state since they were still capable of such "street" behavior. This counselor would have preferred their having been able to connect with painful affects and to own up to their misguided behavior. My response to this counselor was that their behavior upon being discovered/accused made perfect sense in view of their traumatic histories of incest. The fundamental premise of incest is that you "keep the secret." Moreover, in one of the women's lives, when incest was discovered, she experienced a traumatic abandonment, as well as severe public humiliation. I told the counselor that the sexual acting out and the maintenance of a strict code of silence were perfectly logical considering this history. He was taken aback and reported that one of the dismissed men, whom I did not know, was indeed a victim of terrible incest. I explained further. How could one admit to a forbidden, hidden, sexually taboo relationship (within the TC context), particularly when one has learned from past trauma that upon discovery horrible things happen?

Unfortunately, the TC responded to the clients' reenactment of their individual behavioral traumas of incest by banishing them from the TC society. The TC family fell apart and public humiliation occurred. If only a more therapeutic response to this large-scale transference drama within the dysfunctional family TC environment could have prevailed. The TC unconsciously colluded in the repetition of the original trauma and in facilitating the realization of childhood fears associated with the trauma.

The setting of behavioral limits, consistency in responding to behavior that violates established limits, and the occasional dismissal from treatment of clients who have broken important rules seems reasonable. However, my experience suggests that the TC treatment structure—and perhaps treatment within the overall field of chemical dependence—needs to evolve to a level where sexual and other acting-out behavior is more effectively prevented, managed, and transformed. Effective prevention may rest in treatment practitioners' enhanced ability to change not only drug-using behavior and attitudes, but clients' unconscious repetition and mastery of childhood trauma through acting-out behavior.

Other Damon House events expand upon this issue. One of the women in my group therapy session—to be merely punished after dropping guilt for her own behavior—began to talk about her new bad feelings (guilt) for "spilling the beans," which led to the discharge of a friend. She noted that when she was confronted by staff members, they could not understand how her dismissed friend had been holding no guilt for her. How could it be, they had asked, that the dismissed woman knew nothing about the secrets to which my remaining patient had admitted? To me, it was painfully obvious. This woman was yet another victim of childhood incest and sexual abuse. Moreover, she had been reenacting, over the course of several months with the women in my group, the behavior of keeping other adult sexual behaviors a secret, because of her fear of rejection and humiliation and her inability to tolerate intense feelings of shame and guilt regarding her sexual behavior in the crack culture. I interpreted to the group that the real tale of the dismissals and recent crisis at Damon House was the acting out of childhood and adolescent sexual abuse, following the dictum that you keep it a secret within the dysfunctional family.

After group, I was to consult with a male client in crisis. He was one of the men revealed to be engaging in minor sexual behavior by the dropping of guilt, resulting in punishment but without banishment from the TC. Not to my surprise, his partner in kissing behavior was another childhood victim of incest and sexual abuse. Two victims of incest had found each other for mutual unconscious acting out of behaviors derived from their child abuse.

This man's state of crisis is even more telling with regard to the future tasks facing the field of chemical-dependency treatment. He was being seen outside Damon House in individual therapy, in addition to participating in groups and counseling sessions in the TC. The young man said that he had begun having problems about two months earlier. He said that since starting outside therapy, he had wanted to talk about his childhood sexual abuse, but the counselor had repeatedly told him not to talk about sexual issues as these therapists were not equipped to deal with them. This facility offers some of the best outpatient treatment available in New

York City for those on Medicaid; it is the poor person's version of the Washton Institute (see Chapter 3), but pales terribly in comparison. Damon House was contacted by the outside counselor, who wanted to initiate a referral to a psychiatrist for evaluation in light of worsening symptoms.

My assessment revealed that these worsening symptoms involved the emergence of Post-Traumatic Stress Disorder (PTSD). This client described the return of repressed and split-off memories of sexual abuse and physical torture, which comprised his frightening flashbacks.

What percentage of recovering individuals unwittingly trade in addiction and unconscious compulsive behaviors for the overwhelming painful and frightening return of the repressed and split-off memories of child abuse? How many of these clients happily enter treatment for chemical dependence, only to find that the facilitators of the recovery process are unable to handle the return of the repressed and split-off trauma? How many chemical-dependency treatment professionals would know how to respond? Where does the work of a recovering counselor, a certified alcoholism counselor, a psychologist, and psychiatrist begin and end in treating the chemically dependent over the course of different phases of recovery?

The young recovering man presented symptoms of PTSD at a time when he is supposed to be in stable recovery and in pursuit of lifetime recovery. But how will this be possible if the return of what has been repressed, split off, and dissociated is dealt with ineffectively? What are the chances of relapse when one is in recovery one year or 12 years, and the return of traumatic memories, as in PTSD, compromises effective functioning? What kind of clinical technique do we employ when we remove one symptom only to find, months or years later, that we must now face the legacy of childhood trauma in dysfunctional families or some other trauma— such as prostitution in the crack culture, street violence, or participation in a war.

Even before the surfacing of traumatic memories to the degree that they qualified as PTSD, his life played out seductive and sexual scenarios—such as kissing the woman in the TC who was also an incest victim—and unconscious transference dramas repeatedly held sway as the main action of his life. He admits to many problematic situations created by his unconscious acting out of dramas that are derivatives of his childhood and adolescent sexual torture/incest.

The limitations in the overall service delivery system available to chemically dependent clients emerge from this tale. A large hidden population within our chemically dependent patient population is composed of victims of childhood abuse and neglect who are left with the compulsion to repeat aspects of their childhood traumas in an attempt to master states of overstimulation that their childhood egos could not manage. The adult legacy of poor regulation of affect, self-esteem, impulses, and interpersonal behavior can be seen in acting-out behavior such as sexual flirtation and sexual contact. However, other clients may be inhibited and almost phobic in relation to the expression of sexual and aggressive impulses as a consequence of childhood trauma in dysfunctional families.

Most contemporary treatment models serve to peel off the layer of chemical dependence and chemical-related psychosocial deterioration only to reveal clients' underlying poor self-regulation. Evidence of poor self-regulation can be seen in acting-out behavior. Sexual acting out reveals that the chemical dependence layer was just one outward manifestation or layer of symptomatology arising from earlier childhood and adolescent trauma. Recovery remains incomplete for our clients when their underlying problems involving poor regulation of affect, self-esteem, impulses (sexual and/or aggressive), and interpersonal behavior remain. These poor self-regulatory capacities set recovering clients up for dismissal from treatment when they easily act upon sexual (or aggressive) impulses in contemporary interpersonal relationships—impulses prematurely aroused and activated in states that constituted overstimulation in childhood during abuse.

For other clients, once the layer of chemical dependence is peeled off, underlying symptomatology that may emerge can involve Post-Traumatic Stress Disorder, dissociative states, and other compulsive behaviors related to food, sex, or gambling. Clients need therapists who are adequately trained to manage the return of the repressed and split-off. Skilled therapists need to support clients' egos in integrating and working through memories of abuse and trauma.

My model of group therapy (Chapter 4) provides a good starting point for clinicians aspiring to remediate clients' underlying poor self-regulatory capacities and facilitate the integration and working through of traumatic memories. However, individual psychotherapy (such as that described in Part II) with clinicians trained in deploying appropriate clinical techniques must augment group therapy approaches for the subpopulation of the chemically dependent with histories of childhood abuse within dysfunctional families. However, only if we break the code of silence on forms of child abuse can we accomplish the following: (1) recognizing the need for and implementing additional staff training; (2) beginning to analyze our personal and institutional practices for subtle collusion in not breaking the code of silence on forms of childhood abuse; and (3) providing additional treatment interventions (group and individual) that will assist clients in integrating and working through traumatic memories, improving their self-regulation, reducing chances of relapse, and effectively preventing acting-out behavior.

Can the fields of chemical dependency and mental health sufficiently evolve to meet the challenge posed by addicts' underlying child abuse? Will we be better prepared in the 1990s and beyond for the inevitable failures and chronic relapsers from today's weight-loss programs? We must thank Oprah Winfrey for breaking the code of silence regarding her childhood and adolescent sexual abuse—which might begin to direct the researchers, treatment practitioners, and weight-loss relapsers toward exploration of and resolution of this critical variable in the most difficult cases. What will we do if relapse-prevention advances sufficiently actually to keep people clean and sober long enough for rigid defenses and compulsions to give way to a return of what has been repressed and split off? Will we collude with them and only offer punishment for relapse, for sexual acting-out behavior, or for molesting their own children? Will we be tempted to follow the code of silence, as did Freud? Will we misrepresent the "chemical-dependency elephant" as the hard-core addict, as the relapse-prone, unmotivated sociopathic, or as proof of some dogma we rigidly advance for our own personal or political purposes? Fortunately, we are unlikely to call obese middle Americans—who include more men than ever these days, even football coaches—criminal or sociopathic for binging in secret; negative stereotypes might not hamper the evolution of comprehensive weight-loss programs based on a biopsychosocial model of compulsive food disorder.

I ask hard questions because I heard "hard" things recently from this young man. My keeping of confidentiality feels like collusion with our society's dysfunctional will not to break the code of silence on the rampant forms and degrees of child abuse within dysfunctional families. Hard times require hard questions and hard risks—like breaking the code of silence on child forms of torture, abuse, and soul murder. Similarly, it is time for a hard look at where the field is today.

A CRITIQUE

With the current state of disarray of the addictions field, our poor treatment outcomes because programs are not yet designed to meet client needs, our overt hostility toward difficult patients, and our rigid dogmatic stances within our opposing camps, the clients may do us a favor when they relapse. They remove themselves as problems we cannot solve, do not know how to solve, and are too rigid or dogmatic to figure out how to solve. We can blame the difficult, repeat relapsers for their own treatment failure, and even hate them for being narcissistic, inflated, and criminal as they do anything to secure the next high. Again, the real failure may rest in professionals' and researchers' rigid adherence to their own schools of thought and perpetuation of a field of chemical dependency unable to expand to the greater challenge of delivering quality comprehensive mental health services to stigmatized populations.

Until we forge and implement comprehensive and intensive services, providing multimodal interventions delivered with a multifaceted clinical technique (and have some quality outcome-evaluation research to support its widespread implementation) our clients relieve us of a tremendous responsibility and burden by disappearing from or being banished from treatment and relapsing out of sight.

PRAISE AND DIRECTION

The field of chemical-dependency treatment has made tremendous strides and can realize its potential to move the field of mental health toward a unified theory that guides the delivery of comprehensive and intensive services. Chemical-dependency treatment should, and may, find its place as an important subspecialization within psychology that delivers valued mental health services. Advances in the field of chemical dependency show that state-of-the-art mental health treatment must fully consider and address the biological, psychological, and social-environmental factors as being in intricate interaction in producing diverse kinds of mental disturbance. The biopsychosocial approach to addiction embodied in this edited volume shows individual professionals moving the field toward integrating theory and diverse clinical techniques facilitating reconciliation among opposing treatment philosophies/branches, and advancing quality research that permits refinement of treatment models.

Other profound advances in our understanding of basic processes underlying compulsive behavior, as articulated by Wurmser, suggest that the challenge we face is greater than we might have imagined. This required expansion in our basic thinking about the dynamics of compulsive drug use and behavior is daunting, but critical. Wurmser provides answers to questions that lie at the very heart of the matter of compulsive drug use, and I fear our field's ability to apply them clinically requires more of a revolution than even this volume's integration of theory, refinement of clinical technique, and reconciliation of bitter disputes can achieve. But, on a more positive note, the directions in which Wurmser forces us to expand our very thinking on compulsive drug use refreshingly suggests that answers do exist, that explanations can be compelling, and that correct technical interventions appropriate for the most challenging cases are possible.

Future research and clinical work with the chemically dependent need to further integrate and refine the applicability of the concept of phases of treatment and recovery. Research on treatment outcome must establish to what extent specific client-to-treatment and client-to-intervention matching strategies are important for implementation during specific phases of treatment. For example, is the provision of neuronutrients sufficiently effective during a 14-day period of withdrawal, or do clients substantially benefit from extended neuronutrient protocols that begin to span the six months of recovery, which this author calls the phase of prolonging abstinence? Can research confirm that the provision of comprehensive and intensive services covering the phases of withdrawal and prolonging abstinence (altogether a six-month period) sufficiently improves treatment outcome to justify the cost of such programs? Or, will research clarify the characteristics of clients and of programs that constitute "correct" and "incorrect" client-to-intervention matching strategies? In other words, can research that focuses on the client's phase of recovery being negotiated, and on the timing of the delivery of specific treatment interventions, help the field of chemical dependency treatment refine client-to-treatment matching strategies? In this way, can the field move even further away from the critical error of recommending the same treatment for everyone? Can we move toward suggesting for specific clients, with specific characteristics, specific treatment interventions that should be administered during a specific phase of their recovery?

We can move in this direction if we perform thorough enough individualized assessments of clients and create treatment programs that are flexible enough to accommodate individual client's needs. One result might be variable-length treatment programs that recognize that not all clients require professional individual psychotherapy during a phase of prolonging abstinence, but that there are some clients—such as those with histories of severe childhood abuse and trauma—who absolutely need to be matched to such an intervention. Again, research that considers the kinds of issues arising from an appreciation of phases of treatment and recovery can begin to provide data to refine our treatment models.

Front-line treatment professionals also collect invaluable data through their observations. The concept of phases of recovery and treatment can also guide clinicians in codifying their clinical observations. Clinicians observe subtle changes in cognitive, affective, and interpersonal functioning that occur during specific phases of recovery, which guide the timing of the delivery of their clinical interventions. Clinicians learn from the clients "what works" and "when" it seems to work best. We can enrich and strengthen our observational data by considering phases of client recovery and phases of treatment during which interventions seem to work "best." Careful clinical observation and recording of the experience of modifying one's clinical technique during specific phases of recovery in response to the material presented by the client can produce a rich clinical literature. In turn, published clinical observations can permit further refinements in theory and in hypothesis development for research.

As this edited volume reflects, the concept of phases of treatment and recovery plays an important role in the design of "model" treatment programs currently available, and in the way clinicians modify and implement their therapeutic technique, as well as in the way many contemporary researchers collect and interpret their data. The future evolution of the field of chemical dependency treatment may similarly rest in our ability to further refine our treatment models, our clinical technique, and our research hypotheses by asking what should become routine questions: What phase of recovery is the client negotiating? And what specific combination of interventions, tailored to correspond with the client's phase of recovery, should be delivered at this time?

Name Index

Bruvold, W., 5, 6
Bueno, L., 203
Bugen, L., 130, 137, 147
Bulters, N., 194
Burgner, M., 233
Burns, G., 203
Byron, J., 198

Cahalan, D., 256
Calicchia, J., 268
Cancrini, L., 135
Canfield, D., 197
Capo, T., 216
Carlson, R., 197
Carmody, T., 6, 179
Carpio-Cedraro, F., 322
Carroll, J., 42, 137, 147, 315
Carver, C., 145
Catalano, R., 132
Caudill, B., 5
Chafetz, M., 62, 63, 64, 67, 68, 72, 74, 75
Chaney, E., 145
Charness, M., 199
Chasnoff, I., 316
Chavkin, W., 312, 316
Chesselet, M., 203, 213
Chevron, E., 233
Chien, I., 265, 281
Chiolo, L., 204
Chitwood, D., 322
Chodorkoff, B., 64, 68
Cingolani, S., 135
Clark, H., 291, 299, 301
Clavier, R., 197
Cleary, P., 322
Clemmons, P., 243
Climlco, R., 198
Cloninger, C., 189, 190, 218
Cobbs, P., 291, 294
Cohler, B., 240
Colarusso, C., 236, 239
Coleman, C., 316
Comings, D., 218
Compagnoli, F., 135
Constantini, D., 135
Cook, D., 145, 187, 205
Cooney, N., 127
Cooper, J., 256

Corbett, D., 197
Corbett, R., 6, 67, 315
Corbit, J., 153
Corless, T., 6
Costa, P., 140
Cotton, N., 243
Covi, L., 147
Crits-Christoph, P., 256
Cronkite, R., 133
Crow, T., 197
Crowley, R., 62, 67, 77, 300
Cummings, C., 172
Curry, S., 180

Dackis, C., 198, 199
Daigle, R., 317, 319, 320
Daniel, D., 201
Davidson, V., 63, 71, 73
Davis, M., 198, 199
DeFleur, F., 256
DeLallo, A., 192
DeLeon, G., 4, 40, 267, 280, 315
DeQuardo, J., 202
Derby, K., 85, 115-123, 159-169, 337
Derogatis, L., 147
Des Jarlais, D., 5, 322
DeSoto, C., 64
DeVaul, R., 299
Devine, D., 6, 67, 315
DeWit, H., 197
Dhatt, R., 201, 202
Dibb, G., 264, 280
Dickerson, M, 6
Diclemente, C., 128, 145
DiPowato, N., 195
Ditman, K., 211
Dodes, L., 74, 75, 76, 159, 160, 162, 168
Doherty, W., 13
Domura, Y., 201
Donovan, D., 11, 19, 22, 40, 174
Drake, R., 303, 305
Dubrasguet, M., 202

Eckenrode, J., 317
Edgecombe, R., 233
Eiser, J., 180

Eldred, C., 279
Eliot, C., 214
Elmer, G., 199
Elston, S., 192
Errico, A., 194
Ettenberg, A., 198
Evans, K., 330

Fenichel, O., 77, 109
Fenn, C., 136
Fibiger, H., 197
Figley, C., 135
Filazzola, A., 5
Filstead, W., 233
Fingarette, H., 109
Finney, J., 13, 127, 133, 138, 153
Fishbein, D., 215
Fisher, A., 197
Fishman, H., 267
Fitzgibbon, M., 6
Flewelling, R., 317
Folkman, S., 129, 144
Forrest, G., 63, 64, 69, 71, 73, 74
Forster, A., 202
Fossum, M., 145, 146
Fouriezos, G., 197
Fox, R., 243
Fram, D., 182
Frances, R., 64
Frawley, K., 42, 43, 44
Frazier, H., 216
Freud, A., 96, 110
Freud, S., 83
Freudenberger, H., 40
Fridell, M., 109
Friedle, N., 198
Friedman, S., 5, 322
Frohman, L., 213
Frosch, W., 85, 88
Frye, R., 40
Fullerton, D., 213
Fullilove, M., 322
Fullilove, R., 322

Gaho, G., 188
Galanter, M., 299
Gallant, D., 64, 72
Garattini, S., 201

Subject Index

constancy, 232, 233, 234, 238
loss, 265
relations, 83, 85, 116, 117, 164, 175,
  239, 242
adolescent, xviii
relations, deficits, 84
relations, disturbed, 117–118
relations, early, 89
relations, internalized, xvii, xviii
relations, poor, 52
representation, in addicted women,
  232–246
splitting, 233, 234, 239, 241, 244
Omnipotence, 36, 165
Orality, infantile, 73
Outpatient treatment, 248–260
advances, 4
assessment, 31
indications, 30
intensive, xvi, 10, 15–16, 28–37
philosophy, 29
private, 4
process, xv, xvi, 4, 30–32
Overstimulation, 18
aggressive, 106, 108
sexual, 108, 343
traumatic, 102–103

Peer group, 39
identification, 33
importance, 162–163
pressure, 304
support, 33, 37, 39, 130, 148, 160
Personality
alcoholic, 138
antisocial, 62, 63, 116, 191, 252
disorders, 258
ethnic, 293–294
Eurocentric models of development,
  290–291
multiple, 94, 100
organization, 241
premorbid, 36, 63, 76
synthesis, 165
trauma to, 63
Phobias, 49, 55, 76, 93, 94, 102, 104, 110,
  175, 252
enabling, 300–301
primary, 94, 102
Positive Anonymous, 43
Pregnancy, xvii, 4, 40, 315–317

Problem Situations Inventory. See PSI
Projection, 31, 51, 71, 73, 103, 119–120,
  123, 161, 164, 278
recurrent, 51
Promiscuity, 21
Prostitution, 48
Pseudoseparation, 264, 265
PSI, 132, 139, 153
Psychoanalytic theory, vii, xvi
in addiction, 61–77
diagnostic issues, 63–64
Psychoeducation, 10, 22, 23, 24, 33,
  47–48, 82, 171, 177, 303–304,
  317–318
in outpatient treatment, 16
Psychology
of drug use, 92–110
ego, 61, 62
Psychopathology
in addiction, 20, 67
underdiagnosis, 299
Psychosis, 21, 30
exacerbated by drug use, 258
Psychotherapy, exploratory, 110
Psychotherapy, group, xvi, 7, 10, 39, 43,
  176
in aftercare, 37
in detoxification, 22
Psychotherapy, individual, xvi, 7, 10,
  82–90, 176
assessment data, 17
in detoxification, 22
with difficult patients, 83
long-term, xvii
in therapeutic communities, 54–55

QLI, 137, 138tab, 147
Quality of Life Indicators. See QLI

Racism in addiction, 289–296
Rage, 73
drugs of choice, 93
Rape, 48, 51
Rationalization, 71, 73, 164
Reality testing, 24, 34, 166, 244, 245, 280,
  304, 318
Recovery phases, 3–12, 9tab
lifetime recovery, 9, 40
matched to treatment, xvi, 10, 40
need to understand, xvi